Katyn and the Soviet Massacre of 1940

In spring 1940 the NKVD, Stalin's security police, massacred nearly 15000 Polish prisoners of war captured in September 1939 during the Nazi–Soviet war against Poland. The Germans uncovered and publicised the Katyn burial site of the Kozelsk camp victims in spring 1943 during their invasion of the USSR. The Starobelsk and Ostashkov camp victims only had their killing and burial sites at Kharkov and Mednoe near Tver revealed decades later. Another 7300 Poles were shot in Ukrainian and Belarusan prisons at the same time, bringing the total death toll to around 22000.

This study is the first to use Soviet documentation released in the early 1990s to explain how the failure of NKVD interrogation and recruitment attempts along with acute Polish–Bolshevik rivalry led the Stalinist leadership to decide on mass slaughter. In addition to an exploration of the rationale of the Stalinist state, *Katyn and the Soviet Massacre of 1940* gives an authoritative case study of the processes used by Stalin through a detailed accounting of the mechanics of the transportation and execution of the victims. The truth about the massacre was suppressed both by the Soviet Union and by their post-war satellite regime in Poland. But the management of the issue by the American and British Governments after 1943, examined in the second half of this book, also has major significance. The failure by the Western powers to question the Soviet cover-up stands as an embarrassing part of their wider policy of acceptance of Poland's takeover at the end of the Second World War. While the lingering effects of war continue to haunt Eastern Europe, this study is a vital contribution to the debate over how the memory of atrocities can be assuaged by justice for victims through truth-telling, apologies and reconciliation.

Of interest to historical scholars and students of Eastern European and Second World War history, this volume is a fascinating look into a dark and overlooked chapter of mankind's bloodiest century.

George Sanford is a reader in politics at Bristol University and a leading academic specialist on Poland and Eastern Europe. He is the author of ten books, including most recently the *Historical Dictionary of Poland* (2003), *Democratic Government in Poland* (2002) and *Poland: The Conquest of History* (1999).

BASEES/Routledge series on Russian and East European studies
Series editor:
Richard Sakwa, Department of Politics and International Relations, University of Kent

Editorial Committee:
George Blazyca, Centre for Contemporary European Studies, University of Paisley
Terry Cox, Department of Government, University of Strathclyde
Rosalind Marsh, Department of European Studies and Modern Languages, University of Bath
David Moon, Department of History, University of Strathclyde
Hilary Pilkington, Centre for Russian and East European Studies, University of Birmingham
Stephen White, Department of Politics, University of Glasgow

This series is published on behalf of BASEES (the British Association for Slavonic and East European Studies). The series comprises original, high-quality, research-level work by both new and established scholars on all aspects of Russian, Soviet, post-Soviet and East European Studies in humanities and social science subjects.

Katyn and the Soviet Massacre of 1940

Truth, justice and memory

George Sanford

Routledge
Taylor & Francis Group

LONDON AND NEW YORK

First published 2005
by Routledge
2 Park Square, Milton Park, Abingdon, Oxon OX14 4RN

Simultaneously published in the USA and Canada
by Routledge
270 Madison Ave, New York, NY 10016

Routledge is an imprint of the Taylor & Francis Group

Transferred to Digital Printing 2009

Typeset in Baskerville by Wearset Ltd, Boldon, Tyne and Wear

British Library Cataloguing in Publication Data
A catalogue record for this book is available from the British Library

Library of Congress Cataloging in Publication Data
A catalog record for this book has been requested

ISBN10: 0-415-33873-5 (hbk)
ISBN10: 0-415-54594-3 (pbk)

ISBN13: 978-0-415-33873-8 (hbk)
ISBN13: 978-0-415-54594-5 (pbk)

Let us think of these things always and speak of them never.
Sir Owen O'Malley, British ambassador to the Polish Government-in-Exile,
despatch of 11 February 1944

The crime of Katyn, however, occupies a special place in the collective
memory of Poles. It is a great sore, which we have to talk about ceaselessly
– just so that it can be healed.
Speech by the President of Poland, Aleksander Kwaśniewski,
at the military cemetery in Kharkov, 27 June 1998

The worst single unpunished crime in history.
Louis FitzGibbon

One of the most off-handedly ruthless of Stalin's acts.
Robert Conquest

Parallel with the system of terror there developed a system of bluff. This
latter system was born of the necessity to hide the reality from foreigners,
but it led to the wholesale necessity to justify that reality at home.
Final Report by the Polish ambassador in Moscow, Wacław Grzybowski,
6 November 1939

Contents

Tables

Abbreviations

AAN	Archiwum Akt Nowych/Modern History Archive
AK	Armia Krajowa/Home Army
AL	Armia Ludowa/People's Army
CAW	Centralne Archiwum Wojskowe/Central Military Archive
CC	Central Committee
Cheka	Extraordinary Commission/Chrezvychainaya Komissiya (derived from Vecheka/All-Russian Extraordinary Commission for Combatting Counterrevolution and Sabotage; colloquially applied to all later Soviet secret police organisations)
CIA	Central Intelligence Agency USA
CPB	Communist Party of Belarus
CPSU	Communist Party of the Soviet Union (originally (1925–1952) All-Union Communist Party (Bolsheviks), VKP (b))
CPU	Communist Party of the Ukraine
DPA	Department for Prisoner of War Affairs (Upravlenije po Delam Wojennoplennych)
DPSR	*Documents on Polish–Soviet Relations, 1939–1945* (Sikorski Institute)
FCO	Foreign and Commonwealth Office
FO	Foreign Office
FRK	Federacja Rodzin Katyńskich/Federation of Katyn Families
GARF	Gosudarstvennyji Archiv Rossijskoj Federatsii/State Archive of the Russian Federation
GKBZpNP	Główna Komisja Badania Zbrodni przeciwko Narodowi Polskiemu/Main Commission for Investigating Crimes against the Polish Nation
GKSZpNP	Główna Komisja Ścigania Zbrodni przeciwko Narodowi Polskiemu/Main Commission for Prosecuting Crimes against the Polish Nation
GPU	Głavnoe Politicheskoje Upravlenije/Main Political Department
GPU	Gosudarstvennoe Politicheskoje Upravlenije/State Political Administration (1920s security police successor to Cheka)

GRU	Glavnoe Razvedyvatelnoe Upravlenije/Main Intelligence Directorate of the Military General Staff
GUGB	Glavnoe Upravlenije Gosudarstviennoj Biezopasnosti/Main Administration of State Security NKVD
GUKPPiW	Głowny Urząd Kontroli Prasy, Publikacji i Widowislc/Main Department for the Control of the Press, Publications and Entertainments
GULAG	Glavnoe Upravlenie Lagieriei/Main Camps Directorate NKVD
IPiMS	Instytut Polski i Muzeum Generała Sikorskiego/Polish Institute and the General Sikorski Museum
IPN	Instytut Pamięci Narodowej/Institute of National Memory
ISP	Instytut Studiów Politycznych/Institute of Political Studies
KAAR	Kolekcja Akt z Archiwów Rosyjskich/Collected Documents from the Russian Archives
KDZ	Katyń: Dokumenty Zbrodni/Katyn: Documents concerning the Atrocity
KGB	Komitet Gosudarstvennoe Bezpastnosti/Committee on State Security (security police 1954 onwards)
KiW	Książka i Wiedza/Book and Knowledge Publishing House
KOP	Korpus Ochrony Pogranicza/Border Defence Corps
KPN	Konfederacja Polski Niepodległej/Confederation for an Independent Poland
KPP	Komunistyczna Partia Polski/Polish Communist Party
KPRP	Komunistyczna Partia Robotniczna Polski/Communist Workers' Party of Poland
KPZB	Komunistyczna Partia Zachodniej Białorusi/Communist Party of West Belarus
KPZU	Komunistyczna Partia Zachodniej Ukrainy/Communist Party of the West Ukraine
MGB	Ministerstvo Gosudarstvennoe Bezpastnosti/Ministry of State Security (post-Second World War–1954 security police)
MON	Ministerstwo Obrony Narodowej/Ministry of National Defence
MSZ	Ministerstwo Spraw Zagranicznych/Ministry of Foreign Affairs
NATO	North Atlantic Treaty Organisation
NKHBZK	Niezależny Komitet Historyczny Badania Zbrodni Katyńskiej/Independent Historical Committee for Examination of the Katyn Atrocity
NKVD	Narodnyi Komissariat Vnutrennikh Del/People's Commissariat of Internal Affairs (1934–1943)
Oblast	Administrative Region (subdivision of Union Republic)
OGPU	Obedinennoe Gosudarstvennoe Politicheskoe Upravlenje/Unified State Political Directorate (security police 1923–1934)

Okhrana	Czarist secret police
OUN	Organisation of Ukrainian Nationalists
PAN	Polska Akademia Nauk/Polish Academy of Sciences
PFK	Polska Fundacja Katyńska/Polish Katyn Foundation
PISM	Polski Instytut Spraw Międzynarodowych/Polish Institute of International Affairs
PoW	Prisoner of War
POW	Polska Organizacja Wojskowa/Polish Military Organisation
PPR	Polska Partia Robotnicza/Polish Workers' Party
PPS	Polska Partia Socjalistyczna/Polish Socialist Party
PRL	Polska Rzeczpospolita Ludowa/Polish People's Republic
PRO	Public Record Office (Kew, London)
PSZ	Polskie Siły Zbrojne/Polish Armed Forces
PWN	Państwowe Wydawnictwo Naukowe/State Academic Publishing House
PZPR	Polska Zjednoczona Partia Robotnicza/Polish United Workers' Party
RGO	Rada Główna Opiekuńcza/Main Welfare Council
RIIA	Royal Institute of International Affairs (London)
ROPWiM	Rada Ochrony Pamięci Walk i Męczeństwa/Council for the Defence of the Memory of Struggle and Suffering
SB	Służba Bezpieczeństwa Publicznego/Security Service
SDKPiL	Socjal-Demokracja Królestwa Polskiego i Litwy/Social-Democracy of the Kingdom of Poland and Lithuania
SSR	Soviet Socialist Republic
UB	Urząd Bezpieczeństa Publicznego/Security Service (predecessor to SB)
URO	Uchotno-Registratacionny Otdel/Evidence and Records Department
USSR	Union of Soviet Socialist Republics
VOA	Voice of America
WP	Wojsko Polskie/Polish Army
ZPP	Związek Patriotów Polskich/Union of Polish Patriots
ZWC	Związek Walki Czynney/Union of Armed Struggle

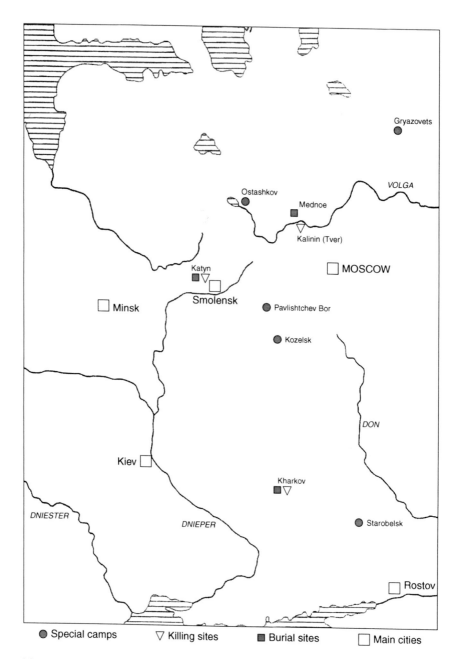

Map of special camps and killing and burial sites.

Introduction

The Soviet Security Services (NKVD) massacred about 14 700 Polish officers and policemen taken from three prisoner of war (PoW) camps called Kozelsk, Starobelsk and Ostashkov in April–May 1940. At the same time another 7300 were killed in NKVD prisons in Belarus and the Ukraine as part of the same operation. We now know, definitely, from Soviet documents released under Gorbachev and Yeltsin, and in particular the crucial decision of 5 March 1940 of the politburo of the All-Union Communist Party (Bolsheviks), that this massacre of almost 22 000 Poles was decided on by Stalin himself. The operation was planned carefully in order to maintain total secrecy and implemented with ruthless efficiency through the transportation of the prisoners of war to three separate killing and burial sites. The Starobelsk officers were shot in the NKVD prison cellars in Kharkov and buried in a nearby forest-park while the policemen and border and prison guards from Ostashkov were killed in Kalinin (now Tver) NKVD prison and buried at Mednoe. The 4400 officers from Kozelsk were transported to the Katyn forest outside Smolensk and buried there. After the German invasion of the USSR Goebbels announced the discovery of the bodies at Katyn with much propaganda fanfare in April 1943. He used the issue as a smokescreen for Nazi war atrocities and as a wedge with which to attempt to break up the alliance between the Western Powers and their post-1941 Soviet ally as well as to scupper any residual chance of Polish–Soviet collaboration.

The above circumstances had crucial consequences. Only a part of the 1940 massacre was revealed through exhumations carried out by German, Polish and International Commission forensic-medical specialists at Katyn in spring–summer 1943. The Soviets used the issue as a pretext for breaking off diplomatic relations with, and then marginalising, the Polish Government-in-Exile in London. The British and Americans refused to take the slightest risk of jeopardising the Red Army's decisive contribution to the Allied war effort against Germany. They, particularly the British Foreign Office, used residual weaknesses in the evidence of Soviet guilt to justify suspension of judgement on the issue of responsibility. Roosevelt and Churchill, although extremely well informed by their own sources, never confronted Stalin over the issue. They went along with his permanent incorporation of the Polish territories occupied in September 1939 and his definition of Poland's new eastern and western frontiers as well as with the eventual imposition, post-war, of Soviet communism and satellite status on Poland. The Soviet Burdenko version of German responsibility for Katyn was presented, but not accepted at Nuremberg in 1946. A Select Committee of the US House of Representatives publicised the 1943 Polish and German evidence of Soviet guilt in 1952 and began to question the Roosevelt administration's role in hushing it up.

The NKVD documents allowing scholars to establish the full details of the planning and implementation of the 1940 massacre became available only from 1990 onwards due to a period of intensive archival collaboration between the newly democratic Polish and Russian republics in the early 1990s. This was supported by judicial investigations and the questioning of surviving witnesses during the same period. As a result of the new documentation and Polish and Russian academic debates of the 1990s studies can now bear authoritative examination of the 1940 massacre; an attempt has been made to remedy the surprising English language neglect of this subject since 1990 in the first half of this book. Gaps still exist over the very top decision making and Stalin's motivation for killing the Poles rather than sending them to GULAG. There are also unclarified issues over the execution stage, especially whether killing and burial were conflated together at Katyn in contrast to their separation in the Kharkov-forest park and Kalinin-Mednoe cases. Much of the detail of the shootings in Belarus still remains speculative because of that country's lack of cooperation since Lukashenko became president in 1994. The parallel story of the Ukrainian executions has, however, taken firmer shape. Other question marks remain over what relevant documentation might still exist in Russia which has not been released, as yet. Crucial material, notably PoW investigation files based on NKVD interrogations in the camps, was allegedly burnt under Khruschev in the mid to late 1950s.

Despite the above residual, almost technical, questions, however, the 1940 massacre, because it concerned both PoWs and foreign nationals, has always had a broad international resonance. It became the most controversial and most examined massacre of the post-1936 Soviet Terror, which also, incidentally, throws significant light on Stalinist policies and mind sets as well as on the NKVD bureaucracy and its techniques in this period. The really big questions have, however, always transcended the purely Soviet and Stalinist dimension. This explains why the second half of this book tackles broader issues, which have had wide contemporary resonance since human rights became dominant features of the post-communist political agenda. The crusade for establishing the historical truth about the 1940 massacre was played out during 1943–1990 against the wider canvas of Great Power politics, first during the Second World War and then, during the period of East–West ideological systemic struggle, in both its Cold War and détente manifestations. The German, American and London Polish documentation was boosted after 1971 by the release of British Foreign Office material. Only the Soviet admission of guilt in 1990 and the release of their documents, however, made it possible to establish the truth about the whole of the 1940 massacre and not just the partial details gleaned from Katyn and the earlier reminiscences of Polish survivors.

The Soviet line on Katyn, established by the Burdenko Commission in early 1944, was imposed on the Polish People's Republic but was not believed by Polish society. It provided dissidents with one of their strongest emotional challenges to the communist state in the second half of its life. After Gorbachev admitted Soviet responsibility in 1990 archival collaboration and judicial investigation brought out most of the facts about the massacre. Since the mid-1990s, however, the emotional and political steam has gone out of the issue with democratic Poland becoming most concerned with issues of commemoration. Russia under Yeltsin and Putin lost interest in further democratisation and in coming to terms with Stalinist crimes.

How do democracies handle the crimes and lies associated with *realpolitik* statecraft under extreme conditions of international conflict and violence? Can elites ever tell the public the truth about the murderous character of necessary wartime Allies or the seamier consequences of military interventions and hope to carry electorates without their normal appeals to morality, principle and truth? Support for human rights, increasing democratic control of national security and mass-media-driven pressures for full and immediate public information have become dominant features in Western democracies since the fall of communism. The recurring internal debates within the British Foreign Office from 1943 onwards about how to handle the inconvenient truth of the responsibility of their wartime Soviet ally for the Katyn part of the 1940 massacre provide a revealing case study. They reveal much about the contemporary dilemma about how traditional elitist and secretive statecraft can be reconciled with these modern pressures.

Democratic values are founded on truth seeking, moral principles and civic participation based on reliable information. The rule of law also implies that perpetrators of criminal acts will not go unpunished. Victims of such acts, the definition of which has now been extended to include groups who have suffered from genocide, massacre or associated atrocities, can now benefit from wider definitions of international law derived from the establishment of international tribunals to deal with post-Yugoslavia and Rwanda. Justice on this dimension, however, goes beyond mere punishment and possible compensation and restitution. Where perpetrators no longer survive to face trial and punishment the memory of past atrocities can be assuaged by full revelation of the historical truth. Justice can thus be done to the memory of victims, and be felt to be done by survivors and successors, leading on to forgiveness and reconciliation, both individual and national.

Sources and style

Access to the Russian archives has become more difficult again, since the mid-1990s. It is, therefore, a fair assumption that the bulk of the relevant primary Russian documentation which has become available concerning the 1940 massacre has been transported to the Central Military Archive in Warsaw. Due to the outstanding editorial work of Professor Wojciech Materski of the Institute of Political Sciences of the Polish Academy of Sciences, the crucial material drawn from this has also been published in the *Katyn: Documents Concerning the Atrocity* series. The London Polish, American and German documentation has long been available; recent government policy has also diminished the number of 'retained' British documents and, one presumes that the bulk of which concerning our subject had become available by the mid-1970s.

The transliteration of Russian names is particularly problematic in the case of this book so I (half) apologise to purists for having adopted an eclectic, mixed and far from consistent policy, particularly between first and second names, which consciously favours polonised and anglicised forms and established endings such as in Trotsky or Gorky over consistency. Imposing uniformity on the Polish is also neither necessary nor desirable hence I ask the reader's indulgence for 'Katyn' in general usage but 'Katyń' in Polish titles, Kozelsk-Kozielsk, Starobelsk-Starobielsk, Ostashkov-Ostaszków and the rest.

Acknowledgements

I am happy to express my sincere gratitude to the Arts and Humanities Research Board for an award under their Research Leave Scheme which enabled me to write this book during the 2003–2004 academic session. I am extremely indebted to the staff of the Central Military Archive and the Modern History Archive in Warsaw as well as the Polish Library in London for their very considerable assistance. I would also like to thank the following individuals for their kindness in helping, supporting and encouraging me in a variety of ways in the difficult writing of this book. For any shortcomings in the handling of the massive detail and the numerous sensitive controversies associated with the subject I take full responsibility: Wojciech Materski, Ryszard Zelichowski, Andrzej Paczkowski, Stephen White, Peter Duncan, Hieronim Kubiak, Bożena Łojek, Marek Tarczyński, Jędrzej Tucholski, Tadeusz Krawczak, Czesław Żak, Zygmunt Kozak, Sławomir Zygmunt Frątczak, Edward Frącki, Richard Sakwa, Zdzisław Jagodziński (+), Richard Little, Jutta Weldes, Anthony Forster, Derek Offord, Jonathan Haslam, Anna Cienciała, Kevin McDermott, Robert W. Davies, Maureen Perrie, Yoram Gorlizki, Andrzej Suchcitz.

1　Poland and Russia

Conflict and domination

The relationship between Poland and Russia has been described as an 'age-old antagonism' which transcended the level of mere conflict between two major Slavonic states.[1] It has been depicted as a historical struggle between different civilisations for political, economic and religious control and, consequently, cultural hegemony over the vast contested borderlands lying between them. Poland was one of the great states in Europe and certainly Russia's (Muscovy's) equal until early modern times.[2] The Commonwealth of Poland-Lithuania controlled much of what is now Belarus, Ukraine, Lithuania and the Baltic States during the fourteenth to seventeenth centuries. The weakening of the state through an excessive form of gentry democracy and the unwise policies of a foreign Swedish Vasa dynasty from the end of the sixteenth century onwards worsened political and social decay. Poland's international position was also shattered by a Swedish onslaught, the rise of Prussia and an uprising in the Ukraine, half of which was lost by the Truce of Andrusowo in 1667. As a result (much of) Poland until 1989 has been dominated, and controlled in different ways, by Russia in its varying incarnations for most of the period since the death of King Jan II Sobieski in 1697 and Peter the Great's modernisation of Russia. But the Polish ethnic and cultural presence in the borderlands (*kresy*) of Belarus and Ukraine remained, until finally removed by Stalin's ethnic cleansing of 1939–1941 and the Second World War border changes and population transfers.

Russian control was camouflaged during the eighteenth century as it made use of collaborating aristocratic landowners and slogans of religious toleration.[3] The central and eastern lands of the Polish–Lithuanian Commonwealth were seized by Russia in the three partitions of 1772, 1792 and 1795. After Napoleon's defeat in the 1812 campaign, a re-established and extended form of Russian territorial control, confirmed at the Congress of Vienna, lasted until the First World War.[4] Inter-war Polish independence survived only from November 1918 until September 1939.[5] Although there is debate on the extent of the autonomy of the Polish People's

Republic (PRL) full sovereignty as well as systemic and international self-determination was achieved only in the Third Republic after 1989. The country's democracy has been consolidated since then and strengthened through EU and NATO membership.[6]

Both Russian policy towards Poland and Polish reactions ran through a wide and varying gamut over time. At one end of the spectrum Czar Nicholas I, after the 1831 Uprising, wanted to steamroll Polish national differences away and to turn the country into the Vistula Province, merely the westernmost extension of a uniformly ruled Russian Empire. His executions, imprisonments, forced emigration and deportations to Siberia began 'the systematic extermination of the Polish presence in the east' that continued until 1945.[7] Something similar was attempted, after the suppression of the 1863–1864 Uprising. Iosif Stalin also took advantage of his alliance with Adolf Hitler from 1939–1941 to partially exterminate, and wholly marginalise, Poland's national elites as a preliminary to establishing Soviet Stalinist communist rule in Poland after 1944.

Hardline policies of Russification, repression and tight uniform control from Moscow did not, however, dominate all the time. Catherine the Great played on domestic conflicts between conservative and reform Polish confederations during the reign of King Stanisław Poniatowski (1764–1795).[8] She was, eventually, forced to share her Polish spoils with Prussia and the Hapsburg Empire in the Partitions. The Congress Kingdom of 1815–1831 gave the Poles real cultural and socio-religious, as well as a degree of political, autonomy. The same was, arguably, true of the PRL under the post-1956 regimes of Władysław Gomułka, Edward Gierek and Wojciech Jaruzelski.[9]

Adam Bromke's depiction of the swings between political idealism and realism from Napoleonic times until fairly recently captured the wide Polish divergences, generation after generation, on the independence issue.[10] Political idealists inspired by historical memories of national greatness felt that the national struggle for independence would be rewarded eventually by a favourable constellation of European forces (as in fact happened in 1918 and 1989 and with the Duchy of Warsaw of 1807–1812). Defeats such as the Napoleonic Legions, the 1831 and 1863 Uprisings and even September 1939 and the 1944 Warsaw Uprising would strengthen national resolve through blood shed by heroes. This Romantic view was particularly strong at moments in the nineteenth century and in the interwar period; but the realist counter-argument predominated more often, especially in the twentieth century. The arguments of Prince Adam Jerzy Czartoryski, Marquis Aleksander Wielopolski and the Organic Work school of the second half of the nineteenth century were reiterated by many Poles during the communist takeover of power (1944–1947), and again after *October* 1956. For them, the 1944 Warsaw Uprising became a symbol of Romantic futility, once the consciousness of Western betrayal and indifference, both in 1939 and at Yalta, seeped through. Post-war Roman Catholic

Primates of Poland, Cardinals Stefan Wyszyński and Stefan Glemp, therefore counselled against violence and favoured compromise from 1956 onwards. Stalin's purges of inter-war communists, the 1940 massacre and associated deportations of Poles also contributed to similar attitudes within the Polish United Workers' Party (PZPR). This was especially so during Solidarity's heyday, Martial Law in 1980–1983, and during the attempted reform period preceding communism's collapse in Poland in 1989.

The Russian threat from the east has also been matched by the German menace from the west. Frederick the Great and his Hohenzollern successors merely questioned the Polishness of Pomerania, Poznań and Silesia. Adolf Hitler's anti-Slavonic racism and drive for Teutonic *Lebensraum*, however, threatened the very existence of the Polish national community during the Second World War. During 1939–1941 Poland faced the maximum moment of danger to its national survival. The Nazis and Soviets came together in the Ribbentrop–Molotov Pact and its secret annexe to carry out the country's Fourth Partition.

The Polish–Soviet War of 1920: was Stalin polonophobic?

Natalia Lebedeva suggests that the main reasons for Stalin's hatred of 'feudal-landowning' inter-war Poland and its officer class are to be sought in 'the bitterness of defeat' in the Polish–Soviet War of 1920. The Stalinist leadership thus regarded the Polish army as its main enemy in the 1930s.[11] Józef Piłsudski's victory before Warsaw, when he outmanoeuvred Tukhachevsky's army by counter-attacking an exposed flank during the third week of August, was crucial.[12] Polish independence only survived for under two decades but this strengthened Poland's political and national consciousness and stimulated social and economic development after 123 years of threefold subordination to foreign powers. The defeat killed off the Bolshevik dream of World Revolution. It prevented the Red Army from taking over a weakened Germany with its strong revolutionary working class movement. Even worse, further Polish victories after Warsaw, notably Edward Śmigły-Rydz's on the River Niemen, forced the Bolsheviks to sue for peace and to accept what Lenin called a 'bandit treaty'. At the Treaty of Riga of March 1921 they had to cede West Belarus and the West Ukraine and accept a frontier close to the so-called Curzon Line.[13] The Versailles system was then completed by the confirmation of this frontier by the Allied Conference of Ambassadors in 1923.

Viachyslav Molotov had this humiliation and the Polish territorial gains dividing the Ukrainian and Belarusan Republics in mind when he famously, if somewhat inaccurately, called Poland 'the monstrous bastard of the Peace of Versailles'. The war and its drawn result reinforced Polish–Russian stereotypes and hatreds of each other. The USSR became committed to revising the frontier whenever a favourable opportunity offered itself. New Marxist–Leninist ideological pressures now reinforced older state and national factors. Independent Poland was regarded by the Bolsheviks as a national and class opponent representing mixed gentry landowning and bourgeois values and interests. Soviet propagandists consistently referred to Poland as *panskaia Pol'sha* (gentry-ruled state). Poland was also both a barrier to the expansion of their system and a potential springboard for Western or Nazi aggression on the Soviet Union. The seventeenth Soviet party congress described Poland as 'the tool and vanguard of Western imperialism'.[14] Poland, however, became less compact ethnically and religiously. After the short initial (fully) democratic interlude until 1926 Piłsudski's ruling *Sanacja* elite never quite decided whether to repress or to win over the one-third of its population composed of national minorities, especially the five million Ukrainians.[15]

The way the 1920 campaign was fought also involved Stalin directly in the blame for its failure. Stalin as Commissar of the South Western Front failed to send reinforcements to Tukhachevsky in time as ordered. He supported the drive by his military commanders, Budienny and Yegorov, on Lwów instead. By the time they changed direction the Soviets had been defeated and were in full flight from Warsaw.[16] As in an earlier dispute, over Tsarytsin during the Civil War, the recriminations became part of the life and death power struggle between Stalin and Trotsky.[17] Volkogonov reports that Stalin extracted, and, presumably, destroyed, the relevant documents on this episode from the Kiev central archives in 1925.[18] The Stalinist victors thus rewrote history, bent ideology to their purposes and used the Security Services to eliminate inconvenient witnesses.

When the full truth about the 1940 massacre came out in the 1990s, some Russians attempted to balance the historical equation as they saw it by discovering a reciprocal atrocity.[19] The Polish Procuracy rejected a belated Russian demand in 1998 that they open a criminal investigation into the deaths of Soviet PoWs during 1919–1921.[20] It has been suggested that Mikhail Gorbachev directed Soviet historians to seek 'a Polish anti-Katyn' in his growing hardline period preceding the failed *coup* of August 1991. A Russian Government Historical Commission investigated the question but denied that it manufactured a counterweight to Katyn.[21] The public claim by the Russian Consul in Kraków, Boris Shardakov, in November 1994 that Piłsudski was as bad a criminal as Stalin as he was responsible for the deaths of 50000–60000 Soviet PoWs in 1920 became something of a *cas célèbre*.[22] The Polish response proved that this was nonsense but Polish public opinion viewed such initiatives as highly provocative.[23] Official documents showed that 66000 Red Army PoWs were returned by November 1921, 25000 decided not to return and another thousand settled permanently in Poland.[24] Only about a third of the 18000 Red Army soldiers who died of sickness in captivity may have done so because of the poor medical and living conditions of the time but the propagation of such anti-democratic themes in Russia caused Polish concern.

Polish and Soviet communism

Communism was weak in Poland, historically, for three main reasons. First, the nineteenth-century revolutionary movement was dominated by the issue of the regaining of national independence rather than the liberation of the proletariat. The vast majority of the Polish Socialist Party (PPS) founded in 1892 supported Bolesław Limanowski's reformism and, after 1906, Józef Piłsudski's nationalist struggle for independence.[25] The First Proletariat's Marxist internationalism was largely symbolic and easily suppressed by the Czarist authorities in the 1880s.[26] The Social-Democracy of the Kingdom of Poland and Lithuania (SDKPiL), founded in 1892, enjoyed wider, if patchy, support in the PPS-Left and the Jewish Bund and had notable leaders like Róża Luksemburg, Julian Marchlewski and Adolf Warski. Others like Feliks Dzierżyński (Dzerzhinsky in Russian), Karol Sobelson (Radek) and Jakob Fürstenberg (Hanecki) went on to become prominent Bolsheviks within the USSR. The inter-war Polish communist parties emerged out of the SDKPiL's roots and tradition.[27] The Bolsheviks favoured Luksemburg's thesis on the economic union of the Polish and Russian proletariats but Stalinists later denounced her libertarianism and warnings against the dictatorial potential of one party rule as Menshevik.[28] Stalin also persecuted the Polish political prisoners repatriated to the USSR, the bulk of whom were of Jewish origins.[29]

Second, atheistic and egalitarian Marxist–Leninist ideology clashed with Poland's strongly Roman Catholic, gentry and national cultural values. Third, communism was associated after 1917 with a hostile power which attempted to conquer the country in 1920. It is true that Lenin accepted Poland's independence and the ending of Czarist rule in 1918. But the USSR, both as a state and through the Third International (Comintern), thereafter threatened Poland's international security and domestic social order, supported national minorities against the unitary state and challenged its eastern frontier.

The Communist Workers' Party of Poland (KPRP) was formed in December 1918 through the amalgamation of the SDKPiL with the PPS-Left. Accused of being unpatriotic and treasonable during the Polish–Soviet War, it never shook off its image as the agent of a hostile foreign power and alien ideology. The Comintern founder and SDKPiL leader, Julian Marchlewski, organised a Provisional Revolutionary Committee (PRC) in Poland on 2 August 1920 on direct Bolshevik instructions.[30] Marchlewski chaired the committee composed of Feliks Dzierżyński, Feliks Kon, Józef Unszlicht and Edward Próchniak (secretary).[31] Colloquially known as the Białystok Provisional Government, this was based in the Red Army-controlled city of that name in north east Poland. It can be regarded as a trial run for the actual Soviet takeover of Poland following its successful and, this time, permanent occupation by the Red Army in 1945. The PRC tried to gain support for the Polish Soviet

Republic by promising workers the nationalisation of industry and mining and peasants land through the breaking up of large estates. Hardly surprisingly, doctrinaire social promises were insufficient to allay Polish distrust of Soviet intentions, especially once the Red Army had crossed the River Bug. The resulting patriotic upsurge demonstrated the irrelevance of the Białystok Committee which retreated back to the Soviet Union in the baggage train of the Red Army. Lessons may have been drawn from this experience. The Soviet takeover of Poland, when it came in 1944–1947, was more sophisticated than the Białystok dress-rehearsal.

KPRP organisation fell to pieces and its membership collapsed at the end of the Polish–Soviet War although major socio-economic discontent allowed it to rebuild.[32] Communists gained some representation in the Sejm and in local councils by functioning on the borderline of legality.[33] The KPRP was re-branded in 1925 as the Communist Party of Poland (KPP). Burks has demonstrated conclusively its weakness within the ethnic Polish and Roman Catholic national core. He explained its disproportionate strength within Ukrainian and Belarusan minorities in terms of 'a traditional or an ethnic tie to Russia' while there were special reasons for strong Jewish support.[34] The Communist Party of the West Ukraine (KPZU) and the Communist Party of West Belarus (KPZB) also emerged as separate and quite strong bodies in the *kresy*.

The communist party was perceived by the Polish nation as a Soviet-controlled agency willing to sacrifice the country's independence and eastern provinces.[35] But its disunited leadership occasionally resisted, or misread, the twists and turns of Comintern policy. The Comintern's right wing and United Front turn in 1922 favoured the emergence of Adolf Warszawski (*pseud.* Warski), Maksymilian Horwitz (*pseud.* Walecki) and Wera Koszutska (*pseud.* Kostrzewa). They accepted the party's earlier mistakes in repudiating Poland's independence and promised to defend it against international capitalism with Soviet support. Leadership support for Trotsky during 1923–1924 led to their disciplining by the Comintern, controlled by Stalin's ally in the first stage of the leadership struggle, Grigorii Zinoniev. It also gained the party Stalin's 'enduring enmity and suspicion'.[36] Their 'May Error' – passivity towards Piłsudski's 1926 *coup d'état* – and support for the rightist Nikolai Bukharin, who was also being defeated by Stalin, allowed Leftists led by Julian Leszczyński (*pseud.* Leński) to control the KPP by the late 1920s.[37] Leński and his supporters Stalinised the KPP and followed Stalin's revolutionary class struggle turn, slavishly, in both domestic politics and the Comintern. The PPS rebuffed their unconvincing overtures once the Comintern returned to United, and then Popular, Front tactics in the mid-1930s.[38]

The culminating point of this analysis concerns the arrest in the early 1930s of prominent KPP activists (notably Jerzy Czeszejko-Sochacki, Tomasz Dąbal, Sylwester Wojewódzki and Tadeusz Żarski) who had sought refuge in the USSR. They were accused variously, and liquidated, on trumped up charges of spying for Piłsudski's Poland, contacts with Polish Intelligence and provocations designed to weaken the KPP.[39]

The KPP was accused of having been infiltrated by Piłsudski's security services while Poland was demonised as a military and subversive threat to the Soviet Union in the Moscow Show Trials. The politburo of the All-Union Communist Party (Bolsheviks), VKP (b), empowered the NKVD on 18 August 1937 to liquidate 'the Polish spying and sabotage ring' POW (Piłsudski's Polish Military Organisation, established in 1917).[40] Recently examined Soviet and Comintern archival documents, notably the diary of Comintern General Secretary, Georgii Dimitrov, confirm that arrests and interrogations of KPP leaders and activists peaked between autumn 1937 and summer 1938. Stalin instructed Dimitrov in November 1937 that 'the dissolution [of the KPP] is one or two year's late. It must be wound up, but this decision, in my opinion, need not be published in the press.'[41] The formal dissolution by the Comintern on 18 August 1938, therefore, merely marked the belated recognition of the KPP's destruction.[42]

The full might of the Comintern was directed to liquidating its organisation and leadership in Poland from the bottom upwards.[43] An initiative group led by a communist youth activist and Spanish Civil War veteran, Bolesław Mołojowec, supported Comintern agents in breaking up the KPP.[44] Mołojowec, after this experience of being licensed by the great *Vozhd* to see plots and conspiracies everywhere, took it upon himself to have his brother, Zygmunt, shoot, Antoni Nowotko, the first leader of the reborn Polish Workers Party (PPR) in German-occupied Warsaw in 1943.[45] The residual (home or domestic) communist leaders, like Władysław Gomułka, who had survived by remaining in Poland, in turn, had him shot summarily in a cellar in Radom.

Dziewanowski's picture of all the KPP leaders resident within the USSR, plus those lured back from abroad, being shot during 1937–1939 has been confirmed by the post-1990 documentation, although estimates range from a few hundred to well over a thousand.[46] Certainly, all the major figures of inter-war communism, Leński, Warski, Kostrzewa and Krajewski, notably those resident at the Hotel Lux in Moscow, perished. The party was condemned at the Eighteenth VKP (b) congress in 1939 as having become completely factional, infiltrated by *Sanacja* and Trotskyite agents and taken over by anti-Soviet elements. The KPP was rehabilitated officially in 1956 in a declaration by five communist parties (the CPSU and PZPR plus the Italian, Bulgarian and Finnish parties) at around the time of Nikita Khruschev's Secret Speech to the Twentieth CPSU congress.[47] The document declared that the KPP's dissolution was 'unjustified' and provoked by false material provided by provocateurs.[48]

Why Stalin dissolved the KPP remains controversial. Weydenthal supports the 'contaminated' party interpretation. The fruitless Stalinist search for a mole, who really existed – (KPP CC candidate member, Józef Mitzenmacher, *pseud*. Jan Alfred Regula, died 1947) – drove the Stalinists to frustrated extremes.[49] Dziewanowski has expressed the most persuasive explanation. Stalin discarded 'an ineffective and unreliable instrument'; he nipped potential opposition to a major new tack in his policy in the bud.[50] By 1938 Stalin realised that the KPP was incapable of either delivering socialist revolution in Poland or acting as an unthinking and fully obedient Soviet agent. He was already envisaging a deal with Nazi Germany in order to prevent it from attacking the USSR as it was being encouraged to do by Western appeasement policy. Munich and the betrayal of Czechoslovakia confirmed his *realpolitik* view that the KPP might obstruct his trumping of the Western Powers through a *rapprochement* with Nazi Germany which would be cemented by their mutual destruction of Poland. The KPP, concludes Dziewanowski, 'one of the last major victims of the great purges, became one of the first victims of the Hitler–Stalin pact'.[51]

Alongside the decision to destroy the KPP in August 1937 Stalin also struck hard at the Polish national minority in the USSR. Totalling only 636 220 according to the 1937 census, although independent estimates range as high as 1.2 million, Polish peasants had suffered heavy repression and mass deportation to Kazakhstan after 1928 due to their strong opposition to collectivisation. NKVD Order number 00485 was confirmed by the VKP (b) politburo on 9 August 1937. An accompanying, 30-page-long 'sealed letter' signed by NKVD Head Nikolai Yezhov depicted Stalinist paranoia about the infiltration of all walks of Soviet life over two decades by POW and the Second Department (Military Intelligence) of the Polish General Staff. While all Poles were to be regarded as under suspicion of collaborating with 'the Fascist-Insurgent, Espionage, Sabotage, Defeatist and Terrorist Activities of Polish Intelligence in the USSR six categories were specified as needing particular attention'.[52] In practice, 'the Poles became the first major Soviet population group to be repressed collectively in 1936–1938 on the basis of nationality rather than class affiliation'.[53] An accelerated procedure was adopted. Initially, a *dvoika*, composed of a local NKVD officer and procurator, confirmed execution by shooting and five- to ten-year sentences proposed by local investigators. These sentences were typed up as information lists, every ten days or so, and sent on to Moscow, for what apparently was very mechanical, almost automatic, confirmation by middle-ranking NKVD officials. This so-called 'album procedure' clogged up by summer 1938, even though the timescale of the 'Polish Order' was extended repeatedly from its original three-month period. As a result the VKP (b) politburo devolved sentencing prerogatives to local republican *troikas* (local party First Secretary, procurator and NKVD Head) in September 1938 to accelerate 'national' operations and to clear the prisons.

It has been estimated that, as a result of the Polish Operation, 111 000 out of 143 000 sentenced during 1937–1939 were shot, the highest percentage of any group.[54] About a quarter of the Polish minority was thus repressed and about a fifth shot, just in this short period. This reflected

Stalin's fear of a potential 'Fifth Column' and a dangerous neighbour in the period approaching the outbreak of war as well as his hatred of Poland's gentry-aristocratic, nationalist and democratic socialist elites. Soviet hysterical fears, typecast preconceptions and indoctrinated hatreds of the Polish *Pans* (gentlemen squires) carried over into the events of 1939–1940. The process by which the PoWs were to be liquidated in 1940 was tried and tested by such Stalinist NKVD actions as the Polish Operation during the Great Terror which produced a type of anti-Polish template.

Inter-war Polish–Soviet relations: the unresolved dimension

Riga's provisional character meant that Russo-Polish relations remained generally hostile during the inter-war period.[55] Poland signed a political and military alliance with France in 1921.[56] She became part of the *cordon sanitaire* blocking the emerging USSR from Western Europe.[57] Poland's two hostile neighbours responded with the Treaty of Rapallo of 1922. They developed secret military collaboration during the 1920s as a consequence of their common interest in subjugating the *saisonstaat* (temporary state) lying between them.[58]

Piłsudski, after his seizure of power in May 1926, however, faced less direct threats. He feared that Western Power *rapprochement* with Germany at Locarno in 1925 and the USSR's re-incorporation in the Western security system and entry into the League of Nations in 1934 would be achieved at Poland's expense. Piłsudski's directives were implemented, after 1932, by Foreign Minister Józef Beck, his closest agent amongst the Colonels.[59] Beck, recognising the unreliability of the French and the lack of interest of the British, attempted to 'balance' between the Great Powers. Poland's 'Two Enemies', Germany and the USSR, were considered equally dangerous. Beck strengthened Poland's tactical position by signing non-aggression pacts with the USSR on 25 July 1932 and Nazi Germany on 26 January 1934. The Soviet pact fitted both partners into the emerging Collective Security and League of Nations framework, favoured by the then Soviet Foreign Minister, Maxim Litvinov.[60] A symbolic gesture of good will it promised peaceful coexistence but only postponed fundamental problems.[61] *Sanacja* (Piłsudski's political camp) also felt threatened by France's bilateral Treaty of Mutual Assistance of May 1935 with the USSR which downgraded the Franco-Polish alliance. Beck supported France over Hitler's remilitarisation of the Rhineland in March 1936.[62] But Anglo-French passivity demonstrated their unreliability and the need to continue the tactical *détente* with Berlin despite Soviet criticism. Marshal Śmigły-Rydz, Piłsudski's successor as commander of the Polish army, revived the Franco-Polish relationship through the Rambouillet Agreement of September 1936. His adherence to Beck's bilateral definition of the alliance precluded harmonisation of relations with the USSR.[63]

Soviet propaganda painted Beck as Hitler's lackey who would join in a
Nazi onslaught on the USSR. This nonsensical picture was given the lie by
Poland's military resistance in 1939. Why it was so widely believed in
Western Europe needs explanation. The reason lies, primarily, in a welter
of misperceptions about Poland, prevalent in European public opinion.
The liberal guilt school of thought, fostered by academics, who really
should have known better, like John Maynard Keynes, also propagated the
idea that Germany had been harshly treated at Versailles.[64] Others, followed 19th-century partitioning powers' propaganda that the Poles were
unbalanced and pre-modern revolutionaries, incapable of ruling themselves. Supporters of Collective Security in the 1930s also had no patience
with, Poland's opposition to the *diktats* of the Great Power Directory.
Inter-war Poland was, then, charged variously with national megalomania
and excessive territorial ambitions, democratic anarchy until 1926, followed by authoritarianism under Piłsudski, as well as bad treatment of
national minorities. Unlike Czechoslovakia or Romania, whose Foreign
Ministers, Beneš and Titulesco, gained political capital by subscribing
enthusiastically to League of Nations shibboleths, Poland was regarded
and badmouthed as a nuisance by the British and French political classes
and public opinion.

Beck refused to subordinate himself to Franco-British appeasement policies which allowed Hitler in 1938 to carry out the *Anschluss* of Austria and
to gain the Sudetenland at Munich. Beck's 'parallel' policy – 'independent' initiatives and brusque *realpolitik* methods in 1938 – gained him an
awful, although somewhat undeserved, historical reputation. It allowed
pusillanimous and hypocritical Western statesmen and muddle-headed
public opinion to cover up feelings of guilt at not standing up to the real
big Nazi bully, Hitler, by discovering a convenient scapegoat. Beck sent a
moderate ultimatum to Lithuania, merely demanding the resumption of
diplomatic relations, in March 1938.[65] The Poles also seized largely Polish-
inhabited Cieszyn in early October 1938 once it became clear that the
Western Powers had abandoned Czechoslovakia. Both episodes could be
defended in terms of their historical backgrounds and circumstances; but
the British and French mixture of moral self-righteousness and suppressed guilt at weakness and failure to stand up to a major opponent
leading to the betrayal of a civilised state produced a syndrome of psychological substitution. The Poles suffered repeatedly from this factor in the
period leading up to 1945, particularly when they were inconvenient
victims of history and circumstances.

Piłsudski's successors, after his death in 1935, understood that a deal
with Nazi Germany would involve massive territorial losses and population
transfers as well as satellite status to the Reich. The Poles knew that
Hitler's demands over Danzig and the extra-territorial road across the
Polish Corridor to East Prussia represented only the thin end of a very
long wedge. They hoped that Hitler could be faced down if Poland and

the Western Allies were sufficiently firm but they had no illusions about Nazi Germany. Stefan Lubomirski, the Councillor in their Berlin embassy, declared that 'Gdańsk is obviously only a pretext for the Germans, behind which lies a huge plan of conquest'.[66] Beck rejected Hitler's demands in a speech to the Sejm on 5 May 1939 emphasising Poland's historical resolve to defend its national honour and to resist aggression. 'We in Poland do not accept the idea of peace at any price.'[67]

On the other hand, when Hitler increased the pressure on Poland in Spring 1939 Beck, having gained the British guarantee of 31 March, saw equally great dangers in, even discussing a Soviet alliance.[68] Śmigły-Rydz is held to have expressed the Polish dilemma in the much-quoted phrase that 'With the Germans, we risk our liberty, with the Russians our soul.' As late as 26 June Wacław Grzybowski, the Polish ambassador in Moscow, reiterated the Polish illusion that Russia would never allow a German victory over Poland nor accept a common frontier with Germany.[69] It is now clear that the Franco-British failure to negotiate an alliance with the USSR in Moscow in summer 1939 was only superficially occasioned by Poland's effective veto of two crucial issues.[70] First, their acceptance of a Soviet guarantee, and second, the right of transit across Poland for Soviet forces either in reaction to, or to forestall, German aggression. Marshal Klimentii Voroshilov put the latter question to the Anglo-French Mission in Moscow on 11 August. Called on to respond positively, in order to save the negotiations, Beck told the French ambassador in Warsaw that he was being asked to endorse 'a new partition': the Soviets would occupy eastern Poland but could not be relied on to fight or to leave.[71]

Short of writing a blank cheque for Stalin there is nothing that Beck or the Western Allies could have done, by then, to head off the accelerated pace of secret German–Soviet exchanges.[72] These culminated in the signing of their non-aggression pact by Foreign Ministers Molotov and Ribbentrop on 23 August 1939 which allowed Hitler to secure his eastern rear for his attack on Poland which began on 1 September.[73] But Hitler gained more than mere Soviet neutrality for the destruction of the Versailles system and the green light to go ahead and unleash the Second World War.[74] The secret protocol to the pact envisaged the Fourth Partition of Poland and delineated the respective German and Soviet spheres of interest (along the Rivers Narew, Vistula and San – the Pysa appeared in later documents). But its real significance was that it committed the new Allies to decide Poland's fate and future division through mutual agreement.

Notes

1 Bohdan Budurowycz, *Polish–Soviet Relations, 1932–1939*, New York: Columbia UP, 1963, p. 188.
2 For general histories of Poland see Norman Davies, *God's Playground: A History of Poland*, Oxford: Clarendon Press, 2 vols, 1981. Jerzy Lukowski and Hubert

Zawadzki, *A Concise History of Poland*, Cambridge: Cambridge UP, 2001. Cf. Edouard Krakowski, *Pologne et Russie*, Paris: Laffont, 1946.

3 Jerzy Lukowski, *Liberty's Folly: The Polish–Lithuanian Commonwealth in the Eighteenth Century, 1697–1795*, London: Routledge, 1991.

4 Robert F. Leslie (ed.), *History of Poland since 1863*, London: Cambridge UP, 1980 Piotr Wandycz, *The Lands of Partitioned Poland, 1795–1918*, Seattle, WA: University of Washington Press, 1975.

5 Antony Polonsky, *Politics in Independent Poland, 1921–1939*, Oxford: Clarendon Press, 1972.

6 George Sanford, *Democratic Government in Poland: Constitutional Politics since 1989*, Basingstoke: Palgrave Macmillan, 2002.

7 M.B. Biskupski, *The History of Poland*, Westport, CT: Greenwood Press, 2000, pp. 25–6.

8 Richard Butterwick (ed.), *The Polish–Lithuanian Monarchy in European Context, ca. 1500–1795*, Basingstoke: Palgrave, 2001.

9 For the dispute over the character of the PRL see Sanford, *Democratic Government in Poland*, Ch. 2.

10 Adam Bromke, *Poland's Politics: Idealism versus Realism*, Cambridge, MA: Harvard UP, 1967.

11 Natalia Lebediewa, 'Operacyjno-Czekistowska obsługa jeńców wojennych', *Zbrodnia nie ukarana. Katyń – Twer – Charków*, Warsaw: NKHBZK, 1996, p. 122.

12 Described by Lord d'Abernon as *The Eighteenth Decisive Battle of the World*, London: Hodder & Stoughton, 1931. Norman Davies, *White Eagle, Red Star: The Polish–Soviet War, 1919–20*, London: Macdonald, 1974. Thomas Fiddick, *Russia's Retreat from Poland, 1920*, London: Macmillan, 1985. Adam Zamoyski, *The Battle for the Marchlands*, New York: Columbia UP, 1981.

13 For the text of the treaty see *Documents on Soviet–Polish Relations, 1939–1945*, London: General Sikorski Historical Institute/Heinemann, 2 vols, 1961/1967, hereafter DSPR, 1, pp. 3–8.

14 Budurowycz, *Polish–Soviet Relations*, p. 189.

15 Antony Polonsky, *Politics in Independent Poland, 1921–1939: The Crisis of Constitutional Government*, Oxford: Clarendon Press, 1972. Richard Watt, *Bitter Glory: The History of Independent Poland, 1918–1939*, New York: Hippocrene, 1998. Timothy Wiles (ed.), *Poland between the Wars, 1918–1945*, Bloomington, IN: Indiana University Polish Studies Center, 1989.

16 Isaac Deutscher, *Stalin: A Political Biography*, London: Oxford UP, 1961, pp. 216–17.

17 Ibid., pp. 201 ff.

18 Dmitri Volkogonov, *Stalin: Triumph and Tragedy*, London: Weidenfeld & Nicolson, 1991, p. 361. Roman Brackman alleges that Stalin's polonophobia was fuelled further by the fact that he had been a Czarist Secret Police (Okhrana) agent and that their file on him had fallen into the hands of Dzerzhinsky and other Russified Poles, *The Secret File on Joseph Stalin*, London: Cass, 2001.

19 Cf. 'Kontr – Katyń', *Biuletyn Katyński*, no. 40 (1995).

20 Zbigniew Karpus, *Jeńcy i internowanych rosyjscy i ukraińcy na terenie Polski w latach 1918–1924*, Toruń: Adam Marszałek, 1997.

21 The Russian historian Boris Nosov confirmed this later although he accepted that Katyn might have, partly, been Stalin's revenge for 1920. 'Szukanie Anti-Katyna', *Gazeta Wyborcza*, 12–13 August 2000, pp. 13–14.

22 Jacek Wilamowski, *Kłamstwo Stulecia: W Cieniu Katynia*, Warsaw: Agencja Wydawnicza CB, 2003, pp. 85–7.

23 For the view of the Katyn organisations see 'Oświadczenie w sprawie rosyyjskich ataków na Polskę', *Zbrodnia nie Ukarana: Katyń – Twer – Charków*, Warsaw: NKHBZK, 1996, p. 473.

24 Wojciech Materski, *Pobocza dyplomacji: Wymiana więźniów politycznych pomiędzy II Rzecząpospolitą a Sowietami w okresie międzywojennym*, Warsaw: ISP PAN, 2002, p. 87.
25 See the entry on the great socialist historian in A. Thomas Lane (ed.), *Biographical Dictionary of European Labor Leaders*, Westport, CT: Greenwood Press, 2 vols 1995, pp. 573–4.
26 Ibid., pp. 1022–3.
27 M.K. Dziewanowski, *The Communist Party of Poland: An Outline of History*, Cambridge, MA: Harvard UP, 2nd edn, 1976, Chs 2–4.
28 John P. Nettl, *Rosa Luxemburg*, London: Oxford UP, 1969.
29 Materski, *Pobocza dyplomacji*, pp. 267–8.
30 Branko Lazich (ed.), *Biographical Dictionary of the Comintern*, Stanford, CA: Hoover Institution Press, rev. edn, 1986, pp. 300–1.
31 Dziewanowski, *Communist Party of Poland*, pp. 92–4
32 Jan B. de Weydenthal, *The Communists of Poland: An Historical Outline*, Stanford, CA: Hoover Institution Press, 1978, p. 14.
33 Tadeusz Daniszewski, *Posłowie Rewolucyjni w Sejmie (lata 1920–1935)*, Warsaw: KiW, 1961.
34 R.V. Burks, *The Dynamics of Communism in Eastern Europe*, Princeton, NJ: Princeton UP, 1961, p. 188.
35 Andrzej Peploński, *Wywiad Polski na ZSSR, 1921–1939*, Warsaw: Bellona, 1996. Communists affiliated with the KPRP/KPP, particularly its underground agents within the CC Technical and Military Departments, supported Soviet espionage activities throughout the inter-war period. They carried out subversive agitation within the Polish army and collaborated closely with Soviet political (NKVD/OGPU) and military (GRU) espionage agencies.
36 Weydenthal, *Communists of Poland*, pp. 20–1.
37 Cf. Kevin McDermott and Jeremy Agnew, *The Comintern: A History of International Communism from Lenin to Stalin*, Basingstoke: Macmillan, 1996.
38 Henryk Cimek, *Komuniści, Polska, Stalin, 1918–1939*, Białystok: KAW, 1990. Józef Kowalski, *Komunistyczna Partia Polski, 1935–1938*, Warsaw: KiW, 1975.
39 Dziewanowski, *Communist Party of Poland*, pp. 147–9.
40 Fridrikh I. Firsov, 'Dimitrov, the Comintern and Stalinist Repression', in Barry McLoughlin and Kevin McDermott (eds), *Stalin's Terror: High Politics and Mass Repression in the Soviet Union*, Basingstoke: Palgrave, 2003, p. 73. Leński, under torture, admitted that he had belonged to POW since 1917 and that 90 per cent of the KPP Central Committee in 1932 had also been POW agents!
41 Ibid., p. 73.
42 The full text of the Comintern resolution was only handed over by the Soviet historians on the Mixed Historical Commission considering 'Blank Spots' in summer 1988, *Polityka*, 9 July 1988, p. 2.
43 For limited official accounts see Kowalski, *Komunistyczna Partia Polski*, pp. 426 ff, and Antoni Czubiński (ed.), *Historia Polskiego Ruchu Robotniczego, 1918–1939*, Warsaw: KiW, vol. 3 1988, pp. 610–13.
44 Weydenthal, *Communists of Poland*, p. 32.
45 One of the greatest *cas célèbres* in the history of Polish communism, this affair remained unresolved during the life of the PRL. Cf. Piotr Lipiński, 'Osiem śmierci Marcelego Nowotki', *Gazeta Wyborcza*, 19–20 July 2003.
46 Dziewanowski, *Communist Party of Poland*, pp. 149–54. Al. An. Myszkowski, 'Słownik biograficzyny komunistów Polskich represjonowanych w ZSSR', *Zeszyty Historyczne*, Paris: Instytut Literacki, 1984, pp. 40–80. This gives 311 biographies of communists repressed in the 1937–1938 purge and estimates that about 600, mainly leaders and activists, perished. See also the additions by S. Ludkiewicz and Lucjan Kieszczyński in *Zeszyty Historyczne*, no. 73, 1985, pp. 56–73 and S.

Rawicz, ibid., no. 74, 1985, pp. 208–29. Cf. 'Stalin, NKWD a Polscy Komuniści', *Polityka*, 2 December 1989, p. 14.
47 *Trybuna Ludu*, 19 February 1956.
48 *KPP: Uchwały i rezolucje V–VI Zjazd (1926–1938)*, Warsaw: Wydział Historii Partii KC PZPR, 1956, pp. 598–9.
49 Weydenthal, *Communists of Poland*, pp. 32–3.
50 Dziewanowski, *Communist Party of Poland*, pp. 153–4.
51 Ibid., p. 154.
52 The categories were: remaining, as yet uncovered, POW members; Polish PoWs who remained in the USSR in the 1920s; all defectors from Poland; political emigrants and political exchange prisoners; former members of the Polish Socialist Party (PPS); and anti-Soviet nationalists in the Polish minority. Nikita Petrov and Arsenii Roginskii, 'The "Polish Operation" of the NKVD, 1937–8', in McLoughlin and McDermott, *Stalin's Terror*, pp. 153–8.
53 Vladimir Abarinov, *The Murderers of Katyn*, New York: Hippocrene, 1993, p. 141.
54 Ibid., pp. 170–1.
55 Jan Karski, *The Great Powers and Poland, 1919–1945*, Washington, DC: UP of America, 1985. James Shotwell and Max Laserson, *Poland and Russia, 1919–1945*, New York: Carnegie Endowment, 1945. Polish examinations are Jerzy Kumaniecki, *Pokój polsko-radziecki 1921*, Warsaw: IKS PAN, 1985. Marian Leczyk, *Polityka II Rzeczypospolitej wobec ZSRR w latach 1925–1934*, Warsaw: PWN, 1976. Stanisław Gregorowicz, *Polsko-radzieckie stosunki polityczne w latach 1932–1935*, Wrocław: Ossolineum, 1982.
56 Piotr Wandycz, *France and her Eastern Allies, 1919–1925*, Minneapolis: University of Minnesota Press, 1962. Piotr Wandycz, *The Twilight of France's Eastern Alliances, 1926–1936*, Cambridge, MA: Harvard UP, 1988.
57 Roman Dębicki, *Foreign Policy of Poland, 1919–1939*, London: Pall Mall, 1962.
58 Aleksandr M. Nekrich, *Pariahs, Partners, Predators: German–Soviet Relations, 1922–1941*, New York: Columbia UP, 1997.
59 See Joseph Beck, *Dernier Rapport*, Neuchatel: La Baconnière, 1951; *Final Report*, New York: Robert Speller, 1957.
60 Text of 1932 pact in DPSR, 1, pp. 14–16. An additional protocol in 1934 extended its life until the end of 1945.
61 *Documents on British Foreign Policy*, London: HMSO, hereafter DBFP, 2nd Series, VII, p. 240.
62 George Sakwa, 'The Franco-Polish Alliance and the Remilitarization of the Rhineland', *Historical Journal*, 16, 1 (1973), pp. 138–9.
63 George Sakwa, 'The "Renewal" of the Franco-Polish Alliance in 1936 and the Rambouillet Agreement', *Polish Review*, 16, 2 (Spring 1971), pp. 45–66.
64 John Maynard Keynes, *The Economic Consequences of the Peace*, London: Macmillan, 1919. Cf. Etienne Mantoux, *The Carthaginian Peace or the Economic Consequences of Mr Keynes*, London: Oxford UP, 1946.
65 George Sakwa, 'The Polish Ultimatum to Lithuania in March 1938', *Slavonic and East European Review*, 55, 2 (April 1977), pp. 204–26.
66 Jan Szembek, *Diariusz i Teki Jana Szembeka*, London: Polish Institute and Sikorski Museum/Orbis Books, vol. 3, edited by Józef Zarański, 1972, p. 671.
67 Józef Beck, *Przemówienia, deklaracje, wywiady, 1931–1939*, Essen: n.p., 2nd edn, 1939, p. 426.
68 Anita J. Prazmowska, *Britain, Poland and the Eastern Front 1939*, Cambridge: Cambridge UP, 1987.
69 Szembek, *Diariusz i Teki Jana Szembeka*, 3, p. 641.
70 Lord Strang confirms the Polish–Allied dilemma in *Home and Abroad*, London: André Deutsch, 1956, pp. 33–4.

71 Léon Noël, *L'Agression Allemande contre la Pologne*, Paris: Flammarion, 1946, p. 423.
72 Geoffrey Roberts, *The Unholy Alliance: Stalin's Pact with Hitler*, London: I.B. Tauris, 1989.
73 Text of treaty and secret annexe: DPSR, 1, 38–40; DGFP, Series D, VII, pp. 246–7. Original Russian documentation is now also located in CAW KAAR VIII.800.21, file 1.
74 Jerzy Łojek, *Agresja 17 września 1939, studium aspektów politycznych*, Warsaw: PAX, 1990.

2   The Sovietisation of East Poland

Invasion and conquest

The course of the German–Polish war of September 1939 does not concern us as much as why the USSR invaded on 17 September 1939 to occupy the eastern half of Poland attributed to it by the Ribbentrop–Molotov Pact. John Erickson's answer is that Stalin moved somewhat earlier than he had intended to, and before he was fully prepared.[1] Steinhardt, the American ambassador in Moscow, considered that the USSR participated in this 'Unholy Alliance' as it feared being left out of the sharing of the spoils.[2] Despite brave resistance, an effective defence of Warsaw and a victory on the River Bzura, the Polish army had been out-manoeuvred and broken up by the German *Blitzkrieg* fairly quickly.[3] Smigły-Rydz ordered his troops to fall back and to regroup in south east Poland, in his general order of 10 September. The aim was to defend a bridgehead with Romania on the River Dniester.[4] This failed to stop the Germans advancing rapidly into eastern Poland, especially towards Lwów, in an attempt to encircle the Polish forces but it precipitated the Soviet invasion.

Diplomatic formalities were carried out in the early morning of 17 September. The Soviet deputy Foreign Minister, Vladimir Potemkin, handed the Polish ambassador in Moscow, Grzybowski, a note (which he refused). This stated that the disintegration and 'internal bankruptcy' of the Polish state had rendered all her international agreements with the USSR 'defunct'.[5] The Red Army had, therefore, moved to liberate its Ukrainian and Belarusan kinfolk.[6] Britain and France initially denounced the Soviet action as unjustified and promised that it would not affect their obligations towards their Polish ally.[7] They also recognised legal continuity in the Polish Government-in-Exile in Angers led by General Władysław Sikorski in late September.

Stalin told the German ambassador Friedrich von der Schulenberg, that there was no place for an 'independent residual Poland' as a buffer state; friction between Germany and the USSR had to be avoided 'in the final settlement of the Polish question'.[8] An interim demarcation agreement thus separated out their military operations and envisaged a German retreat behind the Rivers Bug, Vistula and San.[9] Stalin's long-term territorial wishes were incorporated in the German–Soviet Boundary and Friendship Treaty (including three secret protocols) of 28 September.[10] One of the protocols, confirming Nazi–Soviet solidarity in suppressing all Polish opposition, was stated publicly in their joint governmental declaration, the same day.[11] Stalin exchanged ethnically Polish territories (basically Lublin province and a part of Warsaw province) between the Rivers Vistula and Bug (minus Suwałki) for Lithuania. He did so in order to allay Western susceptibilities about the annexation of indisputably Polish lands.[12] Stalin also gained German agreement to his future incorporation of the Baltic States. In the short term, he returned the heavily Polish-inhabited Vilnius territory to Lithuania in the Soviet–Lithuanian agreement of 10 October 1939. German diplomats considered the German–Russian agreements 'a permanent settlement ... a definitive resumption of their historical friendship', eliminating differences over Poland 'once and for all'.[13]

The Red Army attacked with overwhelming force along the whole length of the 900-mile-long frontier. Over half a million, building up to a million, troops and about 5000 tanks, were organised in two fronts, the Belarusan and the Ukrainian, and seven field armies. They were opposed by about 20 000 lightly armed KOP (Korpus Ochrony Pogranicza) border guards led by Brigade-General Wilhelm Orlik-Rückemann.[14] More sporadic resistance came from up to a quarter of a million disorganised Polish troops who had been pushed into eastern Poland by the German advances.[15]

Polish claims that the Soviet 'stab in the back' sabotaged a major fight back in the second stage of the Polish–German war can now be discounted.[16] Poland's political and military leadership led by President Ignacy Mościcki, Prime Minister Felicjan Sławoj-Składkowski, Foreign Minister Beck, the Commander-in-Chief Marshal Śmigły-Rydz and the General Staff had already decided that the war was lost.[17] They were on the border at Kołomyja and Kuty and sought refuge in Romania during the night of 17–18 September. There, some were subsequently interned, as a result of German pressure, and not allowed to travel on to France as they had intended.

Szawłowski states that 'with its flagrant aggression of 17 September, the USSR committed a breach of at least five international treaties, both bilateral and multilateral'.[18] Śmigły-Rydz, after the above consultation with the President and the Prime Minister, however, decided against declaring war on the USSR and outright resistance to the Soviet invaders. His General Order, issued at 4 p.m. on 17 September, was, under the circumstances, bound to cause confusion. Polish forces were only to fight if engaged by, or called upon to surrender and disarm by, Soviet forces. Their primary aim was to seek shelter in Hungary and Romania as a preliminary to evacuation to France and Britain.[19] General Stachiewicz confirmed the above. He also ordered General Kazimierz Sosnowski, commander of the southern front, to maintain resistance against the Germans.[20] In practice, the Polish forces were caught between the German and Soviet pincers. Left with incoherent orders, numerous units fought sporadic last ditch actions, during what has been called the 'fifteen day war', while retreating before the overwhelming superiority of Red Army numbers, organisation and armour.[21]

Śmigły-Rydz's last order to his troops from Romania on 20 September declared that Polish honour had been maintained by KOP resistance to the Soviet invasion. The priority now was to avoid pointless bloodshed 'in the struggle with the Bolsheviks and to save whatever could be saved' for the future struggle against Germany in the West.[22] The same day German and Soviet troops met on the upper Dniester and closed off the Polish escape route to the south. The Soviets, determined not to allow the Polish armed forces to escape, closed the Romanian frontier on 19 September and strictly forbade the exit of any Polish military.[23]

Śmigły-Rydz's failure to declare war has been criticised on the following grounds: it later allowed the Western Powers to wriggle out of adopting an unequivocal official position towards the Soviet aggression; it spread confusion and facilitated Soviet disinformation; and it demoralised the Polish forces and made them more inclined to capitulate without a fight.[24] Some writers consider that Śmigły-Rydz, through ambiguity and indecision, erred in not declaring the fact of Soviet aggression clearly enough and in not resisting it more determinedly, to establish the point, beyond doubt, in international law.[25] Łojek also argued that the absence of international recognition of a state of war made it easier for the Soviets to mistreat Polish prisoners as counter-revolutionaries rather than as prisoners of war.[26] It is difficult to credit that Śmigły-Rydz should have succumbed to a basic misconception about Soviet intentions and misread Stalin's firm commitment to the German–Soviet alliance to destroy Poland.

Despite later émigré polemics occasioned by the bitterness of defeat, there was no alternative to continuing the struggle in the west apart from surrender to the Nazis or Soviets. After all, about 40 000 Polish soldiers as well as about 20 000 civilians succeeded in crossing over into Hungary.[27] Roughly 30 000 military (including 9276 air force personnel, of whom 1491 were officers), 10 000 civilians and many high political and military dignitaries also escaped to Romania.[28] Significant numbers of soldiers crossed frontiers unofficially and about 47 000 Poles, including 9200 officers, succeeded in making their way to France, Cyprus and the Middle East by May 1940. The 15 000 military who sought refuge in Latvia and Lithuania were, however, imprisoned in the USSR after the Soviet annexation of the Baltic States. They were fortunate to just escape extermination in the spring 1940 massacre.

Confusion reigned as to Soviet intentions. The Red Army, initially, pretended that they were coming as liberators or even as Allies in an anti-German struggle.[29] Polish commanders organised increasing resistance as units were captured. Soviet atrocities occurred, especially against officers. The commander of the Grodno garrison which had resisted the Soviet advance stoutly, General Olszyna-Wilczyński, was shot together with his adjutant, in full view of his wife and chauffeur, when caught fleeing in his car near the town of Sopóckinie.[30]

Nevertheless, Soviet disinformation succeeded to the extent that the Poles often preferred to surrender to the Soviets, rather than to the Germans, notably in Lwów where an exchange of German and Soviet positions occurred. The Soviets, however, failed to honour capitulation agreements. General Langner, the area commander, was, fooled into surrendering his officers to the tender mercies of the NKVD on 22 September although most of the rank and file soldiers went free initially.[31] The officers were rounded up, and eventually ended up in the Kozelsk camp, thus perishing at Katyn, despite the promise that they should be allowed to go home or to move on to Romania or Hungary. The troops of General Mieczysław Smorawiński in Włodzimierz Wołyński, despite signing a capitulation agreement allowing them to leave with full military honours for beyond the Bug, were rounded up on leaving the town and taken into captivity.

Molotov admitted to the Supreme Soviet on 31 October that the 'liberation' of eastern Poland had cost the Red Army 737 killed and 1862 wounded.[32] Polish specialists claim up to 3000 killed and 8000–10000 wounded as well as the destruction of 100 Soviet tanks and armoured cars.[33] Polish military deaths are variously estimated at between 3000 and 7000, with 20000 wounded.[34] An additional thousand to 2500 were executed or murdered in immediate reprisals by both Soviet and harassing Ukrainian nationalist forces.[35] Jaczyński lists a large number of such atrocities, notably cases of revenge for having offered resistance and the immediate execution of prisoners, especially of officers. The Soviets regarded resistance to them as illegitimate and claimed to be merely reclaiming their own West Ukraine and West Belarus.[36] Their fanning of anti-Polish social and national hatred also provoked something close to an ethnic civil war with the Ukrainians with communal atrocities and reprisals on all sides.[37] Symptomatically, such events have had incomparably less resonance in the West than the occasional Polish transgression under similar onset of war anarchic conditions such as Jedwabne in 1941.[38]

The Soviet subjugation of incorporated East Poland, 1939–1941

As a result of the Fourth Partition of Poland the USSR gained 52.1 per cent of the territory and 38.1 per cent of the population of inter-war

Poland (202 000 square kilometres of territory and 13.4 million population). The figures of Poles taken into Soviet captivity are, however, more contentious – the generally accepted figure being around a quarter of a million.[39]

Rigged sham elections were held very quickly on 22 October to demonstrate the popular will of over 90 per cent support in a 'plebiscite' with a farcical 99.7 per cent turnout.[40] The delegates elected to the National Assemblies of the West Ukraine and West Belarus immediately petitioned for incorporation in the USSR within their respective Soviet Socialist Republics.[41] The Supreme Soviet passed the appropriate decrees on 1–2 November.[42] On 28 November it conferred compulsory Soviet citizenship on all inhabitants of the newly annexed territories.[43]

The latter was crucially significant for the treatment of Poles in the Eastern Territories. It laid the legal and formal basis for their ethnic cleansing during 1939–1941 and for Stalin, at Teheran and Yalta, to gain Allied support for the permanent incorporation of inter-war Poland's Eastern Territories within the USSR. It also meant that the Soviets regarded Polish PoWs from this area as a separate category to those originating from German-occupied Poland.

Molotov's claim that the Soviets reclaimed overwhelmingly East Slav territory inhabited by seven million Ukrainians, three million Belarusans and a mere one million Poles is tendentious propaganda.[44] Western scholars, basing themselves on updated 1931 census figures consider that the Polish element was at least four and a half million, at best five and a quarter million – 35–40 per cent of the population.[45] There were also a roughly equal number of Ukrainians, two and a half million Belarusans (or undefined *tutejszy* or Polesians), over a million Jews and smatterings of other nationalities.[46] Poles were overwhelmingly Roman Catholic, Belarusans and Volhynian Ukrainians were Orthodox while Ukrainians in Eastern Galicia were largely Greek Orthodox (Uniate) although identities were often mixed and confused in this border area.[47]

The main aim of Soviet policy during 1939–1941 was to destroy Polish political, social and cultural influence entirely, and to disperse the Polish population throughout the USSR, where it could be controlled effectively.[48] As far as the main theme of this book is concerned 'the crime against Polish officers and policemen was part of the plan for the destruction of the Polish state, it was carefully planned and decided at the highest party-state level'.[49] The establishment of Soviet power was cloaked under the mask of self determination for the Ukrainians and Belarusans who were now united with their respective republics. Polish control of the borderlands would thus be smashed and replaced, resolving the centuries-long historical conflict in Russia's favour, once and for all. Soviet methods took four main forms. The treatment of prisoners of war will be dealt with later. The other techniques of mass arrests, conscription and forced labour volunteering as well as mass deportations are covered here. One

should also note Andrei Vyshinsky's threefold definition of the fate awaiting imprisoned or deported Poles under the Soviet judicial system: total
confinement in corrective labour camps (GULAG), direction to work in
'special settlements' where limited freedom of movement within the local
district was allowed, and exile where an individual worked and lived fairly
normally under NKVD supervision.[50]

Academic study of the subject has, understandably, been heavily
affected by the bitterness and hatred occasioned by these events and by
the wider setting of the East–West conflict. Since the late 1980s, and certainly since 1991, primary Soviet, as well as Polish communist, documentation has become available to scholars. The vast Western academic and
émigré literature of the Second World War and Cold War periods can,
therefore, now be confronted with substantiated alternatives. The new
'official' material, however, needs careful interpretation although such
sources have not changed the well-established picture of the nature and
functioning of the Soviet system overmuch. Official Soviet statistics on the
number of victims of their 'Terror' are significantly, sometimes dramatically, lower than the estimates of 'external' observers. Volkogonov rightly
says that 'the Western and Polish media have given inaccurate figures on
these deportations'.[51]

The repression of the Polish element, especially of anyone regarded as a
leader in any way, started with immediate arrests as soon as the Red Army
entered. Arrests mushroomed in a more systematic way across the length
and breadth of the occupied territories right up to the German invasion in
June 1941. They became mass roundups of specially selected categories designated by the Soviet authorities. Those most at risk were Army officers who
had evaded capture and returned home, individuals who had resisted the
Soviet occupation, frontier crossers, 1920 war veterans and military settlers
as well as political, social, trade union, religious and cultural figures and
members of inter-war Polish organisations. The decapitation of the Polish
elite and its organisational core was followed by the arrests of relatives,
friends, collaborators and anyone named during interrogation. Lastly,
terror moved on to its mass, and more random, phase.

Most of those arrested were eventually executed, or sentenced to
imprisonment, forced labour in a camp or administrative exile under any
of the 14 clauses of article 58 of the Soviet Penal Code (and its Ukrainian
and Belarusan equivalents). The most widely used paragraphs were
number two which defined treason as any form of armed struggle against
the USSR (punishable by death by shooting) and number thirteen which
introduced the ideological crime of 'historical counter-revolution'; the
latter was applied retrospectively to veterans of the Polish–Soviet War and
to any form of service in inter-war Poland which was defined as Fascist and
contrary to working class interests. Paragraphs six on spying, ten on diver-
sion and anti-Soviet propaganda and fourteen on sabotage were also,
much used.

The Soviet legal process was economical, to say the least, and has been well publicised by a vast literature.[52] After intensive interrogation, often involving torture and violence, starvation and other forms of abuse such as threats and blackmail, sentence would be proposed by local investigators and confirmed by 'troikas', special tribunals of three judicial and NKVD officials, on the basis of the indictments and confessions thus prepared. The defendant was normally absent and learnt the sentence, normally five to eight years in a GULAG camp, only subsequently. Some of the death sentences were commuted to labour camp while many were postponed until the spring 1940 clear out. The 11 000 individuals facing the death sentence in Ukrainian and Belarusan prisons, mentioned in Beria's preparatory document for the 5 March 1940 decision, composed the latter category.[53] An authoritative report, prepared for the Polish Ministry of Justice, follows recent Russian sources in arriving at a total figure of 107 140 arrestees between September 1939 and May 1941, 42 662 in West Belarus and 64 478 in West Ukraine.[54] Polish and Russian academics now generally accept that about 110 000 Poles were arrested in this period in the two regions.[55]

After registering all males born between 1890 and 1921 by March 1940 the Soviet authorities called up those born in 1917, 1918 and 1919 in September, and the 1920, 1921 and 1922 cohorts in December. An estimated 200 000 were thus conscripted by this carefully prepared process. The population was, simultaneously, intimidated by threats of capital punishment for avoiding military service and reprisals against families.[56] Conscription meant physical control as well as actual removal of the most vigorous section of the population from which opposition was most likely to come. That they were not trusted by the Soviets is confirmed by the initial induction of the vast majority into labour battalions, not Red Army combat units. There they could be brainwashed, disciplined and worn down by long and hard labour under poor living conditions.

There were three major waves of deportation from the Eastern Territories (plus a fourth one, directed equally at the Baltic States) during 1939–1941.[57] This involved those sections of the civil population, generally whole families, who fell into some category that the Soviet authorities considered potentially suspect and disloyal. As they were not accused of having done anything they were not susceptible to being rounded up and held as PoWs, or to being arrested, sentenced or conscripted. The procedure for dealing with them took the incredibly simple form of deportation by administrative decree to various parts of the USSR.

The mode of deportation was uniform and carried out by 4–6-strong, NKVD-led groups. A family would be woken, given limited time to pack basic belongings and taken by horse-drawn sled or cart to a railway station.[58] There they would be herded onto goods or cattle trains and held in locked wagons during the long journey east or north. The first deportation on the night of 10–11 February 1940 according to older sources carried away about 220 000 (but only 138 619 according to the Soviet NKVD document figures) mainly ethnic Polish military settlers, foresters and various supporters of Poland's cause to the north of European Russia (Arkhangelsk oblast and Komi ASSR) and Siberia (Sverdlovsk, Omsk, Novosibirsk, Tobolsk and Krasnoyarsk oblasts).[59] There they were held in NKVD-run special settlements and employed in forestry related activities.

The second deportation on 13 April 1940 was directed at relatives of inmates of Soviet prisons and labour camps, of PoWs, in both the USSR and Germany, of internees in the Baltic States, as well as of those who had fled outside the USSR. As most of the 59 416 (suspiciously low new NKVD figures) to 320 000 (old sources) deportees were women and children, this time, with low labour productivity, they were transported to village settlements, mainly in northern Kazakhstan, where they could maintain themselves in the local economy.[60] The lower figure corresponds closely to the 22 000–25 000 families of the victims of the 1940 massacre specified in the VKP (b) politburo decision of 5 March 1940.[61] Beria sent the republic Ministers of the Interior, Ivan Serov in the Ukraine and Lavrentii Tsanava in Belarus, detailed instructions on 7 March 1940 regarding the method of deportation and the supervision of the process by operational troikas.[62] Beria defined family members as wife and children but also parents, sisters and brothers if they resided at the same address as the PoW. The same day Beria ordered Soprunenko, his official in charge of the NKVD PoW department, to draw up, within a five day deadline, detailed alphabetic inventories of PoW relatives broken down by residence in German- and Soviet-occupied territory.[63] The result for Starobelsk was information on 1662 families, drawn up by province, resident in German territory. The political aim of this deportation was to apply collective responsibility and to disperse into the wilderness individuals who had been aggrieved by the Soviet arrest of their relatives or who had actual or potential contacts with relatives who had fled abroad. The linkage with the massacre of PoWs in the camps and republic prisons was obvious and direct.

The third deportation, mainly carried out on 29 June 1940, was primarily directed at foreign nationals who had fled from the German occupation of western and central Poland. NKVD sources give a figure of 145 000 refugees from German-occupied Poland as well as 35 000 detained attempting to cross over in the opposite direction. Both categories were normally sentenced to between three and eight years in a labour camp. About three-fifths of the 180 000 (new figures) to 240 000 (old sources) deportees were Jewish while the rest were Polish. As there was a sufficiently high proportion of men this time, they were directed to NKVD run mining and forestry projects in Siberia and Arkhangelsk.

The fourth and last major wave of deportation was mainly from the Baltic States which were occupied by the Red Army in June 1940 and incorporated into the USSR soon afterwards. The much-publicised deportation instructions for the NKVD aimed to eliminate anti-Soviet elements in the broadest sense; it covered 11 well-known categories ranging from former Czarist officials and policemen, White Russian officials and soldiers and members of anti-Soviet parties to Esperantists and philatelists![64] Deportations started on 13 June 1941 and rolled on until they were interrupted by the German invasion on 22 June 1941. Polish communities in Lithuania, especially in Vilnius and Kaunas, were targeted particularly heavily, as were residual Poles in West Belarus. They formed a significant percentage of the variously estimated 87 000–91 000 (new figures, of which 34 000–44 000 were Poles) to 200 000–300 000 (older sources) involved in this deportation.[65] There is evidence that the Baltic States were initially scheduled to suffer massacre and deportation immediately after the same processes had been completed against the Poles in 1940. For unknown reasons repression was postponed for a year. It was then, interrupted by German invasion.

There has been considerable controversy over the number of Poles who, in one manner or another, crossed the inter-war Riga frontier into the USSR proper during 1939–1941. The issue is complicated further by the difficulty in differentiating between ethnic 'Poles' and 'Polish' Jews on the one hand and Ukrainians, Belarusans and others (often of Polish citizenship) making up the total deported. The problem of contrasting ethnic-linguistic and civic definitions of citizenship is best illustrated by the third deportation which, according to old estimates, transported 138 000 Poles and 98 000 Jews, most of whom had Polish citizenship and identified with Poland. How the latter should be counted has caused much debate and was politically contentious. The Soviets, after summer 1941, applied an ethnic definition of Polishness excluding Ukrainians, Belarusans and some Jews from their amnesty and the right to emigrate.

Siemaszko estimates that the four major deportations involved between 980 000 and 1 080 000 individuals. Poles were hardest hit because they were distrusted most by the Soviets along a wider range of ethnic, social, educational and historical dimensions than any other group. One of Siemaszko's estimates, that 13.3 per cent of all Poles, defined by mother tongue, were deported, was previously considered inadequate as it produces about 450 000 Poles deported from the Eastern Territories during 1939–1941, about half the earlier accepted figure.[66] Scholars have in the past started with Bogdan Podoski's 1945 figures, produced by the Culture and Press Department of the Polish Army Second Corps in Italy. He arrives at a global total of 1 692 000 individuals (1 114 000 permanent residents, 336 000 refugees and 242 000 soldiers), of which 58 per cent were Polish speakers, removed in this period from the Soviet-incorporated territories.[67] Wielhorski also arrives at a similar figure of 1 050 000 Poles out of a lower total figure of 1 492 000.[68] Jan Gross's figure is in the middle range, 1.25 million or 9 per cent of the population, in contradistinction to the other Polish émigré estimates which range up to over a million and a half.[69] Significantly, the Katyn survivor Professor Świaniewicz, with his

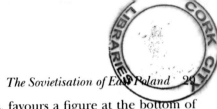

strong personal grasp of Soviet realities, favours a figure at the bottom of the range, 880000.[70]

Since 1991 the above figures, which dominated the academic and political consciousness in the West for four decades, have had to be revised downwards, very dramatically, in the light of new Russian documentation. The NKVD figures reported to Beria and Stalin have been checked by the Polish and Soviet dissident organisations KARTA and Memorial and found to be generally reliable.[71] The new Polish–Russian academic consensus starts with the rock bottom figure that 'only' about 320000 Poles were deported into the USSR proper during 1939–1941.[72]

The final destruction of the Polish presence in the borderlands started with Stalin's purges in the 1930s and continued right up until the frontier changes and population transfers of 1945–1946. Sizeable Polish minorities, and, arguably, historical, religious and cultural residues, still remain in Lithuania, Belarus and Ukraine, but they are mere shadows of their historical forebears. Older Polish sources roughly agreed on the following figures for the various types of repression of Poles involved in this vast historical process of national reconstruction: 1114000 permanent residents of the Eastern Territories and 336000 refugees (from German-occupied Poland) deported; 210000 conscripted and also consigned to the nether regions of the USSR; 250000 individually arrested civilians imprisoned throughout the USSR; and finally, 181000 PoWs captured in 1939, including the 14700 held in Kozelsk, Starobelsk and Ostashkov, to which should be added another 15000 PoWs deported from Lithuania in 1940.[73] To this figure, which already comes to well over two million, are often added the Poles deported from Soviet border areas and generally repressed in Belarus and the Ukraine in the 1930s.[74] The highly contrasting Russian document-based, lowest possible figures are 98000 arrested, 320000 deported and 43000 interned as PoWs.[75] The evidence therefore suggests that the Soviets undoubtedly smashed the political, social and cultural bases of Polish domination in the Eastern Territories during 1939–1941. They made a significant start on their ethnic cleansing of the Polish element which was completed at the end of the Second World War.

Nazi–Stalinist collaboration to destroy occupied Poland

The German–Soviet agreements of 1939 allowed the partners to destroy and partition Poland and to establish a common frontier. This also provided the Nazis, especially the SS, with the conditions for 'a dress rehearsal' for later full blown genocidal violence and policies against Slavs.[76] Having gained Stalin as an ally and secured his rear, Hitler could carry out his air campaign against Britain and the successful conquest of Denmark, Norway, the Low Countries and France in spring 1940. The Comintern swung the international communist movement against the war dividing the French Communist Party. Hitler's gains are obvious – the conquest of Western Europe (apart from Britain) and half of Poland as well as a free hand in Central Europe and the Balkans. Post-1991 documentation and academic debate has refuted Stalin's claims to have utilised the additional time of 1939–1941 for strengthening the USSR before the Nazi onslaught of 1941.[77]

As in the inter-war period German–Soviet collaboration assumed important economic and trade dimensions which generally favoured the Reich.[78] Raw material imports such as oil, iron, copper, nickel and grain supplied the Nazi war effort. It is doubtful if this was counterbalanced by Soviet benefits in drawing on German military technology, especially air-craft, tanks and the import of equipment and munitions.[79]

It is uncontentious that the Allies of 1939–1941 were held together by their mutual interest in destroying, in their respective manners, the Pol-ishness of the areas of Poland which they controlled. The Nazis annexed Western Poland to the Reich and established a *General-Gouvernement* in the remainder. Their policy of ethnic reconstruction was predicated on Teu-tonic resettlement, the extermination of all Polish elites as well as Jews and gypsies and the total subjugation of the rest of the Slav population to slave labour.[80] We have already examined the similar methods of terror used in Sovietising and destroying the Polishness of the erstwhile Eastern Territo-ries during this period. These well-known aspects of Nazi and Soviet rule occasion little fundamental debate except about statistical parameters and specific details. Much discussion has, however, since the fall of commun-ism, concerned their degree of direct collaboration and coordination. Khruschev notes that the Ukraine NKVD chief, Serov, met regularly with Gestapo representatives to discuss Polish PoW exchanges and hints that other topics were discussed.[81]

Some German–Soviet actions that seem coordinated in time were the simultaneous arrests of Polish professors in the Kraków Jagiełłonian and Lwów universities in November 1939. Whether there is a direct linkage between the Soviet April–May 1940 massacre and the A-B Aktion (Ausserordentliche Befriedungsaktion) carried out by the Nazis in the *General-Gouvernement* from May–September 1940 has been much discussed.[82] The latter was also directed primarily at Poland's leadership and intelligentsia stratum and produced notable massacres such as the shooting and burial of 1700 prominent Poles in the Palmiry forest outside Warsaw. At least, an equal number of Polish politicians, academics and representatives of cultural life were murdered at the same time all over the *General-Gouvernement*. Large numbers of others, caught up in mass arrests, were sent to the Sachsenhausen and Auschwitz concentration camps. The Soviets were also busy hoovering up similar social Polish strata in West Belarus and West Ukraine at the same time.

Natalia Lebedeva and Wojciech Materski, with their unparalleled know-ledge of the Russian documentation, argue that the Nazi–Soviet repres-sion of the Polish intelligentsia was, not only mutually agreed, as has been demonstrated in this chapter, but also coordinated in some important respects.[83] The linkage between the April–May massacre of PoWs and the second deportation of April 1940 directed at the relatives of Poles in both Soviet and German imprisonment has always been striking.[84] Three meetings between Gestapo and NKVD specialists concerned with combating Polish resistance certainly occurred in Lwów in October 1939, Kraków in January 1940 and Zakopane in March 1940.[85] Lebedeva and Materski stress the significance of Beria's order of 7 March 1940 to the head of the NKVD Main Department for PoWs. This ordered Soprunenko to draw up a register of the relatives of PoWs – defined as wife, children, parents, brothers and sisters – resident in the German as well as Soviet, occupied parts of Poland.[86] Lebedeva and Materski subsequently uncovered evidence that the Germans had compiled similar lists in their own PoW camps.[87] As these had been exchanged through their respective diplomatic channels they surmise that the exchange of mutual services must have been on the basis of a formal agreement between their police services. Whether anti-Polish collaboration went any deeper has not been confirmed by any German documentation.[88] Further Russian primary evidence on this tantalising question may or may not exist, and, if it does, is unlikely to be revealed until further democratisation occurs in Russia.

Notes

1 John Erickson, 'The Soviet March into Poland, September 1939', in Keith Sword (ed.), *The Soviet Takeover of the Polish Eastern Provinces, 1939–1941*, Basingstoke: Macmillan, 1991.

2 FRUS, 1941, I, p. 206. For German–Soviet exchanges see DGFP, Series D, VIII, pp. 44–5, 76–7.

3 See *Polskie Siły Zbrojne w drugiej wojnie światowej*, 1, Part IV, *Kampania wrześniowa 1939*, London: IPiMS, 1986.

4 Wojciech Włodarkiewicz, 'Przedmoście rumuńskie w wojnie 1939r', *Wojskowy Pregląd Historyczny*, 41, 3 (1996), pp. 43–64.

5 KDZ, 1, no. 7.

6 DPSR, 1, no. 46.

7 British Cabinet decisions of 18 September 1939, PRO FO/371/23103. DSPR, I, pp. 49–51. Andrzej Szcześniak, *Zmowa: IV rozbiór Polski*, Warsaw: ALFA, 1990, pp. 138–9.

8 DSPR, 1, p. 51. DGFP, D, VIII, p. 130.

9 'Protokół niemiecko-sowiecki z 22 IX 1939r', *Zeszyty Historyczne*, no. 27, Paris: Instytut Literacki, 1974, pp. 169–70.

10 DGFP, D, VIII, nos 157, 158, 159, 160. See ibid., no. 193 for the supplementary protocol of 4 October 1939 specifying the new German–Soviet frontier in detail.

11 DSPR, 1, p. 54.

12 Robert Conquest, *Stalin: Breaker of Nations*, London: Weidenfeld & Nicolson, 1991, p. 223.

13 Circular by State Secretary Weizsäcker, 30 September 1939, DGFP, D, VIII, no. 169.

14 On the military aspects of the Polish resistance see *Polskie Siły Zbrojne. . .*, 1, Part IV, pp. 514–90.

15 Czesław Grzelak, *Kresy w czerwieni: Agresja Związku Radzieckiego na Polskę w 1939 roku*, Warsaw: Neriton/WIH AON, 1998.

16 See Generals Kukiel and Norwid-Negebauer in *Zbrodnia Katyńska w świetle dokumentów*, London: Gryf, 1982, pp. 8–9.

17 This is confirmed by the Chief of the General Staff General Wacław Stachiewicz who attended the key leadership meeting on the afternoon of 17 September: 'Pisma', *Zeszyty Historyczne*, no. 50, Paris: Instytut Literacki, 1971, p. 51.

18 Ryszard Szawłowski, 'The Polish–Soviet War of September 1939', in Sword, *Soviet Takeover of the Eastern Provinces*, p. 30.

19 KDZ, 1, no. 6. *Polskie Siły Zbrojne*, 1, Part IV, pp. 530 ff.

20 Stachiewicz, 'Pisma', p. 53. This also applied to the defence of Lwów against the Germans. The orders were categoric, however, that if Soviet troops got there first negotiations were to take place to enable the Polish forces to evacuate to Romania or Hungary.

21 See Ryszard Szawłowski (*pseud.* Karol Liszewski), *Wojna polsko-sowiecka 1939 roku*, London: Polish Cultural Foundation, 1986.

22 Szcześniak, *Zmowa: IV rozbiór Polski*, pp. 11–12.

23 KDZ, 1, pp. 87–8.

24 Stanisław Jaczyński, *Zagłada oficerów Wojska Polskiego na Wschodzie, Wrzesień 1939–Maj 1940*, Warsaw: Bellona, 2000, p. 28.

25 Piotr Żaroń, *Agresja Związku Radzieckiego na Polskę 17 Września 1939r: Los jeńców Polskich*, Toruń: Adam Marszałek, 1998, pp. 62–3.

26 Jerzy Łojek, *Dziejach Sprawy Katynia*, Białystok: Versus, 1988, p. 10.

27 *Polskie Siły Zbrojne...*, 2, Part 1, pp. 19–21.

28 Czesław Bloch, 'Polacy na obcźynie', *Wojskowy Przegląd Historyczny*, 35, 1–2 (1990), pp. 81–2. See also Tadeusz Dubicki, *Żołnierze polscy internowani w Rumunii w latach 1939–1941*, Łódź: Wydawnictwo Uniwersytetu Łódźkiego, 1990.

29 Russian portrayals of the September invasion as a liberation march, not aggression, provoked Polish–Russian polemics as late as the mid-1990s. Cf. Czesław Grzelak, 'Marsz wyzwoleńczy czy agresja?', *Wojskowy Przegląd Historyczny*, 40, 1 (1995), pp. 214–19.

30 Szawłowski, *Wojna polsko-sowiecka 1939r*, p. 87.

31 Langner has been roundly condemned for this, despite his claim that 'we did not fight the Soviets because we were not ordered to do so'. After being sent to Moscow he was allowed to escape to the West via Romania. See Żaroń, *Agresja Związku Radzieckiego...*, pp. 68–78. For Langner's account drawn from his diary see *Niepodległość* (London), no. 28 (1978), pp. 180–208.

32 *Pravda*, 1 November 1939.

33 Szawłowski, 'The Polish–Soviet War of September 1939', in Sword, *Soviet Takeover of the Eastern Provinces*, ch. 2.

34 Czesław Grzelak, *Dziennik sowieckiej aggresji: Wrzesień 1939*, Warsaw: Gryf, 1994, pp. 37–9.

35 Eugeniusz Kozłowski, 'Agresja na Polskę we wrześniu 1939r: próba bilansu strat', *Wojskowy Pregląd Historyczny*, 36, nos 3–4 (1991), pp. 21–49.

36 Jaczyński, *Zagłada oficerów...*, pp. 45–60.

37 Jan Gross, *Revolution from Abroad*, Princeton, NJ: Princeton UP, 1988, pp. 18–21.

38 Cf. Antony Polonsky (ed), *The Neighbours Respond*, Princeton, NJ: Princeton UP, 2004.

39 *Zbrodnia Katyńska w świetle dokumentów*, p. 13.

40 Jan Gross, 'The First Soviet-Sponsored Election in Eastern Europe', *East European Politics and Societies*, 1, 1 (Winter 1987), pp. 4–29.

41 Cf. Wiktor Sukiennicki, 'The Establishment of the Soviet Regime in Eastern Poland in 1939', *Journal of Central European Affairs*, 23 (1963), pp. 191–218.

42 DPSR, 1, pp. 69–70.

43 DPSR, 1, p. 92.

44 DPSR, 1, p. 68.
45 American embassy in Berlin estimates were 5.2 million racial Poles out of 13.2 million: FRUS, 1941, 1, pp. 218–22.
46 Edward Rozek, *Allied Wartime Diplomacy*, New York: Wiley, 1958, p. 37.
47 The area was 81 per cent rural. For the pattern of urban–rural and ethnic settlement see Gross, *Revolution from Abroad*, pp. 4–8.
48 Cf. Albin Głowacki, *Sowieci wobec Polaków na ziemiach wschodnich II Rzeczpospolitej, 1939–1941*, Łódź: GKBZpNP-IPN, 1998. Krzysztof Jasiewicz, *Zagłada Polskich kresów: Ziemiaństwo polskie na kresach północno-wschodnich Rzeczypospolitej pod okupacją Sowiecką, 1939–1941*, Warsaw: Volumen/IISP PAN, 1997. For the wider context see Terry Martin, 'Stalinist Forced Relocation Policies: Patterns, Causes and Consequences', in Myron Weiner and Sharon Russell (eds), *Demography and National Security*, New York: Berghahn, 2001.
49 The editors' view, HDZ, 1, p. 45.
50 Stanisław Kot, *Conversations with the Kremlin and Despatches from Russia*, Oxford: Oxford UP, 1963, p. 30.
51 Dmitri Volkogonov, *Stalin: Triumph and Tragedy*, London: Weidenfeld & Nicolson, 1991, p. 359.
52 Kazimierz Zamorski, 'Arrest and Imprisonment in the Light of Soviet Law', in Sword, *Soviet Takeover of the Polish Eastern Provinces*.
53 *Katyn: Dokumenty ludobojstwa*, Warsaw: ISP PAN, 1992, p. 39.
54 Stanisław Ciesielski, Wojciech Materski and Andrzej Paczkowski, *Represje Sowieckie wobec Polaków i Obywateli Polskich*, Warsaw: KARTA, 2000, p. 12.
55 Aleksander Gurjanow, 'Sowieckie represje wobec Polaków i obywateli polskich w latach 1936–1956 w świetle danych sowieckich', in Krzysztof Jasiewicz (ed.), *Europa NIEprovincjonalna*, Warsaw: ISP PAN, 1999, p. 973. Cf. Krzysztof Jasiewicz, 'Obywatele polscy aresztowani na terytorium tzw: Zachodniej Białorusji w latach 1939–1941 w świetle dokumentacji NKWD/NKGB', *Kwartalnik Historyczny*, no. 1 (1994), pp. 105–34.
56 Keith Sword (ed.), *Deportation and Exile: Poles in the Soviet Union, 1939–48*, Basingstoke: Macmillan, rev. edn, 1996, pp. 10–11.
57 The nomenclature of the area annexed by the USSR is, obviously, historically and politically controversial. This author considers that the terms 'Eastern' or 'Occupied' Territories are appropriate until the 1941 German invasion although West Belarus and West Ukraine appear as appropriate.
58 See Gross, *Revolution from Abroad*, Ch. 6.
59 The Soviet territorial levels, taken from the top downwards, were (Soviet Socialist) republic – autonomous republic – region, province or district known as oblast.
60 Beria's order of 20 March 1940 to S. Burdakov, Interior Minister of Kazakhstan, envisaged 25 000 families, totalling between 75 000 and 100 000 individuals, as being subject to deportation for ten years: KDZ, 2, no. 24. For an examination of the wider fate of Polish women in the USSR see Katherine Jolluck, *Exile and Identity: Polish Women in the Soviet Union during World War II*, Pittsburgh, PA: University of Pittsburgh Press, 2002.
61 KDZ, 1, no. 208.
62 KDZ, 2, no. 2.
63 KDZ, 2, no. 3.
64 Reproduced in Sword, *Soviet Takeover of the Polish Eastern Provinces*, pp. 306–7.
65 Z.S. Siemaszko, 'The Mass Deportations of the Polish Population to the USSR, 1940–1941', in Sword, *Soviet Takeover of the Polish Eastern Provinces*, pp. 225–7. It is a curious historical fact that the young Wojciech Jaruzelski and his family were deported at this time to Barnaul while his father was sent to a labour camp.
66 Ibid., pp. 228–30.

67 P.B. (Bogdan Podoski), *Polska Wschodnia, 1939–1941*, Rome: n.p., 1945; Kraków: 'W', 1989.
68 Władysław Wielhorski, *Los Polaków w niewoli sowieckiej*, London: Rada Ziem Wschodnich RP, 1956.
69 See *Deportacje i przemieszczenia ludności polskiej w głąb ZSRR, 1939–1945*, Warsaw: PWN, 1989, pp. 18–19.
70 Stanisław Świaniewicz, *Forced Labour and Economic Development*, London: Oxford UP, 1965, p. 42.
71 Ciesielski, Materski and Paczkowski, *Represje Sowieckie wobec Polaków i Obywateli Polskich*, pp. 13–14.
72 Ibid., p. 26. For the new literature on the subject consult Stanisław Ciesielski, Grzegorz Hryciuk and Aleksander Srebrakowski, *Masowe deportacje radzieckie w okresie II wojny światowej*, Wrocław: Instytut Historyczny Uniwersytetu Wrocławskiego, 1994. Aleksandr Gurjanov in KARTA, no. 12 (1994), pp. 114–36. 'Sprawozdanie z dyskusji dotyczące liczby obywateli polskich wywiezonych do Związku Radzieckiego w latach 1939–1941', *Studia z dziejów Rosji i Europa Środkowa-Wschodniej*, 31 (Warsaw, 1996). Aleksandr Gurjanov, Aleksandr Kokurin and Krzysztof Popiński (eds), *Droga śmierci*, Warsaw: KARTA, 1995.
73 *Deportacje i przemieszczenia...*, pp. 23–4.
74 Mikołaj Iwanow, *Pierwszy narod ukarany: Polacy w Związku Radzieckim*, Warsaw: Omnipress, 1991. Henryk Stroński, *Represje Stalinizmu wobec ludności polskiej na Ukrainie w latach 1929–1939*, Warsaw: Wspólnota Polska, 1998. Cf. *Polska-Białorus, 1918–1945*, Warsaw: Instytut Historii PAN, 1994, esp. M.P. Kościuk, '"Czynnik Polski" w stalinowskiej polityce represyjnej lat 30. na Białorus' and chapters by A.F. Chackiewicz and W. Michniuk.
75 Ciesielski, Materski and Paczkowski, *Represje Sowieckie wobec Polaków i Obywateli Polskich*, p. 26.
76 A recent study argues that Germany's September campaign against Poland marked the departure from normal civilised canons of warfare. The Poles were perceived as a racial enemy, whose elites were to be murdered while the ordinary population would be ground down and transported around, as necessary: Alexander B. Rossino, *Hitler Strikes Poland: Blitzkrieg, Ideology and Atrocity*, Lawrence, KS: UP of Kansas, 2003.
77 Aleksandr Nekrich, *'June 22, 1941': Soviet Historians and the German Invasion*, Columbia: University of South Carolina Press, 1968.
78 Cf. FRUS 1939, 1, pp. 490–8.
79 Conquest, *Stalin*, p. 225.
80 See Richard Lukas, *The Forgotten Holocaust: The Poles under German Occupation, 1939–1944*, Lexington, KY: UP of Kentucky, 1986.
81 *Khrushchev Remembers*, London: Sphere, 1971, p. 141.
82 Cf. Jacek Wilamowski, *Kłamstwo Stulecia*, Warsaw: CB, 2003, pp. 106–9.
83 Natalia Lebediewa and Wojciech Materski, 'Zastanawiający Dokument: Przyczynek do hipotezy o związku akcji AB ze zbrodnią Katyńska', in *W przeddzień zbrodni Katyńskiej: Agresja sowiecka 17 września 1939 roku*, Warsaw: NKHBZK, 1999, pp. 69 ff.
84 Clearly confirmed, in my view, by KDZ, vols 1 and 2.
85 Conquest, *Stalin*, p. 225. Nicholas Bethell, *The War Hitler Won*, London: Allen Lane, 1972, p. 337 considers that regular meetings took place between the NKVD and Gestapo to coordinate the suppression of Polish resistance.
86 KDZ, 2, pp. 47–8.
87 Lebediewa and Materski, 'Zastanawiający Dokument', pp. 74–83.
88 It also did not exclude the simultaneous existence of a developed Soviet espionage network in Nazi-occupied Poland. See Piotr Kołakowski, *NKWD i GRU na ziemiach polskich, 1939–1941*, Warsaw: Bellona, 2002, Ch. 3.

3   The Stalinist Terror and prisoner of war system

The nature of the Stalinist beast

Comparative communist, including Soviet, studies were riven from the 1960s onwards by the debate about the concept of totalitarianism. Simplifying enormously, one school of thought followed Leonard Schapiro's argument that the essence of communism was that its blend of Marxist–Leninist ideology and communist party practice produced an unending quest for total control over all walks of life.[1] The varieties of different types of fully established communism in 16 different countries following Tito's defiance of Stalin in 1948 and significant changes within individual systems over time convinced many specialists that the concept was being stretched far too much. Could totalitarianism be relative or comparative within the framework of Hannah Arendt's ideal type, as reformulated by Schapiro?

There was, subsequently, a return to the older political studies idea of the authoritarian system.[2] This trend was aided by the flexibility of Friedrich and Brzezinski's six point syndrome.[3] The framework of Marxist–Leninist ideology, the leading role of a disciplined communist party, police repression and monopolies over the economy, mass media and educational systems and weaponry could be, and were, revised and pulled in all directions. The empirical evidence of elite, bureaucratic, social and intellectual-cultural pluralism and the decline of police Terror in Eastern Europe could thus be accommodated.[4] The emergence of various forms of protest and reform currents produced new interpretations of revised balances between the communist party state and society such as the concept of the 'oppositionless state'. Just as a polycentric pattern emerged in the international relations between communist states, so by 1980 a varied spectrum of types of domestic communist political system ranged from Stalinist totalitarianism in Albania and North Korea to pluralist, even democratising, authoritarianism in Yugoslavia, and in different ways in Poland and Hungary.[5]

A key point about the exclusive totalitarian approach was that it allied with right-wing Reagan–Thatcher rhetoric in the 1980s and mobilised

Western public opinion towards regarding communism as fundamentally evil and unreformable.[6] The more flexible comparative communist academic view could, however, be used to explain certain phases in Soviet (1930s until 1953) or East European (1947–1954 for most countries) development as totalitarian, and to point up subsequent evolution away from it. The crimes of the Stalinist Terror, therefore, did not need denial, but their avowal did not necessarily foreclose the legitimacy of reform communist attempts such as Gorbachev's. Perceptions are, however, conditioned by the historical failure of intra-systemic communist reformism. Communist systems have collapsed everywhere apart from China, North Korea and Vietnam (along with Cuba for the duration, if that, of Castro's life). But the historian is obliged to note the different phases of the East–West ideological-systemic conflict which took place from 1917 to 1991. Stalinist crimes, such as Katyn, were used, or in the very odd British case not used, by Western politicians to shape public opinion in differing ways in different countries at different times.[7]

Soviet Stalinism was the classic form of totalitarianism although it is debatable whether it gelled in 1928 (industrialisation and collectivisation), 1934 (Kirov's murder) or 1936 (the qualitative shift into the Great Terror). The academic consensus is that it had certainly assumed its settled 'normal' form by 1940, the year in which Stalin took the decision to massacre the Polish PoWs. It continued until Stalin's death in 1953 (although its character was transformed during the Great Patriotic War). The shooting of Beria and his NKVD associates and Khruschev's qualified denunciation of Stalinism at the 1956 CPSU Twentieth Congress mark the limitation of terror and the emergence of socialist legality.

The release under Yeltsin of official Soviet documents on this period has provoked much academic debate and a significant, if paradoxical, reinterpretation of Stalinism. The previously dominant top-down view, pioneered by Robert Conquest, regarded the tyrannical dictator and his inner coterie as dominating the party, state and other bodies which became mere policy implementing transmission belts. Every so often, party rivals, incompetents or failures and their supporters at all levels were purged by the ruling team as scapegoats for policy disasters or current difficulties.[8] The personal characteristics, experience and feelings of the leader are crucial within such an explanatory framework. Stalin's subjective resentments against Poles, therefore, became significant in such analyses. Khruschev was a transitional leader with considerable scope for personal initiatives but these eventually led to his deposition by the Soviet elite. Brezhnev, however, was in many respects a board chairman who depended upon achieving consensual elite majority support.[9] The one constant factor, in Soviet leadership, according to Archie Brown, has been the decline in the power of successive CPSU First Secretaries since Stalin.[10]

The new interpretation of Stalinism pioneered by J. Arch Getty, Sheila Fitzpatrick, Roger Pethybridge, Gabor Rittersporn and others is largely bottom-up. Stalin is reinterpreted as the spokesman, almost agent, of a new stratum of managerially inclined party *apparatchiks* who replaced – exterminated is the more correct term – the ideologically dominated Old Bolshevik generation. James Burnham's insight of the managerial state blends with Stalinism as a form of modernity competing with Western equivalents.[11] Stalinists within their peculiar mind-sets applied rational managerial criteria to running the Police State, to eliminating all opposition and to achieving goals. All this is the opposite of Hannah Arendt's characterisation of Stalinist totalitarianism as a fundamentally psychotic drive subordinating the individual and intermediate organisations into an undifferentiated mass ruled by the dictator and his agents. The argument that the new leadership generation headed by Molotov, Malenkov, Beria, Kaganovich and their ilk at the different levels of Soviet power and society were Stalin's 'willing executioners' is valid enough. The impression that he became their prisoner, and could not have done otherwise is, however, highly debatable. I agree with E.A. Rees on the purposive character of the interplay between radical policies and the organisational building of High Stalinism in its totalitarian form after 1928.[12] The new social history of the 1930s has demolished older Arendtian concepts of the political monolith and total social atomisation. It has revealed the complex, and somewhat autonomous, nature of the forces in play. But the new revisionism has not shown that Stalin was incapable of being the wholly decisive element in the decision to carry out the 1940 massacre of Poles.[13] On the other hand, the recent emphasis on 'participatory totalitarianism' explains why the Stalinist regime went through intensive interrogation-confessional as well as legal-judicial procedures rather than simply massacring its victims without formalities.[14] Foreign observers noted that the systemic need to maintain legitimacy and internal motivation produced a gigantic 'system of bluff' designed 'to hide the reality from foreigners' but also justifying 'that reality at home'.[15]

By coincidence, the communist party archives of the Smolensk region, where the Katyn massacre took place, were captured by the invading Germans, although in a somewhat damaged and unreliable form. They found their way, thereafter, to America. Unfortunately, they do not contain much on local NKVD personnel, organisation and practices as that body's archives were highly centralised in Moscow. Merle Fainsod's classic study also only covers the inter-war period although he demonstrates the dynamic interaction between the party organisation, the security agencies and the local population, even at the height of the Great Terror.[16] Abarinov confirms that only the party archives fell into German hands; the NKVD oblast records were either destroyed or transported back to Moscow before the German invasion.[17] What has been learnt about NKVD institutional practices since 1990, however, suggests that his surmise that the Smolensk NKVD records contain anything relevant to Katyn is erroneous.

The People's Commissariat of Internal Affairs (NKVD) was established by the Bolsheviks at the outset of their rule. The secret police or Cheka, initially the GPU/OGPU, was not always subordinate to, or part of the NKVD and became an all-powerful and separate body at times. The NKVD which concerns our subject was, however, re-established in July 1934, when the OGPU was incorporated within it. This became Stalin's main instrument of Terror under Genrikh Yagoda and Nikolai Yezhov.[18] Lavrentii Beria, a Mingrelian Georgian, assumed control in December 1938. He brought in supporters such as Merkulov, Kobulov and Tsanava, the so-called 'Georgian Gang', although not all of them, such as Milshtein, were necessarily ethnic Georgian. The NKVD continued as such until April 1943 (with a break from February to July 1941) when the security police became independent of NKVD control under the successive NKGB, MVD and MGB labels.[19] The security police during 1939–1940 were controlled by the Main Administration of State Security (GUGB) of the NKVD. In theory, this was merely an NKVD department. In practice it was infinitely more significant than the other NKVD Main Administrations for Frontier and Internal Troops (GUKV), Corrective Labour Camps (GULAG) and the ordinary police or Militia. Conquest defines the GUGB as 'the central core and overwhelmingly predominant element in the NKVD'.[20] Its departments (Political, Economic, Special, Operations, Foreign and Transport) were generally more powerful than whole Main Administrations such as that for Special Camps (DPA), set up by Beria in September 1939, which concerns us directly in this study.

The Soviet system never had death camps like the Nazi ones at Auschwitz-Birkenau, Bełżec, Majdanek, Sobobór and Treblinka in the *General-Gouvernement* whose sole purpose was the rapid and efficient extermination of large numbers of human beings according to an industrial process of killing and disposal. Many writers, notably Conquest, however, suggest that the Soviet labour camps, particularly those in the Far North Eastern Kolyma and Komi regions situated on the Arctic Ocean, assumed something close to this function after 1936 and that around three-quarters of the Poles sent there died in 1940–1941.[21] Minority nationalities within the USSR, such as the Poles and Ukrainians, sentenced to hard labour or *katorga*, were most at risk of a purposive Soviet policy of being worked to death under poor living conditions. Conquest surmises that death rates per annum in the camps, even under non-*katorga* conditions, could have reached 20 per cent and that around a quarter of the Polish deportees to Kazakhstan perished. Stalin and the NKVD, therefore, had quite an efficient and cheap alternative to outright massacre, particularly as the extensive character of Soviet industrialisation produced a growing labour shortage.[22] This circumstance makes it harder to explain why mass execution of the Polish officers and policemen, however exceptional, rather than the Arctic labour camp option, was resorted to by Stalin. The Rosefield–Wheatcroft debate and the new Soviet documentation has revised downwards most earlier estimates of the numbers held as slave labour in prison camps.[23] One may thus conclude that Kolyma represented an exceptional case which peaked during the Second World War.

It is now generally agreed that Conquest's older figure of 20 million, let alone Medvedev's sensationalist figure of 40 million 'excess deaths' for the Stalinist period probably has to be reduced, like the figures for the 1940–1941 Polish deportations, by a factor of around three. The top estimate is now that anything between four and seven million Soviet citizens, out of a total of about 24 million repressed (executed, imprisoned in labour camps or deported to restricted settlement), over the whole period, were shot during 1929–1953; even that figure includes additional, *ad hoc* and not always properly sentenced and recorded Second World War executions.[24]

NKVD executions, of individuals, or of smallish numbers per night, took place in the basement cellars of their internal prisons on a regular and ongoing basis as penal-judicial investigations were completed and confirmed. Mass executions in outside locations were the exception, not the rule, even during the peak 1936–1941 period. They were resorted to when prisoner numbers escalated out of control as a result of some drive against communist-party-designated enemies. The best-known mass execution and burial sites have been found at Kuropaty outside Minsk and Vinnitsa and Bykovna in the Ukraine. Within Russia, Merridale suggests that the huge sprawling municipal cemeteries of Butova and Kommunarka in South Moscow and Levashova and Preobrazhenskoe in Leningrad were used by the NKVD to bury victims alongside normal civil usage. She surmises that most major cities had 'a sinister new earthwork in its outskirts' covering NKVD burial sites after 1936.[25] Like our specific cases of the Kharkov forest-park, Katyn and Mednoe, burial areas were enclosed and turned into forbidden zones under NKVD surveillance.

Soviet treatment of PoWs captured in Eastern Poland

The Soviet Union's invasion and occupation of Eastern Poland in September 1939 was a clear act of aggression in international law. It contravened its signed obligations under the 1932 Non-Aggression Pact with Poland and the 1933 London Convention on the Definition of the Aggressor. But the Soviets did not declare war, nor did the Poles respond with a declaration of war. As a result there was confusion over the status of soldiers taken captive and whether they qualified for treatment as PoWs.[26] Jurists consider that the absence of a formal declaration of war does not absolve a power from the obligations of civilised conduct towards PoWs. On the contrary, failure to do so makes those involved, both leaders and operational subordinates, liable to charges of War Crimes and Crimes against Humanity.[27] These principles, stated by the Allied victors at Nuremberg, have been re-iterated in the post-1990 Yugoslav conflicts.

The general Polish view, accepted by post-communist Russian scholars after 1991, has been that the Soviet aggression was sufficiently denounced as such by the Polish authorities.[28] The continuity provided by the Polish Government-in-Exile and the blatant character of both German and Soviet aggression in September 1939 meant that Poland in international law should be regarded as an occupied country. The self-serving Soviet argument that as Poland had fallen apart and ceased to exist its captured soldiers should not benefit from PoW status was unsubstantiated. There is now general agreement with the view of the leading Polish authority that Polish soldiers, and associated supporters, should have qualified automatically for PoW status on being taken into captivity.[29] The mature PRL view became that the absence of a declaration of war meant that their status was that of 'internees', as in the case of those who crossed over into Lithuania.[30] This Soviet definition of the latter was also applied to Polish PoWs generally after the Nazi invasion of Summer 1941. The purely legal view and the perception of actual realities, therefore, varied according to time and circumstance. Soviet behaviour and political rhetoric in September 1939 qualified their Polish captives as armed counter-revolutionaries opposing the reassertion of Soviet power over their own territories.[31]

International law regarding PoWs was codified by the Hague Conventions of 1899 and 1907 and confirmed by the Geneva Convention of 27 July 1929. The latter confirmed and widened the principle of humane treatment of PoWs including their living, social, cultural and sanitary conditions, personal security, right to attempt escape and to individual, not collective, punishment through due judicial process. It also specified important principles, which are highly relevant to discussion of the 1940 massacre, in defining who should be regarded as a PoW and thus benefit from the rights of that status. The Red Army resented support for the Polish Army by border guards, local militias, armed policemen (gendarmes in Soviet terminology) and the Polish population. It responded with on-the-spot executions, violence and mass arrests during its advance, especially against officers and individuals perceived as non-workers or peasants. As a point of law it is, therefore, of cardinal importance that the 1929 Geneva Convention clearly extended PoW status to paramilitary and volunteer organisations, the police and civilians taken captive during military operations.[32] The Polish President's General Mobilisation Order of 30 August 1939 called up all reserve officers, territorial militia and auxiliaries. In addition the Council of Ministers decreed the inclusion of the police within the Armed Forces on 12 September. These groups, therefore, qualified for PoW status in the light of international law. The formal extension of these rights to civilian combatants by the 1907 Hague Convention meant nothing to the Soviets. The Red Army committed, what would now be regarded as war crimes, by executing many individuals, of all categories, as 'bandits', along with soldiers caught continuing armed struggle in the rear of the Red Army.

It should also be noted that the institution of 'Protecting Power', a neutral country assuming the responsibilities of care for the PoWs of another country involved in conflict, did not apply to Poles in Soviet captivity during 1939–1941. The British embassy in Moscow, formally looked after Polish interests in the USSR after September 1939 but was prevented from fulfilling this obligation. The Americans felt that representations by them on the 'deplorable' condition of both military and civilian Polish prisoners in the USSR would be rejected by the Soviets, so they did not make any.[33] The International Red Cross was not allowed to carry out its international duties of care over PoWs in any way. The USSR declared that it was not bound to allow Red Cross supervision of PoWs on its territory as it had not signed the 1929 Convention on the Treatment of PoWs and did not recognise the Hague Conventions.

Polish PoWs, when captured, were disarmed and held for a short initial period by the Red Army. As soon as practicable, they were handed over directly to the NKVD whose control over them lasted until August 1941. This openly contravened the Hague and Geneva Convention principles that governments and their armed forces not the security police, should be responsible for PoWs. Red Army treatment of captives depended upon the conditions of war. It ranged from reprisals such as torture, humiliation, robbery and killings through shooting or bayoneting at one extreme to the immediate liberation of rankers at the other. Officers were invariably held and sent up the line for questioning by senior Red Army, and subsequently NKVD, officers. The varied treatment of PoWs in this initial stage was also openly at variance with the humanitarian principles and living conditions laid down in the 'Regulations for the Treatment of PoWs' approved by the Soviet Council of Ministers.[34] One presumes that these regulations were designed as part of the Soviet 'big lie' for propaganda and 'external' use. They also reflected regime self-delusion and its tendency to apply the principle of declaring that black was white as self-justification.

The NKVD Escort Guards were put on a military footing from the outset. The Minister of Defence, Klimentii Voroshilov, ordered the Red Army Military Councils on 19 September to evacuate captives, through back roads in order to avoid clogging up the main military effort. They were to be handed over to the NKVD at the old frontier who would convey them to the Kozelsk and Putivl distributor or filtration camps.[35] Given wartime conditions, prisoners' treatment was extremely poor, and often harrowing, *en route* to the designated collection camps close to the nearest wide gauge railway stations.[36] Here they were handed over to the NKVD Department for Prisoners of War who searched and registered them and began the process of selection by appropriate categories. Officers, policemen, state officials and whoever was recognised as counter-revolutionary were separated from NCOs and rankers. Medical and sanitary conditions as well as food and accommodation were extremely primitive in these hurriedly thrown-up concentration camps. Most PoWs spent up to a few weeks in these camps before being herded by the NKVD Escort Guards onto heavily crowded and slow-moving freight trains or cattle wagons and conveyed, under dreadful conditions, on to permanent camps deeper in the USSR.

Lev Mekhlis, Head of the Red Army's Political Department, informed Stalin on 20 September of the difficulties being faced in occupying Eastern Poland while coping with vast masses of prisoners.[37] Deputy Defence Minister Grigorii I. Kulik proposed initially, as was done between 23 and 25 September, that Ukrainian and Belarusan prisoners, apart from officers, should be released and allowed to go home after registration.[38] Soviet policy hardened, thereafter. Stalin, unconcerned by the overloading of military capacities, supported NKVD ideological-security pressure to control and process all PoWs, rather than to leave them as counter-revolutionary threats in the occupied territories.

One needs to deal at this point with the thorny issue of the numbers of Polish PoWs taken into Soviet captivity. Initial Red Army figures adding up to an incredible 452536, including 18789 officers, can be discounted because of double counting, the inclusion of civilians and militia who had resisted and the normal muddle and confusion of wartime. Molotov claimed 230000 in his 31 October 1939 Supreme Soviet speech while the Red Army newspaper later asserted that 181223 PoWs had been captured.[39] The most widely accepted figure for the initially captured PoWs is 240000–260000.[40] By 2 October about 56 per cent of the 99149 prisoners who had passed through the collection camps had been sent on to NKVD camps.[41] The inflow into the former was curtailed a week later, after which they were run down. We shall examine next how the NKVD organised its PoW camp network but here one should note that the number of PoWs held in NKVD captivity had decreased by mid-November to 39600 out of the 125000 accepted by the NKVD.[42]

Making and administration of Soviet policy towards the Polish PoWs

As one might expect the Germans had made meticulous preparations, within their long-prepared plans for aggression and expansion, for dealing with PoWs.[43] The largely unprepared Soviets were almost overwhelmed by the huge numbers of prisoners taken captive so their initial responses were fairly hand-to-mouth. It did not take long, however, for the leadership to develop their preferred form of organisation for dealing with PoWs and to grope their way towards producing a coherent policy.

Like everything in the USSR, matters concerning PoWs were decided at the highest level by the VKP (b) politburo. This normally merely meant the endorsement of proposals put to them by specific bodies with amendments added by Stalin. Reflecting the influence of the security services in the system, Beria, sent Molotov (chairman of the Council of People's Commissars) proposals, as early as 17 September, ostensibly on behalf of the Red Army Staff. Eight collection camps were to be established in the Belarus and Kiev military districts along with two distributor camps at Kozelsk and Putivl.[44] The politburo also confirmed his proposal to put the NKVD Escort Guards on a war footing.[45] These moves indicated that the Soviet leadership decided from the outset that the Polish officer and police PoWs and their camps would be handled by the NKVD, and not by the Red Army, as laid down in international law.

Thus empowered by Stalin, Beria set about organising a Main Department for Prisoner of War Affairs (DPA) within the Ministry of Internal Affairs (NKVD) in his Order of 19 September; its functions were set out in its statute of the same day.[46] The DPA was quite separate from the NKVD Main Department for Correctional Labour Camps (GULAG). The new department was originally attributed 56 posts – the Head and his two deputies, a 12-strong secretariat, an 8-strong Political Department and 4 special sub-departments for Special Affairs (8 posts), Records and Registration (10), Supply (8) and Sanitation (6). Beria delegated direct oversight of the DPA to his Deputy-Minister of Internal Affairs, Vasilii Vasilevich Chernyshev. He appointed Major of State Security Petr Karpovich Soprunenko as the department's Head with Semen Moiseevich Nekhoreshev as Political Commissar. Ivan Ivanovich Khokhlov and Iosif Mikhailovich Polukhin were appointed as Deputy-Heads of the Department, with the latter being put in charge of the security guards.

Beria also ordered the appropriate NKVD oblast executives, together with GULAG representatives, to establish eight PoW camps and appointed their commandants and commissars. We will focus on three of these NKVD-run special camps – Kozelsk, Starobelsk and Ostashkov – as the centre of our concerns in this study. Together with the other five – Yukhnov (usually referred to as Pavlishtchev-Bor in Russian or Pawlisczew Bor in Polish), Putivl, Kozelchanskii, Yuzhskii and Oranskii – they were initially designated as distributor and filtering, just as much as holding, camps. Two other camps were also established at Gryazovets and Vologda soon afterwards. Soprunenko and Nekhoreshev worked out a model statute, approved by Chernyshev on 23 September, regulating the functions, organisation and personnel of a PoW camp.[47]

While these organisational arrangements were being implemented policy towards the PoWs underwent a number of twists and turns. The Red Army and NKVD leaderships were, initially, overwhelmed by the vast numbers of PoWs. Their concern, to lessen pressure on limited resources, and to utilise PoW labour power as rapidly as possible, was reflected in a draft resolution presented on 2 October by Beria and Mekhlis to the VKP (b) CC Secretary, Andrei Zhdanov.[48] Their main proposals were the release of Belarusan and Ukrainian ordinary-ranking PoWs resident in Belarus and Ukraine; to assign 25000 PoWs to complete the building of the Nowogród Wolyński–Korzec–Lwów road by the end of December; to organise a separate camp for officers; and to hold the most senior officers (lieutenant-colonel to general) and high state and military officials separately from the remaining officer ranks; similar segregation was to be applied to intelligence, counter-intelligence and police functionaries, prison guards and gendarmes. PoWs originating from the German-occupied part of Poland were also to be grouped separately, prior to negotiations with Germany about their return. An expanded and more detailed draft was submitted to Stalin and approved by the politburo on 3 October.[49] The politburo also resolved the following day that the Military Councils of the Ukrainian and Belarusan Fronts should have the power of confirming death penalties on Poles sentenced for counter-revolutionary activity. Polish prisoners were thus sentenced and held in prisons in the Ukraine and Belarus until they shared the same fate in April–May 1940 as their colleagues sent on to the camps. Others were transported to other camps, and in due course retrieved, and directed on to Kozelsk and Starobelsk.[50]

The filtering and segregation principle was applied by Beria directly in subsequent orders which specified PoW categories to be sent to individual camps.[51] Senior officers and officials were to go to Starobelsk and the spies, police and prison guards to Ostashkov (plus military settlers, junior officers and rankers not qualifying for release to the occupied territories as laid down by Soprunenko on 29 October). The original plan was to group ordinary rankers from German-occupied territories in Kozelsk and Putivl. In late October it was decided to exchange ordinary rankers from the German-occupied territories and to direct the remainder to work in camps run by the Ministry of Ferrous Metallurgy. Kozelsk arrived at its final designation as a camp for officers and higher state and military officials at this time. The organisation, life and characteristics of these three special camps will be discussed more fully, later. Three further important issues need to be discussed at this point – PoW releases, exchanges with the Germans and utilisation as forced labour.

In order to cope with the flood of prisoners being taken by the Red Army Chernyshev specified, on 7 October, the categories to be released on the spot, and the methods of their release home.[52] Only ordinary ranks, resident in West Belarus and West Ukraine, were to be freed. Orders for the military commanders strictly forbad the release of officers and directed that they should be sought out rigorously by the Red Army and handed over to the NKVD.[53] PoWs already detained and sent on to the camps were covered by the politburo decision of 3 October. As a result of these decisions about a third of all PoWs held by the NKVD were released during October–November, the bulk of whom went by 18 October. Just under half of the 42 400 released were ethnic Polish.

The principle that the Germans and Soviets should exchange each other's Polish PoWs, originally resident in the other's occupied part of

Poland, was not specified in the secret protocols to the agreement of 28 September 1939. It emerged after that as part of their growing cooperation to destroy Poland. Stalin had already provided Hitler with a sweetener by returning some hundred German communists who had sought refuge in the USSR to the tender mercies of Nazi concentration camps. Their handing over at Brest-Litovsk provided early practice for the NKVD and Gestapo to work out the technique of prisoner exchanges. Beria and Mekhlis drew Stalin's attention, in early October, to the need to segregate the Polish PoWs according to occupation zone. The Kozelsk and Putivl camps were rapidly designated for this holding purpose although few were sent to the latter. Beria estimated, on 11 October, that about 33000, mainly Polish, rankers, were subject to exchange with the Germans.[54] A report, submitted to him by Soprunenko on the 8th, indicated that 6928 in this category were held in Ostashkov, 5470 in Kozelsk, 5030 in Yukhnov, 3521 in Yuzhskii, only 1219 in Putivl, and between 1573 and 2593 in the remaining camps.[55] The politburo approved Beria's proposal to start immediate negotiations with the Germans over the PoW exchange, on 13 October.

Beria's initiative responded to a German Fourth Army offer, on 11 October, to hand over about 20000 Polish PoWs of ethnic Belarusan and Ukrainian origins whose homes were in Belarus and the West Ukraine. This was supported by the German Military Attaché in Moscow who proposed a mutual exchange of their PoWs according to the criterion of zone of permanent residence. Subsequent discussions between Potemkin and Schulenberg agreed that the exchanges should take place at Brześć-on-the-Bug and Jagodzin close to Dorohusk.[56]

The NKVD planners ordered their agents involved in the exchange to check the personal documents of the incomers rigorously in order to identify their designated counter-revolutionary categories of officers, intelligence agents, police, prison guards and gendarmes. These were to be sent to the Yukhnov and Yuzhshkii camps.[57] The outgoers were to be handed over by the Red Army but they were transported to the frontier by NKVD Escort Troops in railway cattle wagons.[58] They do not seem to have made a very good job as they failed to arrive by agreed dates, were deficient in feeding their prisoners and, above all, committed the cardinal Soviet sin of allowing 85 PoWs to escape from the first convoy and 24 from the second.[59] The exchanges began on 30 October, the day after the delayed arrival of the German Exchange Commission, and continued until 23 November. The Soviets handed over 42492 PoWs, 24670 at Brześć and 17822 at Jagodzin, over 90 per cent of whom were ethnic Poles. The Germans during the same period managed to hand over only 13757 PoWs, 10409 at Brześć and 3348 at Jagodzin.[60]

Soprunenko's statement, that all the prisoners accepted by the Soviets from the German-occupied zone were allowed to go home after questioning, is untrue. Some were released, as the NKVD could not cope with holding and feeding the additional inflow, at peak. Most, if not all, were arrested by the NKVD soon afterwards and a large number were sent directly to labour camps. Those identified as counter-revolutionaries were arrested and held in prisons. Their ultimate fates were decided by the interrogation and sentencing process.

In the end the Soviets disposed of three times as many PoWs to the Germans as the other way around, thus gaining a substantial saving in resources. In my view, which counters the previous Polish academic consensus, this was the prime consideration for politicians and war planners on both sides. The dominant recent explanation for the 'Final Solution' of the Jews is that overwhelming population overcrowding in the *General-Gouvernement* led the Nazis to choose the option of industrially organised extermination.[61] The evidence that the Soviets won out in the PoW exchange is that subsequent German efforts in April 1940 to renew the process by returning more of the Poles, which they held from the Soviet-occupied territories, including Lithuania, were resisted strenuously.[62] The Germans probably allowed themselves to be caught out in this way in the first, and only major, round of PoW exchange because of their pressing need for slave labour. Why the Soviets failed to take the opportunity of ridding themselves of at least some of the junior Polish officers at this stage also still has to be explained.[63]

As early as 25 September, the Interior Ministry had ordered that 25 000 PoWs be assigned to the building of the Nowogród Wołyński–Lwów road.[64] Only about 15 000 were officially directed for that purpose. But 10 300 rankers and junior officers were sent to work in iron, copper and manganese mines as well as in quarries in East Ukraine run by the Ministry of Ferrous Metallurgy. There they were held under extremely poor living and working conditions in three main camps.[65] It is true that the interministerial agreement of 14 October 1939 between the Ferrous Metallurgy and Interior Ministries, covering a force of 10 000–11 000, laid down that they be paid the equivalent rates of free hired labour.[66] That such hard and dangerous labour was not a particularly attractive proposition under wartime conditions is shown by the fiasco of subsequent efforts to convert them to contractual free labour status. A report of 19 January 1940 by a government inspection commission stated that only 1541 PoWs were paid by piece-rate; a mere 158 longer-term contract agreements had been signed in the Krivoi Rog basin. The bulk of PoWs showed their dissatisfaction with the conditions, which the commission, privately, accepted as justified, through regular work stoppages in the form of refusal to leave camp for work and malingering.[67] There were major work stoppages against the Soviet rejection of demands to be released home from Christmas Day onwards. The camp authorities reacted, initially, to the refusal to work with about 250 arrests and sent leading troublemakers to Ostashkov.

The Soviet leadership took the Polish refusal to collaborate, in what by Stalinist standards was a fair offer, very badly. They concluded that if

Polish ordinary ranks proved so obstinate, there was even less chance that officers would cooperate. They therefore wound up the East Ukraine labour camps in May 1940 just as the main massacre was ending.[68] About 8000 PoWs were transferred to GULAG camps in sub-Polar north eastern European Russia. There, they were forced to work, with considerable loss of life and great damage to health, on the construction of the main Northern-Pechora railway line.[69] About 2000 were rewarded for being more cooperative by being sent to the Równo labour camp and work on road building projects in Eastern Galicia.[70]

By the end of November 1939 the official Soviet number of PoWs held in all NKVD camps was 39 600 while the end of year figure was 38 710. The three special camps of Kozelsk, Starobelsk and Ostashkov held 15 087 of the former while another 23 623 were held in labour camps. The process of segregating officers to Kozelsk and Starobelsk and policemen and associated categories to Ostashkov was so far advanced as to be almost complete. It then became possible for the NKVD to concentrate on its main political function – euphemistically termed 'the operational-Chekhist servicing of PoWs'. Before we examine that, however, we need to discuss the specific context of the three main special camps which held the PoWs destined to be massacred.

The special camps

Commandants were formally in full control and responsible for everything in their camps but in practice they were subordinate to a whole host of party-state and NKVD policy-making and control-checking officials. As usual in the Soviet system, they were supervised by the camp political commissar and overseen by the Heads of DPA departments and their inspectors as well as by the territorial NKVD executives. The commandants were Vasilii Korolev in Kozelsk, Alexandr Berezkov in Starobelsk and Pavel F. Borisovets in Ostashkov. Their respective commissars were Mikhail Alexeev, Mikhail Kirshin and Ivan V. Yurasov. Such functionaries were not particularly distinguished in terms of intellect, character or personality. Korolev, for example, was criticised for incompetence, lack of dynamism and poor leadership.[71] Kirshin and the Kozelsk Special Department Head, Pavel Borisov, were accused of drunkenness and of lacking authority.[72] Their replacement was proposed by various DPA inspectors but only Borisov and an Economic Department official were actually dismissed. Soprunenko preferred to maintain continuity and strengthened the *Komendatura* with DPA and NKVD provincial agents.[73] The latter overshadowed commandants as did the heads of the camp Special Departments, Hans A. Ejlman (Borisov's successor) in Kozelsk, Mikhail Lebedev in Starobelsk and Grigorii V. Korytov in Ostashkov.

Beria's Order 0308 of 19 September 1939 laid down the organisation and personnel framework for the camps and specified that there should be 134 camp officials per 10 000 PoWs.[74] The commandant was to have a deputy, an assistant and three duty orderlies. The camp chancellery (12 posts) was to oversee the following departments – Special (9), Political (7), Records and Registration (13), Supply (19), Financial (5) and Sanitation (7) – as well as fire fighting and internal security teams. NKVD inspectors reported on the generally low professional and moral level of the camp functionaries. They found difficulty in coping with their professional duties, especially in records, and were often dissatisfied with their relegation in career terms from the cities to the camps.[75] DPA inspectors' reports are littered with criticisms of the camps' senior officials and proposals that they be replaced.

The camp guards, composed of older army reservists and local inhabitants, were poorly equipped and clothed. Their superiors complained of their tendency to get corrupted by getting too close to the PoWs by running errands and providing minor services for them in exchange for jewellery, watches, clothing and the like. Although the Soviets did not recognise the Geneva Convention rights to PoW self-government they tolerated it in practice. Camp and block/barrack Seniors (Elders) were approved, even in the collection camps, in order to provide liaison and coordination. The *Komendatura* also decreased their own administrative and service burdens by allowing PoWs to provide for themselves in everyday aspects of life.

Kozelsk

The most widely known Second World War Polish PoW camp is Kozelsk because its massacred inmates were discovered and exhumed at Katyn in 1943.[76] The similar fate of their compatriots at Starobelsk and Ostashkov came out into the full light of day only in the 1990s. Kozelsk is situated in Smolensk oblast on the Smolensk–Bryansk–Tula railway line, about 150 miles to the south east of Smolensk. The well-known Polish aristocratic Ogiński and Puzyna families had substantial estates there during the Polish–Lithuanian Commonwealth.

The PoW camp was established in early October 1939 and was wound up in July 1941. It was situated about five miles from the railway station and three miles from the town in what during the Polish–Lithuanian Commonwealth had been a fortified monastery with walls, four towers and a wide gate. In the Soviet period this had been converted into the Gorky rest home. The buildings were made up of two quite separate parts. The ex-monastery grounds were made up of four closed and run down Orthodox churches and what had originally been housing for clergy and pilgrims. About 500 yards away, separated from the former by a wood, lay the 'skit' or hermitage, a complex of huts for Eremite monks, where Felix Dostoyevsky had stayed. This had been turned into a rest home for mothers with young children. The layout of the PoW camp was, therefore, well suited for the long-term Soviet purpose of isolating, in the monastery, PoWs originating from German-occupied territory and Lithuania from those coming from the Soviet-occupied areas who were held in the hermitage. In late summer 1939 machine guns were placed in the four towers, elevated sentry boxes were constructed between them and the whole terrain was surrounded by barbed wire.

The Kozelsk camp was initially inundated with up to 12 000 prisoners, mainly rankers, captured in the September invasion. The bulk of these were either exchanged with the Germans or sent to labour camps. Most of the civilians, notably priests and court and procuracy officials, were also moved to Ostashkov with the designation of Kozelsk as an officers' camp. By the end of November the camp's population had stabilised at around 4700 while the officer inflows (4727 during November) from other camps had transformed its composition. This lessened the camp's overcrowding, and living conditions improved considerably. It became an overwhelmingly officers' camp. Four generals, Stanisław Bohaterowicz, Henryk Minkiewicz-Odrowąż, Mieczysław Smorawiński and Jerzy Wołkowicki, as well as rear-admiral Ksawery Czernicki were detained in Kozelsk. Just before its evacuation it held 330 majors, lieutenant-colonels and colonels plus 15 naval captains, 647 army captains and another 3480 lieutenants and ensigns. Military officers thus totalled 4477 out of the 4599 inmates. The latter included five ordinary ranks and nine military chaplains. The 107 non-military personnel were composed of 61 state officials, 37 refugees and nine landowners.

Kozelsk also held the one woman to be murdered from the camps in the massacre. Sub-lieutenant Janina Lewandowska (born 1910), a pilot in the Polish air force, was the daughter of General Józef Dowbór-Muśnicki. Her father was hated by the Bolsheviks and she was transported out of Kozelsk to perish at Katyn. At the age of 20 she had become the first woman in Europe to parachute from a height of over five kilometres. She also had a beautiful and charismatic singing voice which gained her the soubriquet of the 'Poznań nightingale'. Lewandowska had separate quarters and played a full part in the camp's conspiratorial and religious life for which she suffered a period of camp detention.[77] A purely fictional American piece of Katyn literature imagines her camp life and death.[78]

A DPA report of 1 December admitted that much work still had to be done to make Kozelsk suitable as an officers' camp.[79] The conversion of the wooden bunk beds from three- to two-level ones had been completed satisfactorily. The camp's buildings were, however, not suited for winter heating. Sanitary conditions were uneven while there were numerous shortfalls, in food, clothing and water supply because of inefficient pumps. These deficiencies in the camp's domestic economy had necessitated the replacement of the Deputy Commandant. Changes had also been required in the Records Department although a file had already been drawn up for each PoW and photographing and fingerprinting was in train. The strongly patriotic and religious character of most officers was being countered by political work amongst the PoWs – the screening of Soviet films, the availability of Soviet newspapers and question and answer sessions on current issues.

Starobelsk

Starobelsk was a smallish county town in Voroshilovgrad (now Lugansk) oblast in the eastern part of the Ukrainian SSR. It is situated about 160 miles to the south east of Kharkov on the River Ajdar. The PoW camp, established in early October, was located in the substantial rectangular grounds (about 15 acres) of an ex-Orthodox convent and seminary and surrounded by a 1.7-metre-high wall.[80] This in turn was surrounded by a three-metre-wide defence zone and a barbed wire fence. There were ten internal sentry posts equipped with searchlights and machine guns. Sixteen of the enclosed, and very run down, 22 buildings, which included a disused Orthodox church, cottages, sheds, barns and stables, were utilised for PoW occupation. Survivors' accounts confirm that the original accommodation was extremely cramped and flea-ridden. Facilities were initially very poor. Services such as latrines, water tanks and baths had to be built and serviced by the prisoners' own labour.[81] The Poles noted bullet-scarred walls and bones – signs of executions from the Bolshevik Revolution and Civil War. Rotting wooden bunks indicated that the buildings had been used, subsequently, as either a prison or military barracks.

Conditions became tolerable only towards mid-November after Starobelsk had been designated as the main holding camp for officers. The vast initial inflow of rankers was transferred elsewhere. The camp population decreased from 6000, and stabilised at under 4000. Almost all of them were officers including most of the air force and Gas Institute personnel taken prisoner. Just before the evacuation began Starobelsk held eight generals, 497 between the ranks of major and colonel, 843 captains and 2527 junior ranks. As 3884 (including nine military chaplains) out of 3893 inmates were military officers, Starobelsk was even more heavily an officers' camp than Kozelsk.

The camp authorities utilised 300 PoWs, working a 14-hour day in November, to build two additional barracks, with two-level wooden beds, housing 1040. The larger church, which had been used as a granary and whose grain had been exported to Germany, was also later emptied and converted for PoW use. The eight generals (Leon Billewicz, Stanisław Haller, Aleksander Kowalewski, Kazimierz Łukowski, Konstanty Plisowski, Franciszek Sikorski, Leonard Skierski and Piotr Skuratowicz) were isolated and held separately in the town in a house on the corner of October and Kirov streets. All were to perish in Kharkov.[82]

Ostashkov

The town of Ostashkov, situated in Kalinin (now Tver) oblast, was once famous for leather manufacturing. It lies north west of Kalinin on the railway line between Great Luki and Bologoe. The camp was situated about nine miles from the town, again in the grounds of an ex-monastery, but one that this time was situated on the five-hectare-large Stolbnoi Island in Lake Seliger.[83] Saint Nil had lived in a hermitage and was buried there. The Romance-style monastery built on the island in 1864 and the seminary became the centre of a large religious community. Pilgrims, such as Czarina Alexandra, wife of Czar Nicholas II, visited his shrine. The monks were killed and the cult forbidden by the Bolsheviks during the Revolution. The island abounded with Polish connections. The monastery was built by the forced labour of 1863–1864 insurrectionists. Prisoners of the Polish–Soviet wars of 1919–1920 were held there until the Treaty of Riga. After that, like Kozelsk, it was converted into a rest home (and aquatic sports centre) before being turned into a camp for Japanese PoWs in 1939. The Polish prisoners were forced to work in 1939–1940 on the construction of a high embankment and a wooden bridge linking the island to the mainland.

Ostashkov was a general holding camp for Polish PoWs of all ranks from early October onwards. There was a tendency from the outset for civilians arrested for aiding the Polish Army and for officials to be sent there. At peak the camp held just under 8400. The number of inmates was reduced to 6600 by late November through the exchanges with the Germans and the release of civilians and rankers resident in the Occupied Territories. The transfer of officers and ordinary soldiers elsewhere was accelerated after Ostashkov was designated as the main camp for police-men, border (KOP) and prison guards, gendarmes and state and judicial officials.

Prisoners were accommodated in a complex of 22 PoW blocks con-verted from single-storey, decaying and flea-ridden ex-monastic buildings surrounding the Orthodox church. The area was enclosed by a wooden and barbed wire fence with the camp administration being located in buildings outside it. A DPA inspector's report criticised poor camp secur-ity. It was not surrounded entirely by a barbed wire fence and was com-pletely without searchlights. The camp administration was not coping with the pressing accommodation, domestic economic and socio-cultural prob-lems of the prisoners while staff were incompetent, corrupt and poorly motivated.[84] Tishkov was dismayed by the 'chaotic state' of the records department as nobody knew the exact number of PoWs in the camp. He recommended (in vain) that police reservists, ordinary-ranking KOP border guards and reserve officers belonging to the working intelligentsia, from Soviet-controlled territory, be released after scrupulous interroga-tion to identify those involved in anti-Soviet espionage.

PoW numbers and composition

Table 1 shows that the numbers in the three special camps stabilised by late November, once their initial functions as collection camps had passed. Overall, totals did not vary much until the final liquidation began in early April 1940. This, however, conceals considerable inflows and outflows during December and January as the DPA became increasingly rigorous in specifying and defining the categories to be held in them. The 15 March figures of 4594 in Kozelsk, 3896 in Starobelsk and 6364 in Ostashkov total 14854.

Table 2 (page 53) shows that Kozelsk and Starobelsk held 8337 military officers, of the rank of ensign and lieutenant and above, as of 1 April, just before the massacre began. But only 837 (plus an admiral and the 17 naval captains) were majors or higher, 1490 were captains while over three-quarters, 6009, were junior officers of the various grades of lieutenant and ensign-cadet rank.[85] This peculiarly skewed composition is, partly, explained by the higher percentage of senior officers falling into German captivity. This feature provides *prima facie* preliminary evidence that the massacre occurred, for whatever reasons, before the NKVD selection process was complete. It also suggests that the massacre was not aimed primarily to eliminate Poland's officer *corps*, so much as to weaken its general leadership elite.

The reason why Poland's general elite suffered so heavily is that a high percentage of the officers in the two camps were reservists (2252 in Starobelsk alone, mainly from German-occupied territory) and retired officers, a very high proportion of whom were university graduates. The three camps held about 800 medical doctors,[86] 110 university professors and academics,[87] 1000 lawyers as well as numerous vets, writers, and journalists. As the 'flower of the Polish intelligentsia', they had played important roles in all walks of inter-war Poland's public life and would have constituted an important source of opposition to Sovietisation.[88] Madajczyk states that the professional officer corps of the Polish Army was about 18500 in May

Table 1 Number of PoWs in NKVD special camps

Day/month 1939/1940	Total all camps	Total three special camps	Kozelsk	Starobelsk	Ostashkov
29 November	39331	14948	4718	3907	5959
31 December	38710	15087	4766	3916	6291
9 January	38368	15079	4663	3916	6286
20 January	38254	14971	4665	3913	6278
4 February	38117	14990	4702	3910	6378
22 February	38007	14888	4609	3908	6371
16 March	37666	14854	4594	3896	6364

Source: Adapted from KDZ, 1, appendix 1.

Table 2 Composition of the three special camps

	Kozelsk			Starobelsk			Ostashkov			Total three camps
	29/11	20/1	1/4	29/11	20/1	1/4	29/11	20/1	16/2	16/3
Generals	4	4	4	8	8	8				12
Colonels	24	27	26	57	55	55				81
Lieutenant-colonels	79	74	72	130	127	126				198
Majors	258	236	232	321	320	316				547
Captains	653	652	647	853	851	843				1490
Other officers	3419	3404	3480	2519	2528	2527				6009
Ordinary ranks**	78	173	5							5
Admirals	1	1	1							1
Naval captains	17	17	17							17
Military chaplains	7	1	8	12	12	9	11*	5	5	15
Landowners	4	6	9	2	2	2				11
State officials	43	33	61	5	5	5				66
Refugees	131	76	37				35			35 + 67†
Police*** officers							199	281	288	288
Police*** sub-officers							603	740	775	775
Police*** rankers							5016	4932	4924	4924
Military settlers							27*	27	35	35
Prison officials							104	111	189	189
Spies							2	6	9	9
Total	4718	4665	4599	3909	3910	3893	5959	6158	6360	14846

Source: Adapted from KDZ, 1, appendices 2, 3, 4.

Notes

*Estimates

**Qualifying for transfer

***Police headings include gendarmes

† Unclear Ostashkov figures. The best estimate is that there were 35 refugees (possibly increasing to 89), some of whom might have overlapped with a later 'remainder' category of about 67 refugees, state officials and landowners

1939. The country also had another 60 000 reserve officers aged under 50, 39 500 reserve ensigns and 12 000 retired officers liable to general mobilisation. He estimates that over 9000 found themselves in Soviet and 19 000 in German captivity while another 10 000 escaped to the West and the Middle East.[89]

If the composition of Kozelsk and Starobelsk was fairly straightforward, that of the least studied, Ostashkov, brims with anomalies reflecting Soviet uncertainties. The fact that 4924 out of its 6360 inmates, just prior to the massacre, were ordinary policemen of the lowest rank, probably, reflects the Soviet over-estimation of their role, even in a semi-authoritarian system such as *Sanacja* Poland. On the other hand there were only 170 police officers of sub-lieutenant rank or higher and 3109 NCOs compared with 2265 ordinary-ranking policemen.[90] The corresponding figures for gendarmes (military policemen) were 55, 6 and 63, and 8, 60 and 98 for prison guards.[91] The remaining categories demonstrate that Ostashkov was something of a dustbin for a number of individuals which the NKVD was not quite sure how to deal with. Significantly, the vast effort of NKVD interrogations unearthed only nine spies and what they described as provocateurs. It is also unclear whether there was any direct personal animus against the 166 prison guards and 23 prison officials because of their involvement against inter-war Soviet agents.[92] Likewise it is not clear whether the 35 military settlers were all war veterans who suffered collective and symbolic responsibility for 1920 and Polish settlement in the Eastern Territories. The purely civilian category of landowners and state officials seem to have been located in the other two camps while the refugees (border crossers) were divided equally between Kozelsk and Ostashkov. Given time, all the different categories would, no doubt, have been decanted into separate camps. As almost all were shot after transportation from individual locations one concludes that the general category of class enemy and anti-Soviet counter-revolutionary prevailed over individual sub-distinctions.

Although inter-war Poland's population included about one-third national minorities the final national composition of the three Special Camps was overwhelmingly Polish. At the end of February 1940, 3828 out of 3908 Starobelsk inmates were Poles compared with a mere 71 Jews, four Ukrainians and individuals of five other nationalities (Bulgarian, Latvian, Lithuanian, German and Hungarian). The equivalent figures for Kozelsk were 4347 Poles out of a total of 4486, plus 89 Jews, 23 Belarusans, 11 Germans, six Ukrainians, one Czech and one Georgian.[93] There were 6013 Poles out of 6072 Ostashkov inmates while 28 were Belarusans, 23 Ukrainians, four Germans, two Russians and two Czechs.[94] Poles thus totalled 14 188 out of 14 456 or 98.1 per cent. The caveat to this is that around 900 of those massacred may have been heavily Polonised or secularised individuals of Jewish origins while about 40 of the Gryazovets survivors fell into this category.[95]

One should also note that while the three special camps are usually described as PoW institutions they also held a number of civilians whom the Soviets designated as class enemies and counter-revolutionaries. Soprunenko's note of 3 March 1940 gives their number as 148 including 24 priests, 11 large landowners, 71 high state officials, 35 settlers, three factory owners and tradesmen and four others.[96]

Deaths, suicides and escapes

The Nazis pioneered the model extermination camps for Jews and gypsies while large numbers of inmates were also killed in their concentration camps through purposive, as well as casual, individual violence by guards, starvation, sickness and hard labour. The Soviets did not use equivalent death camps to the Nazi ones. Soviet labour camps in the climatically harsh regions of Siberia and Northern European Russia were designed for the purpose of breaking and wearing down, and perhaps eventually killing off, individuals. Polish sources claim a wastage (death) rate of anything between 25 and 60 per cent per annum in 1940–1941 for their PoWs held there. It is, therefore, significant that the regime in the special camps from November 1939 to March 1940, while by no means comfortable, was not specifically designed to kill or grind down. Its insufficiencies were criticised by the DPA and, generally, reflected Soviet poverty and administrative incompetence. Prisoners, up to the rank of major, were forced into heavy labour, contrary to international conventions, both in building and maintaining camp facilities and outside on lumbering tasks. A Kozelsk survivor and medical doctor, reported later, that the behaviour of the Soviet authorities was 'on the whole correct'; the main problem was insufficient and unsatisfactory food.[97] Overall, one gets the clear impression that despite such hardships the special camps' main purpose was to provide a favourable environment for the primary Chekhist tasks of propaganda, indoctrination, interrogation, provocation and the selection of human material which could be useful for Soviet purposes.

Although sanitary conditions were initially very primitive they improved slowly, if only as a result of the PoWs' own efforts and labour. Medical facilities were also put in place. The Kozelsk camp hospital, for example, eventually had 90 beds. A whole raft of camp reports to the DPA reveal a picture of extensive and fairly competent treatment, hampered by the lack of sufficient drugs and medicine, of the more common illnesses such as influenza and stomach problems, along with the consequences of poor hygiene and flea-ridden conditions. Pneumonia and tuberculosis were more difficult to treat given insufficient heating, poor food and inadequate clothing. The authorities did their best to prevent epidemics by providing vaccination against typhus, dysentery and smallpox, especially in Starobelsk. Significantly, Soviet doctors are widely praised in Polish PoW memoirs for their humane, sympathetic and open Slavic approach, particularly with their Polish medical colleagues.

According to articles 11 and 12 of the Geneva Convention food rations for PoWs should be the same as those in the armed forces of the holding power. In practice the Polish PoWs received basic amounts of bread, porridge, cabbage soup and tea supplemented by irregular amounts of salted fish, cabbage and potatoes.[98] Helpings of meat (usually horsemeat) were extremely rare. The meals, prepared by the Poles themselves, whose cooks improvised brilliantly in a difficult situation, had to be eaten uncomfortably on the barrack bunks.[99] The main problem was food pilfering by camp workers, whose own rations were barely better than those of the PoWs, especially of shortage items such as sugar, flour and butter. Conditions worsened after the Finnish–Soviet War broke out when insufficient rations and nagging hunger weakened PoW resistance to sickness. The poor quality of what the camp authorities alleged to their superiors to be a fully sufficient noodle soup provoked protest in the form of a refusal to eat in three barracks (numbers 10, 15 and 20) in Starobelsk on 28 October 1939.[100] Shortages, and breaks in supplies, worsened during the winter causing another food strike, this time in Kozelsk, on 21 January 1940 against a particularly evil smelling *barszcz* (beetroot soup).[101]

A report by the DPA Sanitary Department Head, Sokolov, to Nekhoreshev on 21 February 1940 reveals that 60 PoWs died during the months of October, November and December in all the NKVD camps.[102] Twenty-five died in the three special camps, the highest mortality (16) being in Ostashkov, because of its higher number of older inmates, while six died in Starobelsk and three in Kozelsk. Of the 60 that died in total, 14 died from pneumonia, 12 from tuberculosis, eight from dysentery, six from burst ulcers, four apiece from infections and heart problems, three from cancer and nine from other causes. The most widespread illnesses were influenza, digestion problems (especially in November when the sickness rate doubled) and a variety of skin diseases. Two leading Polish specialists, however, calculate that 40 PoWs died in Ostashkov and 32 in Starobelsk up to the moment that the massacre began.[103] On the other hand a survivor's account claimed that 92 prisoners died in Ostashkov between October 1939 and April 1940.[104]

Suicide was rare, and considered important enough to merit a direct report to Beria, as in the following case. A 41-year-old ensign, Bazyli Zacharski, hanged himself on his belt in Kozelsk on the morning of 2 December as a result of feeling strongly depressed at being separated from his family.[105] A doctor apparently attempted to cut his throat with a razor blade in Starobelsk in October but the NKVD concluded that this was a faked attempt.

The DPA and the NKVD leadership were absolutely paranoid about camp security, the complete isolation of all inmates from the outside world and all escape activity. The actual number of attempted escapes was small. There is no evidence in the NKVD documentation of a single successful escape from our three special camps.[106] Apparently the Poles were lulled into a false sense of security by the prospect of repatriation either to their homes or even to a neutral country or the West. It had also, initially, been relatively easy to escape from the collection camps during the first two to three weeks of captivity.[107] A mentally disturbed prisoner, Józef Augustyn, was shot dead by a sentry at Starobelsk on 11 October when he ventured out into the warning zone and refused to stop when called upon to do so.[108] Two other thwarted escape attempts from Starobelsk and the buying of civilian clothes by officers in Kozelsk in preparation for attempted escapes were reported by mid-November 1939.[109] The first serious escape attempt from Kozelsk was by two sub-lieutenants, Julian Michniewicz and Zenon Rymaszewski, on 7 December 1939. The NKVD report states that they were assisted by a Lithuanian (Antoni Balulis) who had been imprisoned for spying against Poland in the 1930s.[110] The likelihood is that he betrayed them as he survived the massacre and was sent to Gryazovets. Ostashkov reported that no escapes had taken place up to mid-December but made much of escape talk by PoWs, presumably conveyed by an informer.[111] Another informer in Ostashkov alerted the camp authorities to an escape by a policeman and a gendarme on 5 March 1940. The two escapees actually got as far as 15 miles away from the camp before being captured by collective farm workers.[112] The most serious escape attempt in Kozelsk occurred on 16 March 1940 when five PoWs were caught in the act of fleeing the 'Skit', again on the basis of betrayal by an inside informer.[113] The fear of the planning and preparation of escapes by their PoWs loomed large in the consciousness of camp *komendaturas* and their superiors. Much attention, including provocation, was devoted to uncovering even the initial discussion of such activity. As will be noted, the NKVD recruited a network of informers in all three camps who reported the words as well as the actions of PoWs.

Correspondence

PoWs were guaranteed the right to correspondence by articles 36–40 of the Hague Convention. This was in practice impossible during the confusion of the September Campaign and the vast PoW inflows of the distributor camp phase. It was, therefore, only on 20 October, when the situation had settled somewhat, that the Soviet authorities agreed that correspondence could be sent and received. The NKVD did so as it hoped to gather additional information about PoWs' views, their relatives' addresses and situations and foreign contacts from this source.[114] One of their provocations in late December 1939 worked on the rumour, which they spread, that prisoners who obtained foreign visas would be released and allowed to leave the USSR. This encouraged the PoWs to write to friends and relatives, however distant, in foreign countries requesting them to arrange such exit documents.[115] The names and addresses were duly noted by camp special departments in the prisoners' files. The usual Soviet 'big lie' mechanism also applied in regard to addresses. The return address for Kozelsk PoWs, for example, was the Gorky Rest Home, Smolensk oblast Post Box 12!

In practice, incoming and outgoing mail was censored by a political officer in each of the camp's special departments. As the camps had insufficient personnel with the required knowledge of the Polish language the Red Army made up the shortfall by supplying a number of their translators. Despite this the checking of correspondence resulted in long delays. Consequently, the PoWs never knew whether their letter had gone out, and if so, in what censored form. This was the main complaint by the Starobelsk colonels who demanded that PoWs be informed if mail had been confiscated and who also wanted the right to send correspondence once a week, not once a month.[116] The volume of correspondence was quite heavy, though. About 50 000 letters and cards were sent out of Starobelsk and 110 000 communications were received by it from October 1939 to March 1940. On the other hand censorship was not as watertight as desired by the DPA. The military settlers in Ostashkov got wind of the deportation of their families.[117]

The emotional and psychological importance of correspondence is confirmed in all the sources.[118] Some of the correspondence has been published.[119] As one would expect, it is heavily dominated by personal and family matters and sheds little additional light on camp conditions and affairs.

An interesting footnote to this aspect is provided by the case of the Starobelsk translator D. Chekholskii who sent out 30–40 letters to relatives in April 1940 while the massacre was taking place.[120] He also replied to relatives' queries in June assuring them that the PoW was healthy and that they should send inquiries to the DPA address at 2 Dzerzhinsky Square in Moscow. Chekholskii was, apparently, dismissed in June 1940. This might have been another case of NKVD misinformation although, it transpires from their correspondence, that Kirshin and Soprunenko either did not know about it or disowned his initiative. Some of the incoming correspondence after April was sent to the Belarusan and Ukrainian NKVD to assist them in taking measures against any Polish relatives of the murdered PoWs who had not, as yet, been deported to Kazakhstan from their regions.

The cessation of correspondence and rumours that the camps had been evacuated also gave rise to a large volume of inquiries by organisations and individuals outside the USSR. The International Red Cross and Red Crescent, for example, sent Soprunenko on 1 July 1940 a list of names of 220 PoWs whose whereabouts were being sought by relatives.[121] A similar Red Cross inquiry of 10 July concerned 12 doctors held in Starobelsk.[122] Similar inquiries, from within the USSR, some being heartrending appeals by mothers, wives and children to Stalin, were also sent to Kalinin, Molotov and Timoshenko.[123] DPA policy was to ignore all such correspondence and also to order other bodies not to reply. Every such inquiry was marked 'Special Department' which was insiders' code denoting that the individual had been liquidated in the massacre. Much, if not all, of this material was burnt by the DPA Second Department Head, Maklarskii, on Soprunenko's direct orders.

A large amount of outgoing correspondence which had not been cleared before mailings were banned in mid-March 1940, as well as an even larger amount of incoming material which had 'no operational value', was destroyed in August 1940. Soprunenko also ordered the Starobelsk Special Department on 10 September 1940 to destroy all the investigation files of the camp's previous inmates apart from those sent on to Pavlishtschev Bor.[124] This led to the burning of 4031 investigation files plus their card index, 231 pages of interrogation records, documentary records of the PoWs in alphabetical order as well as a variety of orders, correspondence and photographs.[125]

Notes

1 Leonard Schapiro, *Totalitarianism*, London: Macmillan, 1972.
2 Amos Perlmutter, *Modern Authoritarianism: A Comparative Institutional Analysis*, New Haven, CT: Yale UP, 1981.
3 Carl Friedrich and Zbigniew Brzezinski, *Totalitarian Dictatorship and Autocracy*, Cambridge, MA: Harvard UP, 2nd edn, 1965.
4 Ghita Ionescu, *The Politics of the European Communist States*, London: Weidenfeld & Nicolson, 1967.
5 H. Gordon Skilling, 'Interest Groups and Communist Politics Revisited', *World Politics*, 36, 1 (October 1983), pp. 1–27.
6 The best example of a compendium of Stalinist crimes being conflated with the whole of the communist experience and being used for such political propaganda purposes is Stéphane Courtois and Mark Kramer (eds), *The Black Book of Communism: Crimes, Terror, Repression*, Cambridge, MA: Harvard UP, 1999. This is not to argue that post-Stalinist communist states were not guilty of repression, only that they were not, in general, pathologically so, as previously.
7 The issue has also divided the extreme Left. See Paul Piccone's savaging of Victor Zaslavsky's attempt to explain the Katyn massacre in terms of ideologically driven totalitarianism and Stalin's drive for global power leading to 'class cleansing', *Telos*, no. 114 (Winter 199), pp. 3–10, 67–107.
8 I see no difficulty in reconciling the purposive top leadership measures in the classic description by Zbigniew Brzezinski, *The Permanent Purge*, Cambridge, MA: Harvard UP, 1956 with the confused, almost anarchic, social consequences depicted by Gábor Rittersporn, *Stalinist Simplifications and Soviet Complications: Social Tensions and Political Conflicts in the USSR, 1933–1953*, Reading, UK: Harwood Academic Publishers, 1991.
9 Karen Dawisha, *The Kremlin and the Prague Spring*, Berkeley, CA: University of California Press, 1984.
10 Archie Brown (ed.), *Political Leadership in the Soviet Union*, London: Macmillan, 1989.
11 James Burnham, *The Managerial Revolution*, London: Putnam, 1942.
12 E.A. Rees, 'Stalinism: The Primacy of Politics', in John Channon (ed.), *Politics, Society and Stalinism in the USSR*, Basingstoke: Macmillan, 1998, pp. 56–65.

13 Consult: J. Arch Getty, *Origins of the Great Purges: The Soviet Communist Party Reconsidered, 1933–1938*, Cambridge: Cambridge UP, 1985. J. Arch Getty and Roberta Manning (eds), *Stalinist Terror: New Perspectives*, Cambridge: Cambridge UP, 1993. Sheila Fitzpatrick, *Everyday Stalinism*, Oxford: Oxford UP, 1999.

14 Stephen Kotkin, *Magnetic Mountain: Stalinism as a Civilisation*, Berkeley, CA: University of California Press, 1995. Cf. Astrid Hedin, 'Stalinism as a Civilisation: New Perspectives on Communist Regimes', *Political Studies Review*, 2, 2 (April 2004), pp. 166–84.

15 Final Report by the Polish ambassador in Moscow Wacław Grzybowski, 6 November 1939, DPSR, 1, no. 69.

16 Merle Fainsod, *Smolensk under Soviet Rule*, London: Macmillan, 1958. Ch. 8 on 'The Organs of State Security' reveals nothing relevant to our subject except for the capacity of the NKVD functionaries to defend themselves against party complaints and 'the absence of effective Party control of NKVD operative work' at the district level, p. 169.

17 Vladimir Abarinov, *The Murderers of Katyn*, New York: Hippocrene, 1993, pp. 186–9. Cf. Czesław Madajczyk, *Dramat Katyński*, Warsaw: KiW, 1989, pp. 176–9.

18 See Boris A. Starkov, 'Narkom Ezhov', in Getty and Manning, *Stalinist Terror*. This discussion demonstrates the extent and traumatic effects of the internal purge within the NKVD between 1936 and 1940.

19 On these aspects consult, Robert Conquest, *Inside Stalin's Secret Police: NKVD Politics, 1936–1939*, Basingstoke: Macmillan, 1985. Although his account ends in 1939 the techniques, institutional framework and individuals carried over into 1940.

20 Ibid., p. 14.

21 Robert Conquest, *Kolyma: The Arctic Death Camps*, London: Macmillan, 1978, pp. 218–19.

22 See David Dallin and Boris Nicolaevsky, *Forced Labour in the Soviet Union*, New Haven, CT: Yale UP, 1948. Stanisław Świaniewicz, *Forced Labour and Economic Development: An Enquiry into the Experience of Soviet Industrialization*, London: Oxford UP, 1965.

23 Edwin Bacon, *The GULAG at War: Stalin's Forced Labour System in the Light of the Archives*, Basingstoke: Macmillan, 1994.

24 See chapters by Fitzpatrick, Nove and Wheatcroft in Getty and Manning, *Stalinist Terror*.

25 Catherine Merridale, *Night of Stone: Death and Memory in Russia*, London: Granta, 2000, pp. 254–5. There is no way of confirming Memorial estimates that Bykovna contains 200 000 and Butovo 100 000 victims, ibid., pp. 236–7. For the most reliable discussion of general totals of victims of the Stalinist Terror see Bacon, *GULAG at War*, p. 31.

26 See Stanisław Jaczyński, *Zagłada oficerów Wojska Polskiego na Wschodzie, Wrzesień 1939–Maj 1940*, Warsaw: Bellona, 2000, pp. 60–9.

27 Roy Guttman and David Rieff (eds), *Crimes of War. What the Public should know*, New York: Norton, 1999, pp. 97, 107–8, 282–5, 342–3.

28 Marian Flemming, *Okupacja wojskowa w świetle prawa międzynarodowe*, Warsaw: Wojskowa Akademia Wojskowa, 1981.

29 Marian Flemming, 'Status prawno-międzynarodowy jeńców polskich w niewoli niemieckiej i radzieckiej', in Edmund Nowak (ed.), *Niemiecki i radziecki system jeniecki w latach II wojny światowej: Podobieństwa i różnice*, Opole: Centralne Muzeum Jeńców Wojennych w Łambinowicach-Opolu, 1997.

30 Marian Flemming, 'Status prawny żołnierzy na obcym terytorium', *Wojskowy Przegląd Historyczny*, 22, 1 (1977).

31 Cf. Madajczyk, *Dramat Katyński*, p. 16.

32 Marian Flemming, 'Osoby uprawnione do statusu jeńca wojennego', *Wojskowy Przegląd Historyczny*, 34, 1 (1989), pp. 34 ff.
33 FRUS, 1941, pp. 210–11, 225–6, 233–4.
34 KDZ, 1, no. 15.
35 KDZ, 1, no. 10.
36 See Jaczyński, *Zagłada oficerów. . .*, pp. 76–88.
37 *Agresja sowiecka na Polskę w świetle dokumentów: 17 września 1939r*, Warsaw: Centralne Archiwum Wojskowe/Bellona, 1994, 1, pp. 187–92.
38 Ibid., 2, pp. 102–4.
39 *Krasnaya Zvezda*, 17 September 1940.
40 *Zbrodnia Katyńska w świetle dokumentów*, p. 13. Grzelak, *Kresy w czerwieni*, pp. 484–7.
41 *Agresja sowiecka*, 1, pp. 267–9.
42 Soprunenko to Beria, 19 November 1939, KDZ, 1, p. 268.
43 Danuta Kisieliewicz, *Oficerowie polscy w niewoli niemieckiej w czasie II wojny światowej*, Opole: Centralne Muzeum Jeńców Wojennych, 1998.
44 KDZ, 1, pp. 76–7.
45 KDZ, 1, pp. 77–8.
46 KDZ, 1, nos 11 and 12.
47 KDZ, 1, no. 21.
48 KDZ, 1, pp. 125–6.
49 KDZ, 1, pp. 127–32.
50 A note of 23 December 1939 for Chernyshev makes this clear: KDZ, 1, pp. 330–1.
51 KDZ, 1, nos 38 and 39.
52 See Jaczyński, *Zagłada oficerów. . .*, p. 109.
53 'Jeńcy polscy w ZSRR . . . Dokumenty', *Wojskowy Przegląd Historyczny*, 40, 1–2 (1995), p. 417.
54 KDZ, 1, p. 160.
55 Their figures totalled 32 826 held in the NKVD camps to which they added 11 825 still held in the collection camps thus adding up to an optimistic grand total of 44 651 subject to exchange, KDZ, 1, p. 156.
56 Whether the second exchange point, or an additional one, was Przemyśl, remains unclarified, Jaczyński, *Zagłada oficerów. . .*, p. 114.
57 *Agresja sowiecka*, 1, p. 314.
58 Toczewski, 'Wymiana polskich jeńców wojennych pomiędzy ZSRR i III Rzeszą w okresie II wojny światowej', *Łambinowicki Rocznik Muzealny*, no. 15 (1992).
59 *Agresja sowiecka*, 1, pp. 331–4.
60 Ibid., 1, p. 386: cf. KDZ, 1, nos 108, 111.
61 Götz Aly, *Final Solution: Nazi Population Policy and the Murder of the European Jews*, London: Arnold, 1999.
62 Madajczyk, *Dramat Katyński*, pp. 134–5.
63 Sikorski's successor, Stanisław Mikołajczyk, in *The Pattern of Soviet Domination*, London: Sampson Low, Marston, 1948, p. 39, claims that the Germans specifically refused to take Polish officers in the above exchanges.
64 KDZ, 1, no. 24.
65 See Albin Głowacki, 'Z badań nad dziejami jenieckiego obozu pracy NKWD w Równem', *Przegląd Historyczny*, no. 3 (1993); 'Obozy pracy dla polskich jeńców wojennych na wschodniej Ukrainie (w świetle dokumentów sowieckich), 1939–1940', *Dzieje Najnowsze*, no. 1 (1994).
66 KDZ, 1, no. 57.
67 KDZ, 1, pp. 374–9.
68 Natalia Lebiedewa, *Katyń: Zbrodnia przeciwko ludzkości*, Warsaw: Bellona, 1997, pp. 237–8.

69 Sławomir Kalbaraczyk, 'Zbrodnie sowieckie na obywatelach polski w okresie wrześien 1939–sierpien 1941', *Pamięc i Sprawiedliwość*, 39 (1996), pp. 13–35.
70 Z. Shneigert, 'Obozy NKWD jeńców polskich w Małopolsce Wschodniej w latach 1939–1941', *Wojskowy Przegląd Historyczny*, 37, 4 (1992), pp. 118–28.
71 KDZ, 1, nos 61 and 119.
72 KDZ, 1, p. 281.
73 *Komendatura* is defined as the leading NKVD camp functionaries notably the commandant and department heads.
74 KDZ, 1, no. 11.
75 KDZ, 1, pp. 165–7.
76 See Stanisław Jaczyński (ed.), *Obozy Jeneckiej NKWD, ix 1939–viii 1941*, Warsaw: Bellona, 1995, pp. 28–43.
77 *Zbrodnia Katyńska w świetle dokumentów*, London: Gryf, 1948, p. 31.
78 Anthony Jakubowski (*pseud.* Anthony Alexander James), *A Whisper in the Trees*, Santa Maria, CA: Kuma Publishing, 1995. The author characterises his work as 'a fictional account, based on fact of the existence and significance of the only woman prisoner involved in what has come to be known as the Katyn Forest Massacre', *Zawodny Papers AAN*, File 114.
79 Soprunenko and Nekhoreshev to Chernyshev, KDZ, 1, pp. 291–4.
80 Jaczyński, *Obozy Jeneckiej NKWD*, pp. 44–63.
81 Józef Czapski, *Wspomnienia Starobielski*, Rome: White Eagle, 1944, pp. 16–17. Bronisław Młynarski, *W niewoli sowieckiej*, London: Gryf, 1974, pp. 117–24.
82 Another general, Czesław Jarnuszkiewicz, survived as he was sent for interrogation by the NKVD in the Moscow Lubianka prison at the turn of 1939–1940.
83 Jaczyński, *Obozy Jeneckiej NKWD*, pp. 64–81.
84 Tishkov to Soprunenko, 9 December 1939, KDZ, 1, no. 134.
85 Soprunenko reported a total of 8376 officers on 2 March 1940, KDZ, 1, no. 207. This corps was composed of 12 generals and an admiral, 82 colonels, 201 lieutenant-colonels, 551 majors, 17 naval captains, 1498 captains and 6014 lieutenants and ensigns.
86 104 doctors and 26 pharmacists in Starobelsk alone protested to Voroshilov against what Red Cross rules defined as their illegal detention, HDZ, 1, no. 87.
87 Kozelsk definitely held 66 while the estimate is 43 for Starobelsk: Sławomir Kalbarczyk, 'Żołnierze polscy – pracownicy nauki w niewoli sowieckiej w okresie IX 1939–VIII 1941', *Łambinowicki Rocznik Muzealny*, no. 20 (1997), pp. 78–82.
88 Ambassador Romer's testimony, *Hearings*, Part 3, p. 124.
89 Madajczyk, *Dramat Katyński*, p. 9.
90 Soprunenko report of 28 February 1940 on composition of Ostashkov, KDZ, 1, no. 201.
91 These figures are open to dispute and different interpretations. Wanda Roman claims that 103 gendarmes, including 46 officers (a quarter of the inter-war *corps*), were shot: 'Zandarmi Polscy zamordowane na wschodzie (Wrzesień 1939–Maj 1940)', *Wojskowy Przegląd Historyczny*, 41, 3 (1996), pp. 338–46 (names listed pp. 340–6).
92 Only 20–30 communists were executed by the inter-war Polish state for very real acts of violence against it.
93 Soprunenko note of 28 February 1940, KDZ, 1, no. 202.
94 KDZ, 1, no. 200.
95 The civic-ethnic distinction is particularly ticklish in this instance, cf. Frank Fox, 'Jewish Victims of the Katyn Massacre', *East European Jewish Affairs*, 23, 1 (1993), pp. 49–55. Salomon Slowes, *The Road to Katyn*, Oxford: Blackwell, 1992.

96 KDZ, 1, no. 209.
97 Testimony by reserve Lieutenant-Colonel Włodzimierz Missiuro, IPiMS, Kol. 12/3, no. 55.
98 For a survivor's account see Zbigniew Godlewski, 'Przeżyłem Starobielsk', *Wojskowy Przegląd Historyczny*, 38, 2 (1993), pp. 306–31.
99 Jaczyński, *Zagłada Oficerów. . .*, p. 160.
100 KDZ, 1, no. 82.
101 KDZ, 1, no. 172.
102 KDZ, 1, no. 189. See the lists of 27 and 10 names and short biographies in KDZ, 1, nos 184 and 197.
103 Jędrzej Tucholski and Zuzanna Gajowniczek, 'Polscy jeńcy zmarli w Ostaszkowie i Starobielsku', *Wojskowy Przegląd Historyczny*, 37, 1 (1992), pp. 370–3.
104 Jan Bober's testimony, IPiMS Kol. 138/276.
105 Soprunenko to Beria, 7 December 1939, KDZ, 1, no. 133.
106 Roman Wanda, 'Potem był Katyń – akta obozów specjalnych NKWD, Wrzesień 1939–Maj 1940 w zbiorach Centralnego Archiwum Wojskowego', in *Zbrodnia Katyńska: Upamiętnienie ofiar i zadośćuczynienie*, Warsaw: NKHBZK, 1998, p. 106.
107 Jaczyński, *Zagłada Oficerów. . .*, pp. 192–7.
108 KDZ, 1, no. 51 and p. 167.
109 KDZ, 1, no. 109.
110 KDZ, 1, no. 136.
111 KDZ, 1, nos 139, 187.
112 KDZ, 2, no. 14.
113 KDZ, 2, no. 21.
114 See Jaczyński, *Zagłada Oficerów. . .*, pp. 187–92.
115 Colonel Jerzy Grobicki's testimony in J. Czmut (ed.), *Zbrodnia Katyńska: Dokumenty i publicystyka*, Warsaw: Instytut Wydawniczy Związków Zawodowych, 1990.
116 Declaration of 7 January 1940 on the definition of their PoW status and their treatment according to generally accepted principles, KDZ, 1, p. 365.
117 Maklarski to Soprunenko, 16 March 1940, KDZ, 2, no. 15.
118 Jan Stępek (ed.), *Pamiętniki znalezionej w Katynia*, Paris-Warsaw: Spotkania, 1990, pp. 17, 73, 101.
119 Ewa Gruner-Żarnoch and Ryszard Wołągiewicz (eds), *Słowa tęsknoty: Zachowane listy jeńców Kozielska, Ostaszkowa i Starobielska*, Szczecin: Stowarzyszenie Katyńskie w Szczecinie, 1996.
120 KDZ, 2, pp. 362–4.
121 KDZ, 3, no. 1. Other lists of names and individual inquiries followed at various times: ibid., nos 27, 46, 88, 98, 126, 128, 143 as well as from national Red Cross bodies such as the Hungarian, ibid., nos 30, 39.
122 KDZ, 3, no. 5.
123 KDZ, 3, nos 87, 133, 136, 143.
124 KDZ, 3, no. 43.
125 Protocol of the destruction of PoW documents, Starobelsk, 25 October 1940, KDZ, 3, no. 69.

4 The indoctrination, screening/investigation and selection processes

The politburo took a crucial step on the road to the spring 1940 massacre by accepting, on 3 December 1939, the NKVD proposal to formally arrest all officers, of what they contemptuously called the 'former Polish army', registered in the three special camps.[1] This momentous move had ultimately tragic consequences. The Soviet leadership thus categorised the Polish officer *corps* as anti-Soviet and counter-revolutionary criminals subject to Soviet legal procedures of investigation, sentence and punishment and not as ordinary PoWs to be held for the duration of a wartime conflict. This decision was part of the wider policy of extinguishing the Polish state as indicated by its linkage to the deportations and associated arrests in the Occupied Territories. The investigation process against the PoWs was placed entirely in the hands of the NKVD Military Procuracy supported by the camp administrations; sentencing was initially the prerogative of the NKVD Military College.[2]

The ultimate sentence, and the fate, of the officers was, however, far from decided at this stage. The reports of camp and DPA officials on what they called the 'political-moral state' and behaviour of the PoWs, therefore, became of key importance. So did the feedback on the 'operational-Chekhist servicing' of the PoWs mounted by the NKVD from November onwards. This campaign took the following forms; although they were inter-related they took place in parallel and are, therefore, difficult to separate out. The central focus of Soviet concern also shifted over time.

1 The first, and initial, dimension was a propaganda and political-educational campaign. This was designed to sound out the Poles to assess how susceptible they might be to the Soviet system and to indoctrination leading to eventual collaboration.
2 The Soviet state was founded on Marxist–Leninist principles according to which class and social origins determined political allegiances. It was also by the 1930s the most developed police state in human history. The second dimension of NKVD activity, an investigation stage, aimed to build up as comprehensive a record base as possible in the form of individual files for every PoW. This picture of origins,

family connections, political and religious beliefs, behaviour and associations and assignation into appropriate categories would guide the NKVD functionaries in determining the prisoner's sentence.

3 The ultimate purpose of the foregoing was that the initial conversations of the investigative stage should lead on to more intensive interrogation. The process was designed to elicit two things. The main aim was to establish a network of agents and informers who would reveal, by provocation if necessary, all current anti-Soviet organisation, activity and even consciousness. Second, the NKVD had to decide whether a prisoner could become a reliable and useful servant of the Soviet cause. The highest level of the third stage was, therefore, a selection process. Once the decision was taken by Stalin and his inner coterie to massacre the recalcitrant mass of PoWs the process quite literally decided who should live or die.

Political propaganda and indoctrination

The camp authorities mounted a political-educational campaign once the initial flux of the collection stage had passed. They did this out of their own resources, training personnel during October, screening films, sticking up propaganda posters and ordering newspapers and such basic material for instruction as the 1936 Soviet Constitution and Stalin's speeches.[3] The detailed Starobelsk report of 3 December gives a full and representative picture of the social-cultural activity involved. Camp Commandant Berezkov and Political Commissar Kirshin, feeling their positions threatened, attempted to justify themselves to the DPA by claiming that they had implemented all its instructions successfully.[4] Almost all PoWs had been reached in November through discussion of six key political issues, the clarification of Soviet press readings and radio broadcasts and the screening of 13 Soviet films. One blinks at the claim that, wartime or not, the camp library already had 3443 books and took 805 newspapers and 173 journals! The DPA, however, had its own agenda. It intervened directly soon afterwards, despite the completion of the initial filing tasks and promises of an extended political and cultural programme for December.

Soprunenko's extensive report of mid-November 1939 on the state of the NKVD camps paints a rosy picture of the extent of political work in the camps.[5] It also includes PoW responses and questions to the discussions initiated by agitators from camp Political Departments on newspaper articles and radio speeches. One doubts the veracity of the report's claims that the Starobelsk inmates welcomed the Soviet annexation of West Belarus and West Ukraine and inquired whether they could find work and make use of free educational facilities in the USSR. Likewise the Kozelsk PoWs are reported as being very bitter about the hardships of life under the yoke of the *pans* and landowners in pre-war Poland with its high taxes and persecution of Jews, Belarusans and Ukrainians. The latter gives the game away about the individual (and presumably unrepresentative, if not inspired) sources of such statements. The fact that they are reported indicates, however, somewhat more than just Soprunenko writing what his political superiors might want to hear. He also includes a long collection of verbatim statements, without overmuch hostile comment, ascribed to individual Poles by name. He points up the PoWs' wish, and not just the Jewish ones originating from German-occupied Poland, to remain in the USSR or to be repatriated to a neutral country for the duration of the war. He discerned a split between junior and reserve officers, who blamed Piłsudski's system for the September defeat, and the strongly anti-Soviet senior professional cadres. On the other hand camp informers reported what in Soviet terms were provocative counter-revolutionary statements. These concerned the poverty and inferiority of the Soviet system, its lying press and why the Soviet alliance with German fascism would be defeated by the Franco-British alliance which would resurrect Poland's independence.

The tone of the NKVD officials changed significantly by the end of December. They now doubted whether they could re-educate the Poles away from their strongly held patriotism, military discipline and religiosity (which involved the celebration of secret masses in Kozelsk and Starobelsk). They had not shaken the Poles' firm belief in the eventual resurrection of an independent Poland with Western assistance, their hatred of what was dubbed 'Red Imperialism' or their firm desire to leave 'the inhuman land' as soon as possible.[6]

Various open manifestations of a European level of cultural and social behaviour, including protests against the principle, as well as the details, of their captivity, also contrasted vividly with the sullen submissiveness of the Soviet population. Reserve Colonel Tadeusz Petrażycki, a pre-war senator and judge of the Supreme Military Court, had his request that the PoWs be permitted contacts with the Red Cross in order to facilitate correspondence with their families ignored.[7] A protest by 104 doctors and 26 pharmacists against their imprisonment in Starobelsk[8] merely provoked Soprunenko's internal put down of Camp Commandant Berezkov's request for a copy of the Geneva Medical Convention; he was told very curtly to follow DPA directives alone, not that document.[9] On the other hand Brigade-General Franciszek Sikorski's letter of 20 October 1939 from Starobelsk to Timoshenko, Commander of the Ukrainian Front, requesting the early release of the PoWs surrendered to him on the basis of the Lwów capitulation agreement was circulated around the Soviet elite.[10] It is rare to be able to document so closely such a case of bureaucratic pluralism or rather, in this case, elite buck-passing in practice, as Stalin did not declare himself, as yet.[11] Another significant petition, presented by Colonel Edward Saski, and the Starobelsk colonels, made living condition and cultural demands and requested clarification of the status under which they were being held.[12]

Under Soviet totalitarian conditions it was natural that reports from the camps of independent cultural and social activity by PoWs were immediately classified as counter-revolutionary. Camp memoirs make it clear that the officers set up discussion and reading circles from early on.[13] The full blown cultural-educational committee which developed in Starobelsk in late October, chaired by Captain Ludwik Domoń, became known to the camp authorities. Lieutenant-Colonel Mieczysław Ewert lectured on Piłsudski's view of the USSR as a 'prison-house of the nations', which the Poles could split up by supporting the Ukrainians and Belarusans. Sublieutenant Stanisław Kwolek's stirring themes that Poland would regain her independence and frontiers that stretched 'from sea to sea' under Sikorski also occasioned patriotic and religious declamation and singing.

The Starobelsk and Kozelsk authorities attempted to prevent the Poles from celebrating their National Day on 11 November by various chicaneries. The senior officers' call for it to be marked as a work-free day, and by the singing of the National Anthem and religious songs, seems to have been widely heeded.[14] All this brought the DPA's wrath down on Starobelsk in the form of a descent by three inspectors – Trofimov, Yefimov and Yegorov. They reported 'the uncovering in the Starobelsk camp of an anti-Soviet organisation of officer prisoners of the ex-Polish army' to Beria on 25 November.[15] They blamed Commissar Kirshin's passivity. He had lost the initiative by allowing 'the formation of an underground organisation' using cultural activity and talks on sanitary hygiene and the teaching of foreign languages as a cover for anti-Soviet propaganda. Ewert and Kwolek, along with Captain Rytel who had been prominent in organising the 11 November manifestation, were arrested and sentenced by the Kharkov NKVD to eight years' GULAG. Paradoxically, this saved them from the massacre. Ewert and Rytel survived the war. Kwolek died in a labour camp in Komi.[16]

It is quite clear that the officers in Kozelsk and Starobelsk, but not so much the policemen in Ostashkov, organised advanced forms of social, cultural, educational and religious activity. This was done primarily to maintain their spirits and morale as well as to while away the tedious winter hours. This activity, presented in detailed reminiscences by camp survivors such as Czapski, Młynarski and Świaniewicz, has been examined exhaustively, and with great piety, by contemporary Polish scholars.[17] What concerns us most in this study is how this was received and digested by the Soviet authorities. How serious was their designation in Starobelsk of talks to his colleagues by Sub-lieutenant Edmund Czaplicki, a journalist, or of a gathering of officers to celebrate Christmas Eve (*Wigilia* is the most important Polish Catholic feast day) as counter-revolutionary?[18] Did the irritation of the Soviet authorities with the maintenance of customary religious practices such as secret masses and private prayer sessions by the PoWs in Kozelsk lead to the preventive transportation of the chaplains out of the camp on Christmas Eve 1939?[19] We need to assess whether what was accepted as normal legitimate camp activity in German Offlags, including escape attempts, might have contributed to Beria's justification for the massacre of the PoWs in the 5 March 1940 decision. This was that they were fierce enemies, steeped in hatred of the Soviet system, who awaited the slightest favourable opportunity to join in the struggle against it. Moreover, they 'were attempting to continue counter-revolutionary activity, and carrying on anti-Soviet agitation' in the camps.[20] One can only speculate whether Soprunenko's report of the end of December 1939 listing negative phenomena in the camps, or a similar later document, might not have been read by a paranoic and vengeful Stalin on a bad day.[21] Was this what tilted him towards the wholesale massacre option? Or, more likely, was it a hostile comment or drunken harangue by Beria drawn from such reports? Is it possible that the Soviet Stalinist mind-set of 1939–1940 was so rigidly totalitarian that normal Western civilised behaviour and individual autonomy was perceived as a basic social and national threat to which the only answer was extermination?

Investigation, recording and interrogation

Peter Holquist has pointed out that the Stalinists established 'a vast human archive' of their citizens based on questionnaires, censuses and the internal passport system.[22] This process of social and ethnic mapping allowed them to apply increasing levels of state violence from 1936 onwards against whatever categories they defined as hostile. Something similar was developed by the NKVD in the three special camps. The NKVD aimed to build up an information base permitting them to identify and excise unredeemable counter-revolutionary elements. The crucial difference is that almost all the Polish PoWs were ultimately defined as a hostile category and massacred.

As noted earlier, Beria established the DPA and the network of NKVD camps run by it in his directive number 0308 of 19 September 1939 which implemented the politburo decision of the previous day. The Special Department of the State Security Committee (GUGB), headed by Viktor Bochkov with Nikolai Osetrov (simultaneously Head of the Investigation Department) and Alexandr Belanov as his deputies, was assigned the function of identifying both possible agents and collaborators as well as the irredeemably anti-Soviet ballast. The GUGB headed a network of NKVD Special Departments, corresponding to the USSR's territorial framework, whose heads commanded regional special military forces. They also helped the GUGB oversee the work of the Special Departments in the camps. The latter were assigned the key role in maintaining internal discipline and control.

Their joint functions in the 'operational-Chekhist servicing' of the PoWs were defined in Beria's directive of 8 October 1939.[23] Two networks of agents and informers were to be established. One was to report on the political attitudes and morale of the PoWs according to their military rank and place of origin and to support the political-educational drive discussed above. The other, and more important, network, while claiming to support the rebuilding of Poland, was to expose anti-Soviet activity amongst Polish counter-revolutionaries belonging to hostile inter-war political parties, state bodies and social groups. Beria's long list of anti-Soviet organisations covered the whole of the intelligence, security, legal-judicial, police and prison services of inter-war Poland. To these he added membership of a very broad range of what he termed 'fascist-military and nationalist organisations'. Many were associated with Piłsudski and Poland's struggle for independence and her eastern frontiers such as POW, the Settlers' Union, the Riflemen's League, the Youth League and the Union of Reserve Officers. The Polish Socialist Party (PPS), communism's major and much more successful reformist, ideological and political rival on the Left, was included because of its primary commitment to Polish independence. Refugees (kulaks and NEP oppositionists) and émigrés, especially White Russians from the Czarist period, who had sought shelter in inter-war Poland were defined as terrorists and added. Anyone else, regarded as non-Soviet Stalinist was placed in the hold-all category of *provocateur*, including all would-be escapees. The camp Special and Records Departments were to note all this evidence in individual files for each PoW. This would provide the operational basis for revealing further anti-Soviet contacts and linkages. The documentation was to be used by NKVD regional Special Departments to arrest and sentence 'the spies, diversionists, terrorists and conspirators' thus revealed.

The above is an extremely important and revealing document. It further confirms the argument that the Stalinists, from the outset, defined officers and individuals connected with the security, judicial and repressive organs of the inter-war Polish state not as PoWs, but as class enemies. They were to be identified, categorised and bureaucratically arrested and sentenced by the NKVD. Normally, their subsequent fate would have been isolation and a living death in the Siberian labour camps. The decision by the Stalinist leadership to massacre them has to be examined in the light of their German alliance and primary aim of permanently destroying Polish statehood and eradicating all Polish influence from the Eastern Territories. A Kozelsk survivor says that the PoWs were 'interrogated as political criminals'; the NKVD's main purpose was 'to examine them from the political viewpoint'.[24] It is, therefore, crucial to examine what bearing the NKVD's investigative process had, both on the ultimate decision and on its timing.

It would be too tedious an exercise to follow through the bureaucratic process of establishing and developing the PoW files.[25] One should just note that camp personnel often proved not up to the task of building up the record base, which was extremely extensive by March 1940. NKVD documents are full of DPA complaints about the insufficiencies of the

Evidence and Records Departments (URO) in the camps and of measures taken to strengthen their personnel and remedy these deficiencies. Shifts in DPA definitions of categories and criteria for inclusion and in their requests for additional types of information, however, throw light on wider policy aims and priorities.

The camp staff initially could not cope with the implementation of DPA instructions on operational record keeping of 25 September and 1 October.[26] The latter prescribed a standard prisoner's questionnaire (assigned an individual file number) which covered surname, first name, father's name, year and place of birth, social origins, nationality, citizenship, profession/occupation, party political affiliations, education and military rank. Additional information included last military unit, family and work connections. A photograph and description of the prisoner plus date of reception and subsequent activity in the camp was to be attached. This was to be kept by the camp's Special Department while a copy was to go by 20 October to the DPA so that a central file could be established. A more refined form was developed for officers and state officials, once Kozelsk and Starobelsk had been designated as their holding camps.[27] The camps found difficulty in digesting this information and in tackling their subsequent task of producing card indexes. Many of the registration staff were near illiterate sentries whose cards often had to be written out again. Lack of knowledge of the Polish language and of pre-war Polish administrative boundaries and other realities also hampered their work, subsequently. The camps did little more than report numbers of prisoners held, and a basic breakdown by rank, during October. Even that was not always accurate, especially in Ostashkov. Ivan Maklarskii, the Head of the DPA (Evidence and Records) Second Department, therefore strengthened the camps by sending two DPA inspectors to each camp URO with more precise form filling instructions.[28]

Soprunenko instructed the camps to fill in special record cards for senior officers from lieutenant-colonel upwards. Despite his pressure, the record-registration exercise was not completed by 1 December, as he had ordered. The process in Kozelsk was overseen by another DPA inspector, Dmitrii Kabanov. By the end of November 4412 personal questionnaires had been completed and 3240 personal files had been set up, while 109 of the senior officers' files had been drawn up. Work was rather more advanced in Starobelsk and the first-level tasks were gradually completed during December.[29] By early January Soprunenko was asking for additional information to be collected: notably, last position in the former Polish army, previous residence in the USSR, knowledge of foreign languages and residence/visits abroad (where, when and how long).[30] The key question – whether any relatives or friends still lived in the USSR – was clearly connected to the deportation of prisoners' relatives from West Belarus and West Ukraine being planned for the spring. Nekhoreshev's inspection of Starobelsk (at the end of January 1940) revealed that the technical aspects of the record keeping tasks were being handled satisfactorily enough.[31] The DPA thirsted for ever more information about prisoners' political and social-economic affiliations. This exercise was never fully completed, in the DPA's estimation, as shown by continuing instructions and demands for new information during March, right up to the beginning of the massacre.

As we have seen, the NKVD centre sent its senior officials as well as regional functionaries to inspect the three special camps. They were also delegated to carry out particular missions. In early October Nikolai Karelin was sent to Kozelsk, Boris Trofimov to Starobelsk and Kogelman to Ostashkov. They initiated the operational task of establishing the counter-espionage, informational and surveillance networks. This involved recruiting agents within the PoWs and camp personnel as well as in local areas surrounding the camps. Agents were to be supervised by the usual type of on the spot *residents* who maintained contact with the NKVD centre (the GUGB Second and Third Departments and the First (Special) Department of the NKVD USSR). On 31 October Major of State Security Vasilii Mikhailovich Zarubin arrived at Kozelsk, supported by Captain of State Security Alexandrovich, to direct the operational work and to supervise the interrogation of the PoWs. They appear to have recruited about 20 agents and identified individuals willing to collaborate in the formation of Polish military units on Soviet soil. Similar work was initiated by Trofimov in Starobelsk and carried on by Yefimov and Yegorov sent down from the centre. They recruited 70 agents and informers including 41 PoWs.[32] The latter were drawn mainly from junior and reserve officers below the rank of major as well as from national minorities, especially Jews, Germans and Lithuanians. The strict rules regulating recruitment procedures, reporting and meetings were not always fully adhered to, causing the unmasking of some agents. The Starobelsk network was particularly energetic in uncovering counter-revolutionary activity such as the cultural-educational committee already discussed, in identifying and arresting a prominent pre-war OZON leader, Wiktor Kszewski, and in exposing the anti-Soviet ring allegedly led by Major Dembiński and Colonel Żółkowski. They also discovered that four numbers of an underground paper called *Merkury* had been produced while the similar *Monitor* had somehow eluded their notice for 15 issues![33] Grigorii Korytov uncovered similar counter-revolutionary activity in Ostashkov and arrested alleged anti-Soviet agitators. These conspiratorial NKVD activities may seem paranoid, even ridiculous, today; but they were an essential part of the mechanisms of the 1930s Stalinist Terror designed to expose and destroy enemies and to terrify and subjugate the masses.

A larger group of senior functionaries led by Lieutenants of State Security G.I. Antonov and Stepan Belolipetskii descended on Ostashkov in early November. They were charged with preparing individual case files or dossiers on all the camp's PoWs by the end of January so that they could be examined and dealt with by the NKVD Special College (or Extraordinary Tribunal) in Moscow. By the end of December they had produced 2000 such files, 600 of which had been sent to the College with the recommendation of three- to eight-year sentences in a labour camp. What one presumes is a typical specimen dossier against Stefan Olejnik, an Ostashkov inmate, has survived.[34] This shows that policemen were charged under article 58, paragraph 13 of the Soviet Penal Code – struggle against the international communist movement. The one charge against Olejnik, that he had served as a policeman in the town of Borszczów in Volhynia from 1936 to 1939 where he had 'carried on an active struggle against the revolutionary movement', is not substantiated in any specific way. It is unlikely that he was he involved in arresting Soviet agents or Polish working class revolutionaries. Was the mere fact that he had served in the police sufficient to warrant a Stalinist death sentence carried out on, or about, 16 April 1940?

The final stage of the process was mounted by Beria. He sent groups of even more senior DPA functionaries to all three camps on 31 December 1939. Soprunenko went to Ostashkov along with a ten-strong team to support Belolipetskii. Iosif Polukhin, Yakov Yorsh, Filchenko and Ruzyn were sent to Kozelsk, and Nekhoreshev, Rodionov, Ryabchenko and Sergeev to Starobelsk. They completed the case files by the end of the first week of February and sent them to Moscow.[35] Nekhoreshev and his team in Starobelsk also recruited another 31 agents including 22 PoWs as well as three *residents* to maintain contact with them. Together with the interrogation of 270 PoWs, the team succeeded in identifying five General Staff officers, 27 members of hostile pre-war parties and 21 border guards. This mouse of a result apparently pleased them enormously. It allowed them to set up a new collection of about 140 files headed 'enemy'. They continued their favoured activity of exposing anti-Soviet agitation, focussing on the junior officers, through the 'Corrosion' network. As a result the GUGB arrested four more officers.

The contemporary reader may blink at the intensity and dedication with which the NKVD functionaries carried on this apparently pointless espionage work on prisoners over whom they had full control and who they could repress and dispose of as they wished. As late as 7 March 1940 Soprunenko informed Kozelsk commandant Korolev that detailed DPA examination of the investigation files had exposed a further 12 officers in the camp as being intelligence agents and *provocateurs*.[36] One can ask what was the significance of Merkulov's order of 22 February 1940 in the light of such individual decisions which amounted to death sentences? Merkulov directed that all prison guards, intelligence agents, *provocateurs*, settlers, judiciary workers, landowners, factory owners and tradesmen be transferred to NKVD prisons.[37] Was this a pre-emptive NKVD bid to have only these categories shot and to save the officers or *vice versa*, were the officers to be shot and the remainder transported? Was this an early

NKVD attempt to second guess what was firming up in Stalin's mind or did it reflect parts of an already taken decision?

All the foregoing appears even more senseless in the light of the ultimate decision to massacre all bar 395 out of about 15 000 inmates and last-minute additions. The systemic need to justify itself within its own values meant that the leadership was always berating its *apparatchiks* for doing so in a purely mechanical and formal way. For Stalinists, the reality of opposition had to be discovered and illustrated by Chekhist-Bolshevik conspiratorial methods. One should also note the formal bureaucratic-legalism of the whole process. The PoWs had been investigated, interrogated and subjected to NKVD security probing. By 8 February each PoW had had his case condensed summarily in an individual dossier. This material was sent to Moscow for consideration by Beria and his most senior NKVD associates. By 5 March, after they had presented their conclusions to Stalin, the decision to shoot the PoWs crystallised officially in the politburo decision. The Byzantine process of Stalinist top decision making will be examined later in this chapter. The conclusion, here, is that the evidence of the preparatory work suggests that the prisoners' fate was sealed during the 8 February to 5 March time period, most probably towards the end of February, beginning of March.

One can now examine the interrogation process in greater detail in order to elucidate how it contributed to the varied NKVD aims. These were the recruitment of agents and informers and information gathering, especially in order to identify pre-war connections permitting individuals to be classified as anti-Soviet, but also to add specific detail to the individual case files. The main aim was to identify outright opponents of the Soviet system, particularly those who had held functions in the military defence, judicial-police, internal security, frontier defence and counter-intelligence *apparats* of Piłsudski's Poland. Along with anyone supporting independent and anti-Soviet activity or views in the camps they were to be arrested, sentenced and held by the NKVD. The other side of the coin, that of finding individuals willing to collaborate with the Soviet cause, was more problematic. The narrowness of the Stalinist definition of cooperation seems to have produced minimal success. One can deduce that somewhat less than 100 PoWs agreed to become agents and informers. The possibility of eventual collaboration against Germany, as against the Western Powers, seems to have been broached by the interrogators mainly with the most senior officers. One just does not know how many Poles qualified as supporters and sympathisers by intimating that they might be willing to serve in the Soviet armed forces and intelligence services or even to work and settle in the USSR. Only 395 were saved from the massacre, well over a quarter of whom were Germans and Lithuanians. The agents, informers and signers of loyalty declarations to the USSR were included in Merkulov's list of 91 names which covered likely collaborators which the GUGB Second Department hoped to make use of. Others were included in the general list of 161 composed of names proposed by the functionaries sent to the camps. Despite some debate in Poland the identities lying behind such cryptonyms as 'Tygrys', 'Wolski', 'Zuch' or 'Mały' have not, as yet, been revealed.[38]

All PoWs in Kozelsk and Starobelsk were interrogated individually, at least once. Interrogations took place in carefully prepared rooms at all times of day and not just at night as suggested by some sources. PoWs were summoned from the barracks by name, were escorted for questioning under armed guard and were often kept waiting for long periods in order to weaken their psychological defences. Świaniewicz confirms the foregoing points and that the Soviets 'placed great weight on the detailed examination of the Polish officers'.[39] Młynarski describes his interrogation in a dim room in Starobelsk as beginning with an examination of his personal, family, occupational and material details.[40] The chain smoking questioner demonstrated a surprising degree of knowledge of his personal and local details. He utilised any inaccuracies between replies and the written form in order to provoke and elicit further information. Pro-Soviet and anti-Polish harangues were interspersed with questioning about social origins, education and connections designed to categorise the prisoner as a class enemy. Particular attention was paid to service in the armies of the partitioning Czarist Russia or Central Powers during the First World War, the Legions and the 1920 war and to experiences in the inter-war Polish army and the September 1939 campaign. Physical violence was not resorted to in the camps, only in the NKVD prisons, although one outburst of violent methods by NKVD trainees in Ostashkov has been reported.

High-profile prisoners such as Czapski were subjected to two- to three-hour-long interrogations during three to four consecutive nights.[41] This proved just as much a psychologically, as a physically, draining experience. There was no way that the PoWs could defend themselves against their interrogator's charges of being anti-Soviet counter-revolutionaries. The substance of the charges – their Polish patriotism and devotion to the Polish cause, professional qualities and contempt for Soviet tyranny and poverty – was also something that most PoWs did not want to deny anyway. The exceptions usually turned out to be Germans, Jews, Ukrainians, Belarusans and Lithuanians along with a small number of ethnic Poles, who either had grievances against inter-war Poland or succumbed through fear or other circumstances. The retrospective evidence also makes it clear that the number of genuine supporters such as Zygmunt Berling, or even sympathisers, for the Soviet cause in 1939–1940 was infinitesimal. Even Berling seems to have rejected the first two offers of collaboration with the NKVD before consenting to a third. Others, like Air Force Lieutenant Jan Kazimierz Mintowt-Czyż, resisted attempts by the fluently Polish-speaking Alexandrovich at Kozelsk to recruit him into Soviet intelligence work abroad.[42] The mere fact that a dialogue took place may have been sufficient to save him from the massacre.

The top NKVD functionaries used more sophisticated methods in dealing with the senior officers from lieutenant-colonel upwards.[43] Conditions were much more relaxed, particularly in the sessions presided over by the much written and speculated about Zarubin in Kozelsk, which seem to have been closer to discussion periods than interrogations.[44] Pro-Soviet sympathisers like Lieutenant-Colonels Zygmunt Berling and Leon Bukojemski in Starobelsk indicate that they were led into signing loyalty declarations to the USSR through initial discussion of mutual Slavic hostility to Germany.[45] Internal NKVD reports seem to support their own self-justifying accounts. While they were willing to reveal their colleagues' attitudes and state of mind, they did not participate in recruiting further agents. They would not have had much success had they tried. The bulk of Polish officers were almost as rigid in their Polish nationalist attitudes as the NKVD functionaries were in their Sovietism so leftists were quickly identified and shunned. Świaniewicz reports that the officers regarded Polish communists and collaborators with the Soviet occupiers with the 'highest contempt' as 'ordinary traitors'.[46] On the other hand the Soviet authorities, although not the Red Army which was appraised professionally, were regarded rather more as figures of fun. Another complicating issue is that some Polish officers were undoubtedly ordered by their superiors to infiltrate the NKVD networks. Classic counter-intelligence techniques involved the feeding of false information or penetration in order to be better able to combat the enemy.

How, why and by whom was the decision to massacre taken?

Soprunenko proposed the release from Kozelsk and Starobelsk, on 20 February 1940, of about 300 sick and invalid prisoners over 60. He also thought up another category of 'progressive intelligentsia' – about 400–500 agronomists, engineers, teachers and doctors resident in West Belarus and West Ukraine.[47] This highly significant document shows that the decision to empty the camps had already been taken by that date. Beria ordered Merkulov to consult him but for whatever reason they decided against saving these particular categories. They ordered, however, the transfer of 201 inmates comprising 114 prison officials, six spies, two provocateurs, five judiciary workers, 35 settlers, 12 landowners and 27 traders from the three camps to NKVD prisons.[48] This did not save them from being shot as part of the general massacre. They figured on the execution lists, so presumably they were either sent back to the camps or transported directly to the killing sites.

Detailed examination of the NKVD sources for January–March 1940 reveals a dual track. The major, and in fact only apparent, activity involved the NKVD functionaries sent to the three camps in completing the investigation material on the PoWs by the end of January. This was to be presented to the Special College, according to Beria's instructions of 31

December. By 20 January they were receiving instructions to simplify and accelerate the process in order to complete it in time. At the same time Arsenii Tishkov's team was directed to investigate the unrest in the Krivoi Rog and Zaporozhe camps run by the Ministry of Ferrous Metallurgy. Only on 5 March does the wholesale massacre option reveal itself with its attendant changes in procedures and a wholly different set of preparations. Only Stalin and Beria, perhaps just these two, but at most a limited number of closest NKVD associates like Merkulov and Kobulov, would have been privy to the wholesale massacre option before then. After 5 March NKVD preparations involved perhaps some dozen top officials initially during March, increasing to around 200 individuals directly involved in carrying out the massacre during April–May. Earlier explanations, predicated on what André Fontaine called 'an excess of zeal by a subordinate' are now seen to have been complete nonsense.[49] The oft-repeated story that Stalin told Beria to deal with the Polish PoWs and Beria transmitted the order to Merkulov who carried it out literally comes into this category of black propaganda and misinformation based on a total ignorance of Soviet realities.

No document has emerged, and we just do not know if it ever will, revealing what Beria and his top NKVD associates considered doing with the PoWs. They would seem to have been faced with four options. The first can loosely be described as maintaining the *status quo* by holding the officers and policemen in the three camps. This was challenged by the outbreak of the Finnish–Soviet War at the end of November 1938. During December and January the Stalinist leadership believed that a rapid and overwhelming victory would produce large numbers, estimated at 30 000, of Finnish PoWs. A vast amount of evidence shows NKVD preparations for their reception in this period through the evacuation of the special camps. In the event, brave Finnish resistance, making the most of their favourable winter terrain and conditions, meant that only about 800–1000 of their soldiers actually became Soviet PoWs. This was quite clear by early February. One should note, however, that although this invalidates the Finnish PoW explanation it is exactly at this moment in time that the wholesale massacre option was beginning to firm up, if only in Stalin's mind.

On the other hand there is a mass of evidence that at one point, Stalin envisaged even more massive deportations from the Baltic States than actually occurred after their annexation in June 1940. They were to have been accompanied by the mass imprisonment of all military officers and members of the judicial-repressive institutions of Estonia, Latvia and Lithuania. Chernyshev's note of 9 June 1940 indicates the preparations made for the reception of 38 000 PoWs including 5000 apiece at Kozelsk2 and Starobelsk2.[50] The question, therefore, arises – were the Poles killed in Spring 1940 in order to clear the way for a second 'Katyn', with the Baltic States as victims? If so, it remains obscure why this did not happen, and why the major wave of Baltic arrests was postponed until 1941.

Second, the NKVD had implemented the option of using ordinary-ranking Polish PoWs for work on road building in West Belarus and Ukraine and in the iron and steel works of the Donetsk basin. The former demonstrated huge security problems as large numbers of PoWs had escaped. The latter showed the difficulty of converting PoWs into contracted and fairly free labour and the cost of keeping them in work camps. As conditions were nowhere near as closed as in the three special camps it would have been impossible to massacre them while maintaining hermetic secrecy. These PoWs were, therefore, sent to Siberian labour camps instead and thus subjected to the real GULAG in 1940–1941. A parachute *corps* corporal, involved in the Krivoi Rog unrest, was, however, threatened by an NKVD man in April 1940 with the same fate as 'your officers in Starobelsk who will never return home'.[51] One can only surmise that the road construction and metallurgy experiences decided the Stalinist leadership against, even considering, the work option for the officers and policemen.

We now come to the most mysterious and tragic aspects of this discussion. All the evidence suggests that the various levels of NKVD functionaries worked on the assumption that the PoWs in the three special camps would be sentenced to three to eight years' GULAG by the Special College in Moscow.[52] The evacuation of the camps signified their transportation to Siberia or Northern European Russia. It therefore made sense to expose former class enemies and current counter-revolutionaries who would be dealt with separately in NKVD prisons. Only those involved directly in the massacre knew for sure that the truth was otherwise, and even then only after a series of top-level preparatory meetings following 5 March. The meticulous preparations for the massacre, therefore, broke the process up very carefully into separate and distinct stages in order to maintain secrecy.

The final option, which actually materialised, of almost wholesale massacre involves discussion of the psychology of the Stalinist leadership, notably of Stalin himself. The most important level and phase of decision making also remains the most speculative due to the almost complete absence of memoirs or of internal preparatory documentation. The evidence indicates an incredible degree of centralised decision making by Stalin and Beria and provides only indirect circumstantial indicators about the influence of personal advisers. Stalin, for example, must have talked about the matter to Viktor Poskrybyshev, his closest Kremlin aide, who was shot in 1954. As head of the CC Special Sector he would certainly have needed special instructions as to the wording and extent of circulation within the elite of the 5 March decision.

Volume 2 of *Katyn: Documents Concerning the Atrocity*, quite simply entitled *The Massacre*, by contrast, throws enormous light on even the most minute detail of the preparation and mechanisms of the massacre itself. The problem for the scholar is that the hub of power in the Stalinist system was an all-powerful tyrant called Stalin. He inspired and determined decisions in very direct personal and informal ways. It is rare to find written orders emanating directly from Stalin as against their rubber stamping by such bodies as the VKP (b) politburo and secretariat which, by 1940, merely acted as fronts for his will. In such a system participants such as Voroshilov or Kaganovich published party-authorised reminiscences only for propaganda purposes. Khruschev was exceptional in writing, after retirement, somewhat more revealing, if still highly self-serving, memoirs which do not mention Katyn. No top-level Soviet Stalinist from this period survived until democracy when something meaningful might have been revealed. Officials, at both the higher and lower level, such as Soprunenko or Syromatnikov had their own motives for concealing the truth about their guilt and participation in the massacre. Only a half-senile individual like Tokarev, who was on the point of death, spilt some of the beans to the judicial investigators in 1991. The blind Soprunenko, on retirement, lived in Moscow until his death, apparently from cancer, in 1992. He sought refuge in the countryside and refused to give interviews but his daughter Yelena defended him stoutly against the charge that he was the Soviet Eichmann and a 'mass killer'. Yelena declared that her father had never wanted to work in the NKVD and 'just did his duty as an officer according to the rules'.[53]

We shall, therefore, wait in vain for a document to emerge, as in a normal chancellery, entitled 'Kremlin/Stalin to Beria – Options for Dealing with the Polish PoWs'! What in fact almost certainly occurred was the other way around. Beria met Stalin regularly in the Kremlin and, presumably, gave him full progress reports on the behaviour of the PoWs and the conclusions drawn from their interrogation. Stalin also entertained his closest associates, notably politburo members Beria, Molotov, Voroshilov and Kaganovich, and less often Kalinin and Mikoyan, in the evening at his villa at Kuncevo. We just do not know whether it was there, in between much hard drinking, watching films and some clowning, or in the Kremlin, that Stalin and Beria would have mulled over the fate of the PoWs in between considering numerous other issues at various stages of resolution. Beria would have presented the conclusions drawn from the reports of his NKVD and DPA functionaries. From what we know of the somewhat lazy Stalin's haphazard working methods it is most unlikely that he would have asked to see the original documents themselves.[54] In this instance it is most likely that Stalin made up his mind in the last days of February or early March.[55]

The following day, or so, Beria would have had his officials draw up what became his justification for the 5 March politburo decision incorporating the main lines of Stalin's decision and any relevant substantiation and detail. One presumes that Stalin had sight of the initial draft and personally added or deleted whatever he thought appropriate. In this instance, Stalin replaced Beria's name with that of Kobulov as a member of the implementing troika on the draft presented to the politburo. Whether this amendment reflected any wider disagreement remains highly speculative. The corrected document was then put on the agenda of the next politburo meeting although one does not know whether those present would have discussed anything lying outside their respective competences or even whether the matter would have been introduced personally by Beria. What we do know is that the 5 March politburo decision incorporating Beria's proposal was signed personally by Stalin, Voroshilov, Molotov and Mikoyan. An official noted that the absent Kalinin and Kaganovich were 'for' although it is unlikely they were even consulted. Beria himself wrote 'carry out' at the bottom of the original document.

Special Colleges or Tribunals were established by the NKVD in 1934 in order to confirm sentences of up to five years' exile or eight, exceptionally ten, years' labour camp proposed by its Investigation Organs. They could do so in the absence of the accused. In theory, the Special College had to be headed by Beria, or his first deputy, Merkulov, as well as an NKVD plenipotentiary for the Russian Republic, the Minister of the Interior of the republic where the offence had occurred, the head of the Soviet militia and the General Procurator of the USSR (or his deputy). The full procedure was expeditious for individual cases but would have been time-consuming if applied to all 14 700 camp inmates. It involved investigation and interrogation of the accused, the presentation and drawing up of charges and the consideration of sentence by the full panel. The tribunal was not formally given the power of passing death sentences until November 1941. As we have seen, about 600 Ostashkov prisoners had been processed in this way, receiving sentences of between three and eight years; labour camp under article 58, paragraph 13, when this particular procedure was halted.

Soprunenko's proposal to release about 1100 old and sick PoWs along with some other categories resident in Soviet-occupied territory met with a confused reaction. Beria ordered Merkulov to direct various categories of intelligence and prison agents along with civilians to be transferred with their papers to NKVD prisons. At the same time, Beria ordered the Starobelsk commandant to send ten military chaplains, including a rabbi, to Moscow from whence they were returned in time to be included in the massacre. On 26 February Soprunenko sent out a DPA request to camp commandants regarding the completion of the prisoners' financial, social and occupational details on their questionnaires. This information was returned within two days. At that point Nekhoreshev ordered the Kozelsk commandant to send him, by rapid courier, four to five specimen copies of investigation files along with a similar number of files of cases dealt with by their Special Department.[56] Lebedeva argues very convincingly that these files were shown by Beria to Stalin in their discussion, within the following week, preceding the latter's decision to choose the wholesale massacre option.[57] One does not know what other central DPA material or earlier reports apart from the various summaries prepared by the NKVD were submitted by Beria. One also just does not know, and we probably never will for certain, whether Beria initially supported the DPA line favouring isolation and grinding down in the Siberian camps. If, for some reason Stalin had given hostile signals about the Polish PoWs in their preliminary discussions, what evidence we have concerning their relationship would lead one to surmise that Beria would have been equally happy to egg him on and provide supporting evidence to firm up his decision. There is no direct evidence to support his son's argument that Beria earned Stalin's severe displeasure by wanting the Poles to be kept in reserve in case they might come in useful against the Germans.[58]

What we do know is that the decision was taken within the general context of the Second Deportation, particularly of the families of PoWs in the special camps as well as of refugees from German-occupied Poland.[59] Soprunenko was also kept busy in the early days of March in drawing up the statistics and categories which Beria included in the 5 March resolution.[60] What is also revealing about the timing of the decision is that Korytov (the Ostashkov Special Department head) was summoned to a two-day conference in Moscow on 3–4 March which started planning the evacuation of the camps.[61] Preliminary decisions were taken to quieten PoW fears by suggesting that they were being sent home; under no circumstances would sentences be announced within the camps while the transportation operation would be secured by the Escort Guards, not by camp personnel. Korytov reported to his regional superior, Pavlov, that one of the arguments he had used to support the latter was that the convoying exercise would take at least a month. He was, therefore, clearly thinking in terms of Siberia, not massacre. The presence of GULAG representatives and much talk about the 600 Special Tribunal decisions and the need to empty the camps in order to accommodate Finnish PoWs indicate that the planning of the massacre was initiated under cover of the labour camp option.

All that one knows for certain is the outcome. Lebedeva claims to have had sight in the Central Archive of the Federal Security Service of a typewritten draft of Beria's report to Stalin, submitted with a date as early as 3 March.[62] She argues, very convincingly, that the decision to replace the relatively cumbersome, and as yet incomplete, Special College procedure with a very simplified Moscow-based Troika, which could maintain secrecy much more effectively, was taken at this time. We do not know whether there was any last-minute adjustment of the document but the final draft of the 5 March decision is a historic document.[63] It merits exhaustive examination as the Soviets claimed that much of the preparatory documentation was destroyed in 1959 by Khruschev and his security boss of the time, KGB chairman Alexandr Shelepin, so there is little else to go on.

Beria informed Stalin and the politburo that the large number (14 736, 97 per cent Polish) of officers of the former Polish army, policemen, intelligence agents, members of counter-revolutionary parties and organisations and escapees held in the NKVD camps were bitter enemies of Soviet power. They had continued counter-revolutionary activity in the camps and dreamt of liberation so that they might continue anti-Soviet struggle. This preamble was followed by the most up-to-date of Soprunenko's figures on the military prisoners, who were listed as 295 generals, colonels and lieutenant-colonels, 2080 majors and captains and 6049 lieutenants, sub-lieutenants and ensigns. The other categories held in the camps were 1030 police officers and NCOs, 5138 ordinary-ranking policemen, gendarmes, prison personnel and intelligence agents as well as 144 officials, landowners, priests and military settlers. Beria went on to report that 18 632 arrestees were held in prison in West Belarus and West Ukraine, of which 10 685 were Poles; they were composed of 1207 officers, 5141 policemen, intelligence agents and gendarmes, 347 spies and diversionists, 465 landowners, factory owners and officials, 5345 members of various counter-revolutionary and insurrectionary organisations and 6127 refugees.

Beria's conclusion and recommendation was chillingly simple. 'Taking into account that all were hardened and uncompromising [irredeemable] enemies of Soviet power', the 14 700 in the camps, along with 11 000 of those held in the prisons, 'were to be examined by special procedure with the application towards them of the highest form of punishment – shooting.' The examination of the cases and the implementation of the decision was entrusted to a troika composed of Merkulov, Kobulov (replacing Beria on Stalin's suggestion) and Bashtakov. They were to proceed, without summoning the arrested and without presenting charges, on the basis of DPA information for the camp prisoners and Belarus and Ukraine NKVD republic material for the arrestees. The second half of the above document became the politburo decision, passed at its 13th sitting on 5 March 1940 as item 144 of its agenda, which legitimated the massacre in official Soviet Stalinist terms.[64] The next agenda item concerned the preparation of a new sarcophagus for Lenin's body in the Kremlin mausoleum! There is indirect evidence suggesting that the top communist elite was in due course informed quite widely about the politburo decision to massacre the Polish PoWs.[65]

NKVD troikas were used from 1937 onwards to expedite the processing of the huge numbers of individuals repressed during the Great Terror.[66] Apart from rapidity and simplicity they had two other great strengths. The first was their capacity for maintaining secrecy, as investigation, sentencing and execution were kept solely within the NKVD fold. The second, was that they provided the orders for a tried and proven mechanism for the carrying out of massacres by the oblast NKVD. The troika, in this instance, also provided the highly centralised linkage between the decision making by Stalin and Beria and implementation. Vsievolod Merkulov, First Deputy Minister of the Interior and GUGB chairman, and Bachko Kobulov, Head of the Main NKVD Economic Department, were Beria's most intimate associates. They would have been the first to know of Beria's discussions with Stalin and of the way the decision was firming up during February. Unfortunately, from the historian's point of view, they were hardly literary gents and left no records when they were shot, after Stalin's death, at the same time as their patron in 1953. Leonid Fikevits Bashtakov, was not so personally close to Beria as the other two, so he not only survived the 1953 purge but lived long enough to be interviewed by the Russian Procuracy on other matters. Bashtakov refused to see the investigative journalist Vladimir Abarinov, but as Head of the NKVD First (Special) Department he was certainly, at the centre of NKVD affairs. He chose, however, to take his personal knowledge of the 1940 massacre to his grave.

The 5 March document confirms the argument that the killing of the PoWs in the camps and of the arrestees, including civilians, in the Belarusan and Ukrainian prisons formed a coherent whole in the minds of the Stalinist decision makers. The operation thus wholly merits description as the Soviet Massacre of Spring 1940 and justifies examination under a single academic umbrella. Writers, however, have to work within the publishing and other constraints set by the fact that the whole massacre has come to be symbolised by the term 'Katyn' (the victims of a single camp at Kozelsk) in the public mind since 1943. It was only confirmed publicly by Gorbachev in 1990 that the victims of Starobelsk had been buried at Kharkov and those of Ostashkov at Mednoe and that large numbers had been executed in prisons in Belarus and Ukraine at the same time.

The politburo condemned 11 000 arrestees held in prisons in Belarus and Ukraine to death by shooting. Shelepin's 1959 figures, in the documents handed over in 1992, reveal that 'only' 7305 of this quota were actually executed. He also gives a figure of 14 552 victims from the three camps so the whole massacre, according to him, totalled 21 856. The total for the prison shootings is also somewhat less than the number of Poles (10 685) mentioned by Beria. One can surmise that there was a very close, although not quite exact, correlation between Polish ethnicity and those executed. There is also one significant piece of evidence about the missing 3700 or so. Beria and Chernyshev ordered the Escort Guards on 27 February to convoy between 6000 and 12 000 prisoners, who had already been sentenced by the NKVD Special Tribunal as refugees from German-held territory and would-be escapees to it, from the Belarusan and Ukrainian prisons, to GULAGs in Vladivostock.[67] Some of the 3700 may have found themselves added to the 7000 figure not destined for shooting, hence the NKVD flexibility over the bottom and top limits (6000–12 000) scheduled for transportation.

By 1940 Stalin was an all-powerful tyrant who had destroyed all his domestic political and ideological enemies and subordinated the communist party and the security services entirely to his will. He had rewritten history to magnify his role into a veritable cult of the personality and terrorised Soviet society into accepting his massive industrialisation and militarisation programmes. Nobody in his immediate circle, dared to stand up to him, although the wily and totally unprincipled Beria seems to have been more adept than most in handling him.[68] Few would venture to correct him, even on minor points. If Stalin had a phobia about Polish officers he, probably had an even stronger one about policemen and prison guards in general given his shady grassroots revolutionary activity before 1917. There is little evidence in the NKVD documents of the two categories being considered separately as candidates for massacre. Logically, they should have been and the more advanced work on the preparation of the Special College procedure for the policemen may provide a clue. Stalin also believed implicitly, that his deal with Hitler would be long lasting and that it had secured his own, and the USSR's, external position for well beyond the immediate future. The Nazi–Soviet idyll was still continuing in spring 1940. Moreover, Stalin expected that the Western Powers would bog Germany down in a long war. Stalin therefore felt himself in an exceptionally strong position, both domestically and internationally, in spring 1940. It is possible that he got unwontedly carried away by an almost euphoric and exalted feeling that he was at long last allpowerful and beyond all accounting to humanity.

Stalin was thus in a position to order the destruction of almost 22 000 Poles, who were held entirely within his power, if he so wished, either to settle personal scores or to further his political aims. We have already seen that much has been made about Stalin's polonophobia and resentments concerning the 1920 war. Everything that we know about the grimly cautious Stalin, however, indicates that normally, as a self-disciplined and experienced political conspirator, subjective factors would be very subordinate to long-term political aims. In 1940 Stalin wanted to destroy all Polish influence and presence in West Belarus and West Ukraine for ever. As we have seen, motivated by his and Lenin's ideas of 1913 on nationalities policy, he was chary of taking on parts of the ethnically Polish heartland in 1939. Admittedly, he hated Poland's inter-war political and social elites as both a class enemy and a national threat, but he was typical of an entire Bolshevik generation in that respect. Many authorities have, therefore, claimed that massacring about 9000 Polish army officers, many of them university-educated leaders in other walks of life, in 1940 was part of a longer-term Bolshevik tactic of weakening a hostile social and national elite.[69] Neil Ascherson terms it 'an act of selective genocide against a part of Poland's national elite, closely parallel to Hitler's order to exterminate the Polish intellectual class' while Victor Zaslavsky describes it as 'class cleansing'.[70]

All the above may be true, but the key factor is that Stalin was extremely lucky during the Second World War. He survived the German onslaught in 1941 and benefited from the great patriotic upsurge of the Soviet people to turn the tide against the invaders from Stalingrad onwards. The

1940 massacre proved to be an extreme embarrassment during 1941–1943. At peak, in 1943, it endangered the Soviet–Western Powers alliance necessary to defeat Nazi Germany. Had history been frozen at that moment in time the massacre would have been interpreted in terms of Stalin's wilfulness and short-sightedness. After 1944, though, it could be regarded by the Soviet inner echelon as a masterstroke, utilised by Stalin, along with the 1944 Warsaw Uprising, to weaken and outmanoeuvre the London Poles and to Sovietise an ethnically homogeneous Poland within permanently recast new frontiers.[71]

My own view is that the 1940 massacre cannot be explained in terms of these larger historical outcomes and that one has to focus strictly on the context of the time. Here, one has already examined the Soviet de-polonisation of the territories occupied in September 1939. The Nazi–Soviet alliance to destroy Poland's nationhood, certainly Stalin's favoured option in 1939–1940, has also been discussed. An additional, if somewhat far-fetched, explanation is that Stalin destroyed the Polish officers as an additional gauge of friendship for Adolf Hitler. Were the Soviets at their most nervous about Hitler's intentions just before his spring 1940 military campaigns?[72] The official British Foreign Office Historian, Rohan Butler, thus discusses Ulam's thesis that they were provoked by Gestapo 'importunities' into massacring the Polish PoWs.[73] Strong NKVD–Gestapo contacts certainly existed, as discussed at the end of Chapter Two, but the level was primarily one of coordinating the timing of anti-Polish actions. Mutual information also took place, although there is only indirect evidence that the Germans were informed about the 1940 PoW massacre. Himmler and Merkulov met, and no doubt mutually congratulated themselves on the success of their anti-Polish activities, during Molotov's visit to Berlin in November 1940 which otherwise saw the initial political souring of the Nazi–Soviet alliance with disputes over Romania.[74] There has also been much, and so far unresolved, speculation about whether Rudolf Hess brought decisive proof of Stalin's massacre with him during his May 1941 flight to Scotland. Conspiracy theorists argue that this was designed to wean the London Poles away from the USSR and towards Germany as part of Hess's desperate last-minute attempt to achieve a deal between Nazi Germany and the British Empire just before Hitler's invasion of the USSR.

Dr Skarzyński testified to the 1952 US Congressional Committee, that his superior, Dr Gorzycki, the Head of the Polish Red Cross, was ordered by Nazi *General-Gouvernement* officials in late January 1940 to prepare reception camps for Polish officers about to be released from Soviet captivity.[75] That this was only part of the Soviet disinformation campaign is now apparent. Gorzycki received verbal orders to close the camps at Terespol in April or May 1940 as 'the officers won't come back'.[76] Whether the Germans were informed directly by the Soviets or whether they derived this information from their own intelligence sources is unknown. The contrary argument, that the Poles could have been recruited as potential

Allies in an anti-German war also has little credibility in the 1940 context. The evidence that Stalin banked everything on, and believed implicitly in, the permanence of Nazi–Soviet collaboration is borne out by the way in which the German invasion caught him entirely by surprise. Parsadonova's argument that the 1940 massacre was used to scupper a possible reorientation of Soviet foreign policy away from Nazi Germany and towards the Western Powers is thoroughly unconvincing.[77] Post-Soviet speculation, reflecting the confused mood and political currents of 1990s Russia, that Stalin was considering a pre-emptive strike against Germany in 1940 but was disillusioned by lack of Polish support seems absurd at first sight.[78] The GRU intelligence officer and defector to the West Viktor Suvorov's argument that Stalin planned to invade German-occupied Eastern Europe while Hitler was engaged, and hopefully bogged down, in the West was, however, taken seriously by some specialists.[79] Krzysztof Jasiewicz considered that the 1940 massacre was carried out to clear space in the camps for a new wave not from the Baltic States, but from East Prussia and German-occupied Poland, who would have suffered a 'Katyn-bis'.[80]

The above arguments are also refuted completely by the most convincing explanation which can be read quite simply in the NKVD files. Their documents confirm the fiasco of attempting to use Polish PoW labour in European Russia. The PoWs in the special camps laughed off Soviet attempts to indoctrinate them or reduce them to the Soviet level of obedience. Their national, patriotic and religious values and behaviour as well as their individualism and autonomous self-organisation were a continuous affront to NKVD ideas of camp discipline. Most seriously, only small numbers, mainly drawn from marginal ethnic and social levels, were willing to collaborate directly with the NKVD. Had the interrogations taken place after the Nazi attack on the USSR the following summer, the story might well have been different. No doubt, many Poles would have agreed to fight the Germans, even under Soviet auspices, as indeed they did after 1943. But in late 1939 to early 1940 this theoretical possibility could only be hinted at by Zarubin, the most sophisticated of the NKVD officials, to the most senior officers in Kozelsk. Whether the Stalinist leadership really thought that it would be able to recruit a legion of Polish spies and agents for worldwide use seems highly doubtful.[81] Even declarations of loyalty to the USSR were hard to come by under such conditions. At the very end, only about 70 PoWs declared themselves willing to remain in the USSR rather than to be repatriated to the West, through a neutral power, or even to German-occupied Poland.

Boris Levytsky argues that the Stalinists considered that 'the Polish officers represented the master class of Polish magnates (*pany*), who had to be exterminated. The thought that the officers could still be of use to Russia in its war with Hitler simply did not occur to them.'[82] Ronald Hingley agrees that once the NKVD interrogations had proved a fiasco the PoWs 'became liable for execution according to NKVD logic'.[83] A Kozelsk survivor testified that Soviet 'agitation and propaganda had almost no success'. The massacre was decided on as the Polish refusal to collaborate decided the Soviets to dispose of a 'dangerous and inconvenient element', once and for all.[84] Another Kozelsk survivor concluded that Stalinist motivations could be explained straightforwardly as hatred of 'Pańskiej Polska', the tradition of destroying enemies of Soviet power and the reluctance to free political prisoners abroad.[85]

The cost of holding the Polish PoWs in the special camps was relatively high in terms of Soviet security and other resources. That of transporting and holding them in the sub-Polar GULAGs would, however, have represented only a marginal additional drain on Soviet resources.[86] According to Conquest there was no similar genocide of elites in the Stalinist deportation of other nationalities like the Tatars or Chechen-Ingush during the Second World War although leaders naturally suffered most.[87] On the other hand, the Stalinists massacred anything that looked like an alternative national or cultural elite in the Belarusan, Ukrainian and Trans-Caucasian republics during the 1930s. The Polish minority in the USSR was also hard hit by the 1936–1938 purge. All one can say, is that while the 1940 massacre was in some respects untypical of Soviet practice it was by no means outside its more extreme parameters. The contrary view, expressed by an NKVD defector, who knew colleagues involved in the 1940 massacre, is that it was 'a typical operation ... considered entirely routine and unremarkable in Soviet Russia'.[88] The Poles may have been extremely unlucky in terms of the timing of Stalin's decision which, in hindsight, appears unwontedly precipitous in the light of the NKVD documentation. One can argue that he would have been less likely to choose the wholesale massacre option the nearer one gets to summer 1941. Whether there was a special decisive factor – the Finnish War and its frustrations which delayed full-blooded Sovietisation of the Baltic States, personal resentments, internal dissent within the Soviet elite or the German factor – that precipitated the most extreme decision still remains an open subject for discussion.

Notes

1 KDZ, 1, p. 297.
2 Note by Vasilii Ulrich, President of the Military College of the Red Army Supreme Court, 28 January 1940, KDZ, 1, pp. 383–4.
3 KDZ, 1, no. 109.
4 KDZ, 1, no. 127.
5 KDZ, 1, no. 109.
6 KDZ, 1, no. 155.
7 KDZ, 1, no. 62.
8 KDZ, 1, no. 87.
9 KDZ, 1, no. 103.
10 KDZ, 1, no. 69. Jaczyński, *Zagłada oficerów Wojska Polskiego na Wschodzie*, pp. 166–7.

11 Cf. Karen Dawisha, 'The Limits of the Bureaucratic Politics Model', *Studies in Comparative Communism*, 13, 4 (Winter 1980), pp. 300–26.

12 KDZ, 1, p. 407.

13 Józef Czapski, *Wspomnienia Starobielskie*, Rome: White Eagle, 1944, p. 23.

14 Bronisław, Młynarski, *W niewoli sowieckiej*, London: Gryf, 1974, pp. 168–9. Czapski, *Wspomnienia Starobielskie*, p. 30.

15 KDZ, 1, no. 117.

16 Jędrzej Tucholski, '*Sprawa Komisji-Kulturalno-Oświatowej obozu w Starobielsku*', *Wojskowy Przegląd Historyczny*, 38, 4 (1993), pp. 334–44.

17 Jaczyński, *Zagłada Oficerów*..., Ch. 4. Tadeusz Gasztold, *Poza 'Willą rozkoszy': Działalność kulturalno-oświatowa polskich jeńców wojennych w Rosji Sowieckiej w latach 1939–1947*, Koszalin: Pomerania, 1995.

18 KDZ, 1, pp. 347–8.

19 Świaniewicz in *Zbrodnia Katyńska w świetle dokumentów*, London: Gryf, 1948, p. 25.

20 KDZ, 1, p. 470.

21 KDZ, 1, no. 155.

22 Peter Holquist, 'State Violence as a Technique: The Logic of Violence in Soviet Totalitarianism', in David L. Hoffman (ed.), *Stalinism*, Oxford: Blackwell, 2003, pp. 148–56.

23 KDZ, 1, no. 46.

24 Testimony of Wacław Komarnicki, IPiMS, Kol. 12/3, no. 35.

25 See Jaczyński, *Zagłada Oficerów*..., pp. 197–205.

26 KDZ, 1, nos 23 and 33.

27 KDZ, 1, nos 74 and 99.

28 KDZ, 1, nos 105, 107, 114.

29 KDZ, 1, p. 304.

30 KDZ, 1, no. 157.

31 KDZ, 1, p. 386.

32 Natalia Lebediewa, 'Operacyjno-Czekistowska obsługa jeńców wojennych', in *Zbrodnia nie ukarana: Katyń – Twer – Charków*, Warsaw: NKHBZK, 1996, pp. 112–13.

33 KDZ, 1, p. 401.

34 KDZ, 1, no. 158.

35 Soprunenko and Belolipetskii reported on 1 February 1940 that they had prepared 6050 files on the policemen in Ostashkov and that 'all the essential investigative activity had been completed', KDZ, 1, no. 178. This left about 400 cases against the border guards (KOP), judiciary and procuracy workers, landowners, POW members and spies, ibid., no. 188.

36 KDZ, 2, no. 5. The NKVD used the run-up to the massacre to extract information from earlier earmarked individuals but did not want to arouse Polish fears and suspicions by using torture and withdrawing too many individuals prematurely. As part of this policy of keeping things quiet Soprunenko instructed the camp commandants not to arrest any further PoWs for internal infringements without his direct permission, KDZ, 2, no. 30.

37 KDZ, 1, no. 190.

38 Jacek Trznadel, 'Czy ujawniać agenturę NKWD', *Gazeta Polska*, 27 October 1999.

39 *Zbrodnia Katyńska w świetle dokumentów*, pp. 19–20.

40 Młynarski, *W niewoli sowieckiej*, pp. 216–17.

41 Czapski, *Wspomnienia Starobielskie*, p. 42.

42 IPiMS, Kol. 12/3, no. 54.

43 Moszyński, *Obóz w Starobielsku*, p. 4.

44 Stanisław Świaniewicz, *W cieniu Katynia*, Paris: Instytut Literacki, 1976, p. 106.

45 Jaczyński, *Zagłada Oficerów...*, p. 227.
46 *Zbrodnia Katyńska w świetle dokumentów*, p. 21.
47 KDZ, 1, no. 188.
48 KDZ, 1, nos 190, 194.
49 André Fontaine, *History of the Cold War: From the October Revolution to the Korean War, 1917–1950*, New York, 1968, p. 185.
50 KDZ, 2, no. 228.
51 Testimony by Teodor Kuchta, IPiMS Kol. 12/3, no. 39.
52 I concur fully with Wojciech Materski on this point: 'Katyń – motywy I przebieg zbrodni (pytania, wątpliwości)', in *Zbrodnia Katyńska po 60 latach*, Warsaw: NKHBZK, 2000, p. 27.
53 Nicholas Bethell in the *Mail on Sunday*, 17 June 1990: cf. Abarinov, *Murderers of Katyn*, pp. 181–5. Iwona Parchimowicz, 'Czy mogę rozmawiać z panem Soprunienko?', *Polityka*, 12 August 1990, p. 3.
54 For the brilliant literary reconstruction which is, probably, not that far off the truth see Alexander Solzhenitsyn, *The First Circle*, London: Fontana, 1971, pp. 109–46.
55 Świaniewicz, *W cieniu Katynia*, p. 346 agrees with this time-frame.
56 KDZ, 1, no. 199.
57 Natalia Lebediewa, 'Proces podejmowania decyzji katynskiej', in Krzysztof Jasiewicz (ed.), *Europa NIEprowincjonalna*, Warsaw: ISP PAN, 1999, p. 1168.
58 Sergio Beria, edited by Francoise Thom, *Beria my Father: Inside Stalin's Kremlin*, London: Duckworth, 2nd edn, 2003, pp. 54–6.
59 KDZ, 1, nos 204, 208.
60 KDZ, 1, nos 206, 207, 209, 213, 214.
61 Korytov to Pavlov, not later than 4 March, KDZ, 1, no. 215.
62 Lebediewa in *Europa NIEprowincjonalna*, p. 1170.
63 KDZ, 1, no. 216.
64 KDZ, 1, no. 217. The decision is also available in Wojciech Materski (ed.), *Katyń: Dokumenty ludobójstwa*, Warsaw: ISP PAN, 1993, no. 6, while Beria's report is ibid., no. 9. The volume has been published in English as *Documents of Genocide: Documents and Materials from the Soviet Archives Turned Over to Poland on October 14, 1992*, Warsaw: ISP PAN, 1993.
65 Merkulov to CC Special Sector, Second Department, KDZ, 2, no. 38 shows that his copy of the protocols of the politburo meeting, reproduced in a monthly bulletin covering the 17 February–19 March 1940 period, was numbered 41. Cf. Jana Howlett, Oleg Khlevniuk, Liudmila Koshelova and Laris Rogaia, 'The CPSU's Top Bodies under Stalin: Their Operational Records and Structure of Command', Stalin-Era Research and Archives Project Working Paper, University of Toronto 1996.
66 See Oleg Khlevniuk, 'The Objectives of the Great Terror, 1937–1938', in Julian Cooper, Maureen Perrie and E.A. Rees (eds), *Essays in Honour of R.W. Davies*, London: Macmillan, 1995.
67 KDZ, 1, no. 204.
68 See Amy Knight, *Beria*, Princeton, NJ: Princeton UP, 1993.
69 Ryszard Wołągiewicz, *Katyń w albumach rodzinnych*, Szczecin: Stowarzyszenie 'Katyń' w Szczecinie, 1991, p. 82.
70 Neil Ascherson, *The Struggles for Poland*, London: Michael Joseph, 1987, p. 124. Victor Zaslavsky, 'The Katyn Massacre: "Class Cleansing" as Totalitarian Praxis', *Telos*, no. 114 (Winter 1999), pp. 67–107.
71 On the former see Tomasz Strzembosz (ed.), *Stalin a Powstanie Warszawskie*, Warsaw: ISP PAN, 1993 ('Z Archiwów Sowieckich' no. 4). On the latter, Sarah Meiklejohn Terry, *Poland's Place in Europe: General Sikorski and the Origin of the Oder-Neise Line, 1939–49*, Princeton, NJ: Princeton UP, 1983.

72 Adam Ulam, *Expansion and Coexistence*, London: Secker & Warburg, 1968, p. 344.
73 *Butler Memorandum*, paras 31–3. See Ch. 7, f. 45 for full reference.
74 Abarinov, *Murderers of Katyn*, pp. 376–7.
75 Maria Bagińska informed General Marian Kukiel in a letter of 21 April 1943 that the Germans gave similar instructions to the PRC in Brześć-on-the-Bug in March–April 1940, IPiMS, Kol. 12/3, no. 2.
76 *Hearings*, Part 3, p. 402.
77 Valentina Sergeyevna Parsadonova in *Mezdunarodny otnoshenija i strany Central-noj i Jugo-Wostocznoj Jewropy w nachale mirovoj wojny*, Moscow, 1990, p. 64.
78 See R.W. Davies, *Soviet History in the Yeltsin Era*, Basingstoke: Macmillan, 1997, pp. 56–8.
79 Amongst a mass of far from reliable writings see Viktor Suvorov, *Ice-breaker: Who Started the Second World War?*, London: Hamish Hamilton, 1990.
80 Krzysztof Jasiewicz, *Zagłada polskich kresów: Ziemiaństwo polskie na Kresach Pół-nocno-Wschodnich Rzeczypospolitej pod okupację sowiecką, 1939–1941*, Warsaw: ISP PAN, 1998, pp. 143–65.
81 Ibid., p. 156.
82 Boris Levytsky, *The Uses of Terror: The Soviet Secret Police, 1917–1970*, New York: 1972, pp. 151–2.
83 Ronald Hingley, *The Russian Secret Police*, London: 1970, p. 186.
84 Testimony by Colonel Jerzy Grobicki, IPiMS, Kol. 12/3, no. 22.
85 Testimony of Stanisław Dzienisiewicz, IPiMS, Kol. 12/3, no. 14.
86 See Nikita Ochotin and Arsenii Roginsky (eds), *Łagry: przewodnik encyklopedyczny*, Warsaw: Karta/Memorial, 1998.
87 Robert Conquest, *The Nation-Killers: The Soviet Deportation of Nationalities*, London: Macmillan, 1970.
88 A. Romanov (*pseud.*), *Nights Are Longest There*, London: Hutchinson, 1972, pp. 136–7.

5 Course, mechanisms and technology of the massacre

Political and logistical preparations for the massacre

The NKVD had a whole month to prepare the massacre after the politburo confirmed the decision on 5 March. The massacre began with the first transports from the camps in early April and stretched over a period of over five weeks, almost into mid-May. In order to maintain secrecy the process was broken down into three quite separate and distinctly compartmentalised stages. The bulk of camp personnel had no official knowledge of, or direct participation in, the massacre. Their role was limited very strictly to preparing the evacuation of the PoWs with the special brigades and to handing them over 'to the disposal of the NKVD' on the basis of lists phoned to them by the NKVD centre in Moscow. The intermediate stage was that of transportation from the camps to the killing sites. The final stage of execution and burial also did not overlap much in personnel terms with the preceding one. The primary aim of breaking up the massacre into three hermetically sealed stages was secrecy. But the isolation of the final stage was also designed to ensure total manipulated control over the prospective victims right up to the final bullet.

The NKVD documents confirm Zawodny's presupposition that the massacre 'was synchronised in time and centrally directed ... an office in Moscow decided and planned the extermination'.[1] The round of preparatory meetings in the NKVD's Moscow headquarters started with 8–12 top officials coming together on 8 March. The NKVD decision makers and commanders, at both the central and regional levels, had to be informed first, and assigned their tasks. This involved all three stages of organising the PoWs' departure from the camps, their transportation from the camps to the NKVD killing sites, and finally the technical organisation of their execution and burial. The senior NKVD Moscow functionaries, headed by Kobulov and Soprunenko, informed the regional NKVD heads to be involved in the forthcoming operation on 8 March that the 'highest authorities' had decided on the shooting of over 14 000 PoWs. Tokarev testifies that Soprunenko emphasised that the highest priority was secrecy. There were to be no witnesses. Apart from those directly involved in the massacre, no one else was to survive.[2] On 14 March, Kobulov and Soprunenko went over the same ground in greater detail with an enlarged gremium of 15–20 regional officials from the Smolensk, Kharkov and Kalinin oblasts. These included their deputy heads, the district military commanders of the NKVD special units, who had been briefed and prepared by their chiefs. One presumes that the regional functionaries came prepared with specific proposals concerning killing and burial sites, which were discussed and confirmed.

One also presumes that Merkulov and Kobulov, if not Beria himself, must have met with Ivan Serov and Lavrentii Tsanava and their republic NKVD subordinates, but no direct documentary evidence of this has transpired. The relations between Moscow and the Republic First Party Secretaries, Nikita Khruschev in the Ukraine and Panteleimon Kondratevich Ponomarenko in Belarus, are even murkier. One just does not know if, and when, and in what detail, they were informed of the massacre of the camp inmates. They must have been in the know, if not directly involved in implementing the shooting of the arrestees from the prisons within their republics.

Once the central and republican-regional levels had been informed and prepared, the DPA teams in the camps and the camp functionaries were schooled in preparing the evacuation of the camps. This did not necessitate knowledge of the PoWs' eventual fate for the latter, but this probably seeped through to the top *Komendatura* echelons. The commandants, political commissars and heads of the Special Departments of the three special camps conferred in the DPA on 15 March on the technical preparation of the evacuation of the camps. URO heads were also summoned to Moscow, subsequently, and given precise instructions on how PoWs were to be assembled for departure and on the transmission of files. Camp security and censorship of correspondence was also tightened up. The commanders of the camp guards were summoned to Moscow and given appropriate instructions. There is much evidence of intensive DPA contacts with camp commandants, commissars and heads of Special Departments in late March–early April in preparation for the evacuation phase.

The transportation arrangements were largely prepared centrally. The key figure seems to have been Solomon Milshtein, the head of the NKVD Transport Main Department. His detailed plan involved the transportation by rail, from the nearest local station, of the Starobelsk prisoners to Kharkov, of those from Kozelsk to Smolensk-Gnezdovo and of the Ostashkov inmates to Kalinin. The Kharkov-Starobelsk preparations were completed with the railway carriages in place by 23 March.[3] This aspect was closely tied up with the preparation of the Escort Guards who were to assure the security of the convoys from the camps to the killing sites. The Main Department of Escort Troops (GUKV) therefore sent its top functionaries to make the necessary preparations and to oversee their implementation. Alexei Rybakov, head of the GUKV operations department, went to Starobelsk. His deputy, the large and ruddy-faced Alexandr Stepanov, is reported as making quite an impression on the Kozelsk inmates while Mikhail Krivenko, commander of the Escort Troops, went to Ostashkov. We now know which Escort Troop units were directed for convoying duties. A unit of the 136th battalion of Escort Troops commanded by Major Mekhov went to Kozelsk. This was replaced by a unit of the 226nd regiment, 15th brigade, during the operation. Ostashkov was serviced by the 135th independent battalion which was replaced by the 12th company of the 236th regiment. Starobelsk received the 230th battalion of Escort Troops. The Escort Troops did not participate in the actual executions but were responsible for security during the transportation phase and for securing the perimeter of killing sites.

There is hardly any official information about preparations for the execution and burial stage. As transpires from the testimony of the Kharkov prison guard Mitrofan Vasilevich Syromatnikov in 1990–1992, this was based entirely on the personnel and techniques which had developed and been applied by the NKVD since 1936.[4] All that was different was, perhaps, the numbers involved and the five to six week time period into which the operation was compressed from early April until mid-May. For obvious reasons, the identity of individuals involved directly in this stage, especially of executioners, has to be deduced from other than official sources.

On 17 March Beria consolidated the material and psychological preparation of NKVD personnel. He promoted a large number of NKVD officers who had dealt with the PoWs in the DPA and the special camps or who were to play key roles in the forthcoming massacre. Such initial motivation before the massacre was to be paralleled by the handing out of additional financial rewards and decorations on its completion.

Kobulov worked out the draft of the information-decision files to be considered by the Troika. Soprunenko sent them out for rapid completion and return by camp UROs on 16 March.[5] All that was required was information under three headings. The first was surname, first name and father's name. The second – personal particulars – covered year and place of birth, wealth, family, place of imprisonment and date taken into captivity. The third was function and rank in the former Polish army or in the police, espionage or prison services. The final heading, sentence – death by shooting – was fore-ordained by the 5 March decision. In theory, it was to be filled in by the Troika after its considerations had been completed. But one wonders if the Troika even had sight of any, let alone all, of the 14 700 files in the short time available to it before the massacre began. At any rate DPA officials checked the forms and asked camp departments and investigating teams to clear up ambiguous or inaccurate headings. The files were then sent to the NKVD Special Department, whose deputy-head, Arkadii Yakovlevich Gerchovskii, was responsible for their cataloguing. He also, initially, drew up the transportation or death lists. The

Troika confirmed these as they were prepared, on a collective, not individual basis, mainly during April. Lebedeva, who presents the most authoritative picture, cites 9 April 1940 as marking the peak of this simplified and accelerated process. On that day, the Troika confirmed the names on 13 lists, thus condemning 1297 prisoners.[6] Doubtful or special cases, and certainly all those concerning agents, informers or possible sympathisers and collaborators, were considered individually, mainly by Merkulov.

The bureaucracy and book-keeping of death

The process of sending the PoWs from the special camps to the killing sites was, despite his later denials, supervised by DPA head Soprunenko, and his deputy for operational affairs, Ivan Khokhlov. They were responsible for directing the transportation or death lists drawn up by the NKVD Special Department to the camps and for maintaining the single numbered main list. This was accompanied by the euphemistic instruction that the prisoners named on them were 'to be placed at the disposal' of the relevant regional NKVD – Smolensk for Kozelsk, Kharkov for Starobelsk and Kalinin for Ostashkov. The lists, at peak between four and six daily, were delivered to camp commandants by special couriers in sealed envelopes. The actual transportation lists, compiled from these, of those due to depart on any particular day were, however, confirmed by Moscow on each departure day with the reading of every individual name on the list over the telephone. The first of these were lists of 100, 49, 94 and 100 names sent by Soprunenko to the Ostashkov commandant, Borisovets, on 1 April.[7] The 343 named prisoners were transported out of the camp in the first execution convoy on 4–5 March to Kalinin and murdered there the same night.[8] The first list, containing 78 names, was sent to Kozelsk on 2 April. They were included in the first convoy to leave the camp the following afternoon.[9] The first lists also reached Starobelsk on 1 April but the first convoy left only on 5 April. Transportation lists were not in alphabetical order. There seems to have been no particular key to their composition as they contain all ranks, ages and territorial origins. Zawodny, though, discerns a marked tendency for senior officers to be moved out first, from Kozelsk and Starobelsk, suggesting that the NKVD wished to dispose of the leadership element at the outset.[10]

The NKVD documents largely confirm a well-known narrative best publicised by Zawodny, FitzGibbon and the survivors' literature. Masses of statistics and stodgy administrative detail have also emerged. This study is mainly concerned with establishing the broad picture and the main lines of explanation. I have, therefore, not spent overmuch time on reconciling the minor inconsistencies and inaccuracies which litter successive NKVD reports. This has been done by contemporary Polish scholars who continued their crusade for establishing the exact and precise truth into the 1990s.

The document folders, handed over to the Poles by Gorbachev on 13 April 1990, contain the 45 transport lists sent to Kozelsk along with the 65 lists sent to Ostashkov.[11] Information on Starobelsk was retrieved directly from the Russian Archives and published in *Documents Concerning the Atrocity*. Starobelsk received 41 written lists between 3 April and 10 May 1940 containing 3891 names. These were drawn up into 28 transportation lists (25 for 'disposal' by Kharkov NKVD, two for Pavlishtchev Bor and one for Moscow NKVD); dated from 1 April onwards, they led to an uninterrupted flow of daily departures from 5–25 April. They resumed on 2 May with the last major convoy of 235, the final execution convoy numbering 33 left on 10 May, and the convoys finished on 12 May with 20 residual prisoners not destined for execution.

The size of the Starobelsk-Kharkov convoys varies up to a maximum of 260 (three), with five others being in the 200–257 range, six between 150 and 199, five between 100 and 149, three between 50 and 99 and only the last two execution convoys being under 50 at 25 and 33 respectively. The lists include 3888 names, of which 3810 were actually sent.[12] Subsequent DPA reports reveal that Ostashkov had convoyed 6236 out of 6263 names on the lists.[13] This included 98 out of the 99 ordered to be sent to Pavlishtchev Bor.[14] One particularly unfortunate prisoner had been included by mistake in the death convoys and, presumably, killed. No less than 16 of the missing 27 were prisoners who had died earlier in Ostashkov but still figured on the death lists.[15] Mistakes, double counting and earlier sendings to the NKVD in Kalinin accounted for the remaining 11. The equivalent figures for Kozelsk were 4403 sent (including 198 to Pavlishtchev Bor) out of 4419, the shortfall of 16 being accounted for under no less than eight different headings.[16]

There is only marginal dispute about the numbers shot in the spring 1940 massacre. The most authoritative figures are held to be Shelepin's in his note of 9 March 1959 to Khruschev proposing the destruction of the record files.[17] The mature NKVD accounting is that a total of 21857 prisoners were shot, 4421 from Kozelsk at Katyn, 3820 from Starobelsk at Kharkov, 6311 from Ostashkov at Kalinin and 7305 in the Belarusan and Ukrainian prisons. Shelepin's total for the three camps is, however, only 14542, compared to Soprunenko's figure of 15131 contained in a note of 3 December 1941.[18] On the other hand Soprunenko's figures drawn up between 21 and 25 May 1940, just after the massacre, corresponded very closely to Shelepin's statistics.[19] In total 14587 PoWs had been 'placed at the disposal' of the NKVD (i.e. shot), 4404 from Kozelsk, 3896 from Starobelsk and 6287 from Ostashkov. Another 395 had been sent to Pavlishtchev Bor. This corresponds very closely to the numbers executed which have been verified and confirmed by *The Index of the Repressed*: 4410 at Katyn, 3739 at Kharkov and 6314 at Kalinin, totalling 14453.[20] The reason for the discrepancy of 544 between Soprunenko's 1940 and 1941 figures is probably explained by the addition by the NKVD to the death convoys of prisoners from hospitals, their own internal prisons and the Ministry of Ferrous Metallurgy and the road-building camps.

Images of massacre vary enormously. At one extreme one envisages large numbers of anonymous individuals driven to a cliff edge or a forest clearing and machine gunned. This occurred to both Whites and Reds during the Russian Civil War and at the end of the Second World War to Croatian and Slovenian anti-Titoists in Yugoslavia. It is also the picture popularised by films about Nazi and SS atrocities during the Second World War. Other images, are those of Turkish soldiers and peasants slaughtering Armenians during 1915–1916 or hate-filled Hutus descending on Tutsi villages to kill their victims in similarly varied but primitively violent and spontaneous ways. The Soviet 1940 massacre, though, shares one fundamental feature with the trainloads of Jewish and Roma victims brought to be exterminated in Auschwitz and the other Nazi death camps on industrial lines in batches according to a carefully thought out and scientifically organised method. The element of planned, impersonal and unemotional control predominated even though the chosen Soviet method of execution was about as direct and personal a relationship between executioner and victim as one could get. As far as one knows, every single one of the 1940 victims was shot, in the first instance, by an individual NKVD executioner aiming to kill *his* victim with a single shot to the back of the head.[21]

Following on from this, one of the main NKVD socio-technical aims prior to the start of the massacre was to lull the Poles into a false sense of security. This was done by floating various rumours in the camps to fuel illusory hopes and feverish speculation. The camp authorities and guards talked openly from mid-March onwards about the prisoners being moved out. The PoWs from German-occupied territory were encouraged to think that they would be handed over to the Germans, who would then, allow them to go home. For pessimists, rumours were spread that, at worst, they would be transported to more permanent camps, deeper within Russia, while those from the Eastern Territories would be released home. The last-minute appearance of the sick and invalids from the hospitals was also interpreted, in various ways. All the PoWs were, in addition, vaccinated against typhus, dysentery and cholera.[22] Only a madman would do this to someone who was about to be shot would have been the obvious, and planned for, hardly Pavlovian, reaction. Or someone, who was so perfidious that the wastage of scarce medical resources hardly figured compared to the achievement of a larger aim. Every PoW leaving in the departure convoys was also given what by Soviet standards was an almost munificent food ration for the journey. A nice, almost artistic, NKVD touch was that the sardines for senior officers were wrapped up in white foil paper, an unheard of luxury in the Soviet Union of the time.

The fact that the three camps were situated at large distances from each other and lay within different Soviet administrations meant that three individually separate massacres could be organised simultaneously.

The evacuation, transportation, execution and burial of two lots of around 4000 and one group of 6400 PoWs by three different sets of teams made the massacre much more manageable. It also compressed it into just over a five-week period rather than almost four months. As we shall see, shooting between two and three hundred prisoners almost every night, at the rate of one every two minutes or so, for a month was about the maximum strain that even hardened NKVD executioners could cope with. There may be some grains of truth in the widespread reports of suicides, alcoholism and personal breakdowns occasioned by their participation. One suspects that the main reason, however, was the incessant pressure of superiors and, by 1940, the still fresh memory of the continual waves of internal purges of the previous four years. In theory, the larger number of individuals involved in the massacre at three different locations should have increased the problem of maintaining total secrecy. In practice, NKVD internal security and misinformation techniques as well as the mutual self-interest of those involved maintained the veil of secrecy within the USSR. Destalinisation was carefully controlled by the Soviet elites who destroyed much compromising evidence in the mid to late 1950s. Only the fall of communism enabled a few elderly survivors to be confronted by judicial officials in the early 1990s. The dilemma is that the best-informed top officials like Sopruneno squirmed and lied the most in order to deny their personal responsibility.[23] Overall, we are extremely lucky to have even Tokarev's and Syromatnikov's accounts of the killing and burial stage in Kalinin and Kharkov.

The NKVD utilised the same principles and techniques to organise all the stages concerning the disposal of the PoWs from all three camps. The whole process also occurred simultaneously from 1 April until the first week of May with a bit of final clearing up of loose ends during the second week of May. The discovery and exhumation of the Katyn corpses in 1943 and the revelation of the documents by Gorbachev and Yeltsin, however, means that it is now possible to examine the specifics concerning each individual camp. Glimpses and individual touches of detail have long been provided by survivors' reminiscences. The heated and frustrated speculation of the Cold War period, culminating in Fitzgibbon's inspired guess that Kharkov (Dergachii) and Bologoe or thereabouts were the burial sites for Starobelsk and Ostashkov, can now be confirmed, or disproved. The cold facts revealed by the NKVD documentation shed enormous and incontrovertible light on the evacuation and transportation stages. The material can now bear authoritative and near final accounts of these two stages. It is hardly surprising that the Russian authorities have made almost no material available directly concerning the execution-burial stage. At best, an awful lot can be deduced from the remaining material. One also just does not know which sensitive documents were destroyed during the Soviet period. References to them or copies of copies, if that, perhaps still survive in some forgotten provincial deposit and await revelation when Russia undergoes further democratisation.

Starobelsk-Kharkov

The first convoy departed from Starobelsk on 5 April. Camp commandant Berezkov informed, the Polish camp Elder, Major Kazimierz Niewiarowski, at 9 a.m. that its evacuation would begin on that day and continue daily with about 200-strong convoys.[24] He gave the impression that the PoWs would be transported by rail to distribution points in Kharkov, Kiev and Smolensk. From there they would be directed 'home' either to German-occupied Poland or to the Eastern Territories. He explained the relatively small size of the convoys on the grounds of dislocation caused to transport facilities by the Finnish War. The list of those due to travel was telephoned to the camp from 10 a.m. onwards. The 195 named on the first day were summoned to assemble by midday in the commandant's block (number 20) situated in the largest Orthodox church. There they were searched, but apparently, despite survivors' accounts, not too thoroughly, as some personal belongings, particularly letters and notebooks, although no valuables, were found on the corpses when exhumed. What was undoubtedly true was that the roll calls were extremely intensive and repeated in order to ensure that individuals corresponded 100 per cent to the names on the list.

The PoWs were then escorted out through the camp's main gates. It is unclear from a survivor's account whether they were loaded onto awaiting open-roofed lorries or quite literally herded on foot by heavily armed Escort Guards, assisted by baying dogs, to the railway station, about three miles distant.[25] There they were loaded into Pullman carriages with barred and painted-over windows colloquially known as *Stolypynovky*.[26] The individual compartments had been converted to accommodate eight bunks but conditions were extremely cramped as well as dark. There are reports of up to 16 prisoners being squeezed into a single compartment. We do not know how long the prisoners were kept there, before the trains moved out on their 160-mile-long journey to Kharkov. We also do not know how long, and with what breaks, if any, the trains took over what should have been a 4–5-hour journey passing through either Voroshilovgrad (now Lugansk) or Valuyki before arriving at sidings in the Kharkov south railway station.[27]

The Poles were deprived of their belts, coats and any suitcases carrying provisions at this point. Syromatnikov recalled, after half a century, that the prison guards later consumed the confiscated tinned fish finding it very tasty. The Poles were loaded, about 15 at a time, onto prison buses colloquially known as 'black ravens' or *cziorny voronki* which had had their windows painted over. They were transported to the NKVD internal prison, which was also its regional oblast headquarters, situated on Chernyshevskii Street. The four level building with a basement was blown up just before the Germans occupied Kharkov in 1941. We now have Syromatnikov's account of the PoWs' execution and burial, which builds up to a fairly detailed picture as a result of persistent and repeated procuracy questioning.[28] We also have the results of the exhumations carried out in the forest-park in 1991 and 1995–1996.[29] The executions were always completed in a single night, beginning in the evening and continuing very late into the night, or even early morning, particularly when the number of killings was over 250. The Poles, according to Syromatnikov, were never kept in the extremely cramped holding cells for longer than a day or two. As the amount of cell space available was limited to about 250, and already held prisoners, the NKVD were under strong pressure to keep up the killing of the PoWs, as they came in, so as to clear space for the following convoy.

As in the other two massacres every PoW was shot individually in the back of the head by a revolver using German-manufactured 7.65 mm Geco ammunition. Soviet Nagan, not German-manufactured Walther, revolvers are reported by Syromatnikov as having been used in the Kharkov instance. He may have been mistaken as the central NKVD functionaries had learnt from experience that the Soviet TT pistol was unreliable for repeated use as it tended to get jammed. Syromatnikov testified that the prisoners were called out by name and taken individually from the holding cells to another room where they were searched and ordered to take off any remaining caps, jackets and shirts. Their hands were then tied behind their backs. The cord discovered by subsequent exhumations was uniformly about one metre long and had the same type of knots.[30] They were then taken to an ante-room adjoining the execution cell in the basement where another two or three colleagues would already be waiting. The Poles were, by now, fully aware of their fate, because they would have heard the muffled echo of shots. The victims were taken individually through a short corridor into the closed and window-less execution cell where a seated and unidentified NKVD official, rightly or, probably, wrongly described as a 'procurator' by Syromatnikov, rechecked the prisoner's personal details. Tokarev contradicts Syromatnikov directly on this point. As Tokarev is more reliable on most of the detail – the formalities were more likely to have been carried out in the ante, not execution, chamber.

The actual shooting, according to Syromatnikov, was carried out by Timofei Fedorovich Kuprii, who had just been promoted from Junior to Senior Lieutenant of State Security in anticipation of his services in the massacre. Kuprii was the head of the administrative-economic department of the Kharkov regional NKVD. The editors of Volume Two of *Documents Concerning the Atrocity* consider, however, that some of the NKVD officials sent down by Moscow also acted as executioners. Whether Petr Safonov, the head of the regional NKVD, and his deputy, P. Tikhonov, were also directly involved in the shootings is unclear. The central/regional NKVD functionaries may have been confused as 'procurators' by Syromatnikov, while some shooting may have been done in turn. The third person in the cell was apparently a guard whose job was to dispose of the spent bullets and to reload a whole battery of six revolvers. Perhaps his job, along with that of the 'procurators', was also to hold the prisoner firmly so that the shot could be placed exactly. Kuprii seems to have favoured shooting, not in the back of the head as was prevalent elsewhere, but a bit lower down, between the shoulder blades, on the third neck-bone, which resulted in the bullet exiting at the mouth.[31] Optimal results involved much less bleeding. The exhumation evidence is that some prisoners were, shot twice. Some were even finished off by being hit with a rifle-butt, so some sort of desperate final resistance might have been put up.[32] Such prisoners, according to the exhumation evidence, also had their hands tied with barbed wire and additional rope.

When the prisoner had been killed the executioners called out 'allo' and another two guards entered the cell to bind the victim's head and to clear up any blood. They carried the body out on a greatcoat into an adjoining cell where they were stacked on top of each other, or sometimes straight out on a stretcher onto the lorries. Another 'allo' and the next victim would be brought in. Experienced and hardened as the NKVD executioners were one really wonders if a single team of three or four could have kept up the necessary killing rate of one victim every two minutes for 6–8 hours on end. A possible inference is, therefore, that alternate killing teams replaced each other every so often, or, less likely, given the manpower and space constraints, that the killing was done simultaneously by more than one team. Syromatnikov is absolutely insistent that the executions and burials took place solely at night.[33] When they had finished the killers and their assistants washed their hands in methylated spirits. They relaxed with copious amounts of vodka which, presumably, made it easier for them to fall asleep in order to be ready for the next night's grisly work.

The sixth sector of the forest-park lying on the northern outskirts of Kharkov about a mile from the hamlet of Piatichatkii had long been known to specialists as an NKVD burial site. Bodies of Soviet citizens, both pre- and post-dating the 1940 massacre, were found there during the 1990s exhumations. It was always the prime candidate, certainly from the time of FitzGibbon's writings, and it was therefore no surprise when it was confirmed officially in 1990 as the final resting place for the Starobelsk PoWs. Syromatnikov's account, together with the exhumation evidence, means that most aspects of the burial stage are now known and uncontroversial. Pre-1990 rumours that some of the PoWs were shot close to Starobelsk or transported directly to the Kharkov forest-park where they were shot on Katyn lines have now been totally disproved.[34] A Polish second lieutenant, while being held in Starobelsk prison, heard rumours of the shooting locally of Polish PoWs from the Starobelsk camp.[35] Such *canards* concerning Starobelsk were, however, much discussed in the post-1970s FitzGibbon speculation about the true fate of the non-Kozelsk-Katyn victims of the 1940 massacre.[36]

The piles of bodies in the NKVD cellars were loaded, at night, onto covered heavy lorries and driven the short way down the Belgorod road to the forest-park. Syromatnikov states that there were only two such lorries and that about 25–30 bodies were loaded onto each. This means that between four and six round trips per night would have been required during the peak killing period in April. The NKVD section of the forest-park, which was surrounded by a wooden fence and guarded heavily, lies to the right of the road going in the Belgorod direction. There the bodies were stacked in earlier dug trenches. Syromatnikov testified that he was one of a six-man team that took ten days to excavate the largest trench plus a number of smaller ones. When full, the trenches were topped over with white coloured quicklime and covered over with earth.

Extensive exhumations were carried out under the auspices of the Council for Defending the Memory of Struggle and Suffering (ROPWiM) during 1994–1996 which followed up preliminary diggings and investigations in 1991.[37] The main trench was estimated as holding about 1250 bodies, not 500 as claimed by Syromatnikov. The Polish investigators discovered about 60 smaller trenches dug to a standard two metre depth. Only ten held Polish corpses and the remainder held skeletons of Soviet citizens, including women, shot mainly during 1938–1939. All told, the various investigations yielded 15 mass graves containing 4302 bodies. As this is over 300 more than the total of Starobelsk inmates, one supposition is that the additional bodies may be those of Poles shot in Ukrainian prisons as part of the 1940 massacre.[38] The vast majority of graves were 'wet', with the bodies compressed and congealed together by pressure and water, but at least two yielded clear 'dry' skeletons. The graves yielded a certain amount of personal belongings which are now kept in the Katyn Museum in Warsaw. The 1996 expedition was successful in identifying the names of 284 Polish bodies.

Ostashkov-Mednoe

The evacuation of the Ostashkov camp began with the departure of the first convoy on 4 April.[39] There is documentary confirmation, in the form of a cipher telegram sent on 5 April by Kalinin regional NKVD head Tokarev to Merkulov, that 'the first order' had been completed on 343 victims.[40] In other words the first convoy was transported and massacred very rapidly. The last convoy departed on 19 May and Tokarev confirmed the killing of the final 64 on 22 May.[41] Eighteen convoys left Ostashkov between 6 and 29 April during which time 5291 prisoners were transported out.[42] The first two convoys were huge, numbering 494 and 349 respectively. Subsequent ones were smaller but still ranged from 136 to 350, most being very large, around the 300 mark. The Ostashkov convoys were much larger than the ones from Starobelsk. Considerably greater numbers had to be disposed of but the rail travel distance and time were much shorter.

Survivors' accounts confirm that departure lists were communicated as in Starobelsk. The summoned prisoners assembled in the cinema where they were searched and given the standard provisions. From there they were marched out of the camp, across the frozen ice, according to some accounts, to be escorted, once on the mainland, by the usual guards with sub-machine guns and dogs to the railway station. In order to lull them into a false sense of security they were moved out to the melodies of a musical group provided by the camp authorities.

The transportation stage from Ostashkov to Kalinin railway station (now Tver), in the same type of Pullman carriages (Tokarev says that about 5–8 were used daily), was similar to that of Starobelsk except that the route was much shorter. The NKVD documents reveal much more detail, however, such as the names of the convoy commandants (Senior Lieutenants of State Security Pavel F. Dulemba and Nikolai M. Murashov) and the NKVD receiving officers in Kalinin (Lieutenants of State Security Timofei F. Kachin and M.A. Kozochskii). Kachin's regular receipts for the numbers received and Tokarev's confirmation of the 'order completed' on that number are sparsely economical but all the more chilling for that.[43] From the railway station the PoWs were bussed to the NKVD regional headquarters at 2 Soviet Street and held in the basement cells of the internal prison.[44] This building, which later became the Medical Institute, had four floors with a large basement.

The testimony concerning the Ostashkov massacre by Dmitrii Stepanovich Tokarev (1902–1993) is much fuller and much more reliable than Syromatnikov's (1908–1994) for Kharkov. For a start Syromatnikov was basically a senior corridor guard who was eventually promoted to militia lieutenant. While his general description of events is reliable enough he clearly tried to confuse the issue of his direct participation by claiming that he was ill for most of the relevant period. The truth, or a semblance of it in the form of a blind old man's failing memory and excuses after half a century, had quite literally to be squeezed out of him by repeated and increasingly persistent questioning during five separate interrogations by the Soviet, Ukrainian and Russian Procuracies in 1990–1992. Tokarev was far more senior and far better placed as head of the regional Kalinin NKVD to be fully informed than the brutish Syromatnikov. Tokarev was one of the 'highly decorated and richly uniformed thugs', to use Conquest's phrase, who consolidated his career on Beria's coat-tails after 1939 on the basis of services such as the Ostashkov-Kalinin-Mednoe massacre.[45] Syromatnikov was justified in saying that he merely carried out the orders of Kuprii, his superior officer. Tokarev had been a colonel in the border guards before being transferred to the NKVD. He seems sincere in claiming to have been much happier in that service although he continued in the NKVD until 1954 rising to brigade-general rank. Like many others involved in the massacre he was promoted (to captain of state security) just before its start. Tokarev's extremely long and detailed main testimony on 20 March 1991 has been published in a number of sources.[46]

Tokarev emphasised that the Ostashkov camp was controlled centrally by the Moscow NKVD. It was quite independent of the Kalinin NKVD, enjoying a type of extra-territorial status within the oblast. He also denied any direct intervention or activity in the camp, or that any PoW files passed through his office, even when presented with documents from Soprunenko indicating the opposite. Tokarev testified that the Kalinin operation was supervised by three officials sent down from Moscow. Senior Major of State Security N.I. Sinegubov (Deputy Head of the NKVD Transport Department and its chief investigator) seems to have been in overall charge. Mikhail S. Krivenko (Chief of Staff of the NKVD Escort Troops) oversaw the transportation side of the operation in collaboration with Milshtein in Moscow. Major of State Security Vasilii M. Blokhin (a GUGB Administrative-Economic Department functionary and commandant of an NKVD building in Moscow) directed the execution stage. He also, personally, acted as the main executioner, bringing with him from Moscow a whole suitcase full of Walther 2 type pistols used to shoot the Poles. These functionaries took up residence in, and directed operations from, a saloon-sleeping wagon, shunted into the dead end of a railway siding and with telephone connections rigged to it.

Tokarev estimates that about 30 NKVD functionaries of all grades, from both the central-regional and local NKVD levels, were involved in the execution and burial stage. His account of the Kalinin executions differs from Syromatnikov's description of Kharkov in some important respects. Given the different personal and professional factors involved, Tokarev's account should be accepted as more indicative of general NKVD practices. The prisoners were taken directly by prison guards from the holding cells to a red-painted basement ante-chamber known as the 'Leninist room' as it was used for political-agitation work. There, their personal details were checked as in Kharkov. They were, then, handcuffed and led to the adjoining soundproof execution chamber. It is likely that the Kalinin killings were much more brutal and simplified than in the Kharkov case because of the larger sizes of each nightly convoy from Ostashkov. According to Tokarev no procurator was present in the execution room and no formalities such as the reading of sentence took place. The prisoners were quite simply confronted by Blokhin wearing a brown leather cap and leather apron with brown motorcycle elbow-length leather gloves, held down and shot in the back of the head either by him or by Senior Lieutenant of State Security Andrei M. Rubanov (Head of the Administrative-Economic Department, Kalinin oblast NKVD). They were assisted by other prison guards as well as by Tokarev's chauffeur, Sukharev, who allegedly provided him with colourful, almost gleeful, accounts of the nightly killings. The slaughter house methods employed at Kalinin would have taken no longer than a minute or two per individual and could have coped with the numbers involved in a night.

The bodies were then taken out into a courtyard through a secondary entrance by prison guards and drivers where, presumably, the handcuffs were taken off for renewed use, by the likes of another local NKVD driver, Bogdanov. The corpses were then loaded on to five to six waiting heavy lorries which, unlike the ones in Kharkov, were open. Their loads, therefore, had to be covered with canvas. The lorries had a 20-mile drive along the Moscow–Leningrad road to Mednoe a small village lying on the River Tver. There, Blokhin had already chosen an unfenced burial site on the edge of a wood, about half a kilometre from Tokarev's dacha, which was subsequently, watched over by a joint caretaker called Sorokin. Two round trips involving loading and unloading the bodies could just have been squeezed into a single night. As in Kharkov, the bodies were stacked in trenches which had earlier been dug by a mechanical digger worked by two NKVD operatives who came down from Moscow with Sinegubov's team and who assisted in the burials. Tokarev says that about 24–25 trenches, each corresponding to a night's killing, were required. The trenches were then covered over by the mechanical digger but no quick-lime was used and little effort was made to mask the site by planting trees or shrubs. Tokarev liaised with his successor, Senenkov, about the burial site. The latter, and his successors, took precautions to maintain secrecy and to discourage intruders. Unlike Katyn and Kharkov, German occupation of the area was relatively short. Exhumations in the 1990s uncovered 23 mass graves but individual identification was impossible as the bodies had decomposed and fused together by then.[47]

Kozelsk-Katyn

I have left discussion of the Kozelsk-Katyn massacre until last as an enormous literature on it has built up since the Germans announced the discovery of the corpses in spring 1943. Much of the speculation, and all of the Soviet misinformation and cover story, has now been disproved. Its relevance, nowadays, is not so much how this evidence contributed to the struggle for the 'truth' about Katyn; rather it is part of the mechanisms of how that 'truth' was controlled, managed and presented during the period of East–West ideological-systemic conflict up until 1990.

The first convoy of 74 PoWs left Kozelsk on the afternoon of 3 April. The summoned PoWs, assembled in the club where they were given lunch and provisions for the journey. The 800 grams of bread, three herrings and a little sugar were wrapped in white foil paper for the senior officers and ordinary grey paper for junior ranks. They were taken by heavy lorries, on a roundabout route to avoid inhabited areas, to Kozelsk railway station. There they were loaded onto the same type of prison carriages as in the other two cases. The trains passed through Sukhino and Smolensk. The earliest convoys left messages on bits of paper in the carriages as well as on the compartment walls, so the PoWs may have known that they were heading towards Smolensk.[48] Nekhoreshev reported to Merkulov on 22 April that his functionaries had ordered that such messages, as well as accompanying 'anti-Soviet slogans', should be washed off after every journey.[49] At Smolensk the train was broken up into two or three smaller sections, some of which might have waited for up to a night until the NKVD had cleared any backlog in their killing. Were some prisoners taken off at this point to be shot in the Smolensk prison cellars? The bulk of the PoWs were certainly disembarked in a siding at Gnezdovo railway station, about 12 miles from Smolensk, straight onto awaiting 'black ravens' at half hourly intervals. Professor Stanisław Świaniewicz, transported from Kozelsk on 29 April, was taken off the train here and is the sole survivor able to report on the PoWs' journey up to that point.[50]

We are, then, faced with two contrasting versions of the execution stage. The traditional, and until the 1990s unchallenged, *Death in the Forest* view is that they were driven directly to the Katyn forest where they were shot on the edge of previously excavated trenches and buried instantly in one fell swoop. This conflation of the execution and burial stages has been challenged, but not disproved, by the NKVD documentation and by the testimonies regarding the Kharkov and Kalinin prison cell method of killing. One of the surviving prison guards, Petr Klimov, claimed in 1990 that some PoWs were shot in the forest while some were shot in the more usual NKVD manner in the cellars of the NKVD prison in Smolensk.[51] The latter suggestion, which had been repeated in a Polish TV programme, was refuted by Jacek Trznadel.[52] Klimov also asserted that the execution team was led by Lieutenant of State Security Ivan Stelmakh, commandant of the NKVD Smolensk internal prison. Interviews with participants in the massacre, Klimov and the NKVD 'black raven' driver, Ivan Titkov, were reported exhaustively by the Warsaw press in 1990.[53] Other suggestions that they were shot in an adjoining garage with the sound of the shots being muffled by a tractor engine were disproved by the failure of the Polish Red Cross investigators to find any bullet holes in 1943.

We have already seen from the NKVD documents that the bulk of the Kozelsk inmates were transported in 16 convoys to Smolensk (plus one to Pavlischtchev Bor) between 3 and 28 April. The evacuation of the camp was completed between 7 and 11 May when three convoys were directed to Smolensk and one to Pavlischtchev Bor and some residual prisoners were sent to Moscow. A clue to the controversy surrounding the killing site may be provided by an examination of the size of the convoys which were, in general, significantly larger than the ones sent to Kharkov and larger than the Kalinin ones. Seven of the Kozelsk convoys were over 300 (including 439 on 16 April and 411 on 28 April) while another three were between 250 and 299. Given that there is only speculation that the Smolensk NKVD internal prison was used for this particular massacre, and that the NKVD guest house had limited holding facilities, it is probable that the larger convoys, at least, must have been disposed of on the forest site. Lebedeva contradicts Żaron by citing the already mentioned Klimov as saying that a certain number of killings were carried out in the NKVD Smolensk prison at 13 Dzerzhinsky Street and the bodies were then transported to Katyn.[54] This is possible, although there is absolutely no corroborating primary evidence for this suggestion. Świaniewicz reports that the Smolensk prison was 'empty' when he passed through in late April, whatever that might indicate. On the other hand the foremost authority on the Katyn massacre expressed the opinion (in the 1990s) that the first few Kozelsk convoys were killed in the Smolensk prison cellars just as in Kharkov and Kalinin.[55]

There are in fact voices from the Katyn graves. The diary found on the corpse of Major Adam Solski throws crucial light on the time frame of the operation.[56] He was ordered to pack and assemble in the club at 11.40 on the morning of 7 April 1940. There he had lunch and was searched. His convoy left Kozelsk at 2.55 p.m.. We now know from Soprunenko's transportation list of 6 April 1940 to Korolev that he was general number 2159 and number 41 out of 89 names on his list.[57] The latter included Brigade-Generals Bohaterowicz and Smorawiński and Division General Minkiewicz but not Brigade-General Wołkowicki, who, for reasons discussed elsewhere, was not transported to his death. The convoy arrived at the Kozelsk railway sidings at 4.55 p.m. and Solski was loaded into a compartment with 11 colleagues. The train did not move until 3.30 a.m. on the 8th and did not arrive at Smolensk railway sidings until midday. According to Solski's notes they were kept there, until after they were woken at 5 a.m. on the 9th. He then had a 'terrible' journey, pressed into one of 15 small and tight cubicles in a prison van, 'to a wood, something in the character of a summer resort'. A thorough search of the prisoners in his group took place before 8.30 a.m. local time. Solski writes that this was when his watch, ring and money were confiscated. The notes cut off at this point. We are left to imagine poor Solski thrown into the back of a prison van, dragged out and tied up, manhandled and pushed to his knees, shot and thrown into the burial trench from which his corpse re-emerged three years later as number 0490 in a pit containing 2500 bodies. How reliable was his watch (which might have kept, or at least he recorded, both Warsaw and Smolensk time), his timings and his note keeping, though? Does his itinerary indicate the stretched out nature of the process?[58] Did the NKVD use the frequent long stops to catch up on and double check their paper work? Were the prisoners bussed straight to the killing site from Gnezdovo, dragged out and tied or trussed up, depending on the extent of resistance, and then shot, as suggested by Abarinov? Were early morning executions the norm at Katyn? Poignant questions awaiting answers, which may or may not be delivered in the fullness of time.

There is no doubt that the PoWs were driven about three kilometres from Gnezdovo along the Smolensk road to Katyn, a name that has passed into infamy alongside Lidice, Oradour and Srebrenica and which has become the cryptonym for the whole of the 1940 massacre. The NKVD had a wooden guest or rest house here, sometimes referred to as a villa, in the Goat Hills (Kosogorii/Kozie Gory) lying close to the River Dnieper within the Katyn forest. The latter, in another of history's ironies had belonged to the Polish Koźlinski and Lednicki gentry families in the nineteenth centuries. The guest house, along with the adjoining garages, was either burnt down or dismantled in the late 1940s. The local resident and collective farm worker Ivan Krivozertsov testified that the Cheka had used the area as a killing and burial site from the time of the Bolshevik Revolution. It became an enclosed GPU forbidden zone after 1929.[59] The dacha was a holiday and rest house for NKVD functionaries. It was used as an assembly point prior to executions and then as sleeping quarters. He reports that prisoners from Smolensk were brought in by open lorry to dig trenches from early March onwards. This sounds much more convincing than Titkov's unnecessarily sensationalist testimony that 16 army recruits were shot after digging the trenches and burying the bodies.[60] Krivozertsov also says that he, personally, saw, the convoys transporting the Poles from Gnezdovo railway station to Katyn. The local population took it for granted that they were executed there.

Unlike Kharkov, Katyn was a closed site and much further away from the nearest city. The burial site for the Polish PoWs was only 600 yards away from the guest house which was not purpose built for executions like the Kharkov and Kalinin NKVD internal prison cellars.[61] Why the Polish PoWs were not killed in the NKVD internal prison in Smolensk is a question which will probably never be answered satisfactorily. The most convincing explanation is that the local NKVD tradition, and practice, was one of killing prisoners in a closed perimeter with the sounds of gunshot being muffled by the forest. The convenience of conflating the execution and burial stages in Katyn thus outweighed any additional and resultant complications involved in the actual killings themselves.

The main execution team seems to have been Senior Lieutenant of State Security Iosif Grybov (commandant of NKVD internal prisons in the Smolensk oblast), Nikolai Gvozdovskii (assistant commandant of the NKVD Smolensk internal prison) and another NKVD prison commandant, Ivan Stelmakh. The literature has numerous references to this group being strengthened by similar functionaries from the Minsk oblast NKVD. Krivozertsov even suggests that the latter were solely responsible for the actual killings but he seems to have been taken in by disinformation spread by a Smolensk NKVD driver. The Kharkov and Kalinin evidence suggests that about a couple of dozen drivers and prison guards like the previously mentioned Klimov and Titkov were easily recruited or dragooned from the local Smolensk NKVD to support the directing group of executioners and commanders.[62] The oddity of the Katyn case, however, is the absence of central NKVD functionaries to oversee the operation. The apparent delegation of command to the regional level may, however, just reflect a significant gap in the sources.

The absence of major testimony by participants concerning the execution-burial stage in Katyn is more than offset by the importance of the exhumation evidence. This, unlike the other two cases, was carried out in 1943, just three years after the massacre, and not almost half a century later. Although the 1994 and 1995 exhumations discovered some residual personal belongings and trinkets almost everything of any significance had been discovered by the 1943 investigations.[63] Two of the investigators involved also concluded that 'there is no unequivocal evidence as to where the officers were murdered'.[64] The political significance of the International Medical Commission and the Polish Red Cross will be discussed in Chapter Six. Here, we discuss the light thrown on the killings by their work on the exhumed bodies in spring–summer 1943.

The 1943 investigators discovered 8 mass graves ranging in depth from six to 11 feet. They contained between ten and 12 layers of bodies stacked face down. It would appear from the 1943 findings that, as in the ante-rooms to the execution chambers in the Kharkov and Kalinin basements, the PoWs had been searched and deprived of most valuables, at some point, as there was a total absence of rings and watches. The exhumations, however, revealed numerous personal belongings such as identification documents, correspondence, cards, photos and aluminium military tags. This facilitated identification of 2815 (67.9 per cent) of the 4143 bodies excavated.[65] The most important, from the academic viewpoint, were a variety of diaries and notebooks constituting a form of prison memoirs which were collected by the Polish Red Cross Commission in April–May 1943. They were sent to Kraków and, eventually, comprised the Robel collection, discussed in Chapter Six.[66] All entries and dates in them broke off between 6 and 20 April 1940. The significance of this aspect, apart from enriching the historical record and contributing to the reconstruction of the course of events in the massacre, was also politically crucial in one major respect. As the exhumations were carried out either by, or in full sight of, the Polish participants it was proved beyond all question that these were genuine documents. There was no way that such evidence could have faked through insertion after the execution and burial of the Poles. The bodies were also stacked according to the order in which they were reported by survivors as leaving Kozelsk. In other words, an important plank of the Soviet cover story was blown from the start.

It was established in 1943 that the PoWs were shot and buried in their greatcoats and uniforms. Any reconstruction of the course of events must involve a certain amount of speculation but it is most likely that the PoWs were unloaded close to the guest house. What NKVD formalities might or might not have occurred at this point in order to check identities or to seize anything left of value is unknown, except for Solski's note. A certain number (possibly 15–30 at a time) would then have been stuffed into the back of two on-site black ravens who would have driven them the short distance to the burial trenches. There, they would have been pulled out individually, dragged to the edge of, or possibly into, the trench itself, held down and shot in the back of the head in the normal NKVD fashion. Infra-red microscopic analysis established that the revolver was fired against the victim's raised collar or placed directly against the head. In general, the bullet's trajectory was from the back of the neck upwards with the exit point at the front of the skull being between the nose and hair line or an eye socket. The difference from the other two cases is that the PoWs must have heard the shots and seen the terrible sight ahead of them of a colleague being shot and thrown onto the packed rows of bodies already in the trenches. There is much exhumation evidence, including mouth gags, rope-ties and a variety of injuries, to suggest that, although resistance was hopeless, it occurred, especially amongst the younger officers and cadets; the executioners' task was thus rendered messier and more difficult.[67] This, necessitated a certain number of second shots and a significant number of cases where the victim was finally dispatched by a four-edged Red Army bayonet or rifle butt.[68] There is also evidence to suggest that a number of officers were even held down horizontally on top of the corpses, and shot in this terrible position. The 1990s exhumations established more precisely that about a fifth of the victims had their hands tied behind their backs with wire or white rope tied in a double knot. Others had the cord tied around their necks and hands in a standard NKVD procedure where the knot occasioned suffocation, if resistance was offered. The eighth or so thus trussed up had had their heads covered with their greatcoats, or with rags.

Walther pistols were used as in Kalinin with Geco 7.65D mm ammunition, the same as in the other two cases. Zawodny states that some 6.35 calibre bullets were also used.[69] The Germans conceded that this had been manufactured inter-war by the Gustav Genshow ordinance company in Durlach near Karlsruhe between 1921 and 1931.[70] Their claim that the ammunition had been exported to Poland, the Baltic States and the USSR was not refuted supporting the surmise that the NKVD used stocks obtained during the 1939 occupations.[71]

One can conclude that the execution mode at Katyn differed fundamentally from that at Kharkov and Kalinin. It is, therefore, paradoxical and ironic that the German occupation and the evidence unearthed in 1943 turned it into the symbol for the whole massacre. The closed terrain and its acceptable distance from any major population meant that the NKVD could kill the PoWs quite securely out in the open by the burial trenches. It is just possible that the final residual prisoners left over at the end of a day's killings might have been disposed of close by the guest house and then transported for burial. There does not seem to be any obvious practical need for this, however. The executioners did not have far to go to the guest house, after washing their hands in the usual methylated spirits, to eat, get drunk on vodka and sleep off the effects of the day's killings. Kobulov and his central planners, therefore, seem to have had full confidence that the Smolensk regional personnel could be relied on in Katyn because of their experience and favourable local circumstances. If the Minsk NKVD participated, as reported, it might have been primarily for training and 'symbolic' purposes (Belarusans killing hated Polish oppressors!). In a probable attempt at self-exculpation Tokarev stresses that Kobulov, by contrast, at the preparatory March meetings in Moscow, expressed a lack of similar faith in the capacity of the Kalinin NKVD.[72]

The killings in the Belarusan and Ukrainian prisons

It is now generally accepted that the shooting of 7305 out of 18 632 arrestees held in prisons in Belarus and Ukraine should be considered an integral part of the 1940 massacre. Those shot were Polish military officers of all ranks, policemen, factory owners and judicial and civil officials who had been detained either during the September campaign or as part of the subsequent Soviet drive to extirpate the Polish elite in the Occupied Territories. Their fate was sealed in Beria's 5 March 1940 proposal, approved by the politburo, that 11 000 of these counter-revolutionaries should be shot at the same time as the camp inmates. Their cases were to be considered by the same Troika on the basis of evidence provided by the NKVD of the Belarusan and Ukrainian republics. Their formal decisions provided the legitimacy for the transportation or death lists confirmed by the First/Special GUGB Department of the NKVD in Moscow. It is most likely that the files containing specific proposals were produced by the republic Special Departments and their representatives in the main NKVD prisons, in the first instance. Beria's breakdown of the arrestees was that 1207 were officers, 5141 policemen, gendarmes and intelligence agents, 347 spies and diversionaries and 465 factory owners and officials of which 5345 fitted into the catch-all category of members of counter-revolutionary and independence organisations.[73] As we have seen, his residual category of 6127 frontier crossers (refugees from the *General-Gouvernement* and would-be escapees to it) were largely deported to the GULAG.

We have almost no direct information about the preparatory contacts between the Moscow centre and the republic NKVD and political elites. The formal initiating organisational document for this part of the massacre was Beria's Order 00350 of 22 March 1940 on 'the evacuation of the NKVD prisons in the western oblasts of the U(kr)SSR and BSSR'.[74] He ordered that the prisoners held in a number of prisons throughout the two republics should be transported and concentrated centrally. This document also indicates that this transportation and killing operation was directed centrally from Moscow, as discussed below, by Beria and two of his deputy Ministers, Vasilii Chernyshev and Ivan Ivanovich Maslennikov.[75] The evidence discussed below gives the lie to earlier views that there could literally be dozens of execution and burial sites in Belarus and the

Ukraine. 'In each obvod, in various towns and prisons executions were carried out – I would say locally.'[76]

In the Ukraine Beria delegated Major of State Security Pavel Zujev to assist republic NKVD head Ivan Serov. The latter seems to have continued in this role after being nominated as Merkulov's First Deputy-Minister in the independent NKGB formed on 3 February 1940. Three thousand prisoners were to be moved, under reinforced guard, to the central prisons in Kiev, Kharkov and Kherson by the commander of the 13th division of Escort Troops, Colonel Aleksandr K. Zavjalov. Of these 900 came from Lwów, 500 from Równo, 500 from Volhynia, 500 from Tarnopol, 200 from Drohobysz and 400 from Stanisławów. Chernyshev was directed, to draw up a list, also within a ten-day period, of 8000 prisoners held in Ukraine and Belarus to be sent to GULAG. Three thousand of these were to be drawn from the prisons in Kiev, Kharkov and Kherson, presumably in order to make way for the same number of incomers. The latter's arrival in Kiev in late March–early April probably signalled the start of the killings. They needed to be disposed of before the arrival of the Starobelsk prisoners, who, as we have seen, were the last to start leaving camp on 5 April. It is highly probable that the slight delay was caused by this factor.[77] The Kiev victims from the Ukrainian prisons would, on this presumption, therefore have been the first to have been buried in the forest-park.[78]

The arrangements were almost identical in Belarus. Republic NKVD head Tsanava was given the same ten-day period to concentrate 3000 prisoners in Minsk. The largest number, 1500, were from Brześć; as there is no mention of the other most strongly Polish district in Grodno, one wonders if this also included the Poles arrested there. Possibly, the Grodno Poles were killed on the spot, thus making up the difference between the 6000 transported to the central prisons and the number given as finally shot. The remainder were 550 from Wilno, 500 from Pińsk and 400 from Baranowicze. Captain of State Security Alexandr Chechev was delegated to assist Tsanava while Colonel Popov was designated to command the 15th brigade of Escort Troops in the operation. Beria assigned responsibility for overall supervision in Moscow of the transportation and killings in both republics to Ivan Maslennikov, Deputy-Minister of the Interior in charge of Border, Escort and Interior Troops and Vladimir Sharapov (Head of the Main Department of Escort Troops NKVD USSR).

This section of the 1940 massacre has always remained the most mysterious and was the last to have even partial light thrown on it. The list of names of Poles shot in the Ukraine was handed over by General Andrei Homicz (Chomicz), deputy head of the Ukrainian security service (SB), in 1994 and published by the Katyn Committee.[79] The editor, Jędrzej Tucholski, had earlier been instrumental in demonstrating what has now been confirmed by the NKVD documents. This is that the prisoners were not killed in the local prisons where they were held but transported to central execution points, both for reasons of maintaining secrecy and as a unified part of the 1940 massacre.[80] An undated document by Senior Lieutenant of State Security Cvietukhin to Bashtakov reveals that the prisoners were shot according to 33 death lists, with an average of 104 names per list.[81] Wojciech Materski and Natalia Lebedeva also surmise that the relevant documentation has either been removed, destroyed or transferred elsewhere from the archives of the Escort Troops.[82] The 3435 prisoners named on the Ukrainian list were definitely concentrated in Kharkov, Kiev and Kherson but their subsequent killing and burial sites remain unknown.[83] Were only some, or all, shot in the Kharkov NKVD internal prison and buried in the forest-park? There is firm exhumation evidence that Poles were buried at Bykovna and Vladimir in Volhynia.[84] How many, if any, were part of the 1940 massacre remains an open question.

The Belarusans, particularly since 1994 when President Alexander Lukashenko assumed power, have refused to collaborate. Uniformly bad official Belarusan–Polish relations have ruled out the sort of archival and academic collaboration which has been possible with the Russian and, up to a point, the Ukrainian republics. The Belarusans have firmly denied any knowledge or responsibility. Somewhat anomalously, given Lukashenko's pro-Russian and neo-Stalinist stance in every other respect, they have blamed the episode entirely on the Russians. One can only speculate that it is most likely that all the Polish prisoners in the BSSR executions were killed in the NKVD internal prison in Minsk. The exhumations at Kuropaty, outside Minsk, in autumn 1988 indicated that victims of the purge of the Polish urban and professional classes after the Soviet occupation of West Belarus were certainly buried there in late 1939 to early 1940 although no direct link to the spring 1940 massacre was established.[85] There are notable gaps in the evidence concerning the prisoners from the jails in Białystok and Grodno who may have been killed on the spot or in Brest and Minsk after transportation there.[86] Again, there is a strong likelihood, but no direct documentary evidence to support the supposition, that their bodies were buried at the almost symbolic 1930s NKVD burial site for Belarusan nationalists and democrats at Kuropaty.[87] As far as numbers are concerned if one subtracts the Ukrainian 3435 from the general total of 7305 one is left with a figure of 3870 for the Belarus part of the 1940 massacre. This may be too neat a solution, however, particularly as there are a number of additional complicating factors. We have seen that Beria budgeted for 11 000 executions in the 5 March proposal but there seems to have been a shortfall of 3695 in attaining this target. Materski's explanation is fully convincing. Beria thought that a lot more Poles would be arrested and executed. In fact, some were, through their last-minute addition after 4 April, when the 'passportatisation action' began as a preliminary to the second deportation.[88]

Who were the killers? How were they selected and motivated?

One now has a comprehensive picture of who was killed but considerable progress has also been made in answering the question – who were the killers? There is a considerable literature about *Homo Sovieticus* but what concerns us most here is the character of the Second Generation Stalinists who replaced the First Generation Old Bolsheviks in the 1930s. Most specialists discern a shift from ideological-revolutionary belief to managerial and organisational efficiency. The same search for the best technical solution characterised by a Malenkov in party work or a Kaganovich in industry marked a Yezhov, Yagoda or Beria in the organisation of mass Terror directed against the enemies of People's Power.

Wojciech Materski has identified the different levels of the Soviet killing machine as decision makers, planners and different types and levels of implementers.[89] At the top of the pyramid of power headed by Stalin formal responsibility lies with the politburo members (Voroshilov, Molotov, Kaganovich, Mikoyan and Kalinin) who signed the 5 March 1940 document. Beria, of course, formally proposed the decision and acted as the linkman to its planners. Individuals such as Merkulov, Kobulov, Bashtakov, Chernyshev, Maslennikov, Soprunenko and Milshtein, holding the key offices at the top levels of the NKVD, planned the massacre but did not get blood directly on their hands.

The crucial linkmen between the central planners and the implementers were, despite Tokarev's denials, the three territorial heads of the oblast NKVD Executives, all captains of state security – Yemelyan Kuprianov in Smolensk, Petr Sergeevich Safonov in Kharkov and Dmitrii Tokarev in Kalinin. We have already seen how camp officials were strengthened by central officials in the evacuation stage. Likewise, the transportation stage was overseen by 'central' Escort Troop officials.

For obvious reasons, one must be most interested in who were the 'killers' in the execution-burial stage. Materski suggests that the NKVD had a cadre of experienced executioners, who had proved their worth in earlier killings, at both the central and local-regional levels.[90] The former could be 'organisers' like Sinegubov and Krivenko or 'executioners' like Blokhin in Kalinin. Blokhin, although the most junior of the trio, assumed the key role with the death lists being addressed directly by name to him.[91] This confirms the privileged status of 'executioner' within the Stalinist NKVD. Blokhin belonged to the main NKVD Administrative-Economic Department in Moscow. This body was between five and ten times as large as other NKVD departments. There is little doubt that most of the specialist executioners were drawn from this, and the equivalent bodies at different territorial levels. These professional killers like Kuprii in Kharkov and Grybov, Stelmakh and Gvozdovskii in Smolensk doubled up, and camouflaged themselves behind their main functions, as prison and building commandants. Similarly, corridor bosses and prison guards like Syromat-nikov in Kharkov or Andrei Rubanov in Kalinin who had shown both a predisposition and a talent for 'wet work' were quickly identified by their superiors. Such executioners, at both the central and the local levels, were rewarded with promotion, additional premiums and preferential access to housing and goods. The literature also abounds with references to the consequences of their stressed lifestyle, notably alcoholism and high suicide rates. The latter is often rather naively attributed by Polish sources to guilt for their involvement in crimes such as Katyn. Such motivation would be totally exceptional, given their recruitment and hardening processes.

The reliable hard core killers were assisted by a larger number of local NKVD guards, drivers and even clerks. They escorted prisoners and pre-pared and held them down for execution. Those who had a predisposition for doing so, and who had already shot prisoners in the NKVD cellars, might have been allowed to do some of the killing as well, whenever the main executioners felt like a break.[92] This was the case with Sukharev in Kalinin, Tokarev's chauffeur. The supporting cast would then load the bodies on to lorries, drive them to the burial sites as in Kharkov and Mednoe and dump them in the pits. This category is described as 'acci-dental' by Materski.[93] Such individuals were normally ordered and assigned by their superiors. They would have faced severe sanctions, pos-sibly execution and certainly GULAG, had they refused to participate. The aim, as defined by Kobulov at the outset, was that everyone who gained knowledge of the massacre should participate directly and thus assume collective responsibility, designed to maintain total secrecy.

Just as the massacre was preceded by NKVD promotions so its comple-tion was marked by Beria's award on 26 October 1940 of financial rewards for those participating in the operation.[94] Forty-four senior NKVD func-tionaries, ranging from senior major to sergeant of state security, in the Kalinin, Kharkov and Smolensk oblasts received additional monthly salary premiums for 'the effective carrying out of special tasks'. They included names, which will by now be familiar to the reader, like Grybov, Rubanov, Kuprii, Blokhin, Sinegubov, Tikhonov, Krivenko, Pavlov, Stepanov, Kachin and Gvozdovskii. In addition, another 89 ordinary ranks were awarded 800 roubles. This list included Stelmakh, Sukharev, Sorokin and, much to his later embarrassment, Syromatnikov. When questioned on this point by the procuracy he denied all knowledge. The Escort Troops received various commendations and thanks but comparatively miserly special awards of between 25 and 70 roubles.[95] Special camp functionaries were not included although it is possible that they were rewarded separately. It is not likely, though, as they would not have been involved in what in NKVD eyes would have been the most meritorious execution-burial stage.

The lists of those so rewarded above give an indication of the numbers involved in organising and implementing the massacre. They did not include the top NKVD bosses, including the special brigades in the camps (mostly major of state security or more senior). They rewarded themselves through the award of the top Soviet decorations which carried salary and pension supplementation and privilegentsia access to closed-curtain shops, holiday homes and superior housing, educational and medical facilities.[96] Conquest cites an NKVD awards list of 27 April 1940 which includes a number of functionaries who, one surmises, were rewarded for their services to the spring 1940 massacre.[97] Bochkov, Merkulov, Serov and Tsanava were amongst the favoured 12 who received the most prestigious Order of Lenin. Kobulov, Milshtein and the butchers Kuprii and Blokhin were awarded the Order of the Red Banner. Bashtakov, Osetrov, Sudoplatov, Sharapov and Safonov were amongst a much larger number who received the Order of the Red Star. Sinegubov received the Mark of Honour.

Who survived and why: the survivors' testimony and subsequent fate

One of the few *ad hoc* aspects of the massacre concerned the withdrawal of names from the transportation/death lists. The NKVD just does not seem to have been fully in control of information concerning the PoWs who had collaborated or who were marked down as potentially useful. This impression may, of course, be a direct consequence of the absence of relevant documentation. Nor was a coherent policy regarding who was to be spared ever drawn up. Czapski conveys an impression of the centrality of chance and circumstance, as far as ethnic Poles are concerned.[98] This has to be qualified by the evidence that all the PoWs who had been clearly involved in anti-Soviet activities perished. On the other hand, the bulk, if not all, of those who had indicated a willingness to remain in the USSR in the final questionnaire survived.[99] In practice, Merkulov, not the Troika, played the central role on this issue by deciding which prisoners' files would be withdrawn from their consideration.[100] Soprunenko sent the camps, lists of names of prisoners who were not to be transported without his specific permission. He also instructed his chief DPA functionaries on the spot (Zarubin, Mironov and Cholichev), along with camp commandants, not once, but twice, not to evacuate any prisoners regarded as collaborators or potentially useful by the Second, Third and Fifth GUGB Departments, who might have been included on the lists by mistake, without specific instructions.[101]

We now know that the Fifth Department recommended 47, Merkulov's list saved 91 while what can be regarded as an all-purpose general list totalled 161. Which list contained the informers and actual agents as against sympathisers or potential collaborators is unclear. Specific requests, outside these categories, are much easier to identify. The GUGB Fifth Department deputy-head, Pavel Sudoplatov, for example, requested on 7 March that four PoWs, including Jan Lubomirski, be retained in Kozelsk for his department's 'operational activities'.[102] Lists were also corrected as a result of interventions by the German embassy (47 cases) and Lithuanian Mission (19) along with another 24 'Germans', presumably recognised as such by the NKVD.[103] The main lists of survivors totalling 199, containing 107 names from Kozelsk, 63 from Starobelsk and 29 from Ostashkov were sent to the camps on 25 and 26 April with the instruction that the prisoners be transported to Pavlishtchev Bor. Further lists in May of those directed to the same camp totalling another 196 saved 99 from Kozelsk, 15 from Starobelsk and 83 from Ostashkov. The total number of survivors is thus now generally accepted, following Lebedeva, as 395 (made up according to a DPA note of 25 May 1940, of 205 from Kozelsk, 78 from Starobelsk and 112 from Ostashkov).[104] The other estimates, which have previously been much quoted in the literature, are 448 by Zawodny and 432 by Peszkowski and Tucholski.[105] The situation was fluid and a small number of the survivors may have come from prisons or labour camps. Only two individuals were withdrawn from a convoy which had actually left camp.[106] Professor Stanisław Świaniewicz's case from Kozelsk was both dramatic and invaluable for the historical record as he was the sole survivor to witness the first part of his doomed colleagues' final journey. Mikhail Romm, the namesake and cousin of the famous Soviet film director, was also saved by the same order from Merkulov.[107]

The survivors were quartered, for about six to eight weeks, in the otherwise empty Pavlishtchev Bor (also known as the Yukhnov) camp. The accounts of their journeys from the special camps to this transit camp were an important staple of the Katyn literature before 1990, in reconstructing the course of the massacre, but are now of only secondary interest. Filip Iosifovich Kadyshev, the camp commandant, was ordered to hold them in complete isolation and to prevent all correspondence and external contacts.[108] This also facilitated the intensive interrogation of the small numbers involved, which started quite quickly. The process of fragmentation and division into distinct Polish national, German, Jewish and pro-Soviet factions also began in this camp. The atmosphere was bitter and pessimistic. The PoWs did not know, at the time, that the camp represented salvation for them, rather than having missed out on evacuation out of the USSR, as most imagined.

The PoWs were transported out of Yukhnov on 13 June, in a five-day-long train journey, to Gryazovets in Vologda province where they were held until the August 1941 amnesty.[109] In early June 1940 the (now) 394 post-special-camp inmates were composed of one general, eight colonels (including two of police/gendarmerie), 16 lieutenant-colonels, eight majors (including two of police/gendarmerie) and 18 captains (including two of police/gendarmerie). This leading cadre of 52 officers was balanced by 26 lieutenants, 93 sub-lieutenants, 98 ensigns and various NCO ranks plus a varied mixture of 82 rankers, civilians, settlers and the like.[110]

The general, Jerzy Wołkowicki, was spared, not because he had shown any greater willingness to collaborate than his other four colleagues of the same rank in Kozelsk, but because of a purely historical accident. He had participated as a junior officer in the Czarist Navy at the battle of Tsushima in 1904 and gained a legendary reputation for having opposed the surrender of his ship to the Japanese. As the senior officer at Grya-zovets he intervened directly with the DPA over the correspondence, winter clothing and expenses of the PoWs in his charge.[111]

The camp had been disinfected and renovated prior to the Poles' arrival and living and recreational conditions were generally better than previously. The sending of one letter per month and the receiving of correspondence through an NKVD post box in Moscow was resumed in October 1940.[112] From December money could also be sent by their famil-ies to the PoWs. Many of the NKVD officers were transferred directly from the three special camps and quickly undertook an intensive campaign of indoctrination and political education. They formed a strong Special Department, numbering 15, headed by Ejlman who had moved on from Kozelsk, which answered directly to Merkulov, and on practical matters to Soprunenko and the GUGB Fifth Department.[113] The DPA initially judged their work to be 'decidedly unsatisfactory' and riddled with mistakes.[114] Nekhoreshev, however, was soon painting a very rosy picture of the healthy political–moral state of the inmates and of the enthusiasm with which many were studying Stalin's constitution and the Short Course of the History of the Communist Party (Bolshevik)![115] This was a decidedly one-sided view as political polarisation continued to divide the PoWs. A 'Red Circle' of about 50 was formed amongst which Borkowski, Szczypi-orski, Lieutenant Roman Imach and Józef Mara-Meyer were reported as being the leading 'internationalists'. They were opposed by Polish nation-alists led by General Wołkowicki, supported by individuals such as Gro-bicki, Captain Ginsbert, Kazimierz Rosen-Zawadzki, Lis, Domoń, and Rafał Krywko. The NKVD alleged that the latter group used a variety of counter-revolutionary methods to counter the official programme of lectures, dis-cussions and cultural activities.[116] The clash between nationalist and pro-communist factions emerged in rival celebrations of the October Revolution and the Polish National Day.[117] In addition to the foregoing split about 30 individuals went public at Gryazovets with their claims to being German. A dozen were repatriated, after interventions by the German ambassador.[118] The remaining 18 faced the tragic fate of being shunned contemptuously by the Poles and distrusted and imprisoned by the Soviets after Hitler's invasion of the USSR. Conflicts over competing allegiances caused a tense atmosphere leading to numerous fist fights and quarrels.

The inflow of Polish PoWs into Gryazovets from Lithuania, which totalled 2752 by early February 1941, were subjected to the same 'Opera-tional-Chekhist' processing as the PoWs in the three special camps had undergone. By January 1941 the NKVD functionaries had uncovered 31 intelligence agents, of one sort or another, some of whom were transferred for interrogation to the NKVD internal prison in Smolensk.[119] The NKVD focussed its greatest efforts on the Red Corner and transferred about 17 of its most promising members to what later became notorious as the 'Villa of Bliss' outside Moscow. Lieutenant Mintowt-Czyż faced renewed efforts to recruit him by Zhukov, Sudoplatov and Alexandrovich in the Butyrkii and Lubianka prisons in Autumn 1940. Proving recalcitrant, he was beaten before being returned to Gryazovets on Christmas Day.[120] His return alerted the anti-communist Poles to the extent of the NKVD's knowledge about them and the need for greater discretion.[121]

By the spring, the NKVD failure to recruit significant numbers of Poles for their purposes and continuing examples of what they regarded as obduracy led Soprunenko to propose that they be sentenced by the Special College procedure. The option of transportation to the Siberian GULAG for all the other camps contained in a note of 22 May 1941 confirmed that the 364 PoWs were held in a closed camp at Gryazovets and awaited a decision as to where they would be directed.[122] The NKVD authorities vented their spleen on the Poles by reducing food rations and worsening their living conditions. They also scapegoated their own subordinates in true Soviet fashion. Deputy NKVD Minister Sergei Nikoforovich Kruglov inspected Gryazovets in March 1941. He dismissed camp commandant Volkov and reprimanded other camp functionaries, allegedly for incompetence and waste, but possibly for financial corruption concerning meat.[123]

The Gryazovets survivors were saved by the German invasion of June 1941, after which numerous Polish officers were directed to it from other camps. A dozen individuals reacted by applying to join the Red Army immediately. Most felt like breaking out of the camp but were restrained by rumours that a British Mission in Moscow was discussing their eventual transportation to Britain. Wołkowicki wrote to Stalin on 14 July 1941 asking for their transportation to British-held territory and for the camp NKVD to cease harassing them.[124] In practice the Soviets did not officially withdraw from Gryazovets and hand over control to the Poles until 1 September 1941. The visit of Generals Anders and Bohusz-Szyszko to the camp on 25 August, accompanied by General Zhukov, however, marked its actual liberation. After patriotic celebrations the PoWs enrolled in the new Polish Forces except for the 18 'Germans' and an even smaller residual number of communist sympathisers.

One final, but very interesting, footnote to the above discussion concerns the infinitesimally small number of officers who passed over all the hurdles and actually joined the Soviet side.[125] Seven senior officers – two colonels (Eustachy Gorczyński and Stanisław Kunstler), four lieutenant colonels (Zygmunt Berling, Leon Bukojemski, Marian Morawski and Leon Tykociński) and one major (Józef Lis) – were extracted from Gryazovets on 10 October 1940 and sent to Moscow by passenger train. There they were joined by 21 junior officers from the Baltic States contingent held in Kozelsk2. Both groups were quartered separately, but under very good living conditions, as 'guests' of the NKVD in the Butyrki prison in Moscow. The senior officers were interviewed by Merkulov, Reikhman and Yegorov, who eliminated one of the seven who was placed in solitary confinement. The remaining six confirmed, in long conversations in the Lubianka prison with no less a personage than Beria himself, that they were willing to command the new Polish army being formed under Soviet auspices. It was during these exchanges, particularly a supper at which even cognac was served, that the Poles learnt of the fate of their colleagues straight from the head horse's mouth. Asked about the availability of officers from Kozelsk and Starobelsk to officer a proposed Polish armoured corps, Beria came out with the chilling response that they could not be taken into account. He repeated what became the famous phrase that 'we [the Soviets] have made a great mistake'.[126] Merkulov said something similar on a later occasion. 'We have committed an error ... these men are not available.'[127]

The less than magnificent six were transferred on 1 November to what has become dubbed the luxury 'Villa of Bliss' in the Malahovka suburb of Moscow. Their numbers increased to between 20 and 30 at times during the winter. Other potential collaborators arrived having passed through the NKVD interviewing process in the Moscow prisons. Notable figures such as Colonel Morawski and Captain Narcyz Łopianowski were, however, sent back to the Butyrki after displeasing their NKVD indoctrinators. There was also continual conflict between Berling and his small hard core pro-Soviet group and the more patriotic remainder.[128] The successful numbers of the Bliss Academy had been whittled down to a mere 13 by the time of the German invasion. They opted, like the rejects, who were held in the Butyrki and Lubianka before being sent back to Gryazovets, to join the Anders' Army in summer 1941, where they were kept under discreet surveillance.

Berling and his group confirmed their fundamental choice by joining the Union of Polish Patriots and going on to command the Kościuszko Division in 1943. This was considered 'desertion' by the London Polish military authorities who sentenced Berling and two junior colleagues to death *in absentia* on 26 July 1943. The sentence was not confirmed by General Sosnkowski, however, nor was it made public. Berling has always provoked much controversy. He was characterised by another Villa of Bliss inmate as 'a man of excessive personal ambition. Capable, effective and without any scruples.'[129] Berling seems to have surrendered voluntarily in September 1939, to have accepted Soviet offers of collaboration in Starobelsk and to have expressed the wish to the Malahovka group that Poland should become the seventeenth Soviet republic.[130] As commander of the Kościuszko Division he led a badly trained and equipped Polish unit into action at Lenino. The Soviet generals seem to have used the Poles as little more than range-finding fodder for the Soviet artillery. Polish communists subsequently built up a quite unjustified myth about the Polish contribution to the battle although it was precipitated by the Soviet need for a political demonstration before the Teheran Conference. Berling, an ambitious and strong-willed ex-legionnaire of *góral* background as well as a genuine Polish patriot, according to his own lights, however, proved insufficiently amenable. He was stripped of his command in September 1944 after he disobeyed Soviet orders and attempted to succour the Warsaw Uprising. Subsequently, he was forced into obscure retirement by the Polish Stalinists when they came to power who built up the legend of the totally worthless Marshal Rola-Zymierski while conceding control of the Polish army to the fully Soviet Marshal Rokossowski.

Notes

1 Janusz Zawodny, *Death in the Forest*, London: Macmillan, 1971, pp. 154–5.
2 *Katyn: Dokumenty Zbrodni*, Warsaw: Trio, 3 vols 1995–2001, hereafter KDZ, 2, pp. 434–5, 447.
3 Ivan Bezrukov, deputy-head of NKVD Sixth (Economic) Department, to Kobulov, KDZ, 2, no. 29.
4 KDZ, 2, pp. 472–500.
5 KDZ, 2, no. 17.
6 Natalia Lebediewa, *Katyń: Zbrodnia przeciwko ludzkości*, Warsaw: Bellona, 1997, pp. 174–5.
7 KDZ, 2, no. 49 and 51.
8 Tokarev telegram to Soprunenko, 5 April 1940, KDZ, 2, no. 60.
9 KDZ, 2, no. 53.
10 Zawodny, *Death in the Forest*, p. 106.
11 These are reproduced in the appendices to Jędrzej Tucholski, *Mord w Katyniu: Kozielsk, Ostaszków, Starobielsk: lista ofiar*, Warsaw: PAX, 1991, pp. 578–978. Cf. Marek Tarczyński, 'Listy wywózkowe z obozu w Kozielsku', *Wojskowy Przegląd Historyczny*, 35, 3–4 (1990), pp. 313–86.
12 KDZ, 2, no. 196. The Starobelsk lists were first published in *Wojskowy Przegląd Historyczny*, 36, 1 (1991), pp. 284–99: ibid., no. 2, pp. 350–68.
13 KDZ, 2, no. 203.
14 Seventy of these are named in list no. 23 of 13 May 1940, KDZ, 2, no. 186.
15 KDZ, 2, no. 195.
16 KDZ, 2, pp. 327–8.
17 KDZ, 2, p. 416.
18 KDZ, 2, p. 411.
19 KDZ, 2, no. 215.
20 *Indeks Represjonowanych*, Warsaw, 3 vols, 1995–1997.
21 Feminists will not object to the use of the word 'his' which is used advisedly in this context. There is no evidence of a single woman playing any direct role at any stage of the massacre or even reaching the higher directing reaches of the NKVD.
22 Stanisław Świaniewicz, *W cieniu Katynia*, Paris: Instytut Literacki, 1976, p. 105.
23 Soprunenko's Testimony to the Russian Military Procuracy, Moscow, 25 October 1990, KDZ, 2, pp. 423–31. Soprunenko faced a battery of 22 written questions. He showed great skill in denying his personal involvement in the massacre and in downgrading the role of the DPA, generally, compared to

that of the GUGB. He claimed that he was away from Moscow in Vyborg from late March to 25 May supervising the exchange of Soviet and Finnish PoWs and, therefore, could not have any direct knowledge of, let alone involvement in, the massacre. DPA documents, however, went out in his name until 14/15 April. His signature was then replaced by that of his deputy, Khokhlov. See answer to question 11, KDZ, 2, pp. 426–7.

24 Account by Starobelsk survivor Lieutenant Br. Mł., *Zbrodnia Katyńska w świetle dokumentów*, pp. 54–6.

25 Zbigniew Godlewski, 'Przeżyłem Starobielsk', *Wojskowy Przegląd Historyczny*, 38, 2 (1993), p. 329.

26 An unfair attribution. Petr Stolypin (1862–assassinated 1911), Prime Minister of Russia as well as Minister of the Interior (1906–1911), attempted to modernise and industrialise Russia before the First World War. The Bolsheviks emphasised his repression of the 1905–1907 near revolution rather than his modernising constitutional liberalism.

27 For Milshtein's detailed reports on the number of wagons used per night and the time of their departures see KDZ, 2, nos 61, 62, 159.

28 Syromatnikov was questioned on five separate occasions between June 1990 and March 1992 in Chugayev, 50 kilometres outside Kharkov, the first three times by the Ukrainian and, then, by the Russian procuracy. Interviews lasted for between one and six hours, KDZ, 2, appendix 3, pp. 472–500: the first two interviews are in Bozenna Łojek, 'Zeznania Syromiatnikowa', *Wojskowy Przegląd Historyczny*, 40, 1 (1995), pp. 423–38.

29 Andrzej Florkowski, 'Niektóre aspekty badań antropologicznych cmentarzyska NKWD w Charkowie', in *Zbrodnia Katyńska: Upamiętnienie ofiar i zadośćuczynienie*, Warsaw: NKHBZK, 1998.

30 Evidence of the 1995–1996 exhumations, ibid., pp. 66–7.

31 Also confirmed by ibid., p. 67.

32 J. Rosiak, 'Badania elementów amunicji i broni palnej wydobytych w czasie exhumacji w Charkowie i Miednoje', in *Zbrodnia Katyńska: Droga do Prawdy*, Warsaw: NKHBZK, 1992, pp. 351–63.

33 KDZ, 2, p. 474.

34 See Waldemar Siwiński, 'Coraz mniej znaków zapytania', *Polityka*, 12 May 1990, p. 11.

35 Testimony of Kazimierz Olejnik, IPiMS, Kol. 12/3, no. 50. Olejnik was subsequently held in Starobelsk2. He survived as he had earlier been sentenced to eight years' GULAG for belonging to a hostile political organisation.

36 Antoni T. Rekulski, *Czy Drugi Katyń*, Paris: Instytut Literacki, 1980.

37 Andrzej Kola, 'Badania archeologiczne i pracy ekshumacyjne przeprowadzone w 1996 r. w Charkowie w IV strefie leśno-parkowej', in *Ku Cmentarzom Polskim w Katyniu, Miednoje, Charkowie*, Warsaw, NKHBZK, 1997.

38 Ibid., p. 44.

39 Account by Senior Sergeant J.R., *Zbrodnia Katyńska w świetle dokumentów*, p. 59.

40 KDZ, 2, no. 60.

41 KDZ, 2, no. 211. Kachin had confirmed receipt of 249 prisoners on 21 May, KDZ, 2, no. 210.

42 KDZ, 2, no. 152.

43 Something seems to have gone awry on the very last exercise though. Kachin accepted receipt for 294 individuals on 21 May but Tokarev's cipher telegram the following day reports that only 64 had been killed, KDZ, nos 210, 211. Has a final receipt gone missing and were the very last 230 Ostashkov victims finished off more leisurely on the 23rd?

44 Jędrzej Tucholski, 'Transporty śmierci z Ostaszkowa do Kalinina: Materiały do epitafiów katyńskich', *Wojskowy Przegląd Historyczny*, 39, 1–2 (1994), pp. 290–5.

45 Robert Conquest, *Inside Stalin's Secret Police*, Basingstoke: Macmillan, 1985, p. 105.
46 Published as *Zeznanie Tokariewa*, Warsaw: NKHBZK, 1994, as no. 3 in the *Zeszyty Katyńskie* series: KDZ, 2, appendix 2, pp. 432–71. All the evidence in the subsequent three paragraphs is drawn directly from his account, unless otherwise stated.
47 Andrzej Przewoźnik, 'Polskie cmentarze wojenne w Katyniu, Miednoje i Charkowie', in *Ku Cmentarzom Polskim w Katyniu, Miednoje, Charkowie*, p. 10.
48 *Zbrodnia Katyńska w świetle dokumentów*, pp. 41–2.
49 KDZ, 2, p. 224.
50 Świaniewicz, *W cieniu Katynia*, pp. 109–13.
51 Jaczyński, *Zagłada oficerów*..., pp. 287–8.
52 *Tygodnik Solidarność*, 1993, no. 17.
53 *Życie Warszawy*, 3 September 1990, pp. 1, 5: *Kurier Polski*, 3 September 1990, no. 167, pp. 1–2. Both the 85-year-old Klimov and 72-year-old Titkov were tracked down by the dissident Gennadii Zavoronkov and testified before NKVD Major Oleg Zakirov.
54 Lebediewa, *Katyń: Zbrodnia przeciwko ludności*, pp. 209–11.
55 Janusz Zawodny, 'Strategia zbrodni' in *Zbrodnia Katyńska po 60 latach*, p. 16.
56 *Zbrodnia Katyńska w świetle dokumentów*, p. 200.
57 KDZ, 2, no. 69. This document shows that Solski's convoy left Kozelsk on the 8th not the 7th, p. 144.
58 Compare with Abarinov's reconstruction of the various stages of the Kozelsk PoWs' last journey, *The Murderers of Katyn*, pp. 373–4.
59 *Zbrodnia Katyńska w świetle dokumentów*, pp. 202–5.
60 Żaroń, *Agresja Związku Radzieckiego*..., p. 289.
61 Teofil Rubasiński, 'Topografia katyńska', *Wojskowy Przegląd Historyczny*, 35, 1–2 (1990), pp. 286–9.
62 Additional names mentioned in the literature are Belkin, Ustinov and Karl Reinson amongst the executioners and Kuleshov, Nikolai Kostiushenko and Viktor Grigorev amongst the drivers and assistants, Jaczyński, *Zagłada oficerów*..., p. 288.
63 Cf. Marian Głosek, 'Wstępne wyniki badań archeologicznych przeprowadzonych w lesie Katyńskim w 1995 roku' and Marek Dutkiewicz, 'Badania nad mobiliami odnalezionomymi przy szczątkach Polskich oficerów w Katyniu', in *Zbrodnia nie ukarana: Katyń – Twer – Charków*, pp. 20–45.
64 Maria Magdalena Blombergowa, 'Próba oceny prac i metod badań terenowych na cmentarzach Polskich oficerów i policjantów w Rosji', *Zbrodnia Katyńska: Próba bilansu*, p. 95.
65 *Zbrodnia Katyńska w świetle dokumentów*, p. 111.
66 Cf. Stanisław M. Jankowski, 'Pamiętniki znane i nieznane', in *Zbrodnia Katyńska: Próba bilansu*, pp. 113–20.
67 Erazm Baran, 'Uwagi do niemieckiego sprawozdania sądowo-lekarskiego opublikowanego w 1943r.', in *Zbrodnia Katyńska: Droga do Prawdy*, p. 136.
68 In one case even three shots.
69 Zawodny, *Death in the Forest*, p. 23.
70 *Zbrodnia Katyńska w świetle dokumentów*, pp. 107–8.
71 *Amtliches Material zum Massenmord von Katyn*, Berlin: Zentralverlag der NSDAP, 1943, p. 75.
72 Kobulov is reported as saying irritably that 'we did not count on you', hence the strength of the central NKVD contingent in the Ostashkov massacre, KDZ, 2, pp. 434–5.
73 KDZ, 1, p. 470.
74 KDZ, 2, no. 27.

75 Beria requested Transport Commissar Kaganovich on 21 March 1940 to provide the required 630 railway wagons for the deportation of the 8000 and the two concentrations of 3000, KDZ, 2, no. 26.

76 Interview with Colonel Stefan Rodzevich of the Supreme Military Procuracy of the Russian Republic. He probably lied in order to cover up the responsibility of the Moscow NKVD, *Biuletyn Katyński*, no. 37 (1993), p. 4.

77 On the other hand there is a hint in the introduction to KDZ, 2, pp. 10–11, that first death lists arrived in the Ukraine only on 20 April.

78 This view is also shared by the editors of KDZ, 2, p. 85.

79 *Listy katyńskiej ciąg dalszy: Straceni na Ukrainie*, Warsaw: NKZBZK/PFK, 1994.

80 Jędrzej Tucholski in *Biuletyn Katyński*, no. 44 (1999), pp. 3–14.

81 *Listy katyńskiej ciąg dalszy*, pp. xi–xv.

82 Wojciech Materski, 'Katyń – motywy i przebieg zbrodni (pytania, wątpliwości)', in *Zbrodnia Katyńska po 60 latach*, pp. 33–4.

83 Cf. Zuzanna Gajowniczek (ed.), *Ukraiński ślad Katynia*, Warsaw, MSW, 1995.

84 Andrzej Kola, 'Czy w Bykowni pod Kijowem i we Włodzimierzu Wołyńskim spoczywają ofiary zbrodni katyńskiej?' in *W przeddzień zbrodni katyńskiej*, Warsaw: NKHBZK, 1999.

85 Four other killing and burial sites in the Kuropaty forest on the outskirts of Minsk, used by the NKVD between 1937 and 1941, were also discovered at around the same time, Sławomir Popowski, 'Prawda o Kuropatach', *Polityka*, 20 October 1988, p. 13.

86 Daniel Boćkowski, 'Kuropaty – Białoruski Katyń', in *Zbrodnia Katyńska: Pytania pozostałe bez odpowiedzi*, Warsaw: NKHBZK, 2002, pp. 61–5.

87 Jewgenij Gorelik, *Kuropaty: Polski ślad*, Warsaw: Rytm/ROPWiM, 1996.

88 Materski, 'Katyń – motywy i przebieg zbrodni (pytania, wątpliwości)', pp. 35–6.

89 Wojciech Materski, 'Sprawcy zbrodni – definicja i typologia', in *Zbrodnia Katyńska: Problem przebaczenia*, Warsaw, NKHBZK, 2003, pp. 9–21.

90 Ibid., pp. 10 ff.

91 Tokarev's Testimony, KDZ, 2, p. 435.

92 This element of 'self-selection' of roles is confirmed by Christopher Browning's account of the internal dynamics of the Hamburg group of *Ordinary Men: Reserve Police Battalion 101 and the Final Solution in Poland*, New York: HarperCollins, 1992.

93 Materski, 'Sprawcy zbrodni...', p. 14.

94 KDZ, 2, pp. 404–9.

95 The services of the 136th battalion in convoying the Kozelsk PoWs to Katyn were recognised in an order of 21 May 1940 by its Commander and Political Commissar. Four individuals received 70 roubles while another 22 received either 25 or 50 roubles and ten days' leave, KDZ, 2, no. 209.

96 Cf. interview with Sergei Charłamow, 'Ordery za Katyń', *Rzeczpospolita*, 26 March 1990, p. 3. 'Ruble za oprawców', *Biuletyn Katyński*, no. 38/1994, pp. 13–15.

97 Conquest, *Inside Stalin's Secret Police*, pp. 138–44. He lists a mere 31 functionaries identified as being involved in the 1940 massacre. The most authoritative lists since then, which include all the most up-to-date biographical material which has become available since Conquest's time, are to be found in the appendices to KDZ, vols 1, 2, 3.

98 Czapski, *Wspomnienia starobielskie*, p. 28.

99 Berling, *Wspomnienia*, 1, p. 46.

100 Cf. KDZ, 2, pp. 11–13.

101 Soprunenko cipher telegrams of 4 and 7 April 1940, KDZ, 2, nos 57, 73.

102 KDZ, 2, no. 71. The others, who also survived, were Stefan Sienicki, Kazimierz Kazimierczak and Mieczysław Srokowski.

103 KDZ, 2, no. 219. These interventions were not entirely on behalf of their ethnic compatriots. The German interventions saved the aristocrat artist Count Józef Czapski, Wacław Komarnicki, Olgierd Ślizien (Anders' adjutant), Bronisław Młynarski (son of the famous orchestra conductor Emil Młynarski), Adam Moszyński and others such as Stiller, Olizar and Karol Hoffman.
104 KDZ, 2, no. 215.
105 Zawodny, *Death in the Forest*, p. 117. Tucholski, in *Mord w Katyniu*, bases himself on the list provided by Peszkowski, *Wspomnienia jeńca z Kozielska*, p. 48.
106 KDZ, 2, no. 145.
107 Gerchovskii to Khokhlov, 27 April 1940, KDZ, 2, no. 145. Tokarev testified that he received a telephone call from Kobulov's secretary in Moscow after which he had Romm pulled out of the cells where he was awaiting execution, KDZ, 2, p. 445.
108 Soprunenko to Kadyshev, 5 May 1940, KDZ, 2, no. 164.
109 The camp was referred to as camp R-43 in internal NKVD correspondence as part of the drive to maintain secrecy over the 1940 massacre and its residual survivors, KDZ, 3, no. 13.
110 DPA note of 1 July 1943, KDZ, 3, no. 2. The camp commandant produced a list of 365 names on 3 April 1941, which would appear to be those of the survivors from the three special camps still left in Gryazovets, KDZ, 3, no. 132.
111 Wołkowicki to DPA, 26 September 1940, KDZ, 3, no. 49.
112 KDZ, 3, no. 67.
113 KDZ, 3, p. 3.
114 Nekhoreshev to political commissar Sazonov (Gryazovets), 24 August 1940, KDZ, 3, no. 29.
115 Nekhoreshev to Merkulov, 3 September 1940, KDZ, 3, no. 36.
116 Sazonov to Nekhoreshev, Report detailing political work in the camp between July and September, 4 October 1940, KDZ, 3, no. 55.
117 KDZ, 3, no. 77.
118 KDZ, 3, p. 179.
119 KDZ, 3, nos 112, 113.
120 IPiMS, Kol. 12/3, no. 54.
121 Report by camp commandant Volkov on political-operational activity during January 1941, KDZ, 3, no. 116.
122 KDZ, 3, no. 149.
123 Kruglov, Order no. 00339 of 31 March 1941, KDZ, 3, no. 130.
124 KDZ, 3, no. 185.
125 See Żaroń, *Agresja Związku Radzieckiego na Polskę*, pp. 303–12. Zawodny, *Death in the Forest*, pp. 146–53.
126 *Hearings*, Part 4, pp. 431, 555.
127 Ibid., p. 533.
128 Zawodny, *Death in the Forest*, pp. 150–2.
129 Testimony by Rotmistrz (cavalry captain) Narcyz Łopianowski, IPiMS, Kol. 12/3, no. 45. Berling and Gorczyński always took the lead in attempting to convince their colleagues to collaborate with the Soviets, in proposing pro Soviet toasts and in pushing through such gestures as voting for portraits of the Soviet leaders to be put up in the Villa of Bliss.
130 Stanisław Jaczyński, *Zygmunt Berling: Między Sławą a Potępieniem*, Warsaw: KiW, 1993.

6   The struggle for historical truth

Before Katyn': the hinge of fate for Polish–Soviet relations, 1941–1943

The first phase of the Second World War, Nazi–Soviet collaboration to destroy Poland between 1939 and 1941, was followed by the alliance of 1941–1945 between Britain and America and the USSR whose overriding priority was the defeat of Nazi Germany. The German invasion of the USSR allowed the establishment of direct bilateral relations between the Polish Government-in-Exile in London and the Soviet Union between summer 1941 and April 1943. The struggle for the truth about the fate of the missing 1940 Polish PoWs became a central feature of the larger Polish Question – what would be her post-war frontiers and the fate of West Belarus and West Ukraine? Britain and America attempted to mediate a Polish–Soviet understanding which would allow the Poles to contribute to the war effort and incline Stalin to accept an independent and democratic post-war Poland in Europe.[1] Such hopes became increasingly unrealistic as Soviet military power and political prospects strengthened after Stalingrad in late 1942. The London Poles became a nuisance endangering the Allied war effort in 1941–1943. The dumping of an inconvenient historical loser and the handling of the truth about the 1940 massacre, however, caused Western statesmen embarrassing moral and political dilemmas whose consequences affected the origins and course of the Cold War.

Fundamental Polish–Soviet disagreements preceded the ultimate break in their relations occasioned by the pretext provided by the London Poles' request for a Red Cross investigation into the Katyn graves in April 1943. The disagreements concerned the control, size and provisioning of the Polish army formed in the USSR; and the capacity of the London Poles to seek out, organise and bring relief to both the deported civilian and the imprisoned military sections of their community. The confining Soviet totalitarian framework, and the harassment and arrest of Polish officials, resulted in the large-scale evacuation through Persia in 1942; a bitter dispute over the Polish civic and the Soviet ethnic definitions of the citizenship – and consequent political allegiance, of the inhabitants of West Belarus and West Ukraine – reflected the wider political conflict over the character and ultimate fate of these territories; and the Soviet decision to lie about, and to cover up, the fate of the 14 700 officers and policemen massacred in the three camps in 1940 made it impossible for them, even if they had wanted to, to collaborate meaningfully with the London Poles. Stalin thus built up a Soviet-controlled Polish army in the USSR, arrested Home Army officers, forced rankers into the Berling Army as the Red Army advanced into Poland, and remained passive while the Germans suppressed the 1944 Warsaw Uprising. The result was the complete marginalisation of the London Poles.

The documentary sources for chronicling the above story have long been available with the opening of Western archives since the early 1970s and the earlier publication of the Polish documents.[2] The Katyn strand, however, formed the initial cast out of which the protracted subsequent struggle for the truth about the 1940 massacre developed. The ambiguous political agreement of 21 July 1941 re-established diplomatic relations but both sides maintained differing standpoints on the contentious issues of frontiers, territories and the Ribbentrop–Molotov Pact.[3] The USSR agreed to the establishment of a Polish army under Polish command in the USSR but under Soviet military direction.[4] The Supreme Soviet also amnestied 'all Polish citizens deprived of their freedom on the territory of the USSR' on 12 August.[5] The Polish–Soviet Military Agreement of 14 August 1941, however, only opened a long saga of disputes over the size, organisation and ultimate control of the Polish army in the USSR.[6] The Polish–Soviet–British exchanges regarding their political relationship as well as this issue can be followed in detail elsewhere.[7] What concerns us most are the growing complications caused by the 'missing officers'. As Lebedeva says 'the disappearance of the Polish officers and the unwillingness of Stalin and his entourage to give a clear answer to the inquiries of the Polish Government about their fate complicated what were already unclear Soviet–Polish relations and undermined confidence in the Soviet leaders.'[8]

The Polish ambassador in Moscow, Jan Kot, raised the question of the missing officers in a number of exchanges with Deputy Foreign Minister Andrei Vyshinsky in October–November 1941.[9] After these preliminary skirmishes Kot met Stalin in the Kremlin for a conversation on 14 November which forms an important staple of the Katyn literature.[10] Stalin and Molotov cynically played out a well-known comedy scene by pretending to phone the NKVD when Kot asked for the full release of all Polish soldiers.[11] An exchange of diplomatic notes only confirmed the Soviet hard line big lie that 'the amnesty of the Polish citizens has been fully executed' apart from criminals. The Polish reply denied that this was so, requested a list of those detained and protested against Soviet ethnic exemptions and interpretations of Polish communal relief as anti-Soviet activity.[12] Sikorski's visit to Moscow of 3–4 December and meeting with Stalin failed to resolve Polish–Soviet difficulties and to establish a constructive basis for their relationship.[13] Stalin was not used to being challenged and corrected so when Sikorski told him to his face that despite the amnesty numerous Poles were still held in labour camps and prisons he must have squirmed inwardly knowing the truth about the 1940 massacre: 'not one of them' had returned from the three special camps.[14] Their Declaration of Friendship and Mutual Assistance, signed on 4 December, merely committed them to fighting the war against Hitlerite Germany to a favourable conclusion.[15] Sikorski left with the hopelessly optimistic expectation that the Poles would be allowed to freely organise a 150 000-strong army which would become a significant political force favouring a balanced Polish–Soviet relationship within the Great Power alliance.[16] Sikorski's policy was based on the mistaken premise that the Western Allies would repay Poland's military contribution by guaranteeing her post-war security and frontiers against Soviet pressure.[17]

The development of the Polish army in the USSR during 1941–1942 can be traced out in the Soviet documents contained in the November 1992 folder.[18] Beria's note of 30 October 1941 for Stalin revealed that the number of Polish military in the USSR was 40 961 (1985 officers, 11 919 sub-officers and 27 077 ordinary ranks), organised in two infantry divisions, a reserve regiment and an army staff of 508.[19] Beria, at this time, considered that its commanders, Generals Władysław Anders, Mieczysław Boruta-Spiechowicz and Michał Tokarzewski, were collaborating loyally despite being very pro-British.

Was there really a favourable window of opportunity in this period of maximum Soviet weakness – up until the end of 1941 when the Germans were only just repelled from outside Moscow – for the historic revision of Polish–Soviet relations which was genuinely sought by Sikorski and the Western Allies? If there was, the manly presentation of their grievances by the Poles might just possibly have been glossed over by the Soviets were it not for the bind which Stalin found himself in as a result of massacring the Polish officers in 1940. A dictator cannot reveal his crimes and, even less, his mistakes. He cannot afford to be seen to have been caught out in a lie. After playing for time and just surviving in 1941 Stalin subsequently played on the increasing indispensability of the Red Army's contribution to the Allied war effort. This allowed him to subordinate the importance of the London Poles and their forces in the wartime alliance at the price of tactical concessions such as their partial evacuation through Persia. By the time Katyn was revealed by the Germans it was a mere embarrassment to Stalin. He was well on the way to forging the Western commitment to fighting the war through to Germany's Unconditional Surrender and Allied occupation and to Great Power determination of the post-war settlement. He had also excluded the London Poles from having any say over the Polish army in the USSR or over his political forces which returned to

Poland and established communism in the Red Army's baggage train. Could there have been any other outcome? Only if the 1940 massacre had not occurred, fuelling Stalin's need to establish and maintain the big lie on the issue. The situation would also have taken a different turn, as hoped for by Sikorski, if a longer period of military stalemate had continued on the Eastern Front, increasing the need for Polish manpower or if he had received real Western support.

Increasingly bitter Polish–Soviet exchanges about the missing officers continued throughout 1942 against the backdrop of wider events and the continuing controversies over borders and territories.[20] Stalin freed himself from remaining Allied constraints by agreeing to the Polish withdrawal to Persia, which began in spring 1942.[21] The Soviet figures are that 112 171 Poles left the USSR of which 71 202 were military and 40 969 civilians.[22] The rapid deterioration in their relations then came out into the open with the arrest and harassment of Polish community relief officials. The Soviets deemed Polish investigation of the missing officers to be espionage. The citizenship and frontier issues flared up repeatedly.[23] At his meeting with Tadeusz Romer, Kot's successor, on 20 February 1943 Molotov declared brutally that, exceptionally, the Soviets had regarded ethnic Poles resident in West Belarus and West Ukraine as Polish citizens. This privilege could not be extended to Polish citizens 'of the Ukrainian, Belarusan and Jewish nationalities' as 'the question of a Polish–Soviet frontier is not yet settled and is liable to discussion in the future'.[24] Romer's extensive discussion with Stalin in late February merely clarified the conflicting viewpoints on the citizenship, territorial and propaganda issues.[25] The Soviets formed their group of pro-Moscow Poles resident in the USSR into the Union of Polish Patriots (ZPP) in March 1943 under the chairmanship of the writer Wanda Wasilewska. Stalin also organised the entirely Moscow-controlled Kościuszko division in the USSR. Sikorski defended Poland's frontiers, territories and independence while offering Soviet Russia friendly 'co-existence as well as genuine cooperation against the Germans'.[26]

Stalin had, therefore, by April 1943 imposed his control over the Poles in the USSR and excluded the marginalised London Poles from having any say over the Polish army in the USSR or over the fate of the inhabitants of West Belarus and West Ukraine. Katyn now became a godsend, allowing Stalin to complete the above processes and to compromise the London Government-in-Exile's standing with the British and Americans. The pretext for the breaking-off of diplomatic relations was, however, supplied by the very issue – the 1940 massacre – which had stymied whatever little chance there had ever been of Polish–Soviet agreement during 1941–1943.

The diplomatic consequences of the discovery of the Katyn bodies should, therefore, have hardly been unexpected. The way in which the Germans announced, and subsequently attempted to utilise, their discovery of the Katyn section of the 1940 massacre, however, caused important complications as far as the truth was concerned. We now know that the German military unit occupying the Katyn NKVD guest house had reported the presence of Polish bodies in the vicinity during 1942. The Wehrmacht High Command ordered the investigation and exhumation of the graves in order to establish the circumstances and the numbers of those killed only in late March 1943. Whether the Germans waited for the spring to unfreeze the soil, after an exceptionally hard winter, or whether the announcement fitted in with Goebbels' judgement of the best timing for his proposed propaganda *coup*, remains unclear.

Radio Berlin announced, on the morning of 13 April 1943, that the local population had indicated a Soviet execution site at Kosogory, west of Smolensk, to the German occupying authorities. About 3000 bodies stacked in 12 layers, including that of General Smorawiński, had already been uncovered in a huge pit, 28 metres long by 16 metres wide. The Germans also gave the substantially truthful information that the Polish officers were killed by pistol shots to the back of the neck, that they were buried in their military uniforms and that identification would be easy as the Soviets had left documentation on the bodies which had mummified because of local soil conditions.[27] They surmised correctly that they had been transported by rail from the Kozelsk camp. Their presumption that all 10 000 missing officers had been murdered there, and Goebbels' subsequent propaganda use of figures which increased to 11 000–12 000, was, as we now know, mistaken, although self-serving. The Germans aimed to set up a smokescreen for their planned liquidation of the Jewish Ghetto in Warsaw in the second half of April.[28] Their primary objective, that of splitting the Poles and the Western Allies from the Soviets, will be discussed later. They were certainly successful in placing the London Poles in an impossible quandary. As a British Foreign Office official noted in May 1943 'the Polish case has tended to go by default owing to the circumstances in which the Katyn question first became public knowledge'.[29] Eden commented on the second O'Malley report that it was 'puzzling that the Germans should have kept this information bottled up so long'.[30]

The German auspices of the Katyn discovery placed the Government-in-Exile in an impossible situation. It could not accept at face value the immediate Soviet bluster that the Germans were responsible as they had captured and murdered the Polish PoWs in summer 1941, after the Soviet withdrawal from the relevant part of the Smolensk region between 17 and 24 July 1941.[31] The Polish cabinet set out on 15 April what they regarded as the definite facts, confirmed by their excellent sources within the USSR.[32] The Soviets had admitted capturing 181 000 Polish PoWs, of which under 10 000 were regular and reserve officers. About 5000 had been held in Kozelsk, 3920 in Starobelsk and 6570 in Ostashkov. Groups of between 60 and 300 men had been removed, almost daily, from these camps between 5 April and mid-May 1940. The ones from Kozelsk were transported towards Smolensk while 400 were transported to the Gryazovets camp in Vologda district. The document then summarised all the repeated, and fruitless, Polish efforts during 1941–1943 to elicit information from the Soviet authorities regarding the 15 000 Poles held in the three camps when they were broken up. The document made a logical, balanced and unemotional case. The Polish decision to ask for the International Red Cross investigation, however, led to the London Poles being traduced and blamed by the Soviets and the Western Allies at the time, and by others for over half a century.

The end game by Stalin was predictable, rapid and ruthless, despite the Polish Government recalling the German crimes against the Polish nation and denying the Nazis any moral right to speak on their behalf.[33] The Poles also stressed that they were acting completely independently of the Germans. The news was so shocking that 'only irrefutable facts can outweigh the numerous and detailed German statements concerning the discovery of the bodies'.[34] The Poles were unfortunate in that the Germans also asked the Red Cross to investigate at exactly the same time which allowed the Soviets to depict these wholly independent moves as being part of a coordinated conspiracy.[35] *Pravda* attacked 'Hitler's Polish collaborators' on 19 April 1943. Churchill and Roosevelt accepted Stalin's resultant bluster that he was the aggrieved party, in good faith, with the result that the Poles were blamed, both then and subsequently.[36] The best defence is always attack. Stalin broke off diplomatic relations and savaged the London Poles for supporting 'vile Fascist calumny against the USSR' and for colluding with the 'farcical investigation' designed to cover up the Nazis' own 'monstrous crime'.[37] Churchill supported Stalin's opposition to the Red Cross investigation and his argument that it was bound to be fraudulent as it would take place under German control.[38] Churchill's appeal to Stalin, however, failed to prevent Molotov from breaking off relations officially on 25 April.[39] This was despite Eden prevailing upon Sikorski on 24 April to withdraw the request for the Red Cross investigation.[40] Molotov's note argued that the Poles had used 'the slanderous Hitlerite fake' as an attempt to gain territorial concessions at the expense of Soviet Belarus, Ukraine and Lithuania. British reactions will be discussed in the following chapter but the Foreign Office was made fully aware of the London Polish view that following the 1941 Polish–Soviet agreement the Soviets had taken measures 'designed to exacerbate mutual relations'. Polish overtures had met with only 'high handed and brutal acts of the Kremlin. The Katyn affair, seen in this light, seemed to have but changed the timetable for a rupture towards which the Kremlin had been heading for 16 months'.[41]

The 1943 International Commission, Polish Red Cross and German reports

Under Allied and Soviet pressure the London Poles' invitation to the International Red Cross Committee to investigate the Katyn graves was held to have lapsed by the end of April 1943. The Germans, knowing that world opinion was fully aware of their war atrocities in occupied Eastern Europe, therefore set about establishing the credibility of their claim that the Soviets were guilty of this particular crime. To this end they set up an International Commission composed of 12 established academics and experts in forensic medicine. Those who accepted the invitation came from countries outside the Reich, but only the Swiss Dr François Naville was from a non-German-occupied or Axis state. The remainder were: Dr Speelers (Professor of Opthalmology, Ghent University/Belgium), Dr Marko Markov (Instructor in Forensic Medicine and Criminology, Sofia University/Bulgaria), Dr Helge Tramsen (Professor of Anatomy, Copenhagen Institute of Forensic Medicine/Denmark), Dr Saxen (Professor of Pathological Anatomy, Helsinki University/Finland), Dr Vincenzo Palmieri (Professor of Forensic Medicine and Criminology, Naples University/Italy), Dr Edward L. Miloslavic (Professor of Forensic Medicine and Criminology, Agram University/Croatia), Dr de Burlet (Professor of Anatomy, Groningen University/Netherlands), Dr Hajek (Professor of Forensic Medicine and Criminology, Charles University of Prague/Czechoslovakia), Dr Birkle (Judicial-Medical Coroner, Romanian Ministry of Justice), Dr Subik (Professor of Pathological Anatomy, Bratyslava University/Slovakia), and Dr Ferenc Orsos (Professor of Forensic Medicine and Criminology, Budapest University/Hungary). Dr Costedoat, a Vichy Government medical inspector, was present but played no part in the proceedings.

The commission worked in Katyn from 28 to 30 April 1943. Its members were given full freedom to carry out their investigations as they saw fit. The Germans also allowed them to interview local residents. Despite the shortness of their stay the commission examined 928 already exhumed bodies and carried out autopsies on nine fresh corpses.[42] Their final Medical Report was not published separately. The full text is included in the 350-page-long German *Official Material Concerning the Katyn Massacre.*[43] The significance of the document, signed by all 12 participants, was that it confirmed the more detailed German and Polish findings, identifying the bodies and establishing the cause and time of death, discussed below.[44]

The signature of Naville, the independent Swiss witness, was particularly valuable. His further testimony, to the Swiss Council of State in Geneva on 11 September 1946, elaborated on the work, the extent of local contacts and the full independence of the International Commission.[45] This answered a hostile interpellation by Vincent, a communist deputy.[46]

The Council's full support for Dr Naville represented a defeat for the wider Soviet propaganda drive accompanying their attempt to include Katyn as a German war crime at the Nuremberg Trial. The fate of poor Dr Markov, whose native Bulgaria was occupied by the Soviets, was the opposite to Naville's. Markov was forced to recant his evidence. He repeated the Soviet line in February 1945 in a war crimes trial in Sofia, as the price of having charges against him withdrawn.[47] He repeated the performance at Nuremberg.[48] Likewise pressure on Dr Hajek, the Prague forensic-criminologist, induced him to withdraw his signature and to declare that Katyn was a German deed at the war's end.[49] There were also intermediate reactions. A British Intelligence agent, codenamed 'Hamilcar', interviewed Tramsen on his return to Denmark from Katyn. Tramsen stated that he had only agreed to participate as he had been misled into believing that it was a fully independent Red Cross inquiry. He confirmed that he had been given a free hand to investigate the large pit and that none of the papers discovered on the corpses were dated later than 1940. Tramsen also claimed to have insisted on less definite statements in the final report.[50]

The Nazi search for authenticity also permitted a Polish Red Cross (PRC) team of doctors from German-occupied Poland to work in Katyn in April–May. Despite their initial scepticism of German motives, and first hand knowledge of Nazi crimes in Poland, the Poles also confirmed the more detailed German findings.[51] They refused, however, to support German propaganda or to get involved in anti-Soviet activity. There was no final official PRC bulletin as such. Dr Marian Wodziński from the Forensic Medicine Institute at the Jagiełłonian University in Kraków, who as a secret ZWC member had impeccable anti-German credentials, spent five weeks in Katyn from 14 April to 5 June with his assistants. Escaping to Britain at the war's end he confirmed his Katyn testimony. He eventually produced a detailed final draft in 1946–1947, generally described as the PRC Technical Commission report.[52]

Other delegations, including experts in forensic medicine and representatives from various walks of life, from other Polish cities, notably Warsaw, Łódź and Lublin, were also flown in by the Germans during April. The first, on 10–11 April, included Edmund Seyfried and Dr Edward Gródzki (members of the Main Welfare Council, RGO),[53] Dr Konrad Orzechowski (the Germanophile director of a Warsaw hospital), the right-wing journalist Władysław Kawecki,[54] Kazimierz Didur (a photographer) and the writers Emil Skiwski and Ferdynand Goetel.[55] The second, much larger, delegation arrived on 14 April; most of its members returned to Poland on the 16th. It included Father Stanisław Jasiński (Roman Catholic Primate Sapieha's representative), Dr Kazimierz Skarzyński, Dr Adam Szebesta (Deputy-Head of the PRC in Kraków),[56] Dr Stanisław Klapert, and Dr Tadeusz Susz-Pragłowski from the Polish Red Cross, Marian Martens (journalist), Dr Hieronim Bartoszewski, Roman Banach,

Stefan Kołodziejski and Zygmunt Pohorski. The most important accounts were provided by Goetel[57] and Dr Kazimierz Skarzyński, the secretary-general of the Polish Red Cross.[58] Both of them reported back to AK commander General Grot-Rowecki who informed the London Government-in-Exile.[59]

Another notable Polish visitor at this time was the inter-war Germanophile writer and journalist Józef Mackiewicz, on 20 May 1943. He became the main editor of *The Katyn Atrocity in the Light of Documents*, the key émigré publication whose numerous editions were published anonymously with Anders' foreword.[60] Mackiewicz also wrote an important book amongst numerous other writings on the subject.[61] His reports at the time for the Wilno daily *Goniec Codzienny* were the first to attribute responsibility directly to the Soviets. They aroused corresponding controversy including AK charges of collaboration.[62] The German-licensed popular press, the so-called 'reptile press', such as the *Goniec Krakowski*, as well as the AK underground publications, also began to publish lists of names of those murdered as they were identified. This caused nationwide indignation and sorrow as the news spread and as names of identified bodies were announced over German loudspeakers in the streets.[63] The Kraków photographer Kazimierz Didur hid his photographs taken at Katyn during the PRL. They were presented in a full exhibition organised by Władysław Klimczak, the director of the Kraków Photographic Museum, only after communism collapsed, in 1989. In addition, one of Piłsudski's inter-war premiers, Leon Kozłowski, visited Katyn and was encouraged by the Germans to publicise his impressions. More than that, Gauleiter Frank and Nazi occupation officials approached him, and other right-wing personalities, with a view to using Katyn and the Soviet threat as the basis for a German–Polish collaborating Government.[64] This attempt met with almost no positive reaction from the Polish side and was disowned by Hitler, anyway.[65]

The Germans also brought in eight Polish PoWs from their Offlags including Lieutenant-Colonel Stefan Mossor.[66] Arrested and imprisoned by the Stalinists in their military trials he later became a well-known military theorist in the PRL.[67] In addition two American PoWs, Lieutenant-Colonels John Van Vliet and Donald B. Stewart, whose evidence will be discussed more fully, and a British and a South African officer were brought in, in early May.[68] On top of all this traffic by interested Polish parties the Germans also allowed in a large number of neutral journalists, especially from Sweden, Switzerland and Spain. The Vichy writer Robert Brasillach, who was shot at the war's end, also came. The *Reich*'s liaison and press officer on the spot, the Austrian Lieutenant Gregor Slovenczyk, orchestrated the maximum propaganda benefit from these visits. He was uniformly unsuccessful with the Poles although he later attempted to claim the credit for having created the Katyn issue.[69]

The main exhumation work was done by a German Special Medical-Judicial Commission, headed by Dr Gerhard Buhtz, Professor of Forensic

Medicine and Criminology at the University of Breslau. He enjoyed a high reputation in the field of forensic medicine and was to be killed in an Allied air raid in 1944. His investigations and findings were paralleled and confirmed independently by the International Medical and PRC teams.[70] Every detail and conclusion of the forensic evidence was argued and fought over for almost half a century. But it has now become largely irrelevant, insofar as it concerns the central issue of German or Soviet guilt, since Gorbachev confirmed the truth officially in 1990. The same goes for all the valiant efforts from 1943 to 1990 to glean the truth from these details about how the massacre was carried out. The NKVD documents discussed in Chapters 3 to 5 have now revealed in incontrovertibly massive detail how the massacre was planned and how the evacuation of the camps and the transportation of the PoWs to the killing sites was implemented. The remaining gaps concern the central decision making as well as official documentation on the execution-burial stage. The outstanding question left for discussion today forms the staple of the second half of this book. Was the 1943 evidence, despite its German provenance, conclusive and robust enough to indicate Soviet guilt by proving beyond all reasonable doubt that the Poles were killed in spring 1940, and not at a date subsequent to the German invasion of summer 1941?

The German forensic-pathological investigators worked from early April until 7 July 1943 when their investigations were interrupted, allegedly by the summer heat causing an unbearable stench and a plague of flies. The reality was that the Red Army was approaching. The Germans had also got themselves into a propaganda bind by claiming that all the Polish officers had been slaughtered at Katyn. The German team exhumed seven (and eventually eight) mass graves ranging in depth from six to 11 feet, containing 4143 bodies. All the bodies were numbered and 2815 were identified conclusively.[71] They were stacked face down and had been shot in the back of the head with the attendant details described earlier.[72] The bodies were compressed together and had begun to decompose but were easily pulled apart by iron hooks, pickaxes and spades. Any articles found on them were recorded. Each body had its contents secured in an individual manilla envelope, although no valuables such as rings or watches were found. A variety of personal papers, documents, letters, cards, photographs, vaccination cards and cigarette cases as well as tags facilitated the task of basic identification as well as the logging of personal details. The Poles present confirmed these documents as genuine and that no date later than April 1940 appeared. They were also convinced that it would have been impossible for the Germans to have inserted such papers on the bodies due to their presence at many actual exhumations and the decomposed and yellowed state of the material.[73] The questions of the German revolvers and ammunition, signs of the occasional bayonet thrust or rifle butt blow, tied hands, covered heads and gagged mouths filled with sawdust have already been discussed.

The central political issue was, however, clearly that of when the Poles had been killed. As Zawodny says, 'if it could be determined *when* the men were shot, the identity of the executioners would be known'.[74] The Soviets controlled the Katyn forest until late summer 1941 and the bodies were uncovered about 20 months after the Germans occupied the region. The three reports concur that the Poles were killed about three years before April 1943 thus pointing conclusively to a likely killing date of spring 1940 when nobody denied that the PoWs were in Soviet captivity. This was proved by the autopsies on the bodies which confirmed this period of skull and muscle decomposition. The absence of insect remains also indicated that burial had taken place in a cold climate.[75] This conclusion was supported by the documentation found on the prisoners' bodies and by the evidence of local residents. There was one further piece of evidence which lingered in Churchill's mind after reading the secret report by the ambassador to the Polish Government-in-Exile, Sir Owen O'Malley. The spruce trees planted on the pits to camouflage the crime appeared much younger than the trees in the surrounding forest. The Germans brought in an expert forester, Fritz Von Herff, whose microscopic examination confirmed that the trees had been transplanted about three years prior to spring 1940.[76]

An interesting footnote to the above concerned the subsequent fate of the documents and belongings uncovered by the Germans at Katyn, whose contents are discussed separately. After being examined by the International Medical and Polish Red Cross commissions they were packed in nine large wooden cases and transported to Kraków. There, they were stored in the Forensic-Medical Institute, which although supervised by a German appointee, Dr Werner Beck, was in fact run by Professor Jan Zygmunt Robel (1886–1962).[77] The latter and his staff went through and segregated the material meticulously as well as copying and photographing its most important components.[78] They also allowed PRC as well as AK representatives to examine it in secret. The Kraków medical and intellectual *milieu* was, therefore, well informed of its existence and significance.

With the approach of the Red Army in January 1944 Beck received police orders to destroy the material. Instead, he packed it in 14 cases, which were loaded onto two lorries and transported, after an interim stop at Breslau University, as far as Radebeul near Dresden.[79] There, military conditions made further movement impossible. It would appear that the material was burnt by a dispatcher at the railway station. The railwaymen involved, as well as Robel himself, were arrested, subsequently, by the Soviet and Polish security police. Their investigations, apparently, yielded no further result. Some of the copies of this Katyn material were discovered in a Kraków house in 1991 and now constitute the surviving part of the Robel Archive which is stored in the Katyn Institute and the Archives of the Metropolitan Archdiocese in Kraków. A photocopied collection is in the Institute of Military History in Warsaw. The 285 envelopes, containing 1146 pages of material, have been catalogued by Urszula Olech.[80]

Much was made at the time, and during the Cold War, of the evidence of local residents familiar with the Katyn forest. The evidence of Ivan Krivozertsov (*pseud.* Michal Loboda) has already been referred to. His 'suicide' in post-war Britain fuelled much speculation about the nefariously unforgiving memory and long reach of the NKVD.[81] Despite wild and inaccurate rumours Krizovertsov spent the last months of his life at Stowell camp near Gloucester and finally at Easton-in-Gordano outside Bristol. He was found hanged in a neighbouring orchard on 30 October 1947. An inquest held at Flax Bourton police station returned a suicide verdict.[82] This category of evidence is now only of historiographical interest, although it was very important in its time, particularly as the Soviets forced those who remained on their territory and in their control to recant in 1944.

Whether it was reasonable for British and American Governments to actually believe that the Germans fabricated the evidence of Soviet guilt for Katyn will be discussed in the following chapter. Here one will just note that the Germans certainly knew of Katyn for some time before they announced its discovery. Goebbels was also primarily interested in using it for propaganda purposes. He wanted to demonstrate the wickedly murderous character of the Soviets to world and Allied opinion in order to divert attention from Nazi crimes and atrocities. But the primary German aim was to split Poland and the Western Allies away from the USSR. All these Nazi aims were true, but even more unfortunately for the Poles, it did not mean that the Germans had fabricated the truth about Soviet responsibility for Katyn. This particular truth, therefore, suffered for the greater good of Allied victory against Nazi Germany. Finally, one should note that the Germans confused and harmed the London Polish cause in one other respect. The Germans, initially, genuinely thought that all 10 000 officers from Kozelsk and Starobelsk had been murdered at Katyn. They were, therefore, highly embarrassed when their own exhumations only came up with just over 4100 bodies, a figure which we now know corresponds closely to the inmates of the Kozelsk camp.

We do not know whether the Germans had been informed by their Soviet ally of that time about the 1940 massacre of PoWs. They must certainly have known about it from their own sources. The 1972–1973 British Foreign Office memorandum overview of Katyn explains the Nazis' casual and inconsistent announcement of the burial site in those terms. Rohan Butler says that this level of Nazi–Soviet knowledge, if not mutual complicity, explains why 'the Germans would by 1943 have had the Russians trapped since, whatever else the latter said, they could hardly admit to their new Western Allies that they had butchered thousands of Poles at the suggestion, or with the connivance, of the Nazis'.[83]

Some of the German Ministry of Foreign Affairs' telegrams intercepted by British Intelligence during April–May 1940 have now been made public. Their content is predictable although one can appreciate the uncomfortable Anglo-American reactions to them at the time. A German propaganda instruction of 5 May 1943 to all stations ordered that the finding of the 10 000 bodies at Katyn be given 'the widest publicity'. The documentary evidence was to be presented so as to make the world understand 'what the peoples of EUROPE, delivered according to English and North American plans, to the SOVIET UNION, could expect from a victorious, drunken, Soviet army of occupation'.[84] In another circular of 22 May 1943 the Wilhelmstrasse (German Foreign Ministry) crowed over their 'resounding success' in reducing the Soviets to 'fairy-tales about archeological grave discoveries'. Katyn had provoked an open Polish–Soviet diplomatic split. The conflict could not be resolved as the Western Allies had already conceded the Soviet claim to Poland's eastern territories. The episode had exposed Soviet aims. These were 'the bolshevisation of POLAND and indeed of EUROPE, and further that it is still pursuing its claim to the immediate hegemony of eastern and southeastern Europe'.[85] In addition, it had revealed to the émigré Governments in London that banking on the British and Americans to oppose such Soviet ambitions was 'a complete illusion'. Another intercept, just after the Teheran Conference, linked reports of German guilt for Katyn in the British and Soviet press to the Soviet drive to force the Allies 'to adopt a compliant attitude in the Polish Question'. It was designed to force 'an English declaration that even the Polish Question will not be allowed to disturb her alliance with the SU'.[86] German propaganda directives refuted Burdenko's invention of the three interim holding camps through the total absence of any escapes by the Polish PoWs. It instructed that the 1941 execution date should be countered through use of the Buhtz exhumations and the Katyn White Book material.[87] The Germans also made use of Professor Georg von Wendt of Helsinki University who had examined corpses at Vinnitsa in summer 1943. He stated that the same shooting through the skull technique, demanding considerable skill, was evidenced at Katyn as at Vinnitsa. 'This type of execution is used in the Soviet Union only and is completely unknown in other countries.' Only the Bolsheviks possessed 'the skill which makes mass murder by shooting through the base of the skull possible'.[88]

The Burdenko Commission and the Soviet cover story

The Soviets established, in late 1943, an eight-strong Special Commission under the chairmanship of Nikolai Burdenko, after whom it is named, to establish *their truth* about Katyn. Lebedeva says that the initiative came from Georgi Alexandrov who headed the VKP (b) CC agitation and propaganda department. He wrote to deputy politburo member and Red

Army GPU head Aleksandr S. Scherbakov, on 22 September 1943, that preparations should be made to unmask the German provocation over Katyn. A special commission and investigation team should be ready to move in as soon as the Red Army had occupied the area.[89] Burdenko was a member of the Soviet Academy of Sciences, as was the writer (former Count) Aleksei Nikolayevich Tolstoy (1882–1945). Professor Burdenko was chosen, although now deaf, as he enjoyed a world-famous academic reputation as a neuro-surgeon who had founded the Institute of the Mind. Perhaps more importantly, he had acted as Stalin's and Molotov's personal physician. The Central Clinical Hospital of the Red Army was to be named after him. The other members were the Orthodox Metropolitan Nikolai who collaborated with the Soviet authorities in West Belarus and West Ukraine, Lieutenant-General Alexandr S. Gundorov (chairman of the Pan Slav Committee), Ivan A. Kolesnikov (chairman of the Soviet Red Cross and Red Crescent), Academician Vladimir Potemkin (Russian Federation Minister of Education and former Deputy-Minister of Foreign Affairs), Colonel-General Yefim I. Smirnov (Head of the Red Army's sanitary services) and R. Melnikov (Chairman of the Smolensk CPSU oblast executive committee).

Their work, was achieved quickly, in less than a month, as they had the full might of the Soviet state's forensic-pathological, police and other resources behind them. The report issued in Smolensk on 24 January 1944 was obviously conceived and prepared in Moscow. Lebedeva says that Merkulov took personal charge.[90] The Commission's brief was to ascertain and investigate 'the Circumstances of the Shooting of Polish Officer Prisoners by the German-Fascist Invaders in the Katyn Forest', and this they duly did.[91] The two local residents (out of seven) who remained under Soviet control now, hardly surprisingly, changed their testimony. They claimed that their evidence had been obtained by Gestapo beatings and threats. A whole host of new witnesses, totalling about 100, most of them lower-level Smolensk officials and three of the household staff in the NKVD guest house at Katyn, were produced to support the Soviet version and to fill in any gaps.[92] The Soviet medical-forensic team claimed to have exhumed 925 bodies and pronounced on their identity and mode and time of death on this basis.[93]

The Soviet cover story endorsed by Burdenko, which dominated the communist world until 1990, and which was much believed outside it as well, was based on a central lie concerning the time of death. This was that the Poles had been killed two, not three, years earlier, 'between September and December 1941'. Inconsistencies abound on this point as the cover story was manufactured by various hands and rushed out quite hurriedly. Some of the witnesses gave August 1941 as the execution date. This, naturally, raised difficulties and caused further adjustments to the cover story, concerning the winter clothing and military greatcoats in which the PoWs were shot and buried.

The Soviet Burdenko version of Katyn is as follows: it started with some fairy tales about the Katyn forest and the River Dnieper banks being a popular, unrestricted and long-established rest and holiday area for Smolensk citizens. The nub of the Soviet case was that the Polish PoWs were engaged in road building and maintenance work in the Smolensk area in summer 1941. They were housed in three, never exactly located, camps 1-ON, 2-ON and 3-ON, situated 25–45 kilometres west of Smolensk. These camps were a wholly fictitious NKVD invention. They were never mentioned in the Polish–Soviet exchanges of 1941–1943 nor were they reported on by any Pole in the USSR. In the Soviet version, recycled, after two attempts, in a more polished form at Nuremberg, the German 537th Engineering or 'working' battalion commanded by a Colonel Arnes, aided by two lieutenants called Rex (or Rekst) and Hott, established its HQ in the NKVD guest house at Katyn and about 30 German officers took up residence there. This unit was alleged to have captured the Poles (all of them without exception!) and to have brought them to be shot and buried at Katyn. Local witnesses duly confirmed various sightings of Polish PoWs at Katyn and sounds of gunfire during a month-long period. The next stage of the Soviet story concerned the digging up in spring 1943 of the Polish remains by 500 Soviet PoWs, selected from an alleged German prison camp number 126, who were shot, subsequently, by the Germans. The exercise involved the Germans going through the remains and removing any evidence which contained, or indicated, a date later than April 1940. The Germans organised excursions by the local people of Smolensk to view the corpses. Some of them later testified to Burdenko that they were struck by how shiny and relatively unworn the Polish army uniforms looked! After this, the Germans reburied the bodies carefully and concealed any evidence that they had been disturbed.

The above account was supported by the findings of the Soviet Forensic-Medicine team which worked at Katyn from 16 to 23 January 1944. It confirmed that the Poles had been killed by shots to the back of the head by heavy calibre pistols but claimed that this was in keeping with German methods of executing Soviet citizens. The Soviet doctors claimed to have found evidence that the bodies were disturbed in spring–summer 1943 but that the Germans had not been completely thorough in searching the bodies. Nine items dated later than April 1940 were allegedly found, and detailed, in the report. The earliest was a letter dated 12 October (not November as given by Zawodny) 1940 while the latest was an unsent card dated 20 June 1941 addressed to Ulica Bagatella in Warsaw; the remainder included camp 1-ON receipts.[94] The failed sender was the only name (Captain Stanisław Kuczyński, number 53) actually amongst the list of those identified in 1943. The central and crucial conclusion that the Poles were killed in autumn 1941 was asserted simply as having been confirmed by the medical evidence.

The Soviets accepted the false German figure of 11 000 corpses at Katyn in order to confuse the issue and to cover up the threefold locations of the 1940 massacre. This was despite the identification of solely Kozelsk inmates at Katyn by the International and PRC Commissions. The Burdenko version will be discussed further under the Nuremberg heading. Here one can follow Zawodny in pointing to the three major omissions concerning the replanting of the trees, the Soviet-type bayonet wounds and the Soviet origins of the ropes.[95] The weaknesses and inconsistencies in the Burdenko Report were dissected in full in the April 1989 Report of the Polish members of the Joint Polish–Soviet Historical Commission established to examine 'Blank Spots' in their relationship.[96]

The Soviets, like the Germans before them, also invited foreign observers to Katyn. A group of about 20 journalists, all British and American (except for a Frenchman and the Polish communist editor of *Wolna Polska* and subsequent PRL cultural notable Jerzy Borejsza), included John Melby, the Third Secretary of the American Embassy and Kathleen Harriman, the 25-year-old daughter of the millionaire Averill Harriman, who was US ambassador to the USSR at the time. This group was in no position to draw any substantive conclusions. Their trip was short and superficial and the atmosphere was somewhat strained. The silly Harriman girl, however, allowed herself to be used by Roosevelt and the State Department, subsequently, in support of the thesis of German guilt.[97] Another participant in this visit, Alexander Werth, became a well-known Soviet specialist and journalist based in the United Kingdom. The publication of an edited Russian translation of his massive *Russia at War* just squeezed in at the end of the second phase of destalinisation in the USSR in 1966.[98] His criticism of the weak, shoddy and unconvincing presentation of the Soviet case by Burdenko was published as it did not tackle the central issue of Soviet responsibility directly. The British embassy in Moscow reported that the journalists, while initially willing to accept the Soviet case, had not been impressed by what they saw and heard. Witnesses were clearly intimidated and 'told their tale before the same people and repeated it parrotwise'. The Soviet case was based entirely on the credibility of the medical evidence which could not be challenged. Unexpected questions by the journalists caused their hosts 'noticeable irritation'. The embassy was concerned that resulting press criticism of Burdenko might cause Soviet 'explosions'.[99]

One interesting, and much quoted, epilogue to Burdenko surfaced in the Russian exile press in the USA in June 1950.[100] Boris Olshanskii, a Voronezh University academic and Stalingrad and Belarusan Front Red Army veteran, had succeeded in defecting from the Soviet Zone of Germany. Olshanskii claimed to have been a close and long-established family friend of Burdenko's and to have visited the ailing surgeon, who had suffered two strokes, in Moscow just before his death in 1946. Burdenko is reported as having said that Mother Russia's soil was full of Katyns. Stalin had personally ordered him to visit Katyn to refute the German accusation. The medical evidence of 'his spot check' was clearly that all the Polish bodies were four years old. Such unsupported hearsay evidence is unprovable even though it was repeated in 1952 before the US Congress committee investigating Katyn.[101] In words reminiscent of Merkulov's admission to Berling, Burdenko allegedly said that 'our comrades from the NKVD made a great blunder'.

Soviet failure at Nuremberg

The four victorious Allies agreed at the Special London Conference of 26 June–8 August 1945, which prepared the Nuremberg Tribunal, that the USSR would prosecute German crimes against humanity. As they were also responsible for prosecuting atrocities committed in Eastern Europe the Katyn Question fell within their remit. The Soviets had the charge that the Germans killed 11 000 (originally 925) Polish officer PoWs in September 1941 at Katyn included in Count Three of the Allied Indictment of German War Criminals of 18 October 1945. The Chief Soviet Prosecutor, General Rudenko, and his deputy, Colonel Pokrovskii, read the Burdenko Commission report into the trial proceedings as evidence.[102] The American, British and French prosecutors advised Rudenko not to proceed with the charge and included it, with his amended figures, very reluctantly.[103] The court considered Katyn on 13–14 February, and again on 8 March and 1–3 July 1946.[104] Offers by General Anders and the London Government to produce relevant evidence, including crucial witnesses such as Professor Świaniewicz, were ignored.[105]

After considerable legal argument over Pokrovskii's wish to proceed solely on the basis of written affidavits and controversy about the admissibility of witnesses it was agreed that the Soviet and German sides would present three witnesses apiece.[106] The Soviet witnesses were carefully chosen, coached and prepared in Moscow by the Government Commission, chaired by Vyshinsky, who had been given responsibility for managing the Soviet delegation at Nuremberg.[107] Professor Viktor Prozorovskii, the head of the Forensic-Medicine section of the Soviet Ministry of Health, had carried out many of the Katyn autopsies for the Burdenko Commission. He testified that the Poles had undoubtedly been killed in autumn 1941. The astronomy professor Boris Bazilevskii had been nominated as deputy mayor of Smolensk by the Germans and had testified particulars about the alleged camp 126 to Burdenko. He claimed to have heard from his superior, Smolensk Mayor Boris Menshagin, that the Polish PoWs had been shot by the Germans.[108] Bazilevskii asserted that they had been in the Kozelsk camp in August 1940. The most important Soviet witness, Dr Markov, the Bulgarian member of the International Commission, agreed to all Prosecutor Smirnov's leading questions.[109] His evidence that the International Commission had been presented with already exhumed bodies and had signed only under German pressure was to be refuted later by Drs Naville and Tramsen.

The German witnesses demolished the Soviet case against them. Colonel Friedrich Ahrens (not Arnes) demonstrated that he was not in command of the unit at the time that it was held responsible for the massacre as he was on the Western Front.[110] Colonel Albert Bedenk, the Smolensk area commander prior to Ahrens, and their superior, General Eugen Oberhauser, proved the following: the military unit referred to by Burdenko was the 537th Signals Regiment which established a 17–20-strong communications centre in the Katyn guest house in late August 1941.[111] Apparently, they became aware that the nearby forest was an execution and burial site, but at what point in 1942 they learnt sufficiently from local residents to report the presence of Polish PoW bodies to their superiors is unclear. After these exchanges, the Katyn issue quite simply vanished from the Nuremberg proceedings. All mention was omitted from the final verdict on 30 September 1946.[112] Soviet inability to have responsibility attributed to the Germans was a sure indicator of growing disagreements within the erstwhile wartime alliance and the onset of the Cold War. The émigré Polish conclusion that as German guilt had not been established at Nuremberg then the Soviets were responsible by default was, unfortunately, not to prove as compelling as they had hoped.[113]

The US Congress hearings

The Polish community or *Polonia* in the USA was estimated as numbering anything between six and eight million citizens of Polish origins at the end of the Second World War.[114] It did not speak or vote with a single voice but it had traditionally been heavily Democrat and it still represented a powerful political *bloc*. Its flagship organisation, the Polish American Congress (PAC) established in 1944, opposed the Western Allies' acceptance of the establishment of communist rule. Its president, Charles Rozmarek, and its leaders regarded the 1940 massacre as an essential preliminary step by the Soviets in Poland's subordination. Their efforts to have the issue examined were rebuffed by Truman's administration and the State Department on numerous occasions during the late 1940s.[115] The Berlin Blockade, the growing evidence of Sovietisation in Eastern Europe and the consequent onset of the Cold War, however, produced a more favourable political atmosphere.

The turning point came with a series of articles by the journalist Julius Epstein in the *New York Herald-Tribune* during July 1949.[116] Epstein, who became a very assiduous and effective lobbyist for the Polish cause, had his call for an inquiry into the Katyn affair taken up by politicians representing both parties in Congress. Arthur Bliss Lane, the American ambassador to Poland, who had resigned in protest at the country's Sovietisation, spearheaded the establishment of the bi-partisan American Committee for the Investigation of the Katyn Massacre (sometimes referred to as the Lane Committee).[117] He was supported by the Trotskyist writer Max

Eastman. With the trial of Alger Hiss, the start of Senator Joseph McCarthy's anti-communist witch hunt in 1950 and, above all, the outbreak of the Korean War, the resistance of the New Deal liberals to an inquest on Roosevelt's Second World War stewardship was broken. Unfortunately, the cause of the objective truth about Katyn remained highly politicised, but now from a different direction. It was subordinated to the search for culprits in the alleged conspiracy which had sold out Eastern Europe to Stalin. An influential American newspaper wrote that 'a Congressional investigation can add little to the known facts, but it can achieve an important service by discovering who, among the military and civilian officials responsible to Roosevelt and Truman, succeeded in withholding the facts from the American people for so long'.[118] The British FO view centred around the aphorism that the committee's purpose was 'to make anti-Soviet propaganda in the guise of a legal inquiry'.[119]

The House of Representatives voted unanimously on 18 September 1951 to establish a seven-strong Select Committee to 'conduct an investigation of the facts, evidence and circumstances of the Katyn Forest massacre'. All its members, chaired by the Indiana Democrat Ray Madden, represented constituencies containing high percentages of Polish Americans. The other Democrats, who held the majority in the House at the time, were Daniel J. Flood (Pennsylvania), (John) Foster Furcolo (Massachusetts) and the Polish-born Tadeusz (Thaddeus) Michael Machrowicz (Michigan). The Republicans were George A. Dondero (Michigan), Alvin Edward O'Konski (originally Okonski! – Wisconsin) and Timothy P. Sheehan (Illinois). The committee had the normal powers of subpoena over witnesses and documents. Its chief counsel was John J. Mitchell, of later Watergate infamy. The very active young Chicago lawyer and future Democratic congressman from Illinois Roman Conrad Pucinski (1919–2002) became its chief investigator.

The committee held hearings from January to December 1952 during the height of the Korean War so, hardly surprisingly, its evidence and conclusions were related to current perceptions of the Chinese communist threat and North Korean mistreatment of American PoWs.[120] Lieutenant Colonel Donald Stewart, the American PoW who had been brought to Katyn by the Germans, along with Van Vliet, in May 1943, testified his firm conviction that the Soviets were responsible, in October 1951.[121] The committee heard 81 witnesses, read over a hundred witness statements and 183 documents into its report and also heard another 200 interested individuals. The net result was a compendium of seven massive volumes of relevant evidence on Katyn and American–Soviet relations focussed around the Polish Question during the Second World War.

The committee, in order to hear European witnesses, also held hearings in London (in private due to British Government objections), Naples and Frankfurt-on-Main. The most important were members of the International Commission. Dr Palmieri confirmed that all the signs indicated that the Poles had been killed between March and May 1940.[122] The bodies were squeezed together like sardines and it was, therefore, impossible that the Germans could have doctored the documents on them as claimed by the Soviets. Dr Tramsen testified that the mummification of the bodies caused by the pressure of sand and of other bodies on them confirmed beyond all doubt that the Poles had been buried in the winter clothing in which they had been killed.[123] The shape of the cuts on some of the bodies indicated that they had been caused by Soviet-type bayonets. Drs Palmieri and Tramsen, along with Drs Naville,[124] Orsos[125] and Miloslavic,[126] when questioned, confirmed the voluntary nature of their testimony, the absence of German pressure and the unanimous nature of their conclusions that the Poles had been killed in spring 1940. The latter was particularly important. Tramsen and Orsos testified that Drs Markov and Hajek had agreed fully with all these findings at the time.

The committee interviewed almost everyone of significance in the Katyn affair on the American and Polish émigré sides, particularly those whose voices had been muzzled during the Second World War. They included witnesses, some of whom we have already mentioned, and who we will revert to again, such as Lieutenant Colonel Van Vliet,[127] Colonel Henry Szymanski, ex-Governor of Pennsylvania George H. Earle, Major General Clayton Bissell, Justice Robert H. Jackson who had prosecuted at the Nuremberg Supreme Court, Under-Secretary of State Sumner Welles and Ambassadors Averill Harriman and Arthur Bliss Lane. Notable Polish figures included Ambassadors Stanisław Kot, Tadeusz Romer and Edward Raczyński, Generals Władysław Anders, Marian Kukiel, Tadeusz Bór-Komorowski and Zygmunt Bohusz-Szyszko, and Dr Kazimierz Skarzyński. The three German officers questioned at Nuremberg, General Friedrich Oberhauser, Colonel Friedrich Ahrens and Colonel Albert Bedenk, amplified their stories. Kathleen Harriman (now Mrs Mortimer), under extensive questioning by Congressman Machrowicz, changed the view attributed to her by the US embassy in Moscow and the State Department in 1944 and now, accepted Soviet guilt.[128] Her colleague, during the January 1944 visit, Henry Clarence Cassidy, the well-known Moscow Press Bureau chief, admitted that he had reported the Soviet version, even though, he had not been convinced by it.

The committee's interim report of 2 July 1952 had already branded the Soviet NKVD as responsible for committing the Katyn massacre, not later than spring 1940.[129] The British FO deprecated the inconclusive, one-sided and contradictory evidence on which it was based. The committee had 'an obvious political bias and has not been drawn up in an exclusively judicial fashion'.[130] Its Final Report, submitted on 22 December 1952, sent four recommendations to the White House.[131] The Katyn documentation should be sent to all UN delegates. The US Permanent Representative should present the issue at the UN's General Assembly and propose that the International Court of Justice charge the Soviet Union with the Katyn massacre. More generally, the committee recommended the establishment of an International Commission to investigate crimes against humanity. The USSR was denounced for 'one of the most barbarous international crimes in world history'.

Given the growing atmosphere of Korean and Cold War hysteria which fuelled McCarthyism, the committee was now even more concerned to reveal the State and War Department's cover-up of the truth about Katyn which had allowed Roosevelt's White House to follow Stalin's line on Katyn and to abandon the London Poles at Teheran and Yalta. The eight major sources which should have allowed the Roosevelt administration to form a clear picture of Soviet responsibility for Katyn will be discussed further in the following chapter. Here one might note that the committee blamed the administration's 'strange psychosis' and pro-Soviet mindset caused by its overriding desire to maintain the Soviet war effort; this led to the suppression of inconvenient evidence, information and contrary voices as well as the abandonment of Allies. The consequent 'tragic concessions at Yalta' sacrificed Eastern Europe but failed to secure an acceptable post-war settlement based on the Atlantic Charter and United Nations principles. The Republicans used Roosevelt's conspiracy of silence, and worse, over Katyn as part of their 1952 election campaign designed to win over East European ethnic voters away from the Democrats.

Katyn bibliographically – the Crusade for the Truth within and outside the Soviet Bloc

The best public examination of the Katyn evidence which emerged during 1943–1952, until the Russian documentation and Lebedeva's and Abarinov's accounts became available after 1990, was Zawodny's *Death in the Forest*.[132] The British Foreign Office and political elite had, however, the benefit of the second of Ambassador Owen O'Malley's major reports on Katyn.[133] It is worth spending some time on this seven-page-long document as its 12 sections still provide one of the best-informed and most economic and judicious dissections of the 1943–1944 evidence. O'Malley contrasts the German with the Soviet Burdenko method of dealing with Katyn. The Germans brought in a fairly large international commission of pathologists and criminologists to establish their findings and allowed the resultant evidence to be tested by wide-based delegations of Poles. The Burdenko Commission was, however, composed solely of eight Soviet officials and notables aided by five Soviet medical experts. The Germans allowed repeated access to foreign observers and journalists while the Soviets allowed only a single short visit by the Harriman-Melby press group. O'Malley felt that while 'no definite conclusions' could be drawn from the greater breadth of access by the Germans, the fact that the Poles, who hated Germans and Russians equally, were convinced produced a slight initial presumption that 'a guilty conscience' was responsible for the limited and controlled Soviet access. Given the knowledge of the brutality of both German and Russian police methods and their mutual capacity to intimidate witnesses and to produce favourable evidence O'Malley was right not to get involved in this dimension. About nine-tenths of the Burdenko Report was composed of this questionable type of witness statements – another weakness in the Soviet case. The current author agrees that it is 'futile to appraise the trustworthiness of the testimony of witnesses' for both sides. I have, therefore, eschewed doing so, although the reader should remember that an enormous part of the Katyn literature up until 1990 does just that.

O'Malley identified the following discrepancies between the German/International Commission and Soviet forensic findings. Both claimed to have exhumed roughly the same number of corpses, 982 and 925 respectively. The Germans found that there were 'varying degrees of decomposition of the bodies' and that this, together with changes in the skulls, indicated that the Poles had been killed three years previously. The Soviets claimed that as no bodies had decayed or disintegrated they could not have been buried 'for long'; the killings, therefore, took place 'between September and December 1941'. The Germans found no documentation on the corpses dated later than 22 April 1940 – the Soviets discovered papers dated between 12 September 1940 and 20 June 1941. As a result O'Malley dismissed 'as more or less unreliable the verbal accounts of supposed witnesses and the findings of the scientific commissions on both sides'.

O'Malley considered the Burdenko cover story that the Poles had been moved to the three camps around Smolensk in April–May 1940 and had engaged in road building work before being captured by the Germans in July 1941 and shot by them over the following four months as possible, but 'defective'. The 'incredible' flaw in the account was that 10000 Polish PoWs had allegedly lived and worked in the Smolensk region for over a year without a single one ever escaping, even during the confusion of the German takeover. 'Not a single one ... was ever seen or heard of alive again' despite Burdenko's description of German round-ups of escaped Polish prisoners. Apart from the Gryazovets survivors not a single communication was ever received from the three main camps after April 1940 nor was there a single satisfactory reply to over 500 Red Cross inquiries or to the repeated official Polish queries concerning the latter. The conclusions reiterated those stated in his more important report of 24 May 1943: although there could be no certainty as to who murdered the Polish PoWs at Katyn cumulative weaknesses undermined the credibility of the Soviet case. 'The defective nature' of the Burdenko Report 'makes these doubts even stronger than before.'

There is one final piece of hard evidence that was known to Western elites in the 1940s but which only really entered the public domain in the

1990s in a major way with the publication of Wacław Godziemba-Maliszewski's study.[134] The Luftwaffe archives were captured by the Western Allies in 1945 and examined by the British and American Intelligence Services. Reconnaissance overflight photographs of Soviet territory were found amongst other documentation.[135] The British studied them at RAF Medmenham as part of an intelligent assessment exercise called 'Dick Tracy'. The flight path over the area surrounding Katyn was stamped 'Confidential' no less than 11 times. Zawodny's private papers contain correspondence with Godziemba-Maliszewski which concludes that 'at Medmenham they saw ineluctable ground signatures on the terrain of Katyn that existed prior to the German invasion of June 1941'.[136] This is 'first hand evidence' that British and American governing circles knew that 'the elite of their Polish Ally were murdered by the Soviet Union' and not by the Germans.

The literature on Katyn from 1943 to 1990 falls under four main headings.[137] First, there was an enormous amount of personal testimony, mainly by Poles who had been in the USSR during the Second World War or who had been involved with the Government-in-Exile. Second, there were a limited number of studies notably by Zawodny, FitzGibbon and De Montfort who at various times succeeded in synthesising the state of knowledge on the issue at an academically acceptable level. Gorbachev's *Glasnost*, encouraging the growth of a Polish–Soviet campaign to tackle historical 'blank spots' such as Katyn and the Ribbentrop–Molotov Pact, only arrived by the late 1980s. The main work of this period, Czesław Madajczyk's *Dramat Katyński*, was quickly left behind by the documentary revelations.[138] Third, there were numerous sensationalist contributions, some outright forgeries, which purported to shed new light on the massacre. Lastly, there was a growth of dissident literature within the PRL, roughly from the time of the formation of the Workers' Defence Committee (KOR) in 1976. The main inspiration for this movement crystallised with the publication of Jerzy Łojek's pioneering essay by the independent dissident press.[139] After the Solidarity outburst, individuals emerged in the 1980s grouped around the Katyn Committee and publications like the *Biuletyn Katyńskie* who devoted themselves to what can appropriately be called no less than a crusade to establish the truth about Katyn.

The most important memoirs directly connected with Katyn are four works by survivors (Czapski, Młynarski, Peszkowski and Świaniewicz) which throw light on conditions and Soviet organisation and behaviour in the three special camps.[140] A related category are the scraps of diaries and notes kept by PoWs in Kozelsk. Those which have survived were taken from their corpses at Katyn and are now part of the Robel Collection.[141] The general framework for the 1940 massacre and its consequences are covered by a whole string of political memoirs, notably by Anders, Bohusz-Szyszko, Bór-Komorowski, Churchill, Ciechanowski, Goetel, Korbonski, Kot, Lane, Maisky, Mikołajczyk and Raczyński whose full details are set out in the bibliography. For obvious reasons Soviet and PRL memoirs, even exceptional reminiscences such as Khruschev's or, more questionably, Gomułka's, during the Cold War could throw almost no meaningful light on the subject while defectors' evidence usually only muddied already stagnant waters.

The general analyses are drawn on, and considered, throughout this study as are the various falsifications and *culs-de-sac* which plagued the subject before *Glasnost*. The intra-systemic struggle in the PRL for the truth about Katyn and the 1940 massacre will be discussed in Chapter Eight. Here one needs to observe that the primary sources derived from the investigations and reports discussed above set sharp and clear limits for what could be known by the time Zawodny wrote the authoritative Cold War account in 1962. This applied, in particular, to the London Polish documentary collections (notably *Katyn in the Light of Documents*, which under less contested political circumstances would have been accepted as definitive within the strict limits of the available material of the time, and the AK and Government-in-Exile diplomatic documents) which were all published by about 1960. The official publications of German and American Second World War diplomatic documents did little more than confirm the historical context. The subject was given a renewed boost by the publication, according to the Thirty Years' Rule, of some, although not all, its Katyn documentation by the British Foreign Office after 1972. This fuelled the Katyn Memorial controversy but again, FitzGibbon's *Unpitied and Unknown* (1975) marked the limit of what was, or could be, known until Gorbachev. The 1940 massacre thus became a historical quagmire after the respective Polish, Soviet and German templates were established in 1943–1944.[142] Nuremberg and the US Congressional Committee contributed little of additional value. Only the collapse of communism, which permitted the retrieval and publication of key Soviet documents, allowed the basic truth about the whole of the 1940 massacre to be confirmed. The *Katyn: Documents Concerning the Atrocity* series has performed an enormous service in publicising this aspect but important gaps, indicated in this study, still remain. Victor Zaslavsky rightly says that 'the publication of these documents eliminates, once and for all, the mountain of lies and disinformation'.[143]

Forgeries, megalomaniacs, dead ends and pseudo-experts

Apart from official state forgeries, such as the Burdenko Commission, the historiography of the 1940 massacre is littered with two other types of obfuscatory material. One is the appearance of unofficial forgeries or *apocrypha*, a limited number of which proved difficult to expose for considerable periods of time, because of the unclear status of the whole question. The other, given the fog of information and the unclear and malleable framework, is a whole range of testimonies whose significance and/or authenticity was difficult to judge at the time they were offered.

Without any doubt the main example of the first category is the so-called Tartakov forgery, which was first published in an obscure and sensationalist West German weekly in 1957.[144] This purported to be a half-page-long report, dated 10 June 1940, signed by a certain Tartakov, the secretary (*sic!*) of the Minsk oblast NKVD, to the Main Department of the NKVD in Moscow (*sic!*). It reported that the Main Department's orders of 12 February 1940 to liquidate the PoW camps in Kozelsk, Ostashkov and Starobelsk had been carried out, and completed on 6 June. The operation had been directed by an official called Burianov, sent from Moscow. He had used the Minsk security services and the 190th battalion of 'territorial troops' to liquidate the Kozelsk inmates in Smolensk between 1 March and 3 May. Ostashkov had been liquidated by the Smolensk NKVD, secured by the 129th battalion, in Bologoe, who completed the action on 5 June. The Starobelsk prisoners were killed by the Kharkov NKVD, commanded by Colonel Kuchkov and supported by the 68th Ukrainian Rifle Regiment, in a hamlet called Dergachii by 2 June. Copies of the report had been sent to Generals Raikhman (Reikhman) and Zarubin.

The provenance of this leaked document was allegedly the entourage of Prosecutor Martini in Kraków who found this document in his papers after his murder.[145] Despite inquiries by various Russian and Polish scholars and journalists in the 1990s the real source and circumstances of this forgery have never been revealed. Its fabricators seem extremely well informed. The dates and execution locales would have seemed wholly credible in the 1950s and 1960s. The names of the NKVD executioners were thought up but Reikhman and Zarubin certainly existed and, as we have seen, played roles in the massacre and its subsequent cover-up. One can only speculate, that the most likely explanation is that it was produced by a rogue element, probably, made up of ex-members of either West German or American Intelligence, supported by Polish émigrés, although not necessarily of Second World War vintage. There has been speculation that Minsk NKVD personnel were involved at Katyn and, also, that the Nazis had captured their archive, although the latter has never been confirmed.[146]

The Tartakov document is a farrago of lies and inventions which has been disproved completely by the post-1990 Russian and NKVD documentation. At the time, it seemed a fairly credible version of what had happened, and as such was taken seriously by Zawodny.[147] For FitzGibbon the important message in this document was the revelation that the 1940 massacre had been carried out in three separate sites, one for each of the camps.[148] The Nazi and Soviet mystifications that all the PoWs, and not just the Kozelsk ones, had perished at Katyn, was now replaced by firmer evidence that the Starobelsk inmates had been buried at Kharkov and the Ostashkov ones at Bologoe, 70 miles to the north of Kalinin. Although FitzGibbon did not quite get the specific details of the latter right, and gave too much credence to the possibility that some PoWs had been drowned in barges in the White Sea, his interpretation was eventually proved to be on the right sort of lines. FitzGibbon's speculative insight was correct even though his source was totally false.

One of the glaring weaknesses in Butler's FO Memorandum discussed in the following chapter is the author's failure to examine and give due weight to the Polish sources on Katyn. He also conflates the German and Polish versions and does not differentiate and bring out the essential differences between them. In particular, many of the scholarly criteria for privileging primary over secondary, or even tertiary, sources seem to have deserted him on numerous occasions. On the other hand, if either the German or the Soviet party could have done the deed the criteria for judging the importance or relevance of specific witnesses proved very slippery indeed. As a result, the Katyn literature is littered with shadowy, often shady, individuals and testimony which is reported in case it were to prove significant. Clearly, a certain Abraham Vidro's hearsay claim to have heard an NKVD agent (Major Sorokin) boasting in a Soviet labour camp, of his role in the Katyn massacre should have been regarded as potentially less significant than the Menshagin sightings.[149] The same applies to self-publicisers such as Henry Metelmann, a German who fought on the Eastern Front and settled in England. He offered his opinion, gleefully taken up by the British FO, that his military colleagues believed that the Nazis had themselves killed the Poles at Katyn.[150] Another interesting *canard* concerned the existence of an NKVD training film based on the Katyn shootings. In one particularly absurd version it was allegedly shown in the Chinese embassy in Warsaw in 1964 or 1965.[151] Such rumours were potentially less interesting than the claim of a Pole to have befriended Stalin's son, Jakub Dzugashvili, in a German PoW camp. Jerzy Lewczewski told the US Congressional Committee that the latter had told him that the Katyn murders were 'a government necessity'.[152] Zawodny sidestepped the difficulties resulting from the fog of witnesses of varying levels of importance and reliability by concentrating parsimoniously on the central Polish, German and Soviet testimony, hence the convincing character of his account for so depressingly long.

Notes

1 The British role in Soviet–Polish relations in this period is traced out very, perhaps far too, judiciously in Llewellyn Woodward, *British Foreign Policy in the Second World War*, vol. 2, London: HMSO, 1971.

2 For the latter see *Documents on Polish–Soviet Relations, Volume 1, 1939–1943*, London: Sikorski Institute, 1961. Stanislaw Kot, *Conversations with the Kremlin and Dispatches from Russia*, London: Oxford UP, 1963. I am familiar with their originals in the Sikorski Institute in London which overlap with the Hoover Institute's 'Eastern Archive' (Berkeley, California) which has now been micro-filmed and made available in the Archiwum Akt Nowych in Warsaw.

3 DPSR, 1, nos 89, 90, 91, 94.
4 DPSR, 1, no. 105.
5 DPSR, 1, no. 110.
6 KDZ, 3, no. 198.
7 See Anita Prazmowska, *Britain and Poland, 1939–1943: The Betrayed Ally*, Cambridge: Cambridge UP, 1995. John Coutouvidis and Jaime Reynolds, *Poland, 1939–1947*, Leicester: Leicester UP, 1986. George Kacewitch, *Great Britain, the Soviet Union and the Polish Government in Exile (1939–1945)*, The Hague: Martinus Nijhof, 1979. Jan Karski, *The Great Powers and Poland, 1919–1939*, Lanham, NJ: UP of America, 1985. Edward Raczynski, *In Allied London*, London: Weidenfeld & Nicolson, 1962.
8 Natalia Lebediewa, '60 lat fałszowania i zatajania historii zbrodni Katyńskiej', in *Zbrodnia Katyńska po 60 latach*, Warsaw: NKHBZK, 2000, p. 105.
9 DPSR, 1, pp. 173–4, no. 130. KDZ, 3, nos 208, 209. Kot, *Conversations with the Kremlin*, p. 105.
10 DPSR, 1, no. 149. Kot, *Conversations with the Kremlin*, pp. 106–16.
11 The Soviet record, which otherwise corresponds fairly closely to the Polish one, contains no mention of this particular episode, KDZ, 3, no. 212.
12 DPSR, 1, nos 150, 153, p. 230.
13 DPSR, 1, no. 159: Kot, *Conversations with the Kremlin*, pp. 140–55: KDZ, 3, pp. 499–509.
14 FRUS, 1942, vol. III, pp. 100–4.
15 DPSR, 1, no. 161.
16 Sikorski to Churchill, 17 December 1941, DPSR, 1.
17 Sikorski's report of 12 January 1942 to the Council of Ministers, DPSR, 1, no. 171.
18 Wojciech Materski (ed.), *Armia Polska w ZSSR, 1941–1942*, Warsaw: ISP PAN, 1992.
19 Ibid., pp. 19–31. *Polscy jeńcy wojenni w ZSSR, 1939–1941*, Warsaw: ISP PAN, 1992, p. 95.
20 DPSR, 1, nos 177, 192: Raczyński note 49/Sow/42 of 28 January 1942 and Bogomolov note MC57 of 13 March 1942 HIEA AAN.
21 Molotov to the ambassador to the Polish Government-in-Exile, Bogomolov, 21 March 1942, *Armia Polska w ZSSR*, pp. 79–80.
22 Beria to Stalin, 4 April 1942, KDZ, 3, p. 542, no. 240. Also in *Armia Polska w ZSSR*, pp. 91, 107.
23 DPSR, 1, no. 251, p. 426.
24 DPSR, 1, no. 157.
25 DPSR, 1, no. 295, subsequent discussions during March, ibid., 1, nos 299, 300.
26 DPSR, 1, no. 277.
27 DPSR, 1, no. 305.
28 Cf. *Armia Krajowa w dokumentach, 1939–1945*, vol. II, *czerwiec 1941–kwiecień 1945*, London: Studium Polski Podziemnej, 1973, p. 500.
29 Frank Roberts, annotation of 7 June 1943 to O'Malley to Eden no. 51, 24 May 1943, PRO PREM3/353 C6160/258/55.
30 Eden to Churchill, 24 February 1944, FO371/39390 C2099/8/55.
31 Soviet Information Bureau communiqué of 15 April 1940, DPSR, 1, no. 306.
32 Minister of National Defence communiqué, DPSR, 1, no. 307.
33 Polish Government statement of 17 April 1943 concerning the discovery of the graves of the Polish officers near Smolensk, DPSR, 1, no. 308.
34 Minister Raczyński to the Soviet ambassador in London, Bogomolov, 20 April 1943, DPSR, no. 309.
35 Some authors blame the *Daily Telegraph* for breaking the news of the Polish request to the Red Cross on 16 April 1943 ahead of the planned Polish

timetable for releasing the news. This allowed the Germans to get in their request only an hour after the Polish one, thus giving the impression of a joint manoeuvre, as Goebbels had fully intended. Alexandra Kwiatkowska-Viatteau, *1940–1943, Katyn: L'Armée Polonaise Assassinée*, Brussels: Editions Complexe, 1982, pp. 22–3.

36 DPSR, 1, nos 314, 319.
37 Stalin telegram to Churchill, 21 April 1943, FO371/34569 C484569258/55: DPSR, 1, no. 310.
38 Churchill to Stalin, 24 April 1943, DPSR, no. 312.
39 Cf. DPSR, 1, nos 313, 315, 316, 318.
40 FO371/34570 C4668/258/55.
41 Raczyński to William Strang, 8 October 1943, HIEA AAN.
42 Janusz Zawodny, *Death in the Forest*, London: Macmillan, 1971, p. 17.
43 *Amtliches Material zum Massenmord von Katyn*, Berlin: F. Eher Nachf., 1943, pp. 114–35.
44 *Zbrodnia Katyńska w świetle dokumentów*, London: Gryf, 1948, pp. 144–8.
45 Ibid., pp. 150–6.
46 Henri de Montfort, *Masakra w Katyniu*, Warsaw, NKHBZK, 1999, pp. 59–69.
47 Markov also repeated his crucial new testimony, that the barely decomposed state of the bodies indicated that they had been killed much less than three years previously, at Nuremberg on 1 July 1946, *Zbrodnia Katyńska w świetle dokumentów*, pp. 148–50.
48 Louis FitzGibbon, *Unpitied and Unknown: Katyn – Bologoye – Dergachi*, London: Bachman & Turner, 1975, pp. 153–9.
49 Markov and Hajek were lucky, as demonstrated by the fate of the Croatian medical specialist Professor of Anatomy and Pathology Ljudevit Jurak of Zagreb University. He attended the site of the Vinnitsa massacre in 1943 and commented on Katyn in the Croatian press on his return. He was shot by the Titoists for anti-Soviet propaganda after a drum head trial in 1945, www.geocities.com/athens/troy/1791/jurak.html.
50 SD/AK874 of 22 June 1943, PRO HS4/212. The agent also forwarded a detailed diary of Tramsen's activities at Katyn over the 27 April to 4 May period, PRO HS4/137.
51 Cf. De Montfort, *Masakra w Katyniu*, pp. 70–87.
52 *Zbrodnia Katyńska w świetle dokumentów*, pp. 157–88. Apart from the Kraków team other participants included Stefan Cupryjak and Mikołajczyk from the Executive Committee of the Polish Red Cross in Warsaw, the brother of General Smorawiński who personally identified his sibling's body, as well as a number of individuals who had made their separate ways to Katyn (Stefan Kasura, Jerzy Wodziński, Gracjan Jaworowsky, Adam Godzik and Captain Ludwik Rojkiewicz, who later perished in a Nazi street execution).
53 German *General-Gouvernement* officials put the RGO under strong pressure to send a full delegation to Katyn and, after it returned, to establish anti-Soviet collaboration. These overtures were spurned by the pro-London Government Poles, see Bogdan Kroll, *Rada Główna Opiekuńcza, 1939–1945*, Warsaw: KiW, 1985. The Germans apparently had better luck with two actual collaborators, Anatol Słowikowski and Zbigniew Grad, who they flew in separately to Katyn. Both were liquidated by the AK in September 1943 in Warsaw, Jacek Wilamowski, *Kłamstwo stulecia: W cieniu Katynia*, Warsaw: Agencja Wydawnicza CB, 2003, p. 40. Amongst a confusing number of parallel Polish drafts produced by the Katyn visitors, Seyfried's was the earliest. He reported back to the RGO immediately on his return to Warsaw on 13 April, see *Życie Warszawy*, 24 February 1989 ('Historia i Życie' supplement, pp. 1–3).
54 Kawecki survived AK charges of collaboration with the Germans. For his

account of his Katyn visit see *Hearings*, Part 5, pp. 1497–505. Also IPiMS, Kol. 12/3, no. 52.

55 See Jacek Trznadel, 'Głęboko w sumienia świata: Katyń w okupacyjnym "Nurcie" Ferdynanda Goetla', *Wojskowy Przegląd Historyczny*, 37, 1 (1992), pp. 352–5.

56 Szebesta was forced to recant his wartime testimony during the height of Stalinism in the PRL, 'Wywiad z lekarzem Polskim, członkiem tzw: "Komisji Polskiej" zmontowanej przez Hitlerowców dla zamaskowania zbrodni katyńskiej', *Trybuna Ludu*, no. 80 (March 1952), p. 3.

57 *Wiadomości* (London), 23 October, 6 and 20 November 1949. Goetel was a right-wing *Sanacja* member who, nevertheless, went to Katyn with the AK's permission and reported back to them. See *Hearings*, Part 4, pp. 843–7 for his report. Accused of collaboration with the Germans by the communists, he had to take refuge in London. His bitterness at his exile was such that he felt that Katyn justified an anti-Soviet Third World War, *Wiadomości*, 8 August 1951.

58 Testimony of 3 September 1946, IPiMS, Kol. 12/4, pos. 19 also contains an English language version of his report. Kazimierz Skarzyński, 'Katyń i Polski Czerwony Krzyż', *Kultura* (Paris), 9/51 (May 1955), pp. 127–41. Skarzyński's version of the Polish Red Cross Technical Report was published in *Odrodzenie*, 18 February 1989, no. 7, pp. 7–9.

59 *Armia Krajowa w dokumentach, 1939–1945*, vol. 2, *czerwiec 1941–kwiecień 1945* London: Gryf, 1973, pp. 501, 503.

60 See Jacek Trznadel, 'Józef Mackiewicz o Katyniu', in *Ku Cmentarzom Polskim w Katyniu, Miednoje, Charkowie*, Warsaw: NKHBZK, 2002, pp. 47–51.

61 Józef Mackiewicz, *The Katyn Wood Murders*, London: Hollis & Carter, 1951. See his testimony, *Hearings*, Part 4, pp. 867–81.

62 For the AK handling of his case as well as those of Goetel and Skiwski see Stefan Korbonski, *The Polish Underground State, 1939–1945*, New York: Columbia UP, 1978, pp. 142–3.

63 Stefan Korboński, *Bohaterowie Polskiego Państwa Podziemnego jak ich znałem*, Warsaw: Omnipress, 1990. For the debate on the German-licensed press see Lucjan Dobroszycki, *Reptile Journalism: The Official Polish Language Press Under the Nazis, 1939–1945*, New Haven, CT: Yale UP, 1994. Wilno, for obvious geographical borderland reasons, had been an inter-war centre for a realist form of Germanophilism designed to combat the Soviet threat fostered by the Mackiewicz brothers (Józef and Stanisław) and Władysław Studnicki.

64 Richard Lukas, *Forgotten Holocaust: The Poles under German Occupation, 1939–1944*, Lexington, KY: UP of Kentucky, 1986, pp. 112–13.

65 One of the few amusing episodes in this grim period was that the AK printed and displayed thousands of posters purporting to be an official German announcement. This compared 'the bestialities perpetrated by the Soviet assassins of the Polish people' at Katyn with the humanitarian mass extermination methods and marvels of European culture carried out at Auschwitz. Its crematorium alone could handle 3000 corpses a day, ibid., p. 102.

66 Testimonies of Stefan Mossor, IPiMS, Kol. 12/3, no. 56 and Andrzej Bajkowski, IPiMS, Kol. 12/3.

67 For the account of the two officers from Offlag IIC at Voldenberg and Mossor's conclusion 'that there is no doubt that thousands of Polish officers were shot in Spring 1940' see *Zbrodnia Katyńska w świetle dokumentów*, pp. 192–9.

68 The British officer was a Captain Stanley Gilder (RAMC) who was photographed at Katyn and identified in Stewart's testimony, *Hearings*, Part 1, pp. 20–1. Gilder's report was later to be requested by the US Congressional Com-

mittee when it visited London in 1952. The Washington embassy considered the report 'fairly innocuous' and had no objection to its declassification, Sir Oliver Franks to FO, no. 2425 of 8 September 1950, PRO FO371/86679. Although it claimed to be sending it on it has now, for whatever reason, vanished from the file, Chancery (Washington) to Northern Department, PRO FO371/86679 NP1661/10 of 9 September 1950. Gilder and his report was referred to by General Clayton Bissell in his Congressional Committee testimony where he gives the reference number of the document, M19/BM/973, *Hearings*, Part 7, pp. 1854–5.

69 *Le Monde*, 30 November 1945. *Hearings*, Part 3, p. 392.
70 The German report is published in full in *Amtliches Material zum Massenmord von Katyn*, pp. 38–113.
71 Final German Police Report signed by Voss (Secretary, Field Police), 10 June 1943, *Zbrodnia Katyńska w świetle dokumentów*, pp. 98–101. As always in this subject there are minor statistical variations between the various sources.
72 See Zawodny, *Death in the Forest*, pp. 19 ff.
73 The conclusive forensic evidence on this point is summarised by Henri de Montfort, *Masakra w Katyniu*, pp. 120–3.
74 Zawodny, *Death in the Forest*, p. 23.
75 Buhtz report, *Zbrodnia Katyńska w świetle dokumentów*, p. 112.
76 *Hearings*, Part 5, pp. 1491–5.
77 For Beck's testimony see *Hearings*, Part 5, pp. 1511–18.
78 See Stanisław M. Jankowski, 'Pamiętniki znane i nieznane', in *Zbrodnia Katyńska: Próba bilansu*, Warsaw: NKHBZK, 2001, pp. 113–55.
79 Zawodny, *Death in the Forest*, pp. 59–64.
80 'Indeks osobowy do Archiwum Robla', in *Ku Cmentarzom Polskim w Katyniu, Miednoje, Charkowie*, Warsaw: NKHBZBK, 1997, pp. 62–104.
81 Cf. Józef Mackiewicz, 'Tajemnica Śmierci Iwana Krzywozercowa, Głównego Świadka Zbrodni Katyńskiej', *Wiadomości*, 8, 15/16 (20 April 1952), p. 1.
82 This was confirmed in an answer by a junior Home Office Minister to Professor Savory in February 1952, IPiMS, Kol. 12/3, no. 37.
83 FO Historical Papers: History Notes & Occasional Papers. *British Reactions to the Katyn Massacre, 1943–2003*, hereafter *Butler Memorandum*, p. 27.
84 Braun von Stumm no. 117150, circular no. 347 of 5 May 1943, PRO HW1/2344.
85 Sterngracht to All Stations, no. 117825 of 22 May 1943, PRO HW1/2344.
86 Press circular no. 873 of 18 January 1944, PRO HW1/2344.
87 Ministry of Foreign Affairs (Berlin) to All Stations, no. 127768 of 27 January 1994 and no. 27832 of 3 February 1944, PRO HW12/297.
88 Berlin to All Stations, no. 128672 of 28 February 1994, PRO HW12/297.
89 Natalia Lebediewa, '60 lat fałszowania i zatajania historii zbrodni Katyńskiej', in *Zbrodnia Katyńska po 60 latach*, p. 111.
90 Ibid., p. 112.
91 The report is reproduced in full in *Zbrodnia Katyńska w świetle dokumentów*, pp. 114–43, from which all text references are taken. Forty-three files of material concerning the Burdenko Commission and covering 1939–1946 are now available in the Central Military Archive (CAW) in Warsaw, KAAR, VIII, 800.21.
92 See chapter on the Russian witnesses in Jacek Trznadel (ed.), *Powrót rozstrzelanej Armii*, Warsaw: Antyk, 1994.
93 De Montfort, *Masakra w Katyniu*, pp. 109–19 unravels the inconsistencies and falsehoods in the Soviet Report very convincingly.
94 *Zbrodnia Katyńska w świetle dokumentów*, pp. 140–1.
95 Zawodny, *Death in the Forest*, p. 55.
96 'Expertyza', *Polityka*, 19 August 1989, pp. 13–14.

97 *Time*, 7 February 1944.
98 Alexander Werth, *Russia at War*, London: Barrie & Rockliff, 1964.
99 Moscow embassy to FO, 25 January 1944, PRO PREM3/353.
100 Letter to the editor, *Sotsialistcheskii Vestnik*, XXX, no. 6/633 (June 1950) cited in Zawodny, *Death in the Forest*, pp. 157–9.
101 *Hearings*, Part 7, pp. 1939–42.
102 FitzGibbon, *Unpitied and Unknown*, pp. 82–5.
103 Telford Taylor, *The Anatomy of the Nuremberg Trials*, New York: Little, Brown, 1992, pp. 117, 124–6.
104 FitzGibbon, *Unpitied and Unknown*, pp. 91–192. Taylor, *Anatomy of the Nuremberg Trials*, pp. 312–13, 466–72.
105 Władysław Anders, *Bez Ostatniego Rozdziału: wspomniena z lat 1939–1946*, London: Gryf Publications, 10th edn, 1989, p. 414.
106 See the accounts by Zawodny, *Death in the Forest*, pp. 59–76 and De Montfort, *Masakra w Katyniu*, pp. 127–31.
107 Apart from the Soviet Minister of Justice, the Procurator-General and the President of the Supreme Court the commission included Merkulov and Kobulov, two of the Katyn Troika, see Abarinov, *The Murderers of Katyn*, Ch. 5, 'Nuremberg Version'.
108 *Zbrodnia Katyńska w świetle dokumentów*, pp. 122–3. The Soviet dissident Anatoly Marchenko claimed to have met Menshagin in Vladimir prison in the mid-1960s, who allegedly told him that he had personally witnessed the Katyn shootings, *My Testimony*, London: Pall Mall, 1969, pp. 157, 35. This claim was repeated in no. 11/1970 of the underground dissident publication *A Chronicle of Current Events* by the Ukrainian nationalist Svyatoslav Karavansky, cf. Peter Reddaway (ed.), *Uncensored Russia*, London: Jonathan Cape, 1972, p. 222 on the basis of material in the *Samizdat Chronicle of Current Affairs*.
109 International Military Tribunal. *Trial of the Major War Criminals before the International Military Tribunal, 14 November 1945–10 October 1946*, London: HMSO, 1947. Katyn is covered mainly in vol. VII, pp. 425–8, and vol. XVIII, pp. 271–371 and 539–45. See Adam Basak, *Historia pewnej mistyfikacji: Zbrodnia Katyńska przed Trybunałem Norymberskim*, Wrocław: Wydawnictwo Uniwersytetu Wrocławskiego, 1993.
110 *Hearings*, Part 5, pp. 1287–303.
111 *Hearings*, Part 5, pp. 1249–62, 1263–81.
112 *Nazi Conspiracy and Aggression: Opinion and Judgement*, Washington, DC: US Government Printing Office, 1947. Nikitchenko's dissenting opinion on the culpability of the OKW Wehrmacht drew attention to the Nazi 'Nacht i Nebel' order which was implemented in the so-called 'Kugel' (bullet) directive which led to the shooting of PoWs who had been recaptured after attempting escape, p. 187.
113 *Zbrodnia Katyńska w świetle dokumentów*, pp. 262–5.
114 John Bukowczyk, *Polish Americans and their History*, Pittsburg, PA: University of Pittsburg Press, 1998. Frank Mocha (ed.), *American 'Polonia' and Poland*, New York: East European Monographs, 1998. James Pula, *Polish Americans*, New York: Twayne Publishers, 1995.
115 Robert Szymczak, *The Unquiet Dead: The Katyn Forest Massacre as an Issue in American Diplomacy and Politics*, Carnegie-Mellon University PhD, 1980. University Microfilms International, 1985, Ch. V.
116 Congressman Dondero of Michigan publicised Katyn by reading Epstein's *New York Herald-Tribune* article of 3 July 1949 into the House record on 7 and 8 July 1949.
117 Cf. Arthur Bliss Lane, *I Saw Poland Betrayed: An American Ambassador Reports to the American People*, Indianapolis, IN: Bobbs-Merrill, 1948.

118 Editorial in *Chicago Daily Tribune*, 28 January 1952, cited in Szymczak, *The Unquiet Dead*, p. 211.
119 Maddocks, minute of 20 May 1950, PRO FO371/86679.
120 Cf. FitzGibbon, *Unpitied and Unknown*, pp. 206–393.
121 *Hearings*, Part 1, pp. 2–29.
122 *Hearings*, Part 5, pp. 1617–21.
123 *Hearings*, Part 5, pp. 1420–85.
124 *Hearings*, Part 5, pp. 1602–14.
125 *Hearings*, Part 5, pp. 1597–1602.
126 *Hearings*, Part 3, pp. 310–15.
127 *Hearings*, Part 2, pp. 36–62.
128 *Hearings*, Part 5, pp. 2132–49.
129 *The Katyn Forest Massacre: Interim Report of the Select Committee to Conduct an Investigation and Study of the Facts, Evidence and Circumstances of the Katyn Forest Massacre Pursuant to H. Res. 390 and H. Res. 539*, House of Representatives report no. 2430, 82nd Congress, 2nd session, Washington, DC: US Government Printing Office, 2 July 1952, p. 3. Excerpts in FitzGibbon, *Unpitied and Unknown*, pp. 461–82.
130 G. Littlejohn-Cook (Washington embassy) to Northern Department, 30 July 1952, FCO28/100719 1662/17/52.
131 House of Representatives report no. 2505, 82nd Congress, 2nd session, 22 December 1952, pp. 1–12. Reproduced in FitzGibbon, *Unpitied and Unknown*, pp. 449–60.
132 The second half of De Montfort's *Masakra w Katyniu* is somewhat sketchy and the analysis is incomplete as it was interrupted by the author's death.
133 O'Malley to Eden, 11 February 1944, PRO FO371/39390 C2099/8/55. All citations in this and the following two paragraphs are derived from this source. Reproduced in FitzGibbon, *Unpitied and Unknown*, pp. 72–8.
134 Wacław Godziemba-Maliszewski, *Katyń: An Interpretation of Aerial Photographs Considered with Facts and Documents*, Warsaw: Polskie Towarzystwo Geograficzne/Klub Teledetekcji Środowiska, 1995.
135 Cf. Robert Poirier, 'The Katyn Enigma: New Evidence in a 40-Year Riddle', *Studies in Intelligence*, Spring 1981. Poirier was a CIA and NPIC analyst who examined the imagery taken from 17 Luftwaffe aerial reconnaissance sorties during 1941–1944. He demonstrated that the Katyn forest area containing the burial site had not altered during the period of German occupation.
136 *Zawodny Papers AAN*, File 24.
137 For bibliographical essays see Jaczyński, *Zagłada oficerów. . .*, pp. 5–19.
138 Warsaw: KiW, 1989.
139 Leopold Jerzewski (*pseud.* Jerzy Łojek), *Dzieje sprawy Katynia*, Warsaw: Głos, 1980. The officially censored version was published in Białystok in 1982.
140 Józef Czapski, *Wspomnienia starobielskie*, Rome: White Eagle, 1944. Also *The Inhuman Land*, London: Chatto & Windus, 1951. Bronisław Młynarski, *W niewoli sowieckiej*, London: Gryf, 1974. Zdzisław Peszkowski, *Wspomnienia jeńca z Kozielska*, Warsaw: Wydawnictwo Archidieczja Warszawskiej, 1992. Stanisław Świaniewicz, *W cieniu katynia*, Paris: Instytut Literacki, 1976.
141 Anna and Tadeusz Lutoborski (eds), *Pamiętniki znalezione w Katyniu*, Paris-Warsaw: 2nd edn with foreword by Janusz Zawodny, 1990. Stanisław M. Jankowski, *Dzień rozpoczął się szczególnie. . .*, Warsaw: PFK/ZK no. 18, 2003.
142 An awful lot of material, usually of a recycling character, was published in this period. Most of it is now only of interest for our understanding of the perception and management of the Katyn truth, not the truth itself. See the bibliography by Zdzisław Jagodziński, *Bibliografia Katyńska: (książki i broszury)*, London: The Polish Library, rev. 2nd edn, 1982.

143 Victor Zaslavsky, 'The Katyn Massacre', *Telos*, no. 114 (Winter 1999), p. 68.

144 *7 Tage* (Karlsruhe), 7 July 1957. Reproduced in full in FitzGibbon, *Unpitied and Unknown*, pp. 440–1. Zawodny, *Death in the Forest*, pp. 114–15. Wilamowski, *Kłamstwo Stulecia*, pp. 67–8.

145 Wilamowski, pp. 66–8.

146 Józef Mackiewicz, *The Katyn Wood Murders*, pp. 158, 182–3.

147 Zawodny, *Death in the Forest*, pp. 113–15.

148 FitzGibbon, *Unpitied and Unknown*, pp. 431–41.

149 *Butler Memorandum*, paras 60 and 61. W.K. Sorokin was rewarded with 800 roubles for his part in the massacre, KDZ, 2, p. 406, while another Sorokin appears in KDZ, 1, p. 498 and KDZ, 3, pp. 58, 585. Tokarev also mentions S.I. Sorokin in his testimony as the Mednoe caretaker, KDZ, 2, pp. 459–60.

150 *Times*, 27 February 1971: *Butler Memorandum*, para. 62. Metelmann had his memoirs of his Eastern Front experience published as late as 2001, *Through Hell for Hitler: A Dramatic First-Hand Account of Fighting with the Wehrmacht*, London: Casio.

151 Kwiatkowska-Viatteau, *Katyn*, pp. 114–15. I was on my first visit to Poland, studying at Warsaw University, at the time, and interpreted the rumour as a side effect of the growing Soviet–Chinese split and the rise of Moczar's faction.

152 *Hearings*, Part 4, pp. 775–8.

7 The management and control of the truth about the 1940 massacre

The truth and American–British lies, hypocrisy and self-delusion

Postmodernists argue that historical truth tends to be narrativised by an author's subjectivity and the historical context. Consequently, there are no 'real' or 'true' stories.[1] The literal dictionary definition of truth is fairly tautological. *The New Oxford Dictionary of English* (1998) defines it as 'the quality or state of being true' merely adding 'that which is in accordance with fact or reality'. For historians it is normally only a technical problem involving the quality and reliability of sources to establish the basic truth of facts. The 1940 massacre is highly unusual as the basic feature of its truth was the establishment of what would normally be considered mere historical, even statistical, fact. Who killed how many Polish PoWs, where and when have until recently been more primary questions than the normal issues of why, how and with what consequences. The Katyn problematic, however, came to be regarded by Western diplomats and politicians as one of legal-judicial rather than historical truth particularly as civilised people regarded it as a crime just as much as a historical event. The question of who was the guilty party divided opinion for half a century. Before it was resolved satisfactorily, by the admission of the guilty party, what would normally have been subsequent questions of motivation and intent were subordinated to the basic search for the truth concerning the actual crime. This explains why so many individuals and bodies, including the British Foreign Office, were caught up in a political and moral bind which they found difficult to acknowledge, and trapped into applying legal-judicial criteria. In practice, political elites determined their *truth* for Katyn according to changing political needs and circumstances. The triumph of Allied self-interest and realist statecraft over abstract truth in 1943, however, continues to make people feel uncomfortable as it challenges the alleged moral and principled bases of democratic societies.

Having said the above one can discern the following *truths* about Katyn. The simplest was that of the guilty party and its supporters. The USSR always denied responsibility and attributed blame to Nazi Germany. This belief became a test of political loyalty and ideological reliability within its *bloc* and a canon of faith for its supporters outside it. The British and Americans subordinated what is now known to be the actual truth of Katyn to their primary need of maintaining the tripartite alliance and the Soviet war effort during the Second World War. The less-involved Americans were more pragmatic and flexible in handling the issue than the British. The Roosevelt administration suppressed and excluded inconvenient evidence of Soviet responsibility. The pendulum swung in the opposite direction once the Cold War set in. From the 1952 Congressional Committee onwards some Americans used Katyn functionally as propaganda against Soviet totalitarianism in their ideological-systemic-security conflict with the communist bloc.

The British had the closest wartime relations with the Polish Government-in-Exile. They were, therefore, subjected to the most intense barrage of hard evidence pointing to Soviet guilt and faced the greatest dilemma in reconciling truth with *realpolitik* wartime priorities. Lacking French cynicism or American enthusiasm British political elites felt that they could not maintain their perceptions of self-worth and their morally absolutist values unless an element of doubt could be introduced over Katyn. This explains the strength and depth of the Foreign Office commitment to the view that the weight of evidence suggested Soviet responsibility but that in judicial terms it was not quite sufficient to close the issue decisively. The unproven verdict was set in stone. Although challenged, most notably in the early 1970s, it was reiterated by all British political elites and the Foreign Office throughout the Cold War period. The admission of Soviet culpability in 1990, therefore, caused great embarrassment even though, by then, most of the Second World War protagonists were dead. The debate over the official British stance has not been satisfactorily resolved until this day. Zaslavsky rightly says that 'Soviet leaders would not have succeeded for half a century in hiding the truth about the Katyn massacre without Western government complicity'.[2] A British academic goes even further – 'in 1943 the behaviour of the British and American Governments, albeit in extenuating circumstances, amounted to what is called in criminal law conspiracy to defeat the ends of justice'.[3]

The final truth about Katyn is the actual one, the facts about which cannot be seriously contested since 1990, and which is documented in detail in this study. Unfortunately, this had previously coincided with the truth of the aggrieved party, the London Poles and non-communist Polish society during the PRL, so many Anglo-Saxons argued that as self-serving *truth* it was somehow less legitimate.

The abstract truth about the 1940 massacre has, therefore, always been conditioned by international political factors as it was not a purely domestic atrocity like the other crimes of the Stalinist Terror. The international dimension has now been replaced by different intellectual debates and legal frameworks concerning Human Rights, Crimes against

Humanity and the need to render justice to victims and their relatives by establishing Historical Truth within the ex-communist bloc. The latter issue raises the problem of *lustration* of new elites and whether individuals should be prosecuted for political crimes and atrocities committed during the communist era.[4] I argue that the success of democratisation in Russia depends upon a full admission and rejection by its elites and society of the crimes of the Stalinist period. The 'overcoming of history' requires the Russians to come to terms with their Soviet and Stalinist past just as the Germans had to understand their Nazi past in order to reject it after 1950.

One can, therefore, now understand why the truth about Katyn was so carefully managed and controlled for half a century. It was caught inextricably in the central web of the key conflicts and relationships of the twentieth century. Only the collapse of the main self-interested guardian of the anti-truth over Katyn returned the issue to a more normal and less politicised sphere.

America – the pragmatic and utilitarian handling of the truth

The Katyn issue was both extremely peripheral and antagonistic to President Franklin Delano Roosevelt's primary concerns during the Second World War. There is little controversy that he wanted to obtain an understanding with Stalin for the following reasons. First, in order to maintain the maximum Soviet military contribution to the European war against Nazi Germany. Second, at its end, to commit the USSR to what was mistakenly believed, before the atom bombs were dropped on Hiroshima and Nagasaki, would be a long war, involving heavy American casualties, against Japan. Third, Roosevelt subordinated Churchill and British imperialism to these ends and to the strategy which he developed at the December 1943 Teheran and February 1945 Yalta conferences.[5] This conceded Stalin's desired frontier changes concerning Poland and the joint Allied occupation of a demilitarised and denazified Germany. Roosevelt imagined that, in exchange, he would solidify the US–USSR condominium over world affairs within his new proposed United Nations framework and gain Stalin's involvement in the war against Japan. Most controversially, Roosevelt perhaps hoped that Stalin would accept what later became the Finnish type of domestic democratic status based on free elections, not direct imperial control, for the countries which the Red Army occupied at the end of the war. He was warned by Sikorski as to Stalin's real intentions as early as 4 May 1943: 'I fear that what the Soviet Government wants is a Polish Communist Government which would offer them Poland as a Soviet satellite state.'[6] It only became possible to publicise inconvenient truths, such as Katyn, in the West about the erstwhile Second World War ally with the post-1945 Sovietisation of Eastern Europe which initiated the Cold War.

Two key aspects of the American handling of the Katyn issue have now been documented. First, that the Roosevelt administration was informed about Soviet culpability from early on, and second, that it took purposive measures to suppress that truth and to prevent it entering the public domain. The two aspects are linked and can be examined under eight headings identified by Zawodny.[7]

The Americans had little direct involvement in, or knowledge of, the rights and wrongs of Katyn but were quickly informed by Jan Ciechanowski, the Polish Government-in-Exile ambassador in Washington. Polonia organisations were also much involved. Roosevelt chose to lie to the latter, as well as to Sikorski, and his successor, Mikołajczyk, about the real American policy in order to maintain their support for his 1944 presidential re-election campaign. 'To Roosevelt the Polish Question was mainly a question of electoral strategy. The Poles, therefore, stood to gain little support from him.'[8]

The American press, fed with tendentious material by official sources, increasingly depicted the Exiled Poles as troublemaking nuisances while the USSR was painted in uncritically rosy colours. Worrying developments within the American Polonia were identified by the Foreign Nationalities branch of the Office of Strategic Services in a printed report entitled 'The Development of Polish–Russian Antagonism in the United States' in June 1943.[9] This depicted the Polish language press in America as engaged 'in an unbridled campaign of denunciation' of both the Soviet authorities and Russian culture in general after the Katyn revelations. Sikorski's nationalist and conservative opponents were presenting Poland as a civilised and Catholic bulwark defending Europe against Russian Mongols and Tartars. Their most prominent organisation was the National Committee of Americans of Polish Descent (KNAPP) formed in June 1942 and led by M.F. Węgrzynek and Colonel Ignacy Matuszewski, one of Piłsudski's inter-war *Sanacja* ruling coterie. Their newspapers, *Nowy Swiat* (New York), *Dziennik Polski* (Detroit) and *Dziennik dla Wszystkych* (Buffalo), had taken the initiative against the pro-Sikorski Polish National Alliance (PAC) whose main mouthpiece was the *Dziennik Związkowy* (Chicago). The American Polonia was thus becoming increasingly politicised and divided over European and Allied wartime issues. The conclusion that this might become 'a matter of some consequence' in American politics was, no doubt, picked by a White House aide and factored into Roosevelt's domestic electoral and political calculations.

The facts about this presidential cover-up were revealed with the onset of the Cold War. This theme, just as much as the actual truth about Katyn, dominated the proceedings of the Congressional Committee in 1952 which revealed censorship and control of the mass media. The State Department instructed the Office of War Information (OWI) that evidence regarding the Katyn issue was inconclusive. Discussion and a definite view should be avoided as far as possible and German propaganda over the Polish–Soviet split should be countered. In practice the Federal Communications Commission monitored Polish language radio broadcasts and prevented journalists from publicising the London Polish view through use of its Polish Telegraph Agency (PAT) reports. Two journalists who did so, Marian Kreutz (Detroit WJBK) and Kazimierz Soron (Buffalo WBNY), were suspended.[10] OWI head Elmer Davis and Alan Cranston, the head of its Foreign Languages Division, told the Congressional Committee in 1952 that they received no direct orders from the White House or State Department to hush up Katyn. They genuinely believed that it was a German propaganda plot endangering the Allied war effort and, therefore, suppressed discussion on those grounds.[11] Joseph B. Phillips, the State Department official in charge of the Voice of America (VOA), followed the same line as justifying neglect of the issue during the Second World War.[12]

After the evacuation of the Poles from the USSR to Persia the Americans sent an intelligence officer of American Polish origins, Lieutenant Colonel Henry Szymanski, to act as liaison officer with Anders' HQ.[13] He carried out his orders to investigate the Katyn question very thoroughly using all the Polish sources. His report, submitted in late April/May 1942, was backed up by that of the British liaison officer, Lieutenant Colonel Hulls, as well as by Czapski's findings.[14] Szymanski sent the War Department authoritative information on NKVD treatment of the Polish PoWs and their interrogation and selection techniques as well as on the evacuation of the three camps in spring 1940. His conclusion that he agreed with all the Poles in Persia who were convinced of Soviet guilt earned him an official reprimand for the allegedly repetitive and anti-Soviet character of his reports.[15] Szymanski's findings, had already been reported by Ambassador J. Drexel Biddle in an extensive report of 20 May 1943. This spelt out the extent of the evidence of Soviet guilt and the likely manner of their execution of the PoWs from the three camps.[16]

General George V. Strong, Head of US Army Intelligence, was kept well informed on the issue by the Eastern Europe Section head, Colonel Ivan Yeaton, whose bulging file also contained the relevant Polish Intelligence reports. Yeaton testified later that he agreed with Szymanski that the Russians were responsible for Katyn.[17] John F. Carter, one of Roosevelt's special investigators, was commissioned to examine this material and to report directly to the president. His conclusion that evidence of Soviet responsibility was strong enough to justify the London Polish demand for an independent inquiry was accepted privately by both Roosevelt and Under-Secretary of State Sumner Welles. This placed them in the quandary described by Carter: 'The official reaction was that they didn't want to believe it, and that if they had believed it they would have pretended not to.'[18]

Roosevelt also received evidence about Katyn from other sources. His unofficial Special Envoy to the Balkans was based in Ankara as associate naval attaché. George Howard Earle III (1890–1974) had previously been the reforming 'New Deal' Democratic Governor of Pennsylvania from 1935 to 1939 and a senatorial candidate.[19] He was a lively personality and far from being a staid diplomat following the wishes of his superiors. Earle is reported to have told Hitler to his face that he did not like him. The dossier he collected, including Bulgarian sources, pointed overwhelmingly towards Soviet responsibility. He was also one of the first to place Katyn within the larger post-war Soviet scheme for controlling Poland and eliminating its hostile anti-Russian elites. Roosevelt rejected this viewpoint at their 22 May 1943 meeting. He characterised Katyn as 'entirely German propaganda and a German plot' and ignored all Earle's subsequent information on the subject.[20] When Earle threatened to go public in the crucial period between the Yalta and Potsdam conferences Roosevelt wrote on 24 March 1945 categorically forbidding him to do so.[21] He also had Earle transferred to Samoa after this, where he could do no harm, and kept him there until the war in the Pacific ended. Whether this was entirely to do with Katyn or because of Earle's previous secret soundings with the German ambassador in Turkey and the Reich secret services for an early and negotiated end to the Second World War is unclear. In 1952 Earle denounced the pro-Soviet mindset within the Roosevelt administration and the president's willingness to cover up almost any crime committed by the USSR in furtherance of his grand strategy for winning the Second World War.[22]

Because of their timing the Szymanski, Carter and Earle episodes are now much more significant politically than the report filed by Lieutenant Colonel John Van Vliet immediately after his liberation from captivity as a German PoW in May 1945. His visit to Katyn in April 1943 convinced him of Soviet guilt, but he refused to collaborate in any way with German propaganda during his internment. Flown back to the USA he was instructed by General Clayton Bissell, the deputy-head of Army Intelligence, to submit an official report, which he did in late May. This document was significant in the struggle for the historical truth about Katyn because Van Vliet noted the basic facts at the exhumed burial pits in April 1943.[23] The logical reasoning which led this West Point-educated professional officer, with no particular axe to grind, inexorably to an overwhelming conclusion of Soviet guilt was also held to be powerfully convincing by the Congressional Committee.[24]

The committee, though, was more concerned to investigate whether the document had been covered up by Roosevelt's administration. Bissell gave Van Vliet a written order not to discuss the matter without specific War Department permission. The report was marked 'Top Secret'. Bissell claimed that he sent it to Assistant Secretary of State Julius Holmes on 25 May 1945, or, at least, he later 'thought' that he did. The State Department claimed to have no record of it being received and Holmes asserted that he could not remember ever having seen it.[25] The report was quite simply lost, and in limbo – sent, but not received! Despite heavy questioning the committee could not break the stalemate on the actual travels of the report within the administration. It got a clearer statement from Bissell as to his motives for acting within Roosevelt's presidential guidelines as Commander-in-Chief concerning the need to commit the Soviet ally to the war against Japan. Bissell confirmed that he did not need direct orders from his superiors to act against what were perceived as threats to this policy.[26] The Van Vliet report was, therefore, classified at the highest level to prevent it becoming public knowledge and, no doubt, pigeonholed out of harm's way. The committee found no evidence of conspiracy, let alone direct Soviet influence, despite much speculation about the role of Soviet spies and agents of influence within the administration like Alger Hiss. It concluded that the priority of maintaining good relations with the USSR led to the report becoming conveniently misplaced.

The US Government, just prior to Nuremberg, was, therefore, in possession of the Szymanski, Earle, Carter and Van Vliet reports as well as of considerable Polish and British Intelligence material. In addition, it was kept fully informed by its own diplomatic embassy and military intelligence staff. The US ambassadors to Moscow, William H. Standley (1941–1943), and to the Polish Government-in-Exile, A.J. Drexel Biddle (1937–1943), specifically took up the cause of missing officers with the Soviet Government at various times during 1941–1942.[27] They also reported on the growing Polish–Soviet disagreements in full. The Roosevelt administration and the State Department could not, therefore, plead ignorance about the purely historical rights and wrongs of Katyn. The Congressional Committee concluded correctly that a conscious and deliberate political choice had been made to withhold documentation confirming the inconvenient political truth about Katyn and to prevent American public opinion from being informed about the full facts. Its Final Report stated that the evidence at the disposal of the administration 'provided a clear-cut picture of the tremendously important part the Katyn massacre played in shaping the future of post-war Europe'. Growing Polish–Soviet tensions and 'the hopeless search for the Polish officers . . . were brushed aside, on the theory that the search would irritate Soviet Russia and thus hinder the prosecution of the war to a successful conclusion'.[28] A 'strange psychosis' led Roosevelt to sacrifice a loyal ally as well as moral and democratic principles through the fear that otherwise a far more powerful ally might get miffed. The committee, therefore, rebuked various officials, notably Bissell and those in charge of the media, for suppressing public information and debate and producing a conspiracy of silence.

In my view, the fear that the USSR might make a separate peace with Nazi Germany after Stalingrad was absurd. The reality was that Stalin wished to utilise his military victory to the full by occupying Eastern Europe and the eastern zone of Germany, as, in fact, he did. We shall never know whether the earlier publicising of one of his atrocities would have affected his behaviour in any way. What is certain is that a more knowing public awareness in the democracies of the grisly realities of their Soviet ally might have affected their leaders' willingness to bank everything on Stalin's goodwill up until Yalta. The line practised by Truman and the British Prime Minister Clement Attlee became much more realistic and pragmatic after that. The Congressional Committee's hardline denunciation of Yalta as a sell out can now be read in a different way. Up until 1990 progressives were most concerned to prevent the Cold War from getting out of control, especially after nuclear weapons became more frightful with the Hydrogen Bomb and new delivery systems.

> The tragic concessions at Yalta might not have taken place if the Polish officer corps had not been annihilated by the Soviets at Katyn. With proper leadership, the Polish Army could have relieved a great deal of the early reverses suffered by the Allies. The Kremlin's hand would not have been so strong at the Yalta conference, and many of the concessions made because of military necessity [could have been prevented].[29]

The historical outcome – the Sovietisation of Eastern Europe after 1945, the painful survival of communist rule in the region until 1989 and a dangerous East–West systemic and security conflict – is now known. Could this result have been prevented, or even modified, by an Allied policy in which elites shared knowledge of the warts of the Stalinist system such as Katyn with their public opinions and electorates? The dominant answer until recently, which I challenge, was that it would have been too risky because of the Western need to fight a cheap war in terms of lives at the cost of their Soviet ally which had no choice but to incur these enormous losses after the Nazi attack in 1941. I also argue that the problem fundamentally lay with the incapacity of public opinions, especially Anglo-Saxon ones, to stomach what was regarded as immoral *realpolitik* and the relativity of morals and ideals. Elites were thus 'forced' to produce 'noble lies', or self-delude themselves, for a greater good, as in the more generous interpretations of Bush and Blair motivations over the Iraq War of 2003.

As we have seen, the Truman administration was unhappy about the establishment of the Congressional Committee on Katyn although, for electoral reasons, it could not afford to be seen to oppose it openly. The State Department would have opposed the subsequent resolutions empowering and funding its activities abroad, if it had been consulted. But they were by no means uncontested as the House of Representatives votes on these resolutions were 206 to 115 and 233 to 114 in favour. State believed that they raised difficult constitutional, political and propaganda issues. 'This is the first time that an investigating body of a legislature has been attempted to conduct business in a foreign country on matters affecting relations with third countries.' The British embassy in Washington was very happy to hear this and reported that the committee's main purpose is 'to enable Congressmen to let off anti-communist steam'. It had become part of the Cold War's 'psychological warfare' and of competition for the Polish vote; the Republicans were attempting to discredit Roosevelt's 'undue softness' towards Russia.[30] After the committee had visited London, the State Department and the FO congratulated themselves on having succeeded in 'greatly reducing the scope of its activities'. The foreign-policy-making bureaucrats sagely nodded agreement at 'the impropriety of a legislature of one country conducting operations in the capital of another'.[31]

The Katyn issue was, subsequently, treated differently on the public opinion and political elite levels. Katyn was commemorated regularly by the Polonia press which also recycled the available material and produced a growing corpus of reminiscences by survivors of different levels of the Second World War, especially Soviet, experience. The publication of Zawodny's book in 1962 was a milestone marking the limits of what could be established as definitely known before 1990. Katyn became part of the right-wing Republican rollback of communism rhetoric associated with Secretary of State John Foster Dulles. The issue declined in salience thereafter, although Republicans still used it to score points against their Democratic rivals over Roosevelt's policy on Eastern Europe, for two main reasons. First, Soviet responsibility was never fully established in the public mind beyond all question, as it was not internationalised through a United Nations investigation and condemnation. Second, and more significantly, the search for *détente* and for managing the East–West conflict safely, especially after the 1962 Cuba Crisis, gradually squeezed out what came to be regarded as ancient, but still provocative, controversies. Due to the efforts of Congressman Edward Derwinski (Illinois) the 25th anniversary of Katyn, implying Soviet guilt, was, however, commemorated in the form of a US postage stamp in 1965.[32] The campaign to erect a Katyn memorial in Britain was supported very strongly, especially financially, by the American Polonia in the early 1970s. Although there were no Katyn memorials in the USA the PAC contributed 'to the London Memorial rather than erecting one of their own'.[33]

Katyn resurfaced as an issue in America, illustrating the totalitarian nature of communism, with the rise of Polish dissidence and Solidarity in the late 1970s. On the other hand it has been demonstrated that the Polish lobby was weak and divided, easily misled and manipulated for domestic political and electoral purposes and that it had little influence on American foreign policy.[34] There was limited reaction, except in US Polonia circles, to the British Katyn Memorial controversy of the earlier part of the decade and to FitzGibbon's associated publications.[35] This was because the post-Vietnam backlash and Watergate discredited the Nixon brand of Republicanism and allowed Jimmy Carter to develop Great Power co-existence and *détente* to a fuller extent. Carter's replacement by

Reagan and the emergence of Solidarity in 1980 re-ignited the ideological-systemic conflict both between East and West and domestically, within Left and Right. Progressives and Democrats were, as in the late 1940s/early 1950s, again put on the defensive. Oppositionist critiques and revelations concerning Stalinism could be seen as a movement to reform socialism within Poland. The issue of how they should be reported once again caught American officialdom by surprise. Robert Dole, the Republican Senator from Kansas, for example, criticised the VOA for failing to report a dissident writer's (Andrzej Braun) raising of Katyn at the Polish Writers' Congress in May 1978.[36] The founding of the Katyn Institute and the crusade for the truth about Katyn within the PRL will be discussed later. Here, one should note that the American mass media had no inhibitions about equating the crimes of Stalinism with all socialist systems and ideas during Reagan's presidency.

With the fall of communism, politicians and Polonia organisations felt unconstrained in reporting the vast flow of revelations concerning Katyn emanating out of the now democratic Poland and post-communist Russia.[37] Once the main Senate and House resolutions had been passed it was difficult to maintain interest in anniversary commemorations and the like. Congressman Paul E. Kanjorski (Democrat/Pennsylvania) marked the 60th anniversary of Radio Berlin's announcement of the Katyn massacre by recapitulating the findings of the 1952 Select Committee. He had arranged through the Library of Congress for the seven-volume record of its proceedings to be presented to the Polish ambassador in Washington.[38] The Senate passed a major resolution (no. 118) to mark the 60th anniversary on 25 May 2000 which recapitulated the full truth about the 1940 massacre.[39] Later activity, typified by House Democratic Caucus chairman Robert Menendez (New Jersey), publicised PAC Katyn Forest Memorial services and linked Katyn commemoration to tributes to the victims of the 9/11 terrorist attacks.[40]

New massacres in Rwanda and the former Yugoslavia competed for public attention along with revelations concerning half forgotten or neglected ones such as of Jews in Jedwabne in 1941 and of Poles in Volhynia in 1943–1944. None of them could compete against the continuing strength of the Holocaust debate while the post-1980 explosion of concern for human rights in Western democracies produced new frameworks for the study and interpretation of genocide and crimes against humanity. Unlike Britain, however, the Katyn issue has not, since the early 1950s, caused elite embarrassment or major recrimination in the USA.

Britain – defending the indefensible

The Katyn issue raised much more fundamental problems for the British Government and Foreign Office than for the Americans. Poland was Britain's ally right from the outbreak of the Second World War. The

Government-in-Exile was based in the United Kingdom, after May 1940, while its forces operated under general British command. Churchill acted as the spokesman, and Britain as the intermediary, for the Polish cause, in different ways, in relation to both their American and Soviet Allies after 1941. The search for the truth about Katyn, crystallised a number of fundamental disputes concerning Poland's post-war borders and political control of the country as well as the wartime definition and treatment of Poles within the USSR. It faced the British with the need to choose between the interests of their major Soviet and minor Polish Allies as a London Polish–Soviet alliance could not be mediated.

In the longer term, Katyn revealed starkly the clash between *realpolitik* and the principles of international morality and justice promised by the Western Allies as part of their envisaged post-war settlement. The Foreign Office was kept fully informed of the true facts of the Soviet 1939 invasion and subsequent deportations in Poland's eastern territories by its ambassador to the London Government-in-Exile, Owen O'Malley.[41] Frank Roberts noted the 'formidable obstacles in the way of Polish–Soviet reconciliation' and that the 1941 Polish–Soviet agreement was 'little short of a miracle'. His FO colleague Douglas Allen concluded, rather oddly, that the Poles would have to defer to Russia in the east 'if they wish to retain their national identity and independence'.[42]

The hard documentary evidence about the debate within the British elite concerning the handling of the Katyn issue was largely revealed on two occasions. Much of the material became available in the Public Record Office, under the Thirty Years' Rule, in the early to mid-1970s. The debate at that time was fuelled by FitzGibbon's publications and by the Katyn memorial dispute. After the fall of communism some additional British intelligence and cabinet material became available, although knowledge of the new Russian sources and the Polish debate remained surprisingly limited. The FCO mounted major apologias defending the official 1943–1990 British line, notably in 1996 and 2003. It became easier to accommodate Katyn within the Blair Government's rhetorical pretensions to an ethical foreign policy. Public opinion became sensitised to human rights and crimes against humanity as a result of atrocities in post-Yugoslavia, Africa and the Middle East.

The immediate and primary British reaction to Goebbels' revelation of the Katyn graves in April 1943 was the understandable wish to deny the Nazi enemy any political or propaganda benefit from the issue. Given the extent of German atrocities against the Poles the British had no reason for doubting that the Nazis were capable of murdering large numbers of Polish officers, particularly under the savage conditions of the Eastern Front. It took far longer for the British, under Polish pressure, to consider that the Germans might be innocent in this particular instance, and that the Soviets might be responsible. Even then, there were confused and divided reactions over how to handle the London Polish–Soviet split and much residual self-delusion that the rift might be healed. The overwhelming consideration was that nothing should be done to annoy the Soviet ally or to take the slightest risk of endangering the Red Army's contribution to the Allied war effort.

We now know the long-term outcomes and costs of this overriding, if understandable, Western priority. The war against Germany was won at the cost of the lives of relatively few British and American soldiers compared to the Soviet losses. Perhaps, it was inevitable, that America and Britain should concede Stalin his ill-gotten territorial gains derived from the Ribbentrop–Molotov Pact and the 1939–1941 period of collaboration with Nazi Germany. It might also have been inevitable that the way the Second World War was fought would result in Red Army military occupation, and consequent Soviet political control, of Eastern Europe (including East Germany) and the Balkans (except for Titoist-controlled Yugoslavia). Western geostrategic options during the Second World War, the delaying of the Second Front and the absence of military offensives establishing a Western military presence in Central Europe and the Balkans were paid for by the East European peoples in the form of almost half a century of Soviet communist control. The 'cheap lives' option and strategy may have been inevitable for the hard-pressed democracies, especially the British who, additionally, struggled to defend their Imperial commitments in Africa and the Middle East. Roosevelt's territorial and frontier concessions over Poland at Teheran and Yalta also absolve him from later revisionist charges of hardline responsibility for the Cold War.[43] On the other hand, Western failure to tie Stalin down over the political future of Eastern Europe during his period of military weakness meant that Roosevelt had no cards left to play at the end-of-war conferences apart from a simple-minded banking on Stalin's goodwill. Realist theorising in international relations suggests that a critical awareness of the real motives of the Stalinist partner would have come sooner if the Western elites had come to terms with such Soviet brute realities as the 1940 massacre. Certainly, there was no need to encourage Western public opinion to love 'Uncle Joe' and Soviet Russia as against appreciating the Red Army's contribution. Earlier and stronger Western pressure on Stalin would, conceivably, have resulted in a smaller sphere of Soviet control, a longer time scale for its full blooded imposition or just possibly, and this is a paradox of realist theory, a more benign or mixed, possibly Finlandised, form in some countries.

The British Foreign Office made available on the world wide web in 2003 the previously unpublished internal memorandum by Rohan d'Olier Butler, the historical adviser to the Secretary of State from 1963 to 1982.[44] He was charged in 1972 with the brief of bringing together and assessing all the information which successive British Governments had received since 1943 regarding Katyn.[45] Dennis MacShane, the Labour Minister for Europe, whose father, like mine, was a Pole of Second World War vintage, noted correctly in his foreword that it 'gives an accurate account of what the British Government knew about Katyn, and why they maintained the public line about the massacre throughout the Cold War'. Butler's defence of the official British line, that the evidence was not sufficiently conclusive to justify the condemnation of the USSR, is, however, challenged by my study, as is his confirmation of the status quo in 1973. Mac-Shane conceded that the failure to revise the standpoint angered those who wanted 'to see justice done'. His second major consideration pointed up the issue's contemporary relevance in the light of the Blair administration's commitment to open government. 'This is more than a historical compilation. It raises the issue of how ministers and officials handle public discussions about crimes and allegations of crimes against humanity.'

Butler sets out the basis of the wartime documentation on Katyn in his first section where he notes the 1943–1947 German, International Commission, Polish Red Cross, Burdenko and Skarzyński Reports as well as the London Polish compilations discussed in the previous chapter. He discusses their merit and the British wartime reactions in the light of the syntheses provided by Owen O'Malley's two main reports, Professor B.H. Sumner's assessment of Burdenko, Dennis Allen's proposed reply to an October 1945 parliamentary question and F.B. Bourdillon's April 1946 memorandum. Butler notes the two most salient political repercussions of the 1943 Katyn revelations rather coyly. He judges the propaganda coup for the Germans less important than the complications which Katyn raised for Anglo–Soviet relations.

Sir Archibald Clark Kerr, the British ambassador in Moscow, discussed the British dilemma. He warned of a 'pretty savage' Soviet reaction, the exacerbation of Polish–Russian tension and the probable rupture of relations. Kerr confirmed that Soviet 'anger and unconvincing terms of Russian denial suggest a sense of guilt' while 'in a horrible way' the German version seemed to be confirmed by the evidence provided by the Poles.[46] Kerr went to the heart of the problem in this despatch. Katyn was 'disturbing for it is uncomfortable to reflect upon the consequences of an enquiry which might show that guilt was there. I feel, therefore, that to pursue the proposal made to the International Red Cross might be to court something little short of disaster.' Butler claims that this was the only comment made by Kerr on Katyn and that the Moscow embassy failed to present any subsequent assessment of the Katyn documentation. 'This considerable omission was noticed in the Foreign Office at the time, but it was judged prudent not to ask that it be filled.'[47] This is by no means true. It seems to have been largely designed to cover up the ambassador's embarrassing, although honourable, suggestions that the Poles should be informed in good time that the loss of their eastern territories was inevitable. The official British line was, therefore, to condemn the cynical hypocrisy of the Nazis for attempting to use the atrocity to disturb Allied unity. Anthony Eden did so in the House of Commons on 4 May 1943.[48]

The official and public policy was to use the inconsistencies and gaps in the Katyn evidence to justify a policy of non-attribution of guilt. The London Poles were worked on, at the same time, to desist from seeking satisfaction on the issue, for the greater good of Allied unity.

It is revealing that Butler restricts himself very strictly to examining the internal FO debate and neglects the wider policy framework set by Churchill, Eden and the Cabinet. Key aspects such as Churchill's exchanges with Sikorski, when the latter confronted him at their luncheon, with Raczyński present, on 15 April 1943 with 'a wealth of evidence' regarding the massacred PoWs, therefore, do not appear in his later public account. Churchill's alleged advice to the London Poles was to make the best of a bad, although not quite hopeless, situation. Churchill's later claim to have told Sikorski that 'if they are dead nothing that you can do will bring them back' is, probably, not strictly true.[49] At their 15 April meeting Churchill observed that the Katyn announcement 'was an obvious German move to sow discord between the Allies'. The facts were 'pretty grim' but the priority was to avoid 'unnecessary provocation' of the USSR. The Allies would talk to Stalin about Poland's frontiers once their military situation improved. Sikorski, who was being attacked by his fellow Poles in London and the Middle East for being too conciliatory, replied that the matter was 'extremely urgent and the present situation could not be allowed to continue for long'.[50] Churchill, however, on 23 April approved the Soviet ambassador in London, Maisky's, condemnation of the Poles as 'a foolish race who had always mismanaged their affairs'.[51] Their 'feckless government' could not understand the folly of a nation of 20 million provoking one of 200 million. Churchill concurred by conceding that the Poles' invitation to the Red Cross was 'grotesque' and 'absolutely unacceptable to HMG'. He went on to say that grim things happened in war and that the affair of the missing officers was indeed grim. 'But if they were dead they could not be resurrected to life.' Was this, one wonders, the real source of his later claim to have used the same phrase to Sikorski, presumably on 15 April, which finds no confirmation in the Polish primary sources?

Behind the scenes, however, a major debate had rumbled on within the FO about the truth and guilt of Katyn sparked off by Ambassador O'Malley's first despatch of 24 May 1943. This, perhaps the single most important document in the Katyn controversy, was released into the public domain only in 1972.[52] O'Malley arrived at a verdict of almost certain Soviet guilt by rejecting the unreliable witness evidence, as he was to do in his second report of 11 February 1944. He focussed on the arguments presented by the London Poles that the consistent Soviet failure to give any satisfactory reply to their barrage of enquiries during 1941–1943 concerning the missing 15000 PoWs (including the 9000 officers) pointed to Soviet guilt, not incompetence. O'Malley went on, in the first 13 paragraphs of his despatch, to rehearse the arguments about the winter clothing of the uncovered corpses and the evidence found on them, the ending of PoW correspondence in April 1940, the impartial conclusions of the International and PRC Commissions, the total absence of any trace of the Poles in German camps or occupied areas and the holes in the pre-Burdenko Soviet cover story. O'Malley concluded that, despite the confusion about the number of victims buried at Katyn, whether the Poles were massacred in one, two or three places and whether some were sent on to Siberia, 'the cumulative effect' of the evidence undermined Soviet protestations of innocence.

Dennis Allen commented on the front of the document that this was 'a brilliant, unorthodox and disquieting despatch'. He commended the useful and skilfully assembled 'examination of the evidence' in the first section. This supported the conclusion that 'a strong presumption exists that the Russians were responsible'. In common with most other middle-level FO bureaucrats he faulted O'Malley's 'sometimes partial and obviously defective' reconstruction of the Katyn massacre in the five-paragraph-long middle section. Here O'Malley stressed the significance of climatic factors and 'the presumptive evidence of Russian guilt' provided by the little conifers covering the grave. The latter appeared to have been planted well before the German occupation of the Smolensk region in 1941. The Soviet behaviour over this 'burning question' for the Poles was characterised by Frank Roberts, head of the FO Central Department, in May 1943 'as to say the least very odd and disingenuous'.[53]

O'Malley explained the political reasons for the massacre as lying in the Soviets' continual struggle with a national and class Polish enemy from the Polish–Soviet war of 1920 right up to their annexation of Poland's eastern territories in 1939. Perhaps it was a particularly Irish love of horse breeding which led him to use excessively colourful language about Stalin's wish to rid himself of a dangerous breeding elite. Phrases about stallions siring 'a whole herd of hostile Christian thoroughbreds' and Stalin sending 'all this turbulent bloodstock to the knackers' provoked middle-class English objections, and raised hackles, even in 1943. This 'final ghoulish vision' and the middle section was dismissed by Allen as designed 'to arouse anti-Soviet passions and prejudices in the reader's mind'.

If Allen and his FO ilk were put off by such vivid metaphors, they were infinitely more perturbed by O'Malley's six-paragraph-long conclusion about the importance of morality in international and domestic politics. He conceded the reasons, such as the need to maintain Allied unity and the Soviet war effort, which led to a 'dislocation between our public attitude and our private feelings' that was, probably, 'deliberate and inevitable'.[54] He warned that double standards and lying caused confusion and undermined faith in democratic principles as foreign policy was now less of a wholly elite affair than previously. There were 'valid reasons' for behaving externally as though 'a monstrous crime' had not been committed by a friendly foreign government. O'Malley recommended, however, that for the moment sentiments of truth, justice and compassion should be kept 'within our own hearts and minds where we are masters'. They should be kept alive as guidance for current questions of dispute in Russo-Polish relations and for an end-of-war settlement that would 'vindicate the spirit of those brave, unlucky men' who had perished at Katyn.

Allen commented that the above proposal that the British should follow the London Polish example of 'allowing our heads to be governed by our hearts' was 'a devious argument'. However, although he rejected O'Malley's prescriptions his précis is worth citing in full as it represents the contemporary case against the FO line:

> he [O'Malley] recommends, while recognising the present necessity of avoiding public accusations of our Russian allies, that we should at least redress the balance in our own minds and in all our future dealings with the Soviet Government refuse to forget the Soviet crime of Katyn. Our future dealings with the Russians should in fact be governed by the moral necessity of 'vindicating ... and justifying the living to the dead'.

Exactly! Allen could not have foreseen that what were apparently moral arguments in 1943 turned into realist ones when the true face of Soviet Stalinism became clearer after 1947.

The other FO annotations on the despatch record that Frank Roberts considered the presumption of Soviet guilt to be 'a very awkward matter', particularly as the Allies intended to prosecute war criminals at the war's end. He proposed that only the factual first section, and even that with some omissions, should be circulated to the War Cabinet; the remainder was calculated to work up 'the maximum prejudice against the Soviet Union'. William Strang, however, considered it a powerful piece of work which deserved to be read. He therefore proposed that the whole document be circulated to King and War Cabinet. The resultant debate according to Butler produced an elite consensus based on what the FO Permanent Under-Secretary Sir Alexander Cadogan called 'a presumption of Soviet guilt'.[55]

The above conclusion was endorsed at the top by Churchill and Foreign Minister Anthony Eden, but mainly on the basis of O'Malley's February 1944 second report. Whether this was really so, in their own minds, however, has been confused by all their subsequent caveats designed to prevent them from having to acknowledge this conclusion openly in public. Churchill set the gnomic and economic tone for their exchanges – 'This is not one of those matters where absolute certainty is either urgent or indispensable.'[56] Eden, while seeming to endorse O'Malley's conclusion, was quick to qualify it with the prevailing FO observation that 'the evidence is conflicting and whatever we may suspect, we shall probably never know'.[57] The key factor was that Churchill and Eden did not raise the Katyn issue a year later at Yalta. Their basic assumption was that Stalin was a genuine long-term ally who should not be offended. Churchill had confirmed that the Soviets should be supported publicly over the Katyn revelations and that the Poles should be whipped into line for the greater good of the Allied war effort. 'This is the only line of safety for the Poles and indeed for us ... there is no use prawling morbidly round the *three year old* graves of Smolensk.'[58] The phrase which I have italicised demonstrates that Churchill, unlike Eden, had no personal doubts as to Soviet guilt for the massacre. The consequences of this policy were that uncomfortable topics like Katyn, which could have been used as tactical bargaining ploys in the dialogue with the Soviets, were kept firmly under wraps. Together with Roosevelt, the Anglo-Saxons rushed at Teheran to agree on Poland's new eastern frontier, closely following the Curzon line.[59] Admittedly, Churchill stressed to Stalin in a private conversation why Britain felt so strongly about Poland. His emotional appeal, based on history and culture, left the Soviet dictator unmoved. Although it was established that her wartime frontiers could be agreed between the Allies the ambiguity between Soviet and Western conceptions of the character of post-war Poland, and who would control it, was never really broached.[60] All that one can say is that, although Churchill had a better understanding of the character of the Soviet dictator, he deferred to Roosevelt's softly, softly strategy in his exchanges with Stalin at Yalta.[61] History is full of paradoxes. One of them is that the inter-war bull in a china shop Churchill facing up to Stalin directly might have achieved better results! That Churchill was perfectly capable of applying *realpolitik* when it suited him is borne out by his earlier 'spheres of influence' agreement with Stalin in Moscow in October 1944.[62]

All this explains Churchill's laconic, resigned and mournful reaction to O'Malley's reports. He ensured that what he described, on 27 June 1943, as this 'lamentable tale' (the first report) was circulated to King and War Cabinet while the second report also went to Roosevelt and Dominion Governor Generals, High Commissioners and Prime Ministers.[63] He had noted after his return from Teheran, on 30 January 1944, that 'I think that Sir Owen O'Malley should be asked very secretly to express his opinion on the Katyn Wood inquiry', in other words on Burdenko. Churchill's personal conclusions on probable Soviet guilt already seemed to have firmed up. This was indicated by his inquiry 'how does the length of time the birch trees had grown over the grave fit in with this new tale?'[64] He also laid down the dual line between the public and private dimensions of Katyn as far as British policymakers were concerned. 'All this is merely to ascertain the facts, because we should none of us ever speak a word about it.'[65] His central reflection endorsed and paraphrased O'Malley's conclusion to his second report of 11 February 1944:

> Let us think of these things always and speak of them never. To speak of them never is the advice which I have been giving to the Polish

Government, but it has been unnecessary. They have received the Russian report in silence. Affliction and residence in this country seem to be teaching them how much better it is in political life to leave unsaid those things about which one feels most passionately.[66]

As well as having O'Malley's two reports Churchill was also sent a thorough, and largely correct, ten-page-long examination of the Polish source material and the diplomatic course of events by Professor Douglas Savory on 17 February 1944. Savory concluded that 'the Polish Government was fully justified in demanding that an impartial inquiry be held and the facts be verified by an international body'.[67] In addition Churchill also had the Burdenko Report in translation and the FO analysis at his disposal.[68] He was, therefore, as well informed as any outsider could be at the time. He also took some weeks in early 1944 to digest the material and mull over his conclusions. Nobody can, therefore, claim that his decision to subordinate the Katyn issue completely to the Grand Strategy for winning the War was hastily taken or ill informed. One would, perhaps, need a fuller analysis of his relations with Roosevelt to understand this question. If he had any inner qualms or reservations, he certainly never revealed them, except very marginally with the Polish leaders in London. Churchill was positively misleading about Katyn in his post-war memoirs in order to defend the open verdict line in public. He writes that everyone is 'entitled to form his own opinion' on the basis of a vast literature such as the memoirs by Anders and Mikołajczyk.[69]

It was easier for Churchill than for his foreign minister to affect Olympian detachment. Eden was continually and directly affected by the FO's defensive and typically British liberal squirming to maintain balance and a veneer of principle when faced by the most brutal facts of *realpolitik* in international politics. Psychologically, like many of his FO officials, he also succumbed to feelings of sublimated guilt which manifested themselves as irritation with the London Poles. As victims of history they found themselves being blamed for all sorts of sins before they passed from the historical stage. Eden considered O'Malley's report to be 'pretty explosive and in some respects prejudiced'.[70] O'Malley himself was disappointed that his second report had not been printed. He expressed his profound disagreement with the suspension of judgement line and the Research Department conclusion, on which it was ostensibly based, that 'the truth will never come to light'.[71]

It is clear from the Butler Memorandum that the FO used two prominent medical authorities, Lord Adrian and Sir Bernard Spilsbury, to weaken the forensic findings of the International Commission as to the date of the Katyn shootings. The FO undermined Dr Orsos' categoric view of the issue with the totally irrelevant claim that he was anti-Semitic and suggested that he had masterminded the International Commission report 'in a sense agreeable to the Germans'.[72] The FO, therefore, inclined to the view endorsed by O'Malley and Sir Bernard Spilsbury that the strictly medical evidence should be regarded as inconclusive.

The main FO examination of the Burdenko Commission was a Research Department memorandum of 17 February 1944 produced by Professor H.B. Sumner, a well-known academic scholar on Russia.[73] Sumner accepted Burdenko's claims as to the amount of time which his experts allegedly spent over the exhumations at Katyn. He noted that the Commission added nothing new in terms of explaining the Soviet failure to produce the missing Polish officers after 1941 or over the cessation of camp correspondence in April 1940. On the other hand he considered, rather convolutedly, that the nine new documents allegedly found on the bodies argued in favour of the Soviets; they obviously would have included material later than 20 June 1941 in order to incriminate the Germans if they had been forging documentation! Sumner's verdict on Burdenko was that it made out 'a good, though not conclusive, case for the perpetration of the massacre by the Germans'.

The FO officials were divided in their responses to this conclusion.[74] Cadogan objected strongly to calling Burdenko's Commission 'a strong one' while Allen endorsed Sumner as 'a good paper'. Roberts considered that 'this useful paper fastens on the weaknesses in the German case, which indeed have always been apparent, but it does not to my mind dispose of the weaknesses in the Russian case'. Oliver Harvey considered that Sumner provided 'an objective analysis of the Soviet case', which was stronger than first thought. To the FO mind it provided balance to O'Malley's excessive anti-Sovietism and one-sided endorsement of the Poles who had allegedly plumped 'headlong for the German case'. Sir William Malkin, the FO Legal Adviser, latched on to the centrality of the nine additional documents found by the Soviets. 'We are unlikely ever to know the truth about this', he wrote. His conclusion that 'it should, at any rate, justify a suspension of judgement on our part' proved authoritative. It was endorsed by Cadogan and Eden in the covering note to the Sumner Memorandum circulated to King and War Cabinet. 'The truth may never come to light. But meanwhile the evidence at present available would seem to require a suspension of judgement in regard to the whole affair.'[75] This, according to Butler, 'represented the considered view of the Foreign Office', that judgement on Katyn should be avoided.[76] This line was maintained subsequently despite being weakened by an appreciation of the Harriman-Melby delegation's failure to authenticate the nine documents. It was not strengthened by excessive FO attention to flimsy reports concerning Nazi fabrication facilities at Sachsenhausen and the preparation of Polish bodies for sending to Katyn.[77] The FO also lent a ready ear to rumours that Poles in Upper Silesia considered the Germans, not the Soviets, responsible for Katyn. By the time of discussion of the Butler Memorandum, the best-placed FO official concluded that the Burdenko Report was 'simply incredible' and a 'pretty shoddy and inept production'. Tonkin dissected the nine documents claimed to have been found by Burdenko's team in 1944. He concluded that seven were false or doctored while the remaining two were presented out of context.[78]

The initial British reaction to the raising of the Katyn issue at Nuremberg was that it would be 'difficult and inappropriate' for HMG to take the initiative in the matter. Hector McNeill, the Parliamentary Under-Secretary for Foreign Affairs, confirmed this standpoint in the House of Commons on 10 October 1945 – 'as the victims were of Polish nationality and the site of the crime is on Soviet soil'.[79] Lord Chancellor Jowitt did likewise. He stated that 'the perpetrators had not been discovered', in a written Lords reply, on 19 December 1945, to a question by Lord Mansfield.[80] The internal Foreign Office debate centred on Dennis Allen's paper of 25 October 1945; this summarised the earlier debate in preparation for an adjournment debate to be initiated by Major Guy Lloyd MP, which did not, in fact, take place.[81] Allen recommended that the passive suspension of judgement line be continued although 'the Russians have produced *prima facie* evidence in support of their case'. Dean, however, wanted as little as possible of the Katyn evidence, from both sides, to be mooted at Nuremberg. Thomas Brimelow, the later ambassador to Warsaw, then in the Northern Department, agreed with Allen but succeeded in muddying the waters in one significant respect. He argued that Burdenko might indicate that *some*, although not *all*, of the Poles were killed at Katyn after March 1940. 'The Soviet investigations inculpate the Germans without entirely exculpating the Soviet authorities.' The Solomonic judgement that, perhaps, both totalitarian powers were responsible in some measure reinforced the FO preference for suspending judgement. Public statements remained problematic. For Brimelow – 'we cannot do more than say that there is a *prima facie* case against the Germans. We may feel that there is also a *prima facie* case against the Russians, but we cannot say so.'[82]

The British legal team at Nuremberg were, consequently, instructed to leave the preparation of the Katyn case 'severely to the Russians'.[83] Sir Hartley Shawcross attempted to persuade the Russians against including Katyn in the Nuremberg indictment and was concerned by the problems that would arise if evidence were called.[84] The FO line was, however, attacked, both from within and from outside. Sir Reader Bullard, the ambassador at Teheran, reported on 15 February 1946 his personal belief, based on consultations with the Poles in Persia, that the Soviets were responsible for Katyn. He considered that 'it would be unfortunate if the Russians managed to fob it off on the Germans before a court in which the British share is so important'.[85] The internal FO reaction was that Bullard contributed nothing new. A whole horde of officials confirmed in their annotations that it was essential not to 'blow' the Soviet case in public (J. Galsworthy/Northern Department); any acceptance of the German case over Katyn would be 'calamitous' (Frank Roberts). While holding aloof from the issue, it was politically desirable to appear to support the Soviet case in British dealings with them (Patrick Dean).

The London Poles also mobilised in order to get their evidence presented at Nuremberg. Count Raczyński handed over the London Polish 'Facts and Documents' file on the missing PoWs to the FO on 4 March 1948.[86] Hankey (Warsaw embassy) commented on this file that he wished that the Russians would drop the Katyn issue as 'the whole thing stinks. But we can't butt in.' He also sent the FO the Skarżyński Report of the Technical Commission of the Polish Red Cross which had visited Katyn.[87] This was summarised and commented upon by F. Bourdillon who confirmed that the Polish commission accepted 'irrefutable evidence of direct Soviet responsibility for the Katyn massacre'.[88] Their account followed the German version and was corroborated by local witnesses, the exhumations and evidence concerning the cessation of correspondence and the documentation found on the corpses. Bourdillon, however, was not convinced by the German Report or the treatment of the visiting delegations to Katyn. For him, the Germans 'had something serious to hide' and were solely interested in Katyn's publicity value.

The contemporary FO reports on the Nuremberg proceedings and the questioning of the three Soviet and three German witnesses discussed in the previous chapter now read extremely oddly.[89] Perhaps, the sense of justified historical retribution for Nazi war crimes overwhelmed their critical faculties. They failed to notice and to draw the appropriate conclusions from Bazilevskii and Markov reading out prepared statements undeviatingly, as in a Moscow show trial. In general, the British legal team accepted the Soviet case unquestioningly, while their generalisations provided much useful ammunition for future supporters of the FO line of suspending judgement and freezing responsibility for Katyn. The Soviet case was reported as having emerged 'much enhanced' and 'although not of course conclusive the evidence emerged strongly in favour of the Soviet case and the German report was largely discredited and their evidence unimpressive'.[90] Hankey was left to tell Count Raczyński that the British lawyers at Nuremberg had 'been impressed by the weight of evidence produced by the Russians to show that it had in fact been done by the Germans and that the Russians had very much the best part of the argument'.[91] If this was so, it is not corroborated by the subsequent recollections of participants.[92] Butler also fails to reconcile the 1946 FO and legal view with the Soviet failure to have Katyn ascribed to the Germans in the Nuremberg Tribunal's final judgement. He quotes Chief Justice Jackson's view to the Congressional Committee that neither the German nor the Soviet sides were happy with their performance over Katyn at Nuremberg. Churchill's charge that the Soviets did not grasp the opportunity to clear themselves by fastening the guilt conclusively upon the Nazis seems typically disingenuous.[93] The FO at the time, and Butler subsequently, also dismissed the strictures of the Oxford academic G. Hudson on the Soviet legal performance at Nuremberg.[94] The pertinent points made by another academic, writing for the Royal Institute of International Affairs, that all the crucial Polish Government-in-Exile evidence had been ignored while Rudenko had twice shifted his testimony at Nuremberg, were also shrugged off.[95]

The FO assumed an incredibly superior and patronising attitude towards the 1952 US Congressional Committee. Even with the onset of the Cold War, Bevin refused requests in 1950 by the Scottish-Polish Society and General Anders for an International Commission to investigate Katyn.[96] The stock FO objections were twofold. First, such a commission would not get very far without Soviet collaboration, which it was bound not to get. Second, 'as a propaganda stunt Katyn is too closely identified with Dr Goebbels'; the 'only advantage to be gained from reopening this issue would be propaganda material for use against Russia'.[97] The Washington Embassy was convinced that, although the Russians were the culprits, they had very successfully outmanoeuvred the Poles. It reported that the Congressional Committee had been established for domestic political reasons and that it was not taken seriously by the State Department.[98] The FO derided the sensationalist appearance of a hooded John Doe figure, who claimed to have witnessed the Katyn shootings on a totally impossible date. It was more convinced by the contributions of Skarzyński, Olshanskii and Justice Jackson. Eden and the British Cabinet also rejected, on 9 April 1952, the committee's request that it be allowed to hold formal hearings in the UK and that HMG should release the relevant secret documents.[99] The committee's Interim Report was pooh-poohed by a Northern Department official as totally predictable and based on inconclusive and contradictory evidence. He considered, nevertheless, that Soviet guilt seemed increasingly probable although his immediate superior restated the FO line that the circumstantial evidence of Soviet culpability was strong, although not conclusive.[100] Nobody responded to the single official whose annotation, that 100000 surviving relatives of victims of the massacre deserved an answer, raised the moral and human dimension. The demand, in a motion signed by 120 MPs led by Professor Sir Douglas Savory, that HMG should support the raising of the Katyn issue at the UN and before the International Court was resisted, stoutly.[101]

Both the British FO and the American State Department were perturbed by the committee's wish to hold formal hearings outside the USA, notably in London. This led to a great swirl of exchanges within, and between, both administrations in April 1952 over the facilities to be accorded and O'Konski's request for the release of documents. The Home Office was reported as being 'considerably disturbed' to hear that O'Konski and Pucinski were on their way to London to arrange the committee's sessions and foresaw a whole raft of constitutional, public order and practical problems.[102] The problems of perjury, libel, privilege and the voluntary summoning of witnesses were discussed at the FO on 4 April by a gathering of legal experts from the FO, Home Office and Lord Chancellor's Office chaired by Sir Roger Makins.[103] It was agreed that the committee could have no legal or binding status in the UK. Requests for facilities, support or documentation had to come formally from the US Government. The latter had, in fact, just occurred when Gifford, the US ambassador in London, met Sir William Strang in the FO and handed over an official note asking that eight separate pieces of information or documentation be made available to the committee. Most concerned the names and addresses of various British, Soviet and Polish witnesses, notably that of Krivozertsov and the British officials who had interrogated him. The requested documents concerned any Soviet material dealing with Katyn and a certified copy of the report by Colonel Hulls, a wartime British military representative in the USSR.[104] The FO reply of 10 April discussed the problems of perjury and privilege as well as of political demonstrations and counter-protests, which threatened 'embarrassing consequences'.[105]

Faced by all these difficulties the committee held wholly private and informal hearings in the Kensington Palace Hotel.[106] It heard 32 witnesses, including Anders and Raczyński, had these depositions certified by the US Consul in London and, contrary to British wishes, marked the end of proceedings by holding a press conference. The State Department was none too pleased by the intrusion of the legislative arm into foreign affairs. US Ambassador Gifford told Eden that 'he had done all he could to reduce the significance of these hearings'. Both agreed to dampen down coverage by the BBC and VOA.[107] Madden and Gifford withdrew their requests when HMG confirmed that it was not their policy to release confidential documents of the Second World War period. Exceptions could only be made to a friendly foreign government, not a legislature. Otherwise 'denial of such material to the British parliament would appear anomalous'.[108]

The FO reacted negatively to numerous letters during Nikita Khruschev's visit to the UK in 1956 suggesting that he should be approached about Katyn. He was touchy on the subject and its raising would be guaranteed to sabotage the visit.[109] Reform within the communist bloc and détente under Khruschev and domestic-national communism in Poland under Władysław Gomułka subsequently took the sting out of the Katyn issue in Britain. The FO Information Research Department (IRD) background paper of April 1956 concluding that Western opinion held the Soviets responsible for Katyn was denied any official status.[110] The Head of the Northern Department confirmed in 1960 that 'it cannot be represented as embodying the official view of HMG'.[111] This was in response to a private query by the Earl of Arran whether the time was not now ripe for HMG to acknowledge Soviet guilt for Katyn. In reply, Lord Lansdowne, the FO parliamentary under-secretary of state, declared that HMG 'never subscribed to the conclusions' of the Congressional Committee which had no judicial status. Lansdowne confirmed that the FO had never held 'the unequivocal view' that the Soviets were culpable although the 'weight of the evidence tended to incriminate them'. Judgement was suspended because of the confused state of the question; 'no new evidence has appeared to justify any change of attitude on our part'.[112]

Sir George Clutton, in his valedictory despatch in 1966 after six years as ambassador in Warsaw, predicted correctly that widespread and deep 'discontent, frustration and resentment' would lead to either an explosion or a slow collapse during the next few years. While condemning the mediocrity of Gomułka's leadership team, apart from Prime Minister Józef Cyrankiewicz, he sent his colleagues a glowing encomium about the continuing vitality of the Polish nation. 'A people of great generosity of heart, of ease and elegance, of culture and unbounded talent; a people innately aristocratic in the best sense of the word, with a sense of equality and without a vestige of that inferiority complex which is the curse of modern nationalism.'[113] The FO, however, noted that the rise of new forms of national communism, associated with the Partisan faction headed by the Minister of the Interior, Mieczysław Moczar, had revised domestic interpretations of Poland's Second World War experience.[114] This renewed internal debate about whether the non-committed line on Katyn should be changed.[115] In particular, the contradiction between the 1956 IRD Brief and the official public policy of non-attribution of guilt, which had already provoked 'sharp minuting' on the files in 1960, was noted openly in the internal exchanges. 'I am afraid that the position is that we all know that the Russians did it but we are not prepared to say so officially.'[116]

There were two main, and interconnected, reasons for the rebirth of public interest in the Katyn issue in Britain in the early to mid-1970s. First, the release of Foreign Office documents in the Public Record Office under the Thirty Years' Rule provided critics of the FO line with new and specific material. A major article by Ian Colvin in the conservative and anti-communist *Daily Telegraph* appeared on 17 August 1972 under the heading 'Russian Guilt for Katyn Reaffirmed'. It summarised O'Malley's first report in full and described the consternation which it had caused in official circles. The *Telegraph* reported Churchill's enjoinder for secrecy and for the issue not to be allowed to damage Allied–Soviet relations. It also embarrassed the FO by latching on to the circulation of O'Malley's despatch of February 1944 to the War Cabinet in the form of a blurred and smudged typescript in a sealed box.[117] It pointed out that Bourdillon's memorandum and the Burdenko Report were, by way of contrast, printed and distributed far more widely. Colvin also exposed the FO's successful quest to preserve a sense of 'valuable ambiguity' on the issue in order to maintain the suspension of judgement line.

Second, there was a last wave of major activity within the aging Second World War Polish *emigracja* which joined with anti-communist conservatives like Airey Neave MP in a drive to reopen and commemorate the

Katyn issue. The campaign centred on a proposal to erect a Katyn memorial and was supported by a series of publications on Katyn by the well-known Catholic publicist Louis FitzGibbon. Symptomatically, Butler dismissed the first of these, *Katyn: A Crime without Parallel* (1971), as entirely derivative, if not clumsily camouflaged plagiarism, from the London Polish 1965 English language documentary compilation *The Crime of Katyn*. FitzGibbon's *The Katyn Cover-up* got equally unenthusiastic reviews.[118] The press campaign included television programmes on Katyn on the BBC on 19 April and 13 October 1971 and some notable newspaper articles.[119] Amongst the latter, a review of a new edition of Zawodny's *Death in the Forest* considered that evidence of Soviet guilt was 'overwhelming' while the massacre's primary purpose was to eliminate a hostile class elite.[120]

A debate on Katyn also took place in the House of Lords on 17 June 1971.[121] Lord Barnby was widely supported in his plea for a new government statement 'establishing beyond contention the authorship of the Katyn massacre' and for a UN investigation or declaration.[122] Lord Hankey, with his wartime and Warsaw embassy experience, declared that he, personally, had no doubt as to Soviet guilt. But in purely legal terms 'there is a legitimate residual doubt, and I do not think that it has been possible to clear it up on the evidence which has hitherto been released'.[123] The veteran Labour Party left winger Emmanuel Shinwell took the Western democratic socialist line against the communists. Katyn was 'only one incident in a much larger series of crimes'. The massacre had been part of a 'deliberate policy' to exterminate Polish leaders which had also been demonstrated by Soviet passivity during the Warsaw Uprising of summer 1944.[124] Lord Aberdare, however, reiterated the stock government line that it had no standing in the matter and took no official view on Katyn.[125] Aberdare objected to the Government making 'a definite pronouncement' as the 'only result of a new enquiry would be to reopen old wounds'. The subject was best left to the free media, academics and historians.[126] This line failed to mollify the critics. Most notably, the Earl of Arran accused HMG during the debate of 'funking' the issue.[127] Lord St Oswald also wrote on 7 July to Foreign Secretary Alec Douglas-Home, saying how affronted he had been by Aberdare's reply which left Katyn as 'the great unexpiated crime of the Second World War'.[128] Douglas-Home's subsequent meeting with Neave and St Oswald merely reiterated that the Government would not shift its position and saw no reason why it should be expected to act as the 'arbiter' of purely historical disputes. The Foreign Secretary gave his *realpolitik* game away, however, by claiming that HMG criticised or opposed Soviet actions, such as its naval presence in the Indian Ocean or by expelling its spies, whenever the British national interest demanded it.[129]

The FO (now FCO) also stiffened its defences in response to pressure from Lord St Oswald and Airey Neave in July 1971.[130] Its internal brief on the subject accepted that the working assumption, or presumption, that the Soviets 'were probably the guilty party' had strengthened over the years. But it defended the line that HMG should continue not to state this publicly or officially. There was no serious political analysis of why this should be so. As during the Second World War, there was no discussion whether telling the truth about Katyn would endanger détente or harm British–Soviet relations in any substantive way. This is what the constructivist school in international relations calls 'a silence' masking a 'common sense' approach to issues.[131] British administrations considered the proposition as self-evident and as flowing naturally from their perception of the national interest. Constructivist interpretations explain this in terms of their social and cultural mind-set. FCO officials considered that their problem was only how to avoid appearing 'inconsistent or disingenuous' in public as a result. For them, 'the inherent weakness' of the St Oswald–Neave position was that no investigation was necessary, if the facts about Katyn were generally well known and accepted. On the other hand, a new enquiry's findings would not gain universal acceptance without the collaboration of the Soviet and Polish Governments, which would not be forthcoming. Should HMG really be expected to express a public view if the evidence was still incomplete and controversial?[132] Butler accepted the logic of the above arguments and he also endorsed the conclusion. 'We see no advantage in breaking the silence that we have preserved for nearly 30 years on the Katyn massacre.'[133]

The FCO therefore opposed Neave's attempts to have Katyn discussed by the UN General Assembly or to get the International Committee of the Red Cross involved.[134] Sir Anthony Royle, the Under-Secretary for Foreign Affairs, rejected the former of Neave's suggestions in the House of Commons on 12 July 1971. Neave's Early Day Motion on the subject, eventually signed by 193 MPs, only stiffened the FO line that nothing would be gained by 'provoking the Soviets unnecessarily'; the priority 'was to respect, above all, the wish of the Polish [communist] Government that the incident should be regarded as closed'.[135] Neave was leant on by the FCO, with appeals to support the British national interest, during 1972 to influence his parliamentary supporters and the project's organisers to ensure an anodyne inscription on the memorial. He also had his role as a Patron of the Sue Ryder Foundation threatened quietly in a very British sort of way.[136] Royle declared that the Katyn project was now 'a major irritant in our relations with the Poles'. The latter did not understand the autonomy of local government and public opinion in a democracy. Neave remained obdurate and wanted the Soviet and Polish bluff to be called as Soviet threats had not always materialised. He denied that he wanted to damage Britain's relations with communist countries. His motivation was solely 'the recognition of a serious injustice' and one could go too far to cover it up. He promised a fight if HMG attempted to stop the memorial project.[137] Neave was blown up by (what is generally held to be) an IRA bomb outside the House of Commons on 30 March 1979 when he was the Shadow spokesman on Northern Ireland Affairs. Although no proof of Soviet complicity has emerged one may wonder if his role in the Katyn affair might not have been an additional factor, somehow contributing to his selection as an assassination target.

An extremely sparse form of the FCO's dilemma found its way into the public arena as a footnote, tucked away, just like an embarrassing detail in a publication in a communist state, in a new edition of Llewellyn Woodward's officially authorised history of the Second World War.[138] The FCO praised his 'measured reference to Katyn having occurred in 1940' and prepared to cover its back with the argument that only the author was responsible for such public statements.[139]

The 25th anniversary of Katyn in 1965 stimulated efforts within the Polish community in the UK to collect funds for its commemoration in some sort of permanent memorial. This resulted in a sculpture, whose inscription read 'to the victims of Katyn', in the main Polish church in London, Saint Andrew Bobola, in a chapel dedicated to the Holy Mother of Kozelsk.[140] The following year a plaque was also unveiled in the Polish church in Leicester. This strand became intertwined with public polemics over Katyn. FitzGibbon's letter to the *Daily Telegraph* (28 January 1971), anticipating publication of the first of his books on Katyn, provoked Feliks Alexeev, the London correspondent of the Soviet *Novostii* news agency, into trotting out the standard Soviet Burdenko line.[141] This led to a spate of press rejoinders and exchanges, notably by the LSE academic specialist on Soviet dissidents Peter Reddaway, who offered sightings of the previously discussed Menshagin in evidence. The Lords debate and the two BBC programmes marked the peak of public interest. The latter on 19 April 1971 occasioned protests by the Soviet and Polish embassies and led to the cancellation of a proposed visit by Charles Curran, the Director of the BBC, to Poland.[142]

Edward Heath's Government was too preoccupied with growing social and economic problems to contemplate additional complications in British–Soviet relations after it expelled over 100 alleged Soviet spies in 1971. The plea by the Federation of Poles in Great Britain in May 1971 arguing the case for Soviet responsibility in an *aide-mémoire* and calling on 'the Free World to condemn the perpetrators [of the massacre] loudly and clearly' received a cool reception.[143] The FCO in its internal debate on the memorial proposal warned that it would cause 'grave offence' to both Soviet and Polish Governments and harm trade and economic collaboration.[144]

FitzGibbon and his friends, supported by London Poles such as General Stanisław Kopański, kept the campaign going by establishing an Anglo-Polish Committee, which quickly transformed itself into the Katyn Memorial Fund in 1972.[145] Chaired by Lord Barnby with Airey Neave and Lord St Oswald as deputy chairmen and the tireless FitzGibbon as secretary, it received a strong worldwide response for its appeal for funds. The Fund's British Patrons included the Marquess of Salisbury, the Earl of Arran, Viscount Monckton, Sir Tufton Beamish MP and Winston Churchill MP, plus all the leading figures in the Polish émigré Government. The Fund's prime objective was to erect a major permanent memorial to the victims of Katyn, understood as englobing 'the 10000 others'. This involved much discussion before a sub-committee composed of Count Adam Zamoyski, Adam Treszka and FitzGibbon decided that a solid obelisk would be best for practical reasons as it would be difficult to vandalise and bird droppings would slide off. Finding a suitable site proved more difficult, for a mixture of bureaucratic planning and other reasons. This stimulated suspicions that hostile government or pro-Soviet forces were at work. Douglas-Home steered Neave away from the idea that the memorial might be sited in a royal park by making it clear that the required governmental permission would not be forthcoming. He advised that obelisks and plaques did not count as statues and did not need such permission. Proposed sites in Hammersmith, at Wormwood Scrubs (opposite the prison), at Battersea (next to the funfair) and close to the Brompton Oratory proved either unsuitable or impracticable.

The Katyn lobby, however, persuaded Sir Malby Crofton, the Conservative council leader of the Borough of Kensington and Chelsea, to offer a plot of ground close to Saint Luke's Church in Chelsea. This proposal was sabotaged by the local Anglican Diocesan Advisory Committee. It objected that disturbance of tombs might distress local residents and that the proposal was 'not in keeping with the Church's principle of reconciliation'. Chapman Pincher, a well-known, although sensationalist, right-wing journalist of the time, termed these 'most ridiculous reasons'.[146] The Committee was, however, encouraged by the inflow of funds, and the speed with which £8000 out of the original target of £10000 had been raised, to opt for a more ambitious design costing £35000. The St Luke's proposal was effectively rejected (adjourned to seek public consultation), after a long waiting period by the London Diocesan Consistory Court after prolonged hearings before the Archdeacon of Middlesex during summer–autumn 1974. Why the Church of England and parts of the British establishment should object so strongly to the 1940 date designating the Soviets as responsible has been explained by some outsiders in terms of British national pathologies such as ingrained anti-Catholicism. Despite testimonials from Drs Tramsen and Palmieri, Prince Eugeniusz Lubomirski and a Lutheran Kozelsk-Gryazovets survivor, Władysław Jerzy Cichy, the Chancellor of the London Diocese finally ruled, on 15 January 1975, against the appeal for the memorial. The proposed memorial was ruled to be a 'building', which would have breached a borough covenant to maintain an open space.

The Katyn memorial proposal provoked a very full, heated and somewhat irritable discussion within the FCO. It also had British–Polish–Soviet diplomatic repercussions. The Department of the Environment (DoE), when consulted at the outset, stated that its policy 'was to avoid adding to the number of statues already in central London' as well as to ensure that all the appropriate planning regulations were satisfied.[147] The FCO line was that St Luke's Garden was preferable to the Cromwell Road triangle site but that it would be even better if the Royal Borough Council denied permission. The sponsors could then be steered towards an even less conspicuous site, preferably on privately owned land.[148] Its main concern, apart from the memorial's location, was its inscription, especially if a 1940 date imputing Soviet responsibility were to be included. Douglas-Home was unsuccessful in getting Neave and Barnby to abandon this central point.[149] By the end of 1972 the FCO line had hardened around the judgement that 'the Katyn project involves no benefit, and much damage, to British interests'. It should be discouraged while its inscription should not carry the 1940 date or any other imputation of Soviet responsibility. The Polish émigrés should build it in a church or private place while the Americans should contribute to have a memorial built in the USA which had many more Poles.[150]

Soviet and Polish diplomatic protests, notably Polish Foreign Minister Stefan Olszewski's intervention when he met Douglas-Home in New York in September 1972, stimulated FCO attempts to defuse and neutralise the issue. Two most pressing objectives were identified: the memorial should be 'inconspicuously sited', and it should not 'be provocative in any respect, particularly in its inscription', which should not include any mention of the 1940 date.[151] The same official suspected the motives of the memorial's organisers and feared for its consequences upon British–Polish–Soviet relations. Bullard, the son of the wartime ambassador to Teheran, recommended that the FCO mobilise opposition to the St Luke's site and that it should be ground down through bureaucratic obstruction and inertia. The officials resisted calls for Truth and Morality in international relations as they considered that this would benefit only Polish émigrés and the Germans![152] The FCO turned down requests for donations by governmental figures and discouraged approaches to official figures.

In the end, the Royal Borough offered the Katyn Committee a site at Gunnersbury cemetery in West London close by the Chiswick flyover over the M4 motorway, in the so-called 'Polish corner' where General Bór-Komorowski, amongst others, is buried.[153] A 20-foot-tall obelisk of black Nubian granite, following the design of architect Ryszard Gabrielczyk, whose godfather had perished at Katyn, was erected in 1976. Built by the firm of Gilbert and Turnbull at a cost of around £21 000, its foundation stone was laid on 1 July and had two documents concerning Katyn inserted into it. The obelisk had a white eagle engraved into it with the crucial and much contested date – '1940' – below it. The two inscriptions in the plinth at its base were in Polish and English. The latter read

factually – 'In remembrance of 14500 Polish prisoners of war who disap-
peared in 1940 from camps at Kozielsk, Starobielsk and Ostaszkow, of
whom 4500 were later identified in mass graves at Katyn near Smolensk'.
The main inscription, 'Sumieni świata woła o świadectwo prawdzie' (the
conscience of the world calls for a witness to the truth), had been chosen
as the campaign's battle cry at the outset.

Well out of the way, the insult by the British establishment, was com-
pounded by an official, although not wholly observed, ban on former, as
well as serving, officers of the British Army appearing in uniform at the
unveiling ceremony on 18 September 1976. For many London Poles this
was a bitter reminder of the British Government's refusal to allow their
servicemen, who had fought in the Polish Corps under British command
during the Second World War from Tobruk to Monte Cassino to Arnhem,
to participate in the 1945 Victory in Europe parade. The unveiling ceremony was, however, carried out with considerable pomp by the Polish *emigracja*, for whom this was very much a last hurrah with most of their main
personalities, such as London President Ostrowski, present. Other notables included the old and frail Kozelsk survivor General Wołkowicki,
General Bohusz-Szyszko who had also just survived the massacre, Cardinal
Rubin who represented Polish Primate Stefan Wyszyński as well as a
number of English supporters, mainly right-wing Conservative MPs and
peers. Amongst the many wreathes were three from the Churchill family;
'Remembering the men who died at Katyn and with deep apologies for
our cowardly government' (which one – wartime or contemporary?) com-
plemented – 'In memory of our gallant Polish Allies murdered at Katyn in
1940' as well as a tribute to Victor Cazalet, who died alongside Sikorski in
Gibraltar in 1943.

One of the most controversial issues in the Katyn debate in Britain in
the 1990s concerned the intelligence reports received on the subject
during the Second World War. There were two aspects to the question.
First, did they make the issue of Soviet responsibility abundantly clear?
Second, if they did, were they sabotaged or doctored, either by 'traitors'
and Soviet agents of the ilk of Burgess, Maclean and Philby, or by others
for more prudential reasons?[154] *The Katyn Massacre: An SOE Perspective*,
published in February 1996, gave a particularly thin and unconvincing
answer to the 'cover-up' charges.[155] It noted the general policy of making
Special Operations Executive (SOE) files available in the PRO from 1993
onwards. The fourth batch released in March 1995 covered Poland and
the USSR along with Czechoslovakia and Hungary under the HS 4/1-381
classmark. The FCO paper fails to mention the Soviet documentation,
already made public, by then, under Gorbachev and Yeltsin. It does not
even make it wholly clear, for the benefit of non-specialists, that Katyn was
only one of the three burial sites in the 1940 massacre.[156] Their short and
superficial apologia on the substantive issue was that the SOE line 'is the
same as that in the Foreign Office files, but more exaggerated in

emphasis'.[157] Both were most concerned to avoid supporting German propaganda and to maintain the Soviet alliance. They conceded, implicitly, that this had to be at the cost of what the London Poles considered to be the objective truth and their interests. This argument may have been justified by *realpolitik* considerations during the Second World War but after Poland had been 'sacrificed' (p. 8) and Sovietised and the Cold War set in, the argument became a positively weasel one. The 1996 FCO paper can, at best, be regarded as a piece of delaying bluster and a smokescreen, reflecting the paralysis of the dying stages of the Major Government. The FCO retreated behind it while catching up with the post-communist revelations in Eastern Europe.

The most striking feature of an examination of the actual SOE material released so far is the limited volume and unattributed character of the relevant documents. Some of the reports, however, flatly contradict the thesis of a harmonious unity of view between the FO and the SOE. They go well beyond a mere presumption of Soviet guilt.

> SOE interests require the firm support of the Poles even at the risk of offending Soviet susceptibilities. General war interests would not be prejudiced thereby as Russia's participation in the war was not of her own choosing, and it may similarly be thought that the decision whether to continue fighting or not, would not in the case of Russia be affected by the clear and firm statement of Allied policy in Eastern Europe.[158]

Such a firm statement that the defence of the interests of the minor Polish ally could be harmonised with what the major Soviet ally was going to do anyway is completely missing from the FCO discussion. The truth and morality aspect surfaced in the debate around the O'Malley reports. FCO stonewalling and embarrassment over the 1940 massacre issue during the 1990s was, eventually, alleviated by the publicising of the Butler Memorandum on the world wide web.

Notes

1 Hayden White, *The Content of the Form: Narrative Discourse and Historical Representation*, Baltimore, MD: Johns Hopkins UP, 1987.
2 Victor Zaslavsky, 'The Katyn Massacre', *Telos*, no. 114 (Winter 1999), p. 94.
3 G.G. Hudson, 'A Polish Challenge', *International Affairs*, 36, 2 (April 1950), pp. 214–21.
4 George Sanford, *Democratic Government in Poland*, Basingstoke: Palgrave, 2002, pp. 219–25.
5 FRUS, *Diplomatic Papers: The Conferences at Cairo and Teheran 1943*, Washington, DC: Government Printing Office, 1961. *The Conferences at Malta and Yalta*, Washington, DC: Government Printing Office, 1955.
6 DPSR, 2, p. 6.
7 See Zawodny, *Death in the Forest*, pp. 178–88. Robert Szymczak, *The Unquiet*

Dead: The Katyn Forest Massacre as an Issue in American Diplomacy and Politics, Carnegie-Mellon University PhD, 1980 (Ann Arbor, MI: University Microfilms International no. 4012, 1985), Ch. VI.

8 Jan Ciechanowski, 'Sikorski's Role as a Statesman and Commander-in-Chief during World War 2', in Keith Sword (ed.), *Sikorski: Soldier and Statesman,* London: Orbis, 1990, p. 109.

9 US. G.406 sent by Washington embassy to FO on 3 July 1943, PRO HS137. An earlier draft sent in late May was considered 'disquietening', PRO FO371/34577 C6027/258/55.

10 *Hearings,* Part 7, pp. 2012–22.

11 *Hearings,* Part 7, 1996, p. 2285.

12 *Hearings,* Part 7, pp. 2258–60.

13 An earlier attempt by the Americans in spring 1942 to send Szymanski as liaison officer to the Polish High Command in Kuibyshev had been rebuffed by the Soviets, FRUS, 1942, 3, pp. 123, 549.

14 Szymanski's 'An Overview of Polish–Russian relations', concluding that they were marked by 'irreconcilable differences', WSM/Is. IG No 3600, was relayed by the US Cairo embassy only on 15 June 1943. It was submitted to the Congressional Committee, *Hearings,* Part 3, pp. 453–8.

15 *Hearings,* Part 3, pp. 416–505.

16 Hardly surprisingly, this document, Biddle to Roosevelt and Secretary and Under-Secretary of State, no. 316 of 20 May 1943, was much publicised by the Congressional Committee, *Hearings,* Part 7, pp. 2092–7.

17 *Hearings,* Part 7, p. 1934.

18 *Hearings,* Part 7, p. 2249.

19 Earle was Minister to Austria from 1932 to 1934 and, after his spell as Governor, also Minister to Bulgaria, 1940–1941. Pennsylvania had previously been a rock-hard Republican state so many of the sources mistakenly describe Earle as a Republican during his period in office. See *Pennsylvania Governors: Past to Present,* www.phmc.state.pa. us/bah/dam/governors/earle.asp?secid=31.

20 *Hearings,* Part 7, p. 2204.

21 Ibid., p. 2201.

22 Ibid., Part 7, pp. 2207–10.

23 A supplementary report written by Van Vliet in May 1950 was read into the *Congressional Record,* 11 December 1950, p. A6665 by Representative John E. Rankin of Mississippi.

24 Typically, the British embassy in Washington downgraded the significance of Van Vliet's report. The only real bit of fresh evidence for it was 'the condition of the corpses' shoes', Jamieson (Washington embassy) to FO, 9 April 1952, PRO FCO 100719 NP16661/9.

25 *Hearings,* Part 2, p. 67.

26 *Hearings,* Part 7, pp. 2302–6.

27 FRUS, 1942, III, pp. 104–5, 146, 150–1, 154–6, 163, 174–5, 177–8, 183.

28 *House Report,* no. 8205, 82nd Congress, House of Representatives, 22 December 1952, p. 3.

29 Ibid., p. 5.

30 Sir Oliver Franks (Washington) to FO, no. 324 of 31 March 1952, PRO FCO28/100719 NP1661/4.

31 FO to Franks (Washington), 10 April 1952, PRO FO371/97631 Au1661/13.

32 Lee Edwards, 'Amerykańskie poglądy w latach 1951–1991 na kwestię zbrodni Katyńskiej', in *Zbrodnia Katyńska po 60 latach,* Warsaw: NKHBZK, 2000, p. 90. Derwinski had earlier in 1962 publicised the findings of the 1952 Congressional Committee on Katyn as part of the attempt to establish a House Com-

mittee on Captive Nations, see Louis FitzGibbon, *Unpitied and Unknown*, London: Bachman & Turner, 1975, pp. 395–6.

33 B.L. Crowe (Washington) to Tonkin (EES), 27 October 1972, PRO FCO28/1947 U3/18.

34 Stephen A. Garrett, *From Potsdam to Poland: American Policy toward Eastern Europe*, New York: Praeger, 1986. Symptomatically, this book does not contain a single reference to Katyn.

35 The City of Toronto also unveiled a Katyn memorial in September 1980. Despite Soviet protests Pierre Trudeau's Government did nothing to prevent this although it did not participate officially in the ceremonies. Another memorial was unveiled in Adelaide with the 1940 inscription, without any complications, on 17 September 1977 in front of the Dom Polski. See Andrzej Szczygielski (ed.), *Pomnik Katyński w Adelajdzie*, Happy Valley, South Australia: Stowarszyszenie Polskich Kombatantów w Australia, 1981.

36 Szymczak, *Unquiet Dead*, pp. 298–9.

37 Janusz Zawodny commented that he always believed that moral values and respect for human life would overcome the conspiracy of silence in a democracy like the USA, 'Covering Up the Katyn Massacre Tore at Democracy', *Chicago Tribune*, 27 April 1990.

38 *Congressional Record*, 3 April 2003, pp. E660–1. Allen Paul, author of *Katyń: Stalin's Massacre and the Roots of Polish Resurrection*, Annapolis, MD: Naval Institute Press, 2nd edn, 1996, seems to have inspired (or benefited from) this junket in order to boost the publication in Warsaw of the Polish translation of his book.

39 Proposed by Senators Helms, Mikulska, Roth and Biden, *Zbrodnia Katyńska Próba Bilansu*, Warsaw: NKHBZK, 2001, pp. 207–9.

40 *Congressional Record*, 25 September 2003, p. E1899. Senator Jon Corzine carried out a similar eulogy of 'one of the most heinous war crimes in history' in the Senate, *Congressional Record*, 16 September 2003, pp. S11562–3.

41 Particularly by O'Malley to Eden, 29 April 1943, PRO FO371/34571 C4850/258/55, a major and extensive report.

42 Annotations to ibid.

43 Cf. Gabriel Kolko, *The Politics of War: Allied Diplomacy and the World Crisis of 1943–1945*, London: Weidenfeld & Nicolson, 1969, pp. 99–104.

44 FO Historical Papers: History Notes and Occasional Papers, *British Reactions to the Katyn Massacre, 1943–2003* (hereafter Butler Memorandum), www.fco. gov.uk/servlet/Front?pagename=OpenMarket/Xcelerate/ShowPage&c=Page &cid=1049114089000.

45 Rohan Butler (1917–1996) was a Fellow of All Souls and Senior Editor of the Foreign Office *Documents on British Foreign Policy* series as well as of the post-war volumes on *Documents on British Foreign Policy Overseas*. As holder of the prestigious post of Historical Adviser (which had been in abeyance from 1929 to 1963) he enjoyed a magisterial reputation within the Foreign Office and was called upon to overview and give independent assessments of such issues as the status of Szczecin (Stettin) and the relinquishment of Abadan. His first draft of the Katyn memorandum (35 paragraphs) was circulated for internal debate in September 1972 while the final version of 68 paragraphs, revised in the light of internal FO discussion, was printed for internal circulation (DS 2/73) on 10 April 1973. The final draft is at PRO FCO28/1946 (also FCO28/2309).

46 Kerr to Eden, 21 April 1943, PRO FO371/34569 C4396/258/55.

47 *Butler Memorandum*, p. 9.

48 Hansard, 5th series, H of C, vol. 389, col. 30.

49 Winston S. Churchill, *The Second World War*, Vol. IV, *The Hinge of Fate*, London: Cassell, 1951, p. 679.
50 PRO FO371/34568 C4230/258/G. The FO informed Kerr on 19 April (telegram no. 397) that the Poles have 'little confidence in Soviet denial of German allegations', PRO FO371/34568 C4230/G.
51 Pol43/12 in PRO FO371/34569 C4586/258/55.
52 O'Malley to Eden no. 51, 24 May 1943, PRO PREM3/353 C6160/258/55. Also in FO371/34577 C1660/258/55.
53 Allen and Roberts, annotations to ibid.
54 O'Malley report, pp. 6–7.
55 *Butler Memorandum*, p. 12. The comments by FO officials were publicised for a Polish readership by Madajczyk, *Dramat Katyński*, pp. 146–9.
56 Churchill to Eden, 25 February 1944, PRO PREM 3/353 M.1777.4.
57 Eden to Churchill, 26 February 1944, PRO PREM3/353 PM/44/100.
58 Churchill minute of 28 April 1943 to Eden, PRO FO371/34571 C4798/258/G55.
59 Record of Churchill–Roosevelt–Stalin conversation, Soviet embassy, Teheran, 1 December 1943, Foreign Office, Historical Papers No 48, 'Churchill and Stalin: Documents from the British Archives 1943'.
60 Churchill–Stalin conversation, Teheran, 28 November 1943 in ibid.
61 See the PRO PREM3/356/3 file on the conversations on Poland's frontiers and government at Yalta.
62 Churchill, *Hinge of Fate*, Ch. XV.
63 Churchill had inquired of Eden on 15 July 1943 whether the first O'Malley report had been sent to Roosevelt. Eden replied the following day that he was against sending it officially through the Washington embassy – 'if it were to find its way into unauthorised hands, the reactions on our relations with Russia would be serious'. In a letter to Roosevelt of 13 August 1943 Churchill described O'Malley's report as a 'grim, well-written story, but perhaps a little too well written. Nevertheless, if you have time to read it, it would repay the trouble. I should like to have it back when you have finished with it as we are not circulating it officially in any way', PRO PREM 3/353 M.51/4.
64 Eden's reply the following day was that the best evidence suggested a 1940 planting, ibid.
65 Ibid.
66 O'Malley to Eden, 11 February 1944, PRO FO371/39390 C2099/8/55.
67 The Savory Report is in PRO PREM 3/353. Dennis Allen cut Savory's report down for the benefit of the FO consensus on the grounds that 'there is nothing whatever new' in it. The Polish enquiries were 'only an element in the story – although quite an important one', Note of 8 December 1945, FO371/47734 N17514/664/9.
68 PRO PREM3/353 C2957/8/G of 26 March 1944.
69 Churchill, *Hinge of Fate*, p. 681.
70 Eden, 16 July 1943, PRO FO371/34580.
71 O'Malley letter to Cadogan of 13 April 1944, PRO FO371/47734 N16482/664/55.
72 *Butler Memorandum*, para. 12.
73 FO371/39393 C2957G/8/55 of 4 March 1944. Annex B of the *Butler Memorandum*, pp. 1–8.
74 Annotations with various March 1944 dates to ibid.
75 Ibid.
76 *Butler Memorandum*, p. 17.
77 Ibid., paras 18–23.
78 D. Tonkin (EES), 1 November 1971, PRO FCO28/1947 ENP10/1.

79 *Hansard*, H of C, vol. 414, col. 250.

80 PRO FO371/188794.

81 PRO FO371/2309 N16482/664/55, reproduced in *Butler Memorandum*, Annex C.

82 Annotation to ibid.

83 Richard Beaumont (FO) to Colonel Phillimore (British Junior Counsel), 25 January 1946, N568/108/55, cited in *Butler Memorandum*, p. 29.

84 Shawcross to Foreign Minister Ernest Bevin, 28 December 1945, PRO FO371/56474 N108/108/55.

85 Bullard (Teheran), Telegram no. 210, 15 February 1946, FO371/56474 N2111/108/55.

86 FO371/71610 N2599/108/55.

87 Annotation of 10 April 1946, FO371/56476 N4406G/108/55.

88 N5269/108/55 of 10 April 1946, reproduced in *Butler Memorandum*, Annex D.

89 FO371/56474 5675/5676.

90 British War Crimes Executive, Telegram of 6 July 1945 for Dean and Scott-Fox, FO371/56476 N8817/108/55.

91 Hankey to Raczyński, 4 March 1948, PRO FO371/71610 N2599/2599/55.

92 A participant, K. Duke (EERD), noted a quarter of a century later that his recollection of what the British legal team had thought of the Soviet evidence at Nuremberg was, now, 'rather different'. Bullard to Brimelow, paper on Butler Memorandum 16 October 1972, PRO FCO28/1946.

93 Churchill, *Hinge of Fate*, p. 681.

94 G.F. Hudson, 'A Polish Challenge', *International Affairs*, 36, 2 (April 1950), pp. 214–21.

95 S. Lowery in *Survey of International Affairs, 1939–1946: The Realignment of Europe*, London: RIIA, 1955, p. 147.

96 G.W. Harrison of the Northern Department expressed a dissenting voice on 23 May 1950 in the FO debate about the response. 'The fact, however, that we have played down the Katyn murders during the war is not necessarily a good reason for playing it down today', PRO FO371/86679 NP1661/1.

97 Edward Tompkins (Washington Embassy) to Northern Department, 27 September 1951, PRO FO371/94780 18255/1/51f NP1661/3. The internal FO annotations on his report ranged from 'difficult to see what useful purpose this can have ... no justification in raising these ghosts ... one of Goebbels' masterpieces' (Tonkin) to 'the real evidence at Katyn was carefully obliterated by the Russians in 1944. There seems no useful purpose in raising these ghosts now' (L.H. Massey).

98 Ibid.

99 See PRO28/LCO2/5172. Eden also formally minuted his dislike of the committee and its proceedings.

100 G. Littlejohn-Cook, minute of 30 July 1952, PRO FCO28/100719 1661/13. Cf. *Butler Memorandum*, paras 54–5.

101 PRO FO371/188794. Also FO/371/100719 NP1661/15 of 13 August 1952. Cf. Savory letter in *Daily Telegraph*, 13 August 1952.

102 Note by H.A.F. Hohler (FO), 1 April 1952, PRO LCO2/5172.

103 Ibid.

104 No. 5310 of 4 April 1952, PRO LCO2/5172.

105 PRO LCO2/5172.

106 *Hearings*, Part 4, pp. 503–968. This includes an appendix which reproduces the London Government-in-Exile's file on 'Polish–Soviet Relations, 1918–1939'.

107 Eden to Sir Oliver Franks (Washington), 17 April 1952, PRO LCO/2/5172 AU1661/14.

108 R. Cecil to Franks (Washington), 5 May 1952, PRO LCO2/5172 AU16661/23.

109 Haigh minute of 23 April 1956, PRO FO371/122671 NP1661/3. The Government also prevailed on the British Council to ban the showing of a film on Katyn on their premises which the FO considered 'political propaganda', cf. *Times*, 25 April 1956.

110 Contained in PRO FO371/714.

111 R.H. Mason of 10 October 1960, PRO FO371/188794 NP1661/2.

112 Lansdowne letter of 30 November 1960 to Arran, ibid., NP1661/2.

113 Clutton to FO, 1 August 1966, PRO FO371/188748.

114 The Polish debate about its historical dilemmas and defeats and how they should be responded to in the present was given a new twist by Zbigniew Załuski in *Siedem polskich grzechów głównych*, Warsaw: MON, 1962 and also by his *Przepustka do Historii*, Warsaw: MON, 1967. An article by another writer associated with this trend, Wojciech Żukrowski, in *Miesięcznik Literacki* (September 1969) raised particular discussion within the FO.

115 See Miles-Pakenham correspondence, PRO FCO28/714 ENP3/303/2.

116 R.O. Miles to J.N. Henderson (Warsaw), 30 April 1969, PRO FCO28/714 ENP/1.

117 Churchill himself had complained about receiving a 'smudged flimsy' of O'Malley's report on 26 February 1944 in the weekend before he read it. He also laid down that it should 'be circulated to the War Cabinet Ministers only, in a box from hand to hand' on 3 March 1944, PRO PREM3/353.

118 *Butler Memorandum*, para. 63.

119 Ian Colvin in *Daily Telegraph*, 5 July 1971 and 17 August 1971. Lord Nicholas Bethell in *Sunday Times* (magazine), 28 May 1972.

120 Gabriel Ronay, 'The Soviet Massacre of Poland's Elite', *Times*, 29 January 1971.

121 PRO FCO28/1475 and 1476 for the FO's extensive preparations for the debate and for dealing with Lord Barnby's question. For the debate see *Hansard*, 5th series, House of Lords, vol. 320, 17 June 1971, cols. 737–75.

122 Ibid., col. 737. The latter call was taken up in the US by Congressman Pucinski and *Polonia* and Captive Nation associations, FitzGibbon, *Unpitied and Unknown*, p. 398.

123 *Hansard*, 5th series, H of L, vol. 320, col. 754.

124 Ibid., col. 771.

125 This declaration was repeated on 29 June and 21 July, *Hansard*, 5th series, vol. 320, col. 773 and vol. 321, col. 961.

126 Ibid., col. 773.

127 Ibid., col. 776.

128 PRO FCO28/1476.

129 FO Brief for Douglas-Home meeting of 19 July 1971 with Neave and St Oswald, PRO FCO28/1477.

130 *Butler Memorandum*, paras 66–7. PRO FCO28/1476 for the handling of Neave's question of 12 July 1971 in the House of Commons.

131 See Jutta Weldes, *Constructing National Interests: The United States and the Cuban Missile Crisis*, Minneapolis: University of Minnesota Press, 1999, Ch. 7.

132 *Loc. cit*, f. 128, PRO FCO28/1477.

133 *Butler Memorandum*, p. 44.

134 M.S. Barker-Bates (UN Department), 14 June 1971, PRO FCO28/1475, ENP10/1.

135 J.L. Bullard to Sir Thomas Brimelow (Warsaw), 11 June 1971, PRO FCO28/1475, ENP10/1.

136 Bullard brief for Royle–Neave meeting, 16 October 1972, PRO FCO28/1946.

137 Royle–Neave meeting of 17 October 1972, PRO FCO28/1947.

138 *British Foreign Policy in the Second World War*, London: HMSO, II, 1971, p. 626.

139 R.N. Hankey (Soviet Section RD), 24 May 1971, PRO FCO28/1475 ENP10/1.

140 This led middle-rank FO officials, exasperated by the later Katyn memorial controversy, to express the view that as 'there is already one Katyn memorial in London, there would not seem to be an overwhelming reason to have a second one', Tonkin to Bullard, 21 May 1973, PRO FCO28/2308.

141 *Times*, 8 February 1971.

142 G.G.H. Walden (EES), 17 July 1971. PRO FCO28/1475, ENP10/1.

143 PRO FCO28/1475.

144 Bullard (EES) to Wiggin, 11 July 1972, PRO FCO28/1945. Bullard was particularly concerned that the proposed inscription would be 'a gratuitous irritant'. His favoured option was to relegate the memorial to a Polish cemetery or private place.

145 For the whole of this episode see FitzGibbon, *Unpitied and Unknown*, Chs 5–6.

146 *Daily Express*, 6 April 1973.

147 B.J. Bennett (DoE) to FO, 20 June 1971, PRO FCO28/1945.

148 S.W. Martin (EES) to Brimelow, 23 August 1972, PRO FCO28/1945. Martin had earlier pointed out that the Cromwell Road proposal could, if the need arose, be sabotaged by civil servants on the 1851 Exhibition Commission.

149 Martin (EES) to Brimelow (Warsaw), 12 June 1972, PRO FCO28/1945.

150 Bullard (EES) to Logan, 2 December 1972, PRO FCO28/1947 ENP10/1.

151 Bullard to Brimelow, 25 September 1972, PRO FCO28/1946 ENP/10/1.

152 Bullard to Brimelow, 8 October 1972, PRO FCO28/1946 ENP10/1.

153 See Louis FitzGibbon, *Katyn Memorial*, London: SPK/Gryf, 1977.

154 The allegation that Sikorski's death in the Liberator bomber in Gibraltar in July 1943 was not an accident was fuelled by Philby's presence as Head of British Intelligence in the Iberian Peninsula at the time. Louis FitzGibbon has also pointed out that Vyshinsky was in Gibraltar on 4 July 1943 on his way back to Moscow. FitzGibbon considered that Sikorski was regarded as a potential nuisance, if not a threat, to long-term Soviet plans for the post-war takeover of Poland and that he was bringing back crucial evidence concerning Katyn from his visit to Anders in the Middle East, letter in *Daily Telegraph*, 20 November 1973.

155 History Notes, no. 10. FCO LRD – Library and Records Department, 1996.

156 KDZ volume 1 was published in 1995 and by then, Polish and Soviet academics had invalidated the paper's assertions that the Katyn and total massacre numbers had never been established.

157 FCO LRD, no. 10, p. 6.

158 PRO SOE HS4/137, 1943 reports on Katyn Massacre and Polish–Soviet relations. The Polish-British Historical Commission's publication of Second World War intelligence reports in July 2005 merely represented a much belated sop to Polish susceptibilities.

8 Soviet and Polish communist control of the truth about Katyn
The conflict with national memory

Soviet 'management' of the truth about Katyn

The renewed public interest in Katyn in Britain in the early to mid-1970s, especially the proposed erection of a memorial to its victims in London, provoked a strong Soviet and PRL diplomatic reaction to its various aspects. The CPSU politburo discussed the question on 15 April 1971. It confirmed instructions for the Soviet ambassadors to London and (when appropriate) to Warsaw to express Soviet 'surprise and indignation' to the British FCO against the forthcoming BBC broadcast and the 'slanderous' publications appearing on the issue. The politburo reiterated the standard Burdenko line on German guilt claiming that this had been recognised at Nuremberg. The FCO was to be asked to take appropriate steps to prevent the circulation of material designed by its authors to worsen relations between Britain and the USSR.[1] The Central Committee was informed that the Polish 'friends' would be seconding the above actions.[2]

Ippolitov, the Soviet Counsellor in the Warsaw embassy, thus protested against the forthcoming BBC2 broadcast, even before it took place. His note demanded that the FCO 'take due measures in order to prevent the dissemination in Britain of the above slanderous materials'.[3] The British ambassador in Warsaw, Thomas Brimelow, replied that the Soviets should not prejudge the issue. While the BBC was an independent body it would be informed of Soviet representations. The complaint and warning was repeated in early April.[4] Kozyrev, the Soviet Deputy-Minister of Foreign Affairs, repeated stock phrases about the provocative anti-Soviet campaign taking place in London, in September 1972. He expressed the hope that HMG 'would take all appropriate measures to prevent the erection of the memorial in London to the victims of the Katyn massacre'.[5] This was taken a step further by the Soviet ambassador in London, Mikhail N. Smirnovsky, in his meeting with Douglas-Home on 7 March 1973.[6] He reiterated Kozyrev's protest against the Katyn memorial proposal and campaign. His demand that HMG 'take all appropriate measures to see that the so-called memorial is not erected' met with what by now had become the standard response: the inscription had not been authorised officially, the Government had no control over local government bodies and the project should be ignored by governments and starved of publicity.[7]

The Katyn controversy abated, and died away, in Britain with the unveiling of the Katyn obelisk in Gunnersbury cemetery in 1976. The Soviet leadership, however, decided in April to take Douglas-Home's advice and to forego further official diplomatic moves. The Soviet Foreign Office and the CC Foreign Department were to coordinate a more effective response with the Poles.[8] 'The aim was to counter and neutralise anti-socialist and anti-Soviet actions and campaigns in the West in connection with the "Katyn Affair".'[9] The growth of domestic dissidence in Gierek's Poland, especially strong intellectual opposition to a constitutional amendment laying down Polish–Soviet friendship, made the Brezhnev leadership particularly sensitive on this point. Significantly, this politburo decision also instructed the KGB to give Western ruling circles an unofficial warning. 'The renewed use of anti-Soviet falsehoods, of various origins, would be regarded by the Soviet Government as especially provocative, and as being aimed to worsen the international situation.'[10]

The mature Brezhnev line on Katyn is set out in a detailed document, of uncertain, but likely CC secretariat, origins included in the 1992 Yeltsin folder.[11] Almost certainly written in March 1976, it responded to developments in Britain and the early signs of growing dissidence in the PRL. After restating the official line on the Polish PoWs having been killed by the Germans in autumn 1941, Goebbels' propagandist use of the issue and the authoritative character of the Burdenko Report, the document repeats the false claim for communist bloc usage that German guilt was recognised at Nuremberg. The main brunt of the argument aimed to discredit the US Congress Committee's findings as well as the O'Malley Report whose release was fuelling the Katyn debate in Britain. Knowing Soviet practices, one wonders what really lay behind the concluding emphasis on the anxiety which the anti-Soviet campaign over Katyn was allegedly causing Gierek's leadership team. The claim that this had led the Poles to request consultation with their Soviet comrades 'on the means for counter-acting the propaganda pressure of hostile centres' might equally well have meant exactly the opposite. Were there leadership voices on the Polish side asking for a lancing of the Katyn boil who had to be brought to heel? What we do know is that despite being weakened by his climbdown over a failed price increase in summer 1976 Gierek subsequently did little to clamp down effectively on the intellectual, as against working-class, dissidents who propagated the Katyn theme.

The Soviet drive to control the truth about Katyn involved erasing its name, as much as possible, from maps and publications. The reference to it in the 1953 edition of the *Soviet Encyclopedia*, a concise summary of the Burdenko case, was dropped in 1973. Strict censorship instructions dictated how Katyn should be written about following the standard Burdenko version, whenever it became absolutely essential to mention the subject in the mass media. The Soviet authorities also tried to confuse the issue of their failure to erect a full memorial at Katyn by publicising the significance of a village with a similar sounding name. Khatyn, a small and otherwise obscure village in Belarus, about 30 miles to the north east of Minsk and 160 miles west of Katyn, was suddenly favoured with massive Soviet media attention from 1969 onwards.[12] Khatyn was one of 136 Belarusan villages where all the inhabitants had been slaughtered by the Nazis during the Second World War. A large memorial complex was built in 1969. It became the focus of the usual compulsory factory and school visits, media publicity and a brochure, available in no less than six languages. President Richard Nixon's unwise visit to Khatyn during his 1974 trip to the USSR allowed his hosts to publicise the Khatyn memorial.[13] The Soviets thus attempted to discredit the Katyn memorial campaign in London and to confuse Khatyn with Katyn in Western minds.[14]

The Gorbachev/Yeltsin fes and how the truth was revealed

The State Security Committee (KGB) chairman Aleksandr Shelepin sent CPSU First Secretary Nikita Khruschev an important note on the documents concerning the 1940 massacre on 9 March 1959.[15] Shelepin reminded Khruschev that the executions had been carried out on the basis of decisions taken by the CPSU politburo on 5 March 1940 and by the Special Troika which it established. The investigation files for 21857 executed Poles, along with other relevant material, had been stored in a sealed room in the KGB headquarters. No information had been released on the affair to anyone since 1940. Shelepin considered that the files did not now have any 'operational or historical value', either for the Soviet organs or for their Polish friends. 'Quite the contrary, any unforeseen indiscretion whatsoever, could lead to the deconspiration of the operation which had been carried out, with all the undesirable consequences which this would entail for our state.' Any such leak would undermine the Burdenko version blaming the Germans. Shelepin therefore proposed that all the evidence files on the individuals shot in 1940 should be destroyed. Answers to any future queries from the CPSU CC or the Soviet Government could be drawn from the protocols of the Special Troika and the documents implementing its decisions. Not constituting a large amount they could easily be stored in the First Secretary's Special File. Annexed to the foregoing material in the 1992 folder was a four-line-long draft decision, implementing the above, to be submitted for approval by the presidium of the CC CPSU.[16] No written documentation confirming the destruction of the evidence files has emerged. All that one has is the reported testimony of a former KGB Colonel in 1994–1995 that Khruschev gave verbal orders that the investigation files be destroyed.[17] The Special Troika protocols have also not been found.

The process which led Gorbachev to reveal the truth of Soviet responsibility in 1990 and to begin the process of releasing the relevant documents was by no means straightforward. As with many other steps in his reform process, which has been amply discussed elsewhere, he had to be pushed and bounced into taking this momentous step by others.[18] A key role was played by academics and journalists outside the communist party *apparat* who were encouraged and protected by reformists such as Aleksandr Yakovlev within it. The key documents, handed over by Chief Archivist Pikhoya to Wałęsa on 14 October 1992, throw a somewhat selective, and far from continuous, light on a number of key episodes by which the truth about the 1940 massacre emerged between 1988 and 1991.

The first of these concerns the last ditch effort by Gorbachev and Jaruzelski to rescue the Polish–Soviet relationship from the odium being heaped upon it by *Glasnost* revelations of Stalinist crimes.[19] The CPSU politburo endorsed a number of suggestions, in preparation for Gorbachev's visit to Poland of 11–14 July 1988.[20] The building of a memorial complex to the victims at Katyn, with Polish collaboration, and the easing of travel visits to the site by relatives had been proposed by Foreign Minister Edward Shevardnadze supported by two leading reformists, Yakovlev and V.A. Medvedev.[21] This, apparently, responded to repeated requests by Jaruzelski and other prominent PZPR figures, notably Mieczysław F. Rakowski, Marian Orzechowski and General Józef Baryła. The conservative ex-KGB Chairman (1982–1988) Viktor M. Chebrikov, however, proposed that a memorial should also be erected to the 500 Soviet PoWs allegedly shot on the site, according to the Burdenko version, after having been forced by the Germans to carry out their exhumation work. The decision to build the Katyn memorial complex was agreed by Gorbachev and Jaruzelski in Warsaw and confirmed by the CPSU politburo on 1 September.[22] Gorbachev, conceding that many Poles considered that Stalin and Beria were guilty of Katyn, also promised a meeting of Polish intellectuals, held in Warsaw's Royal Castle on 14 July 1988, that he would accept the truth. The way ahead was for historians to carry out a scrupulous investigation to determine the truth about the tragedy.

Gorbachev's leadership was stimulated into the final year-long stage of considering the Katyn question during spring 1989 by a report from Valentin Falin, the head of the CPSU CC International Department.[23] He noted that an ROPWiM delegation, headed by its chairman, General Roman Paszkowski, was planning to collect a symbolic urn of soil from Katyn at the end of March, for reburial in Warsaw. 'The Katyn affair was disturbing social peace in Poland' in the run up to the Round Table which had just opened. As the Poles attributed responsibility to Stalin and Beria, the attempt by Jaruzelski's leadership to balance loyalty to the Soviet Union with the satisfaction of Polish society through such gestures should be supported. Foreign Minister Shevardnadze took up Falin's conclusion that the Polish press and opposition were demanding the clarification of the wider problem of the fate of the Starobelsk and Ostashkov PoWs. He conceded that the Soviet side in the Joint Historical Commission during the previous two years had stood still. They had not been authorised to resolve the Katyn 'Blank Spot' by being given the documents with which to challenge Burdenko.[24] The situation had now become so critical that Polish Official Press Spokesman Jerzy Urban attempted to quieten the academic and press furore by accepting *de facto* that the PoWs had been killed by the Soviets in spring 1940. Shevardnadze's crucial conclusions for the politburo, supported by Falin and KGB chairman (1988–1991) Vladimir A. Kryuchkov, deserve quotation in full:

> We will, probably, be unable to avoid clarifying the tragic affairs of the past to the PRL leadership and Polish society. Time, in this instance, is not our ally. It may become useful to say how matters were in reality and who, specifically, was guilty of what occurred, and thus close the matter. The cost of taking such measures will, in' the last analysis, be less in comparison to the losses incurred by the current delay.

Thus primed, the politburo instructed the KGB, the Ministry of Foreign Affairs and the CC Departments of International and Ideological Affairs on 31 March to prepare proposals, within a month, on the 'further Soviet tactical line on the Katyn question'.[25] The subsequent report of 22 April, however, reflected either the confused state of the available documentation or undecided and negative responses by the actors and institutions involved.[26] It reported that only a part of the 12000 (*sic!*) Polish officers massacred in 1940 were killed at Katyn. Polish and Western sources indicated that the remainder perished at Bologoe and Dergachii. The Soviet procuracy, in collaboration with the KGB, should be instructed to carry out a scrupulous investigation in order to finally clarify the affair. Hopes that positive results could be achieved, and announced, before Jaruzelski's working visit to Moscow of 27–28 April, proved unrealistic.[27] The procuracy investigation, as discussed in the next section, was to grind on, in one form or another, until 1993, when it practically came to a halt.

As a result of dogged detective work and nosing around in the archives by academic historians during 1988–1989 the CPSU apparatus was mobilised into suggesting to Gorbachev that the time had come to accept Soviet responsibility for the 1940 massacre, publicly. The unstated problem was, however, how to massage the embarrassing fact that he probably already knew this from the contents of the personal file which was handed on directly from the outgoing First Secretary to his successor. Falin reported on 22 February 1990 that Natalia Lebedeva, Valentyna Parsadonova and Yurii N. Zoria had been permitted to work in the party's Special Archive and the Central State Archives of the USSR Council of Ministers as well as of the October Revolution (TsGANKh).[28] They had uncovered previously unknown NKVD DPA and Central Executive of the Escort Troops documents of the 1939–1940 period concerning Katyn. This material confirmed that the fate of over 14000 Polish internees in the special camps at Kozelsk, Starobelsk and Ostashkov had been considered on various occasions by Beria and Merkulov and the investigation teams which had prepared material for the NKVD Special College. The internees had been placed at the disposal of the relevant oblast NKVDs during April–May 1940, under conditions of the highest secrecy, on the basis of centrally drawn up lists using a single general numbering system. The lists were accompanied by the order that agents, informers and individuals having potential operational value should be excluded and retained. Unlike usual practice, commandants were ordered merely to mark in their camp index that the prisoners had departed.

Falin noted that the prisoners held in the three camps up until April–May 1940 did not appear in any subsequent NKVD statistics. Their personal files were worked over by the NKVD First (Special) Department and stored in its archive. The historians' findings, with the implicit conclusion that they had been shot by the NKVD, had now been accepted for publication during June–July.[29] This would create a radically new situation. The authorities, faced even with these partial documentary revelations, could no longer defend the Burdenko version. They should take advantage of the forthcoming 50th anniversary of the 1940 massacre to revise their position. Although the direct orders concerning the Katyn tragedy had not as yet come to light, sufficient evidence had been found to discredit Burdenko. The indications were that the massacre was the responsibility of the NKVD and, personally, that of Beria and Merkulov. 'The necessity of liquidating the political aspects of the problem and at the same time to prevent emotional outbursts' led Falin to propose that Jaruzelski be told of the new developments. He should also be consulted over how Soviet and Polish society could best be informed.

Although we lack further documentation concerning the subsequent debate it is clear that the Gorbachev leadership accepted Falin's proposal. On 13 April 1990, Katyn Memorial Day commemorating the 1943 German announcement, the TASS agency made the above policy public. In a historic statement it expressed apologies and declared that Katyn was 'one of the heaviest Stalinist crimes'.[30] The two folders of documents handed over by Gorbachev to Jaruzelski on the same day, during his Moscow visit, however, barely constituted a start in documenting this new reality.[31] The 14 793 names of the victims in the three camps nevertheless went far beyond Moszyński's list, which was particularly incomplete for Ostashkov with only 1200 names.[32] The 1990 documents have been categorised under the following additional headings by the leading authority on the subject.[33] NKVD notes and correspondence concerning PoWs; 45 transportation lists, containing 4419 names, sent to Kozelsk with the order that they be placed at the disposal of the Smolensk NKVD[34]: a directory of 4031 personal files of Starobelsk inmates.[35] The 1990 files and TASS announcement were not a direct disavowal of Burdenko or an explicit admission of Soviet guilt for the 1940 massacre, although they were understood as such by the Poles. Gorbachev did so only implicitly, by opening up the way for that conclusion to be documented.

Soviet communism collapsed and the USSR broke up after the failed coup of August 1991. The President of the new Russian Federal Republic, Boris Yeltsin, banned the CPSU and revealed its crimes politically by accusing it before the Constitutional Court. He also opened the archives to historians.[36] This broke the final barrier on access to the relevant documentation concerning the 1940 massacre, particularly as the issue was used to discredit Gorbachev's hesitations, and possible insincerity, on the subject. Yakovlev reports Gorbachev as having handed over the sealed envelope on Katyn to Yeltsin in December 1991 in a manner which indicated that he had long known its contents and implications.[37] The crucial 42 documents concerning Katyn were handed over by Pikhoya to Wałęsa in Warsaw on 14 October 1992. The photocopies of the original Russian documents along with their Polish translations were quickly published in full, as well as in the order given, by the Institute of Political Sciences of the Polish Academy of Sciences. They came from the so-called 'Set No 1' in the First Secretary's Special Archive (Osobyi Arkhiv) which had been incorporated into the Presidential Archive of the Russian Republic (APRF) on 31 December 1991. The nine key documents included the shattering 5 March 1940 politburo decision but not the records of the NKVD Special College or Katyn Troika. This somewhat sparse material was clearly selected according to Yeltsin's political criteria of his current struggle with communism, so there is no way of knowing how complete the material is.

On the other hand, these documents settled the issue of Soviet responsibility for the 1940 massacre and outlined its general parameters beyond all doubt. The remaining documents concerned the subsequent Soviet cover up and defensive actions. Only two documents deal with the Shelepin–Khruschev exchanges of 1959 on the burning of the investigation files. This left the issue in a particularly incomplete, unsatisfactory and unresolved state. The British Katyn memorial dispute, by contrast, was reasonably well covered in the 12 documents examined earlier. The final 18 documents covered the evolution of the Katyn question within the communist leadership during 1988–1991 as well as the early stage of the procuracy investigation. This group is largely significant in revealing the hesitant and uncertain attitude of Gorbachev's central party bureaucracy to the issue. It also shows the importance of reform communist patrons such as Yakovlev and Falin for letting the academics loose into the archives. A somewhat wider range of Second World War topics was covered in the 60 documents brought back from Moscow in November 1992 by Professor Marian Wojciechowski, the Director of the Main Polish State Archives.[38]

Katyn in post-communist Russian politics: the Procuracy investigations

Early in the life of the democratic Third Republic the Polish Council of Ministers decided on 24 September 1989 that its diplomats and procuracy should work to accelerate the Soviet investigation into Katyn. Józef Żyto, the General Procurator, wrote on 9 October 1989 to Soviet Procurator Alexandr Sukharev, requesting officially that an investigation be opened into the killing of the Kozelsk, Starobelsk and Ostashkov PoWs. Sukharev gave a vacillating reply and seemed to be playing for time while the Gorbachev leadership made up its mind on the issue. Events had, however, slipped sufficiently out of Moscow's control for the Ukrainian Provincial Procuracy in Kharkov to announce on 22 March 1990 that it was opening an investigation into the mass graves, mainly concerning the Polish officers from Starobelsk whose bodies had recently been discovered in the sixth section of the Kharkov forest-park. Gorbachev's handing over of the first folder of NKVD documents to Jaruzelski and the TASS announcement of 13 April 1990 transformed the situation concerning the 1940 massacre fundamentally. This facilitated the appointment of an investigation team in Kharkov, which started work in early May.

Polish Foreign Minister Krzysztof Skubiszewski's conversations with Gorbachev and Shevardnadze during his Moscow visit of 10–16 September 1990 accelerated the Soviet Procuracy investigation into the fate of the Polish officers held in the three camps. Gorbachev enjoined the Procuracy, KGB and Ministry of the Interior to 'ensure conditions for finding and examining archival materials connected with the repression of Poles, who found themselves on the territory of the USSR in 1939, and to present the appropriate conclusions'.[39] The Main Procuracy of the Soviet Army associated the Polish Procuracy with the Soviet inquiry by asking it officially, on 25 December, to open a supporting investigation. The Minister of Justice, Aleksander Bentkowski, had already appointed deputy Procurator General Stefan Śnieżko to oversee the Polish inquiry into Katyn, and he moved smoothly into his new role. Together with a military procurator, Colonel S. Przyjemski, and procurator Henryk Stawryłło from the Ministry of Justice, he met the Soviet investigation team in Moscow on 18–20 December to ascertain the progress being made and to coordinate further actions and meetings.[40] The main Polish investigation work was carried out by Śnieżko's two assistants, procurators Zbigniew Mielecki and Kołodziej. They assembled the Robel Archive, took numerous depositions and facilitated exhumations in Kharkov and Mednoe in July–August 1991 and Katyn in November 1991.[41]

The Soviet Military Procuracy, headed by Colonel Aleksandr Vladimirovich Treteckii, was at its most active during this period in tracking down and interviewing surviving participants and witnesses such as Tokarev, Soprunenko and Syromatnikov. By May 1991 Gorbachev was informed of the investigators' preliminary conclusion. This was that the Polish PoWs from Kozelsk, Starobelsk and Ostashkov had been shot during April–May 1940 on the basis of a decision by the NKVD Special College. Witness statements indicated that there was also a party decision signed by Stalin so the Procuracy requested that this document be sought out in the party archives and sent to it. The Soviet Procuracy had also agreed, at their joint meeting on 19 April, to Śnieżko's request for further exhumations and that photocopies of all the relevant documentation be made available to the Polish side.[42] Gorbachev, buffeted by the ongoing party battle between reformers and hardliners, thus found himself pressed to the wall on the Katyn issue by these developments. Considerable evidence – formal complaints that the Katyn investigation was being hindered by hardliners – indicates that this conflict was replicated within the Military Procuracy.[43]

There is no direct evidence that Gorbachev learnt the truth about the 1940 massacre from the contents of the First Secretary's Special File only in December 1991, as he claimed. Officially, he would have had to unseal special envelopes and sign a usage list in order to do so, but it is difficult to believe that he would not have had a good look through the Special File on becoming First Secretary in 1985. There was considerable controversy, therefore, over whether he actually knew the truth from 1989, at the latest, as claimed by Yeltsin, or earlier.[44] Events, however, conspired against him taking the final decision on the issue. After the failed August 1991 *coup* the newly reorganised Procuracy of the Russian Republic took over. The Katyn investigation was assigned to Lieutenant Colonel Anatolii Yablokov, who the Poles considered as effective and sympathetic as his predecessor. As we have seen, repeated questioning produced key evidence in the transcripts of the Tokarev and five Syromatnikov interviews, qualified written answers by Soprunenko and recollections by secondary figures such as Klimov and Titkov.

The peak period for Polish–Soviet–Russian judicial, archival and academic collaboration was from 1990 until about 1993, after which activity diminished, contacts became more formal and the issue increasingly lost its political salience. The question marks still remaining over the politically selective character of the folders of Katyn documents handed over by Gorbachev in 1990 and Yeltsin in 1992 have already been noted. The absence of the PoW individual investigation files was noted early on. Not everyone was convinced, particularly the Katyn pressure groups by the accompanying record of their intended destruction by Khruschev and Shepilov in 1959.

Given such enormous gaps, in both the judicial evidence and the academic record, the most promising avenue for further progress seemed to lie in the field of archival collaboration and the exchange of documents. Forty-three out of the 150 volumes of evidence gathered by the Soviet Military Procuracy were brought to Poland by 1992.[45] An enormous amount of photocopied documentation, 240 000 pages, of which about 70 000 concern the 1940 massacre, was also brought to Poland by the Military Archival Commission (WKA). The key development for historians, at least, was the visit of the Head of the Archives of the Russian Republic, Professor Rudolf G. Pikhoya, to Warsaw in April 1992. The agreement which he signed with the Main Direction of the Polish State Archives produced joint Russo-Polish archival cooperation culminating in the publication of the main documentary source for the first half of this book. The three-volume *Katyn: Documents Concerning the Atrocity*, published in Warsaw in 1995, 1998 and 2001 (with a fourth volume envisaged as completing the series in 2005), has now established itself as the primary source for elucidating the historical context to, the organisation and implementation of, and the consequences of the 1940 massacre. The Central Military Archive in Rembertów, on the fringe of the Warsaw conurbation, now also holds photocopies of the original documents from which they were selected.[46] On the other hand, only the first volume of the parallel Russian versions has been published, despite the terms of the original agreement.[47] Professor Pikhoya was dismissed from, or eased out of, his post as Chief Archivist of the Russian Federation in early 1996. Amy Knight has demonstrated how the security services acted as 'gatekeepers' to the archives by 'controlling what documents are to be released and who has access to them'.[48] They collaborated with conservative *apparatchiks* in Yeltsin's Russia to maintain society's 'collective amnesia' on Stalinism.

The emergence of Peasant-Left (PSL-SLD) governments in Poland after 1993 saw a crucial shift in the way in which the 1940 massacre issue was dealt with. Once Boris Yeltsin had consolidated his power, after the Duma revolt in 1993, he had to compete with the communists and Zhirinovsky's extreme nationalists. His interest in fostering wider democratisation, by compromising the communists through revealing Stalinist crimes, also diminished as it might have threatened his presidential power. Bożena Łojek is correct to point out that the possibility of identifying and prosecuting surviving perpetrators, thus establishing the historical truth about the episode and of achieving a measure of justice within the legal-judicial framework, passed away for good in the mid-1990s.[49] It was largely replaced by the campaign to commemorate the massacre through appropriate monuments at the burial sites as well as in cemeteries and churches. Prime Minister Waldemar Pawlak entrusted this effort to Stefan Śnieżko. He was appointed chairman of the Committee to Commemorate the Katyn Crime, established on 19 August 1994.

The Katyn pressure groups, notably the PFK and NKHBZK in Poland and Memorial in Russia, were consequently faced with diminishing public support for their calls for the Russian and Polish criminal investigations to continue to clarify the problem. The PFK and NKHBZK sent a memorandum to the Polish Government in October 1994 stating that the Katyn investigation had reached 'a critical stage'. The Russian Republic, as the successor to the Soviet state, bore full responsibility for the atrocity; it had not released all the relevant documentation and evidence and should be prevailed upon to do so.[50] The Katyn lobby received no reply to this, as well as to a string of further declarations, during the 1990s.[51] Exhumations were resumed in the three burial sites under ROPWiM auspices in 1994 but without any procuratorial presence or participation. Only the Ukrainian Procuracy took an interest in the parallel Bykovna exhumations in 1996. By that time Treteckii and Yablokov had been replaced by M. Anisimov and his assistant S. Szalamayov in the Russian Procuracy investigation.

The Polish Katyn lobby were also concerned by numerous attempts by Russians, taking advantage of the new political and press freedoms, during the mid- to late 1990s, to deny Soviet responsibility for the 1940 massacre. This could take a blatantly polemical and primitive form, accepting the Burdenko version in full, as with Mukhin's *Katyn Detective* in 1995.[52] But it could also unconsciously echo the British FO's reservations about parts of the evidence, especially the forensic-medical findings, not establishing Soviet guilt conclusively. The Committee of Experts servicing Yablokov's Russian Procuracy investigation concluded in 1993 that the exhumation evidence established the fact of the crime but did not give a full answer as to its date or the perpetrators and their motives.[53] Pointing out the gaps and inconsistencies in the evidence might have been understandable before 1990. The Katyn lobby was, however, quick to point out that doing so after Gorbachev's admission and Yeltsin's release of the NKVD evidence was a wholly perverse, and politically motivated, attempt to cloud and mitigate the issue of Stalinist guilt. Professor Felix Rudinskii, for example, had defended the CPSU against Yeltsin's charges of criminality and genocide before the Constitutional Court in 1992. He argued in 1998 that the CPSU should be cleared of responsibility for Katyn. His main argument was that the documents handed over to the Poles and the signatures on the 5 March 1940 decision had never been checked to see if they had been falsified.[54] He also argued, in a method associated with the Holocaust revisionist David Irving, that there was no documentary, and signed for, evidence that successive First Secretaries of the CPSU, including Gorbachev, had received the secret package, so it could easily have been tampered with.

The London Government-in-Exile and the Home Army

As noted in Chapter 6, two delegations of Poles, followed by individual visits, went to Katyn in April 1943 and confirmed that the missing Polish PoWs had, almost certainly, been massacred by the Soviets. The Government-in-Exile and the AK gave the Polish Red Cross and the Main Welfare Council some leeway in their dealings with the Germans. Apart from that, however, as evidenced by Mackiewicz's suspended death sentence and AK condemnation of the 'reptile press', all German overtures for anti-Soviet collaboration were rebuffed. The London Government's delegate in German-occupied Poland, Jan Stanisław Jankowski, issued a declaration on 30 April 1943 accepting Soviet responsibility for Katyn but denouncing German attempts to exploit the massacre for propaganda purposes.[55] The breaking off of diplomatic relations by the Soviets worsened the prevailing gloomy atmosphere by indicating that Stalin wanted not only to destroy Poland's elites but also to maintain a free hand in controlling Poland's future fate through subservient agents.[56] This mood of cynical pessimism and lack of belief in Western support helps to explain the AK's desperate last throw in the summer 1994 Warsaw Uprising and the grim resistance, however quixotic, by its successor WiN and other movements in the camouflaged civil war up until 1947.

The Polish Government-in-Exile kept its British ally fully informed of the German propaganda campaign over Katyn in occupied Poland. The main Polish theme was that the Polish people and their leaders 'engaged in a life and death struggle against Germany – have consistently refused to collaborate in any way with the Germans'. They started to prepare for the Red Army's entry into Poland, however, by ordering the AK on 25 October 1943 to get ready for a general uprising at the appropriate time. Mikołajczyk's Government, therefore, gave the Allies ample notice of their wish to incorporate what became the *Burza* (Tempest) strategy, leading to the summer 1944 Warsaw Uprising, 'in the general strategic plans of the Allies'.[57] AK sources recorded the German initiatives over the sending of the delegations from occupied Poland to Katyn and the unsuccessful German propaganda drive to utilise the Soviet massacre to convince the Polish people to volunteer for work in Germany and to shift sides against Bolshevik barbarism.[58] The keynote conclusions noted the total 'absence of any political engagements' or guarantees in favour of Poland or 'definite solutions of the Polish question as an alternative to Bolshevik oppression' by the Nazis. The result for the Poles was that 'the Katyn propaganda offensive has only been to confirm them in the feeling that there is no essential difference between their Eastern and Western oppressors'.[59]

Katyn and the PRL

The massacre of the Polish PoWs in 1940 had important consequences, both for Polish–Soviet relations and for the way in which communist power was established in Poland.[60] The Polish Army in the USSR was largely staffed by Soviet officers as the number of Gryazovets survivors who collaborated was minuscule. Colonel, later General, Zygmunt Berling, after whom the army was popularly called, was, politically, a largely figurehead commander of the Kościuszko Division in 1943–1944.[61] He was sidelined, subsequently, as even he, did not prove a reliable enough stooge, like Marshal Michał Rola-Żymierski, for the Stalinists.[62] Most of the Polish officers in the West, and a large percentage of those who had been in

German captivity, did not return to an increasingly communist-dominated Poland after 1945. Those who did were distrusted and usually purged by the Muscovite faction of the PPR/PZPR led by Bolesław Bierut.[63] Consequently, the Polish army had to be staffed by Soviet officers during the Stalinist period. Hardly surprisingly, one of the most powerful (and successful) demands of the Polish *October* of 1956 was that the Russian officers and specialist 'advisers', led by Defence Minister and PZPR politburo member Marshal Konstanty Rokossowski, should 'go home'.[64]

Berling and a Union of Polish Patriots delegation visited Katyn on 30 January 1944 in order to reinforce the launch of the Burdenko line.[65] A Starobelsk survivor, who had personally heard the notorious phrase about the Soviet 'mistake' in 1940 from Beria's own lips, no Pole was better informed than Berling about the real truth of the fate of his colleagues.[66] His Faustian pact with the Soviets was not made easily, but he has been roundly condemned for trotting out the lies required by the Soviets at Katyn calling for vengeance against the German perpetrators of the crime.[67] The Soviet authorities took up this theme by collecting money to fund the establishment of a tank unit designated as the 'Avengers of Katyn'.

The PPR gradually built up its monopoly of power in Poland by about the 1947 election under the shield of the Red Army and the Polish communist political and security bodies which supported it against residual Home Army and domestic opposition. The Provisional Government, headed by Edward Osóbka-Morawski (PPS), also included non-communist figures like the Peasant Party (PSL), and ex-London leader Mikołajczyk as Deputy Premier. There was, therefore, a period of genuine coalition and mixed power sharing until 1947, with the communist drive for monopoly power being particularly contested under ambiguous near-civil-war conditions. This explains why the PPR attempt to organise a contra-Nuremberg supporting the Soviet version of Katyn proved such a fiasco in this period and why it was not relaunched during the short classical Stalinist period of about 1948–1954. The evidence suggests that Minister of Justice Henryk Świątkowski and Attorney General Jerzy Sawicki sounded Mikołajczyk out in 1945 about the possibility of a Katyn trial under Polish auspices. Mikołajczyk's refusal to collaborate in establishing the Burdenko version of Nazi German guilt was probably instrumental in Moscow, according to Zawodny, eventually dropping the issue.[68] Numerous articles, however, appeared in the pro-communist press propagating the Burdenko line during 1945–1946.

Campaign preparations for the show trial also included pressurising the Poles who had visited Katyn to retract their original positions and to support the Soviet line, as Hajek in Czechoslovakia and Markov in Bulgaria were doing. As we have seen, Dr Szebesta also did so, as did the RGO official Edmund Seyfried. The right-wing writer Ferdynand Goetel, after interrogation by the Military Procuracy, very sensibly fled to the West, along with other key Katyn witnesses like Mackiewicz, Skiwski and Wodziń-ski.[69] Robel was arrested and questioned and, for a while, feared that he would be liquidated surreptitiously like Professor Martini (discussed below).[70] Robel's assistant, Dr Marian Cioch, sought refuge in hiding from the NKVD and Polish police and procuracy arrests and investigations of the Kraków *milieu* before leaving Poland in September 1945. Bolesław Drobner, the pro-communist PPS chieftain in Kraków, was reported to have said that the Government had decided to put Cioch, Szebesta, Father Jasiński and Dr Prągłowski on trial and to sentence them to death for col-laborating with the Germans over Katyn.[71]

Numerous Poles during this period were having to make difficult choices and having to decide whether to stay and survive in a Soviet com-munist Poland or to seek refuge in emigration. The degree of accommo-dation to or even buying into, what became the PRL after 1947 naturally varied according to personal beliefs and circumstances. Only this, can explain a basic mistake by the communists which produced one of the most mysterious episodes concerning Katyn in Poland itself. Roman Martini, the procurator of the Special Court in Kraków, was much involved in prosecuting Gestapo agents who had committed crimes under Gauleiter Frank's rule in the *General-Gouvernement*. He was, therefore, com-missioned by Świątkowski in 1945 to prepare the judicial processing of the proposed Katyn trial. Martini was, however, a man of independent charac-ter who refused to act as a communist stooge in stage managing a show trial demonstrating Nazi German guilt and Soviet innocence of the crime. His energetic and thorough investigations, which involved taking testi-mony from key witnesses such as Skarżyński, led him to the opposite con-clusion, and this made him potentially dangerous.[72] He was murdered on 28 March 1946 in his apartment at 10 Krupnicza Street in Kraków by a young couple during an alleged burglary.[73] Nineteen-year-old Stanisław Lubicz-Wróblewski claimed to have killed Martini as the latter had seduced his 17-year-old girlfriend Jolanta Słapianka. Whether this motive was true or not, and both are usually regarded as naïve pro-communist sympathisers, Słapianka received a 15-year jail sentence. Her boyfriend was allowed to escape, but was caught, and conveniently disposed of, by being executed for another murder in Kraków, in July 1947.[74] The complicity of the authorities in mounting the affair, and in using impressionable young people in this way, whatever their personal or political motives, is indu-bitable.[75] There has, hardly surprisingly, been much speculation about the degree of involvement by Soviet and Polish security agencies.

The most significant aspect of the Martini affair, however, concerns the German documents which are alleged to have come his way during the investigation. Whatever they were, they did not include the subsequently manufactured Tartakov forgery. The claim that it was retrieved by Martini's friends immediately after his murder, before the Soviet or Polish security agents could get there, however, provided a credible provenance.

Whether Martini actually visited Minsk, Kharkov and Smolensk in order to obtain these documents seems highly unlikely given the confused end-of-war conditions. If the NKVD had been on the ball he would certainly have discovered documents proving German, not Soviet, responsibility!

The Martini affair and the failed show trial demonstrated a basic dilemma facing the Polish communists which lasted during the whole life of the PRL until it faded away in 1989. Their dependence upon the USSR meant that they publicly had to accept the Soviet dogma of German guilt for Katyn, as expressed by Burdenko, unquestioningly. This was demonstrated most slavishly in the Stalinist publication by Bolesław Wójcicki.[76] Polish society wavered somewhat on the issue, while memories of German occupation atrocities were still fresh. But with the passage of time, especially after 1956, the overwhelming societal belief strengthened, whenever the issue was raised, that the Soviets were responsible. 'The horrible crime at Katyn became a symbol of Polish–Soviet relations' and an extremely harmful one at that, as it was an additional factor undermining the legitimacy of communist leaderships.[77]

The Polish Stalinists were as servile over Katyn as over most other issues. They arrested various individuals, most of whom were family relatives of Katyn victims or directly connected in some other way. A court in Łódź sentenced Zofia Dwornik, a student at the Film School, to a year's imprisonment in 1951 for telling her friends that the NKVD had murdered her father who had been held in Starobelsk and her brother-in-law who had been detained in Kozelsk. Two of the wartime PoWs taken to Katyn by their German captors in 1943, who had thus become convinced of Soviet guilt, were jailed for longer terms.[78]

The Muscovite Stalinist leadership of Bolesław Bierut fully abetted Soviet condemnation of the US Congressional Committee. Its hearings were reported as having 'aroused greatest possible interest in Poland' and as having led to increased listening of the VOA. The regime responded with a string of bitter articles accusing the US of reviving Goebbels and of 'whitewashing the real murderers' in order to make the Wehrmacht respectable as an anti-Soviet force. The Burdenko Report was republished, but without overmuch comment, as 'individual Poles say that the Russian story is patently absurd'.[79] The Korean War exacerbated US–Polish relations even further. The State Department sent the Polish embassy in Washington a formal protest on 21 March 1952 against an 'abusive press release', dated 3 March, attacking the Madden Committee. This was described as 'a calculated and completely baseless attack on the US and its Congress', which had 'exceeded the limits of propriety'. In view of such 'outrageous and improper action' the embassy was told to cease publication of such releases.[80] The polemics continued, however, when the Madden Committee adjourned to London. Radio Warsaw attacked O'Konski as a paid agent of Hitler and Goebbels while the committee was accused of treating London as the capital of an occupied country.

Condemnation of Nazi war crimes and atrocities in Poland continued unabated during the life of the PRL; it remained one of the communist system's few popular themes during reform periods right up until the mid-1970s.[81] This theme was publicised particularly strongly by the Stalinists and Moczar's Partisan faction. Institutionally it was propagated by the Main Commission for Investigating Crimes against the Polish Nation (GKBZpNP). The communist elite after 1956, however, held very mixed, sometimes schizophrenic, views as to their Soviet patron. The dominant elite tendency during the 1960s and 1970s became one of letting the Katyn question lie dormant as much as possible. No real effort was made to force the Poles to accept the Soviet line as long as it was not questioned in public.

There has been considerable controversy over whether Władysław Gomułka seriously considered changing the Katyn dogma, along with his other major policy and ideological revisions after October 1956. The idea appears in the reminiscences of his interpreter, Erwin Weit, who was allowed to leave for the West in 1969.[82] According to Gomułka's falsified memoirs, *My Forty Years*, published in Israel, Khruschev supposedly suggested during their 1956–1957 meetings that the Katyn boil should be lanced and blamed on Stalin along with other issues that provoked Polish anti-Soviet reactions. There is no evidence whatsoever for this in either the Polish or Soviet communist party documents. On the other hand, a FO official considered a report in a Polish émigré weekly in 1956, that Gomułka had told a Union of Socialist Youth (ZMS) delegation that he had refused Khruschev's suggestion to that effect, 'plausible enough'.[83] Gomułka denied the suggestion, categorically, just before his death during the Solidarity uproar in 1981 and so does Andrzej Werblan, his extremely well informed biographer. Khruschev also does not mention directly either Katyn or the Ukrainian prison shootings in either volume of his memoirs, even though he was First Secretary of the Ukrainian Communist Party at the time.[84] Reports that he established a commission to investigate Katyn after his Twentieth Congress speech, to see whether it should be accepted as yet another of Stalin's crimes, were never confirmed.[85] Such ideas may, or may not, have been floated in 1956, but there is no doubt that if they were, the communist leaders turned them down as they would have 'dangerously inflamed anti-Soviet feeling in Poland'.[86]

Suggestions that Moczar's Partisan faction wanted to harness Polish nationalism to the communist cause in the mid- to late 1960s by such gestures as admitting the Soviet responsibility for Katyn also remain speculative.[87] One can argue that Gomułka probably genuinely believed in his denunciation of the London Government-in-Exile for what he called their 'Katyn provocation'. He compared it to the Nazi burning of the Reichstag in 1933.[88] The objective truth about Katyn did not worry him one iota. He condemned the London Poles in Realist terms for allowing their emotions to lead them to support Hitlerite propaganda and to break with the USSR.

There is no evidence that the Katyn revelations had, in 1943, thrown him and his home communist colleagues in Warsaw 'into a fresh state of confusion and moral crisis'.[89] Gomułka was successful in persuading Khruschev and the Soviet leaders in 1956 that he could pacify society and maintain the essentials of communist rule in Poland. It is unlikely that he would have taken any additional risks, either in inflaming Polish society and its restless intellectuals or in raising doubts about his orthodoxy in Soviet minds. He tightened his grip and the PZPR's leading role about a year later, and subsequently.[90] The 'insistent chant' of 'Katyn, Katyn, Katyn' which greeted his speech in front of the Palace of Culture on 24 October 1956, after the crisis had passed in Poland, but while it was just beginning in Hungary, probably only strengthened his authoritarian tendencies.[91] When asked about Katyn at numerous public meetings in 1956 Gomułka replied that *raison d'état* demanded that Poland remain silent on the question.

The censorship agency excluded discussion of Katyn as much as possible from the public sphere after 1957, but individuals were no longer repressed for private discussion, as in Stalinist times. The release and return to Poland during 1956–1957 of considerable numbers of Poles, including Jews, who had been forced to remain in the USSR at the end of the Second World War, despite expectations, brought no new revelations about Katyn. Moczar's private whispering campaign in the late 1960s failed to convince the FO. It noted that 'Russian responsibility for Katyn is generally accepted in Poland ... if the Polish Government could possibly make anti-German propaganda out of it, they would'.[92]

Gomułka's downfall in December 1970 and his replacement by Edward Gierek signalled the introduction of consumerist policies, a more relaxed domestic and external atmosphere, greater autonomy for the Roman Catholic Church and increasingly flexible Polish–Soviet relations.[93] Gierek faced a dilemma and 'a huge burden' over Katyn. He genuinely wanted to gain popular support after the December 1970 Baltic seacoast shootings. He was too weak politically, however, to persuade the ossifying Brezhnev leadership that 'the old inheritance of Stalin's crimes should fully be exposed by a revelation of the true facts in this case'.[94] Major political change and reform from the top was ruled out by the invasion of Czechoslovakia and the bloc-wide orthodoxy summed up in the Brezhnev Doctrine. Transformation, therefore, had to be informal and was restricted to the levels of society and public opinion. With the passing away of the Second World War generation the intensity of emotions and issues such as Katyn weakened for the mass of society, including workers and peasants, as long as prosperity continued.

After the experience of Dubcek's failure and the 1968 Warsaw Pact invasion, Gierek had to prove his loyalty to Moscow in international and communist bloc affairs in order to be allowed to consolidate his regime domestically. All Soviet protests against the Katyn debate and memorial proposal in Britain were, consequently, supported to the hilt by PRL diplomats and politicians. The Councillor and Press Attaché of the Polish embassy in London complained to the FCO on 9 April 1971 about 'a one-sided and tendentious campaign being organised in Britain on the problem of Katyn'. The Poles had already complained directly to the BBC about the Katyn programme. They regarded it as part of the drive aimed at 'disturbing Polish–Soviet relations' and fostering a Cold War atmosphere.[95] As we have seen in the previous chapter, the FCO concurred and considered that the problem was the memorial's sponsors, not the Katyn issue itself, except for the controversy over the proposed 1940 inscription date. Brimelow, told by the Polish ambassador in London that the memorial would cause offence to both the Soviet and Polish Governments, replied, rather resignedly, that HMG was powerless to intervene in the actions of local councils and private citizens.[96] The issue reached the highest level when Stefan Olszewski, the Polish Foreign Minister, met his British equivalent, Alec Douglas-Home, in New York on 25 September 1972. Olszewski described the Katyn memorial as a 'matter of some political delicacy' and an 'unnecessary irritant'. It might trouble the improvement of British–Polish relations by causing 'lasting damage' to British–Soviet–Polish relations, so he urged that 'a convenient solution' be found. Douglas-Home replied that he had discouraged the memorial project and hoped that it would not attract much attention in the UK if governments ignored it.[97] Their exchange was interpreted by the FCO as meaning that 'progress in Anglo-Polish relations is dependent on solution' of the Katyn memorial question.[98] The First Secretary of the Polish embassy in London also regretted that the issue was bedevilling British–Polish relations and wanted MPs supporting Neave's Early Day motion to be warned off.[99]

The British embassy in Warsaw reported that Katyn was still officially a taboo subject and that there was no memorial to its victims in Poland. Society, though, had found a way around this. Local citizens had dedicated open ground in Warsaw's Powązki cemetery to their memory.[100] The ambassador also noted that the Katyn issue continued to cloud British–Polish relations. Until the Poles were sure that the problem had passed 'without raising a storm of publicity and Soviet ill-will' they would 'find it difficult to make any move which appears to be aimed at bettering relations with Britain in the political (as distinct from the economic) field'.[101] This was a reference to British competition for Polish contracts, notably one for £100 million for building the Ursus tractor works outside Warsaw. The Katyn memorial dispute kept Anglo-Polish relations 'distinctly frosty' during 1972 and was reckoned by the embassy to have cost the UK three other major contracts.[102] This was a continuing theme since 1970 when 'the greatest concern' was 'over how political explosions would affect development of Britain's trade with Poland'.[103]

The memorial issue subsided on the diplomatic front as the Gierek regime opened up to both its own society and the outside world and resigned itself to the erection of the Katyn memorial. By mid-April 1973, the PZPR CC Secretary in charge of foreign relations, Ryszard Frelek, conceded that 'normal' British–Soviet relations would suffice to permit good Anglo–Polish relations. The damage to Britain's relations with Poland and the USSR was precisely what the Katyn memorial's sponsors had intended.[104] Biały, a diplomat at the Polish embassy in London, strengthened the point. 'Those who were behind the proposal for a Katyn Memorial were not relatives of those who suffered; they were rather political troublemakers trying to sow discord between the Soviet Union and Poland.'[105]

The strange linkage and interplay between domestic, economic and international affairs was amply illustrated by an exchange within the FCO in February 1973. Bullard wanted to protect the Ursus tractor contract by having the FCO inform the Borough of Kensington and Chelsea of the international implications of the Katyn memorial, and particularly of the significance of the 1940 date on its inscription.[106] His political and FCO superiors Julian Amery MP and Thomas Brimelow disagreed. They feared that direct FCO intervention might lead to parliamentary questions. Amery did not want to place himself in a 'position where the FCO could be quoted in public as having sought to appease the Soviet Government by trying – almost certainly unsuccessfully, to stop the memorial'.[107]

The Katyn movements: from political dissidence to democratic lobby

Political contestation such as the Workers' Defence Committee (KOR) and demands for liberalisation of the system emerged within the intelligentsia in 1976, well before economic collapse provoked the Solidarity outburst in August 1980.[108] The flourishing dissident press discussed a whole range of previously taboo subjects including Katyn. The opposition groups agreed that the truth had to be revealed about the massacre and its perpetrators condemned. The Roman Catholic Church supported this, by saying masses, in various major cities, for the victims of Katyn in spring 1979.[109] Although the official line was maintained, there was greater official willingness to discuss the issue after 1975 and it crept into the public sphere at the 1978 Writers' Union Congress.

The process was stimulated by a censorship official, Tomasz Strzyżewski, from Kraków, who succeeded in defecting to Sweden. The wide-ranging censorship instructions of the Main Department for the Control of the Press, Publications and Entertainments (GUKPPiW) which he took with him were published by the dissident KOR press in London in 1977 and widely publicised.[110] The censorship agency set out the following instructions for writing about Katyn, in which Strzyżewski had a direct personal interest as his grandfather had perished in the 1940 massacre: 1) Under no circumstances, nor in any way, should the Soviet Union be blamed for the massacre or any responsibility be imputed to it. 2) The favoured formulations to be allowed in academic works, biographies and memoirs were 'shot by the Hitlerites at Katyn', 'perished at Katyn' and 'died at Katyn'. The only permissible dates of death had to be later than July 1941. 3) The term 'prisoners of war' was to be replaced by 'internees', although it was permissible to name the Kozelsk, Starobelsk and Ostashkov camps as the places where the internees were held before being captured by the Hitlerites and shot at Katyn. 4) All obituaries, announcements of religious masses and other commemorations of Katyn as well as doubtful issues had to be approved by the GUKPPiW. The existence of any infractions was not to be revealed publicly.[111]

The censorship revelations stimulated KOR, on the 40th anniversary of the Soviet invasion of Poland, into issuing a statement on the 'Crimes of Genocide committed by the Soviet Union against the Polish Nation'.[112] This condemned the Ribbentrop–Molotov Pact and the Soviet deportations of Poles in the occupied Eastern territories as well as the repression of the large numbers in Soviet captivity during 1939–1941. KOR traced out the position regarding Katyn and the missing officers from the three camps and blamed the Soviet Stalinist regime for this 'crime of genocide'. It cited the censorship regulations as evidence that the Polish communist Government was continuing its refusal to throw light on 'Katyn and other Soviet crimes'; as such it was 'an accessory to hushing up the crime and making it impossible to trace the perpetrators of the genocide'. KOR called for 'the *whole truth* to be revealed'.[113]

Soviet dissidents within the USSR, notably V. Bukovskii, V. Nekrasov, P. Grigorenko, A. Amalrik, N. Gorbanevskaya and P. Litvinov, along with exiles in Paris, also accepted Stalinist responsibility for Katyn.[114] Leaflets calling for the commemoration of the 40th anniversary of Katyn appeared, subsequently, in many Polish cities in April 1980. The anti-Soviet demonstrations of early August included a Katyn protest in the Powązki cemetery in Warsaw. The issue of commemoration provided the emotional, as against the economic protest and anti-corruption, drive behind Solidarity from the outset. The Gdańsk shipyard workers demanded a monument to commemorate 'the fifteen thousand Polish soldiers murdered by the Soviet Government in Katyn' alongside their primary demand for memorials to the victims of the December 1970 Baltic seacoast shootings.[115]

Katyn had also been mooted by the nationalist and anti-Soviet ROPCiO opposition which became the Confederation for an Independent Poland (KPN) – led by Leszek Moczulski. This movement refused to 'self-limit' itself like Wałęsa's strand of Solidarity. It called openly for independence, condemning Soviet control and crimes against Poland. Katyn was publicised, along with the Nazi–Soviet Pact of August 1939, at their inter-war independence day manifestation before the Tomb of the Unknown

Soldier in Warsaw on 11 November 1980. Their stalls sold photos of the Katyn graves, alongside those of their hero, Marshal Piłsudski, all over Poland during 1980–1981. The Young Poland movement, led by arrested activists such as Andrzej Czuma and Wojciech Ziembiński who were closely linked to the KPN, issued a significant statement on Katyn in Warsaw on 8 April 1980. This declared that Katyn was 'an important symbol of all the Poles murdered and persecuted' by the Soviets in Poland's occupied Eastern territories during 1939–1941. Real reconciliation with Russia could be achieved only if Poland regained her sovereignty. The Russians should accept the truth about their historical relations which involved numerous 'Polish wrongs at Russian hands'. The crime of Katyn was the responsibility of Stalin and his terror apparatus which the Russian people should reject while facing up 'to the duty to square accounts with the past'. The silence of the Polish communist leaders and their selective memory was a hypocritical 'insult to the whole Polish nation'. It was 'impossible to remember Palmiry and to forget Katyn'.[116]

Jan Kubik argues that the breaking of the public silence over Katyn was one of the most spectacular features of the Solidarity period. The PRL's taboo regarding the massacre 'became for society a symbol of the Soviet rulers' true intentions in their dealings with Poland'.[117] Katyn appeared repeatedly in Solidarity's press, especially its local publications, and the issue was raised in negotiations with the Government. Along with the problem of political prisoners it played a prominent part in the activities and publications of the newly formed independent Union of Students. Key documents, such as the O'Malley report, were published by the dissident press in Nowa Huta between 1979 and 1981. A simple cross and plaque had marked Katyn in the Powązki cemetery. The Katyn Civic Committee associated with Solidarity's Mazowsze branch replaced this with a solid memorial on 31 July 1981. This was quietly demolished by the authorities during the dark of the following night.[118] Fruitless discussions with the communist authorities over a permanent memorial dragged on until martial law. An individual called Walenty Badylak was reported as burning himself to death *à la* Jan Palach in Kraków's main square on 21 March 1980, allegedly as a protest over the official cover-up of the truth of Katyn. Politically, Solidarity's grassroots feelings and pressure over Katyn surfaced at its First Congress in Gdańsk-Oliwa in September–October 1981.[119] The building was festooned with Katyn posters while memorabilia on the subject were sold in the corridors.

Jaruzelski and the military suppressed Solidarity successfully during the State of War of December 1981 to July 1983 but his regime, although more flexible and less ideological than its predecessors, could do little more than contain the political stalemate during the 1980s. Gorbachev's coming to power in 1985, and his policies of *glasnost* and *perestroika*, however, meant that reform and policies aimed at gaining social support also became possible in Eastern Europe as Soviet control weakened. Not only unpublished doctoral dissertations and the opposition press but also some official publications began ascribing the guilt for Katyn to the Soviet security services from the mid-1980s onwards.[120] Jaruzelski himself wrote that Stalin's anti-Leninist policy towards Poland in 1939–1941 had caused numerous tragedies, which needed to be clarified.[121] The official level, therefore, saw a last gasp attempt to fill in the so-called 'blank spots'. The radicals in the Jaruzelski regime aimed to salvage the Polish–Soviet relationship by defusing popular discontent with the lies and silences concerning such issues as the Nazi–Soviet Pact of 1939, the Soviet invasion of 1939, the 1939–1941 deportations from the Eastern Territories, the KPP's dissolution by Stalin, the 1944 Warsaw Uprising and the fate of the Polish minority in the USSR.[122]

Katyn and the 1940 massacre loomed increasingly large in the Historical Commission's work, reflecting opinion poll findings in summer 1988 that Polish public opinion considered it the most neglected and contentious of the 'blank spots'.[123] The influential reform weekly *Polityka* was allowed to report that 81.6 per cent of adult, and 85.7 per cent of young, Poles had heard of Katyn; compared to the 1944 Warsaw Uprising, almost twice as many considered it a 'Blank Spot'. But the censorship did not permit it to indicate the proportions of those who thought that the Soviets, rather than the Nazis, were responsible. By 1988 the Polish communist elite agreed with PZPR politburo member Marian Orzechowski that the clarification of Katyn was the key to the healthy readjustment of the Polish–Soviet relationship.[124]

The Polish–Soviet Historical Commission, established in late spring 1987, was chaired on the Polish side by the moody and loud-voiced Professor Jarema Maciszewski. It was composed of other PZPR academic notables, mainly nationalist-minded military historians, such as Marian Wojciechowski, Tadeusz Walichnowski (who had gained a bad reputation as an 'anti-Zionist' in 1968), Włodzimierz Kowalski and Bronisław Szyzdek.[125] Czesław Madajczyk took the greatest interest in Katyn and published his *Dramat Katyński* (KiW, 1989), which began to open up the issue, just before Gorbachev's 1990 revelation.[126] What effect this book might have had, as well as the Polish historians presenting their Soviet colleagues on the commission with a report indicating that the Polish PoWs had been killed well before the German invasion of 1941, in precipitating Gorbachev's decision remains speculative. At any rate, the Polish communist academics, although admittedly spurred on by the demise of Polish communism in 1989, unlike the British FCO and Government, just about managed to get their retraction of the official pro-Soviet line in before Gorbachev lifted the curtain on the issue of guilt. This was the Katyn Report prepared by Professors Maciszewski, Madajczyk, Wojciechowski and Ryszard Nazarewicz in April 1989, which examined in detail, and rejected, the Soviet Burdenko case.[127] Even official apologists declared, just before the Round Table started, that social impatience meant that the

Katyn discussions could no longer be held behind closed doors.[128] Before long well-known figures such as the historian Andrzej Ajnenkiel, were writing that despite the absence of Soviet documentation it was clear that Katyn was a Soviet deed. It was also necessary to clarify the exact fate of the Starobelsk and Ostashkov inmates.[129]

The first dissident organisation specifically devoted to Katyn, the Katyn Institute, animated by the sculptor Adam Macedoński in Kraków in 1979, wanted to break the conspiracy of silence over Katyn. It called on the Council of State and the Government to investigate Katyn, to pursue the guilty parties and to provide compensation for relatives of those murdered. The publication by the underground of Jerzy Łojek's *Dzieje sprawy Katynia* under the pseudonym of Leopold Jerzewski in 1980 also inspired the opposition *milieu* in Warsaw to coalesce in the Civic Committee for the Building of a Monument to the Victims of Katyn.[130] Łojek (1932–1986) was a Warsaw University historian and the author of respected, if controversial, academic studies of the 3 May 1791 constitution and attempts to reform the Commonwealth, just before the final partitions of Poland. He also ran the modern history workshop in Mazowsze's Centre for Social Studies, Solidarity's Warsaw region branch. His animating role, after his premature death in 1986, was taken on by his widow, Bożena, a historian of the theatre.

Under Jaruzelski, the Katyn *milieu* was composed of varied independent academics and trade unionists along with relatives of victims of the 1940 massacre who grouped in locally based 'Katyn Family' organisations. A dominating role was played in the latter by Marek Tarczyński and Father Zdzisław Peszkowski, a Kozelsk survivor, who acted as their unofficial, and then official, chaplain. Between October 1989 and February 1990 these individuals and tendencies organised in what emerged as the Independent Historical Committee for Examination of the Katyn Atrocity (NKHBZK). The indefatigable Bożena Łojek became its secretary while its other committee members were Andrzej Chmielarz, Stanisław M. Jankowski, Jerzy Jackl, Andrzej Kunert, Adam Macedoński, Marek Tarczyński, Jacek Trznadel, Jędrzej Tucholski and the national independence politician Wojciech Ziembiński.[131]

The three 'Ts' – Tarczyński, Trznadel and Tucholski – in particular played key roles in the Katyn story, through their writings and activities, during the 1990s. Tarczyński, as editor of the academic quarterly *Wojskowy Przegląd Historyczny*, was able to publish a huge amount of the newly available documentation on the 1940 massacre along with short biograms of its victims and other academic and personal contributions in the journal. He also edited the bulk of the volumes in the key *Zeszyty Katyńskie* series. The committee's aims, set out in its founding communiqué of 6 November 1989, were to organise studies and to support the newly democratic public bodies in the search to establish the truth about the 1940 massacre. As such it became the central pressure group and lobby on the subject in

Poland. The activities, initiatives and writings of the individuals associated with it form an essential part of the skein in this study.[132]

The NKHBZK was very closely associated with two other bodies with whom it often had overlapping membership. The Polish Katyn Foundation (PFK), set up at about the same time as the former by roughly the same individuals, also included the prominent conservative nationalist politician, and premier in 1992, Jan Olszewski. It had two primary aims. First, to raise funding for the construction of a Polish Chapel and Sanctuary as part of the Polish Military Cemetery in Katyn. This effort ran into financial difficulties in the late 1990s despite a generous subsidy by Premier Jerzy Buzek on the 60th anniversary of the massacre. Second, to establish a Katyn library and archive which would stimulate academic study of the 1940 massacre of PoWs in Soviet captivity.[133]

The second aim was achieved, very quickly, with the establishment in 1993 of a Katyn museum, sited in a military museum run by the Ministry of Defence within a 19th-century Russian fort in Sadyba, a southern suburb of Warsaw.[134] Its exhibition rooms, housing exhumed items, photographs, terrain mock-ups and other Katyn, Kharkov and Mednoe material, were visited by between 8000 and 17 000 members of the public annually between 1994 and 2000.[135] The museum organised a large number of events and special exhibitions to publicise the 1940 massacre and to keep its memory fresh in the context of demands for the full truth and justice.[136] PFK supported the *Zeszyty Katyńskie* series which had published 18 volumes by 2002 as well as the journal *Biuletyn Katyński* published by the Katyn Institute in Kraków.

The other body which the NKHBZK collaborated closely with, especially after the young Kraków historian Andrzej Przewoźnik became its secretary in 1992, was the Council for the Defence of Struggle and Suffering (ROPWiM). This body organised exhumations in the burial sites in 1994–1996 and 1999 and collaborated in drawing up plans and inscriptions for the military cemeteries.[137] In addition to the above, the NKHBZK was supported in its central initiatives by a network of territorially based 'Katyn Families' all over Poland who directed their own local activities.[138] Although they were largely autonomous, they all sheltered under the umbrella of the Federation of Katyn Families (FRK) chaired by the indispensable Bożena Łojek. In 2000 they had 27 branches and eight local circles, including a branch in Chicago.[139] Independent groups also existed in Canada, Czechoslovakia, Britain, Israel and Australia. As the Polish branches were very dependent upon a small number of motivated individuals, many of them, like the branches in Gniezno, Nowy Sącz and Wałbrzych, died natural deaths. New ones were slower to emerge.

With democratisation, Katyn became part of the anti-totalitarian rhetoric of the political forces who were not associated with the PRL but who attempted to discredit successor communist forces, such as the Alliance of the Democratic Left (SLD) and Polish Peasant Party (PSL), who were. The First Senate of the Third Republic, elected in 1989, contained 99 Solidarity senators out of 100 and was, therefore, very active in point scoring, agenda setting and issue appropriation in this regard. The First (1991–1993) and Third (1997–2001) Sejms, which were dominated by anti-PRL forces, joined in this effort. Nobody in Poland attempted to absolve the Soviets of blame for Katyn after 1989. The issue, however, became emotionally a truly national one only after President Aleksander Kwaśniewski and younger SLD personalities co-opted the issue after 1995. The SLD-PSL dominated Second Sejm passed a resolution on 9 June 1995 paying tribute, on the 55th anniversary, to the victims of Katyn and other Soviet killing sites. It thanked all those who had kept its memory alive during the years of 'silence and lies' and condemned the criminal system of Soviet communism. The Sejm hoped that 'revealing the full truth about Katyn, establishing responsibility for it and appropriate commemoration at the places of tragic death' would serve to improve relations between a free Poland and a democratic Russia.[140]

The Sejm and Senate resolutions marking the 60th anniversary in 2000 were much fuller. The former thanked all those who had contributed to revealing the truth about the 1940 massacre, especially Polonias, relatives of the deceased and the Federation of Katyn Families, the US Congressional Committee and Russian democrats. It noted that the guilty had not been punished while legal responsibility still had not been fully established. The Senate used stronger language about the need to settle accounts. It condemned 'not only the cowardly silence but also the disgraceful falsification of the truth, not only by the communist authorities in Poland and the Soviet Union, but also by certain influential circles in the West'.[141] In addition, President Kwaśniewski apologised, on behalf of the successor PRL camp, for all those who for whatever reason of fear, personal benefit or totalitarian propaganda had kept quiet or falsified the truth about Katyn.[142]

From 1990 onwards the Polish Procuracy took a close interest in the investigations of the Soviet, Russian and Ukrainian Military Procuracies into Katyn. As we have seen, the questioning of Tokarev, Soprunenko, Syromatnikov and other surviving participants, and witnesses to the 1940 massacre, aroused huge interest in Poland. The mass media paid close and continuing attention to the statements and visits to Moscow, Kiev and the burial sites of Deputy Procurator-General Stefan Śnieżko, the main figure concerned with Katyn in the Polish judicial organs. The tardiness and lack of specific results of these proceedings, however, led Justice Minister Jan Piątkowski, representing the Christian Nationalist Party (ZChN) in the already defeated government of Hanna Suchocka, to utilise Katyn as a political issue just before the September 1993 election.[143] He announced on 2 September that the Warsaw Procuracy would carry out an independent investigation of the 1940 massacre, demanded the extradition to Poland of the three main surviving executioners and removed

Śnieżko from the case. This maverick, and totally unconsulted, move was criticised by Wałęsa's presidential office, by other coalition government partners, notably Foreign Minister Skubiszewski, as well as by the FRK. Śnieżko himself was reinstated, not in the Procuracy investigation, but by being given the chair of the Katyn Commemoration Committee after the 1993 election. The Polish Procuracy inquiry was taken over for a while by Professor Aleksander Herzog, and subsequently by Procurator Szustakiewicz, but it petered out like the judicial investigation in Moscow.

The issue of the *lustration* of individuals seeking public office, elected or appointed, assumed a new salience in the Government of Włodzimierz Cimoszewicz in the mid-1990s. The outcome involved electoral declarations of collaboration with the security services during the PRL by candidates. An Institute of National Memory (IPN) was also established by Jerzy Buzek's (AWS-UW) Government after 1997.[144] The IPN was initially monopolised by Solidarity, Catholic and nationalist opponents of the PRL. They were temperamentally and politically sympathetic to the Katyn lobby. The latter's hopes that the issue would be revived and that the investigation would be organised and coordinated much better were, however, to be disappointed. The IPN chairman, ex-Solidarity senator Professor Leon Kieres, confirmed that the collection of evidence concerning the 1940 massacre was the IPN's main task. Apart from reorganising the material inherited from the GKBZpNP, he failed to push the issue on the parliamentary level. Professor Witold Kulesza, the chairman of the GKSZpNP (successor to the GKBZpNP), however, held some meetings for the activists involved. His reply to an NKHBZK expression of disquiet, and some searching questions, at the way in which the Katyn investigation was fading away, merely outlined the residual contacts being maintained with the Russian, Ukrainian and Belarusan Procuracies.[145]

The official position, confirmed again in September 2000 by Minister of Justice Lech Kaczyński, was that the 1940 massacre was not subject to any statute of limitations. The IPN would continue to assemble documentation and encourage new exhumation work, especially in the Ukraine and Belarus, in order to throw fresh light on the fate of the PoWs shot in those republics. Politically, however, the issue had almost died. This was confirmed by the SLD's victory in the 2001 election. Leszek Miller's Government clearly felt that the question should be left to the historians and for commemoration by public opinion. The steam behind the judicial investigations had, however, almost completely evaporated, except, potentially, in the laggard Belarusan case. General Alexandr Savenkov, the Chief Military Procurator, confirmed to Kieres in Moscow in August 2004 that the authorities of the Russian Federal Republic considered that they had now completed all investigations on their own territory regarding the 1940 massacre. They would be happy to make the full 156 volumes of final documentation available to the Poles.[146]

The 1940 massacre had been identified with the PRL's subordination to the Soviet Union and became a powerful emotional and political symbol of the apparent incapacity of communism to come to terms with its Stalinist crimes. The belated attempt to do so in the late 1980s was overwhelmed by systemic collapse in both Poland and the USSR. The top limit of documentation of the historical truth by the newly democratic Polish and Russian republics seems to have been achieved by about 1993. Since then the issue has become dominated by commemoration rather than judicial retribution, personal compensation of relatives or even the pan-European process of apology and reconciliation between nations. Further breakthroughs in documenting remaining aspects and details of the historical truth remain dependent upon fuller stages of democratisation in both the Russian and Belarusan republics.

Notes

1 *Katyń: Dokumenty Ludobójstwa: Dokumenty i materiały przekazane Polsce 14 października 1992r.*, Warsaw: ISP PAN, 1992, no. 14. The Polish Foreign Office (MSZ) was also to be informed of these instructions.
2 Foreign Minister Andrei Gromyko, politburo circular of 12 April 1971 sent for confirmation by the Central Committee, *Katyń: Dokumenty Ludobójstwa*, no. 15.
3 Sir Thomas Brimelow (ambassador to Warsaw) to Bullard (FO), 16 April 1971, PRO FCO28/1475 ENP10/1.
4 Douglas-Home to Warsaw, 9 April 1971, PRO FCO28/1475 08552/ENP/10/1.
5 Sir John Killick (ambassador to Moscow) to FO, telegram no. 1438 of 13 September 1972, PRO FCO28/1946. The official intervention in the form of an 'oral communication' is appended as telegram no. 139. The basis of the *demarche* was the CPSU politburo decision of 8 September 1972 approving the note, *Katyń: Dokumenty Ludobójstwa*, nos 16 and 17.
6 The politburo decision and instructions of 2 March 1973 are also available in ibid., nos 19 and 20.
7 Douglas-Home–Smirnovsky conversation of 7 March 1973, PRO FCO28/2308 ENP10/2.
8 The official Soviet line was that the Polish comrades had proposed this initiative to the Soviet ambassador in Warsaw, but one somehow doubts it, CPSU politburo circular of 30 March 1976, *Katyń: Dokumenty Ludobójstwa*, p. 75.
9 Protocol no. 3 of the CPSU politburo sitting of 5 April 1976, ibid., no. 22.
10 Ibid., p. 73.
11 Ibid., no. 24.
12 Louis FitzGibbon, 'Khatyn – another hoax', *Journal of Historical Review*, 1, 3 (Fall 1980) available at www.jhr.org. Association with a publication propagating Holocaust revisionism, even denial, could only have done harm to the Katyn cause and strengthened the British establishment's doubts about FitzGibbon's 'soundness'.
13 Benjamin Fischer, 'The Katyn Controversy: Stalin's killing field', *Studies in Intelligence* (Winter 1999–2000), p. 64.
14 *Daily Telegraph*, 3 July 1974.
15 Shelepin to Khruschev, 9 March 1959 in *Katyń: Dokumenty Ludobójstwa*, no. 10.
16 Ibid., no. 11.
17 KDZ, 2, pp. 14, 420.
18 Richard Sakwa, *Gorbachev and his Reforms, 1985–1990*, Hemel Hempstead: Philip Allan, 1991.

19 See George Sanford, 'Polish–Soviet Relations', in Alex Pravda (ed.), *The End of the Outer Empire: Soviet–East European Relations in Transition, 1985–90,* London: RIIA/Sage, 1992.
20 Excerpt from CPSU politburo sitting no. 119 of 5 May 1988, *Katyń: Dokumenty Ludobójstwa*, pp. 82–5.
21 Note no. 434/os of 26 April 1988 for the above politburo meeting, ibid., pp. 86–9.
22 Excerpt from sitting no. 130 of 1 September 1988, ibid., pp. 96–9. At the same time *Intourist* and the Soviet Ministry of the Interior worked out simplified non-visa travel arrangements for relatives, ibid., nos 27, 28.
23 Falin note KC 05619 of 6 March 1988, ibid., pp. 108–13.
24 Note nos 17–204 of 22 March 1989, ibid., pp. 102–7.
25 Excerpt from politburo session no. 152 of 31 March 1989, ibid., pp. 100–1.
26 Note nos 17–305 of 22 April 1989, ibid., pp. 114–15.
27 A draft CPSU politburo decision no. 09287 'On the Katyn Issue' gave the Soviet Procuracy, the KGB and various ministerial archives until 1 August 1989 to report back, ibid., pp. 116–17.
28 Falin to Gorbachev of 22 February 1990, ibid., pp. 119–25.
29 Summaries of Lebediewa's findings were published during the spring, particularly in *Moskovskie novosti*. They were reproduced in detail by the now completely free Polish press, notably 'Dowody zbrodni Katyńskiej', *Polityka*, 31 March 1990, p. 14.
30 Typically, the gesture was spoilt somewhat by being broadcast in the last TV news at one in the morning, when the audience was, presumably, at its smallest. Jaruzelski himself, together with representatives of the three branches of the Polish armed forces, who fired three salvoes in honour of 'those who had fallen without blame', visited Katyn on the 14th, on his way to Kiev, *Polityka*, 21 April 1990, p. 13.
31 Jarema Maciszewski, 'Katyń: Nieznane dokumenty', *Polityka*, 28 April 1990, p. 3.
32 Adam Moszyński, *Lista Katyńska: Jeńcy obozów Kozielsk, Ostaszków, Starobelsk. Zaginieni w Rosji Sowieckiej*, London: Gryf, 1989.
33 Wojciech Materski (ed.), *Kremlin versus Poland, 1939–1945: Documents from the Soviet Archives*, Warsaw: ISP PAN, 1996, pp. 5–6.
34 These were published in the *Wojskowy Przegląd Historyczny* during 1991–1993. Also *Katyń, Starobielsk, Ostaszków, Kozielsk: Najnowsze Dokumenty NKWD*, Paris: Editions Dembinski, 1990.
35 Reproduced in Jędrzej Tucholski, *Mord w Katyniu: Kozielsk, Ostaszków, Starobielsk. Lista ofiar*, Warsaw: PAX, 1991.
36 For the full story of the struggle for historical truth on the Soviet period see R.W. Davies, *Soviet History in the Yeltsin Era*, Basingstoke: Macmillan, 1997.
37 Victor Zaslavsky, 'The Katyn Massacre', *Telos*, no. 114 (Winter 1999), pp. 71–2.
38 They were published by ISP PAN in its five-volume 'Z archiwów sowieckich' series between 1992 and 1995. See bibliography for full titles.
39 Order no. RP-979 of the President of the USSR, 3 November 1990, point 8, *Katyń: Dokumenty Ludobójstwa*, pp. 126–31.
40 Report of 22 January 1991 by USSR Procurator General N. Trubin to Gorbachev, ibid., pp. 134–7.
41 Z. Mielecki, 'Dowody zbrodni katyńskiej odnalezione w Polsce w latach 1991–1992', in *Zbrodnia Katyńska: droga do prawdy: historia – archeologia – kryminalistyka – polityka – prawo*, Warsaw: NZKHBZK, 1992.
42 Trubin to Gorbachev, 17 May 1991, *Katyń: Dokumenty Ludobójstwa*, pp. 140–5.
43 Complaint by Procurator A. Rozanov to Gorbachev, 28 February 1991, ibid., pp. 146–7 and 148–51.

44 Davies, *Soviet History in the Yeltsin Era*, p. 45.
45 *Stan i perspektywy badań nad losami żołnierzy polskich w ZSSR w latach 1932–1958 w aspekcie działalności Wojskowej Komisji Archiwalnej*, Warsaw: Part 1, 2000.
46 See Stanisław Jaczyński, 'Stan badań nad problematyką Katyńską' and Wanda Krystyna Roman, 'Potem był Katyń', in *Zbrodnia Katyńska: Upamiętnienie i Zadośćuczynienie*, Warsaw: NKHBZK, 1998, pp. 84–97 and 98–117.
47 Rudolf G. Pikhoja (ed.), *Katyn: Plenniki neobavlennoj vojny*, Moscow: Demokratia, 1997.
48 Amy Knight, 'Guardians of History', in *Spies Without Cloaks: The KGB's Successors*, Princeton, NJ: Princeton UP, 1998, pp. 190–1.
49 Bożena Łojek, 'Śledztwo Katyńskie – zaniechania i zagrożenia', in *Zbrodnia Katyńska: Pytania pozostałe bez odpowiedzi*, Warsaw: NKHBZK, 2002.
50 'Memorandum PFK i NKHBZK', in *II Półwiecze zbrodni: Katyń – Twer – Charków*, Warsaw: NZKHBZK, 1995, p. 69.
51 See Łojek, 'Śledztwo Katyńskie...', pp. 25–7.
52 In an interview for *Tygodnik Solidarność*, 25 April 1997, p. 8, Natalia Lebediewa attacked engineer Mukhin's lack of historical education and skills and regretted that his book had been published by Struve, an otherwise serious right-wing publishing house. She also confirmed the overwhelming documentary basis establishing NKVD guilt.
53 *Rosja a Katyń*, Warsaw: Karta, 1994, pp. 60–1.
54 Felix Rudinskii, 'Katinskaja tragedia', *Pravo*, no. 1 (1998), pp. 77 ff.
55 Stefan Korboński, *The Polish Underground State, 1939–1945*, New York: Columbia UP, 1978, p. 147.
56 Kazimierz Skarzyński, 'Katyn i Polski Czerwony Krzyż', *Kultura* (Paris), no. 5/91 (1955), pp. 127–41.
57 *Aide-Mémoire* of 30 December 1943, PRO HS4/137.
58 See Marian Marek Drozdowski, 'Polska podziemna i Rząd Polski wobec zbrodni Katyńskiej', in *Zbrodnia nie ukarana: Katyń – Twer – Charków*, Warsaw: NKHBZK, 1996, pp. 91–107.
59 Unattributed note of 20 August 1943, PRO HS4/137.
60 Soviet documentation became available in Polish translation during the 1990s in two series published by Wojciech Materski, Wojciech Roszkowski, Andrzej Paczkowski and their ISP PAN colleagues: 'Z Archiwów Sowieckich' (5 vols, Warsaw 1992–1995) and 'Dokumenty do dziejów PRL' (13 volumes, 1992–2000 continuing).
61 Stanisław Jaczyński, *Zygmunt Berling*, Warsaw: KiW, 1993.
62 Stalin described him as a provocateur and an Anders' agent and demanded that his wife be sent to Moscow as a hostage; protocol of PPR politburo meeting of 14 December 1944, Aleksander Kochański (ed.), *Protokoły posiedzeń Biura Politycznego KC PPR, 1944–1945*, Warsaw: ISP PAN, 1992, p. 75.
63 The military were the major group to suffer from the comparatively limited number of death sentences passed by the Stalinists after 1947, only about half of which were carried out, once the near civil war conditions had eased.
64 See the relevant entries in George Sanford, *Historical Dictionary of Poland*, Metuchen, NJ: Scarecrow Press, rev. 2nd edn, 2003, pp. 18–19, 232, 129–30, 162–3.
65 Another, junior and less well informed member of the group, Tadeusz Pióro, from Colonel Leon Bukojemski's artillery brigade, however, wrote in a major article published just before the start of the Warsaw Round Table, that it was natural that he should accept the Burdenko Report on trust. His father, a colonel in the medical corps, had also been held at Starobelsk with Bukojemski, so he was brought along to strengthen the Soviet case that the Starobelsk inmates had also been shot at Katyn, 'W lesie Katyńskim', *Polityka*, 18 February

1990. This article provoked considerable published correspondence of a completely novel type on the subject, *Polityka*, 18 March 1989, p. 14.

66 Zygmunt Berling, *Wspomnienia*, Vol. I, *Z łagrów do Andersa*, Warsaw: Dom Wydawniczy, 1990. Vols II and III were published in 1991.

67 Zawodny, *Death in the Forest*, p. 170.

68 Ibid., pp. 170–1.

69 *Hearings*, Part 4, p. 768.

70 Wodziński also suffered the same threats before fleeing abroad: testimony of Władysław Kawecki, IPiMS, Kol. 12/3, no. 52.

71 Testimony of Stefania Wanda Cioch (cousin) in London on 29 March 1946, IPiMS, Kol. 12/3, no. 9.

72 The Skarżyński testimony is dated 2 July 1945, Jacek Wilamowski, *Kłamstwo Stulecia*, Warsaw: CB, 2002, pp. 132–6.

73 Józef Bratko, *Dlaczego zginąłeś, prokuratorze?*, Kraków: Stowarzyszenie Twórcze – Krakowski Klub Artystów Literacki, 1998.

74 Wilamowski, *Kłamstwo Stulecia*, pp. 68–9.

75 Cf. Stefan Korboński, *W imieniu Kremla*, Paris: Instytut Literacki, 1956, pp. 100–1.

76 Bolesław Wójcicki, *Prawda o Katyniu*, Warsaw: KiW, 1952 and 1953.

77 Konrad Syrop, *Spring in October: The Polish Revolution of 1956*, London: Weidenfeld & Nicolson, 1957, p. 4.

78 Hieronim Majewski to six years in 1950, also in Łódź, and Mikołaj Marczak to two years in Rzeszów, Andrzek Kaczyński, 'Kłamstwo, milczenie, prawda: Zbrodnia Katyńska: Prawda nie znał tylko ten, kto nie chciał', *Rzeczpospolita*, 12 April 2000.

79 Warsaw embassy to FO, 4 March 1952, PRO FCO28/100719 NP1661/2.

80 Washington embassy to FO, 24 March 1952, FCO28/100719 NP1661/3.

81 Cf. Tadeusz Cyprian and Jerzy Sawicki (eds), *Sprawy polskie w procesie norymberskim*, Poznań: Instytut Zachodni, 1956.

82 Erwin Weit, *Dans l'Ombre de Gomulka*, Paris: Laffont, 1971, pp. 88–90.

83 *Tydzień Polski*, 21 August 1965. D. Tonkin (EES), 18 September 1972, PRO FCO28/1946 ENP10/1.

84 *Khruschev Remembers*, London: Sphere, 1971. Vol. 2, *The Last Testament*, Harmondsworth, UK: Penguin, 1974.

85 *Times*, 17 April 1956.

86 R. Baker (Warsaw Embassy), letter of 13 May 1971, also R.T. Jenkins (EE Section RD), 17 May 1971, PRO FCO1475, ENP10/1.

87 Neil Ascherson, *The Struggles for Poland*, London: Michael Joseph, 1987, p. 174.

88 Political Report to First PPR Congress, 7 December 1945, Władysław Gomułka, *Artykuły i Przemówienia*, Vol. 1, *Styczeń 1943–Grudzień 1945*, Warsaw: KiW, 1962, p. 453.

89 Hansjakob Stehle, *The Independent Satellite: Society and Politics in Poland since 1945*, New York: Praeger, 1965, p. 28.

90 See Richard Hiscocks, *Bridge for the Abyss? An Interpretation of Developments in Post-War Poland*, London: Oxford UP, 1963, Chs 9–11. Stehle, *The Independent Satellite*, Ch. 4.

91 Syrop, *Spring in October*, p. 146.

92 R.O. Miles, minute of 20 December 1968, PRO FCO28/714 ENP/3/303/2.

93 Cf. Keith John Lepak, *Prelude to Solidarity: Poland and the Politics of the Gierek Regime*, New York: Columbia UP, 1988. Vladimir Wozniuk, *From Crisis to Crisis: Soviet-Polish Relations in the 1970s*, Ames: Iowa State UP, 1987.

94 *Neue Zürcher Zeitung*, 29 April 1971.

95 Douglas-Home to Warsaw, 13 April 1971, PRO FCO/28/1475 08552/ ENP10/1.

96 Brimelow, note of 24 January 1972, PRO FCO28/1945.
97 Douglas-Home–Olszewski conversation, P3/548/7 of 5 September 1972, PRO FCO28/1946 ENP/10/548/10.
98 Tonkin to Logan, 28 September 1972, PRO FCO28/1946 ENP10/1.
99 Tonkin to R. Baker (Warsaw), 19 October 1972, PRO FCO28/1947 ENP10/1.
100 Frank Brenchley (Warsaw) to FO, 1 March 1973, PRO FCO28/2308 FM28002.
101 Brenchley to FO, 1 March 1973, PRO FCO28/2308 FM2614202.
102 Warsaw embassy, Annual Review for 1972, FCO28/2288.
103 Warsaw embassy, Annual Review for 1970, FCO28/1430 256736.
104 Brenchley to Bullard (FO), 24 April 1973, PRO FCO28/2308 ENP10/2.
105 S. Martin (EES), 26 July 1972, PRO FCO28/1960 ENP25/1.
106 Bullard to Brimelow, 13 February 1973, PRO FCO28/2308 ENP10/2.
107 Note by M. Goulding, 15 February 1973, PRO FCO28/2308 ENP10/2.
108 Andrzej Jastrzębski (ed.), *Dokumenty Komitetu Obrony Robotników i Komitetu Samoobrony Społecznej KOR*, Warsaw-London: PWN/Aneks, 1994.
109 Jan Józef Lipski, *KOR: A History of the Workers' Defense Committee in Poland, 1976–1981*, Berkeley, CA: University of California Press, 1985, p. 351.
110 *Czarna księga cenzury PRL*, London: Aneks, 2 vols, 1977–1978.
111 Ibid., vol. 1, p. 63. The obituary of General Smorawiński, for example, was heavily censored in *Tygodnik Powszechny* in July 1981.
112 Peter Raina (ed.), *Independent Social Movements in Poland*, London: Orbis Books, 1981, pp. 289–92.
113 My italicisation, as I toyed initially with the idea of using the phrase as the title of this book.
114 Jerżewski (Łojek), *Katyń*, pp. 53–4. Kwiatkowska-Viatteau, *Katyn*, pp. 120–2.
115 Symptomatically, the workers got confused as to whether Katyn had occurred 30, or 40, years previously, Timothy Garton Ash, *The Polish Revolution: Solidarity*, London: Granta, 1983, p. 44. The issue was also raised at earlier workers' protests, notably in December 1979, Antony Kemp-Welch, *The Birth of Solidarity: The Gdansk Negotiations, 1980*, Basingstoke: Macmillan, 1983, p. 198.
116 'The Murder of Polish Officers by the Soviet NKVD in the Katyn Forest', in Raina, *Independent Social Movements in Poland*, pp. 426–8.
117 Jan Kubik, *The Power of Symbols against the Symbols of Power: The Rise of Solidarity and the Fall of State Socialism in Poland*, University Park: Pennsylvania State UP, 1994, p. 222.
118 Kwiatkowska-Viatteau, *Katyn*, pp. 133 ff.
119 George Sanford (ed.), *The Solidarity Congress, 1981: The Great Debate*, Basingstoke: Macmillan, 1990.
120 Wilamowski, *Kłamstwo stulecia*, pp. 76–7.
121 *Kommunist*, no. 11 (July 1987).
122 George Sanford, 'Polish–Soviet relations', in Alex Pravda (ed.), *The End of the Outer Empire: Soviet–East European Relations in Transition, 1985–90*, London: Sage/RIIA, 1992, Ch. 4, especially pp. 108–10.
123 CBOS poll in 'Białe plamy – Katyn', *Polityka*, 13 August 1988, p. 3.
124 'Polacy i my', *Polityka*, 15 April 1989, p. 13.
125 T. Szajna, 'Addressing "Blank Spots" in Polish–Soviet relations', *Problems of Communism*, 38, 6 (November–December 1988), pp. 49 ff.
126 The Historical Commission was criticised on all sides for its slow and cumbersome progress. Cf. Artur Hajnicz in *Tygodnik Solidarność*, 16 June 1989. Eugeniusz Duraczyński in *Polityka*, 13 June 1987, 29 September 1987 and 24 October 1988.
127 Printed as 'Ekspertyza', *Polityka*, 19 August 1989, pp. 13–14. One should note

the date, just before the assumption of power by Tadeusz Mazowiecki's Government, which marked the fall of communism in Poland.

128 Ryszard Wojna in *Rzeczpospolita*, 8 February 1989.

129 *Polityka*, 11 March 1989, p. 10. The joint commission was wound up in May 1990. The Polish contribution was summarised in *Zbrodnia Katyńska: Z prac polskiej części Komisji Partyjnych Historyków Polski i ZSRR*, Warsaw, 1990.

130 The companion volume was *Agresja 17 Września*, also published by the underground, Warsaw: Głos, 1979, with numerous re-editions.

131 See their biographies in *Katyń: problemy i zagadki*, Warsaw: NZKHBZK, 1990, pp. 211–15.

132 For an insider's account of its work see Bożena Łojek, 'Dziesięcolecie działalności Niezależnego Komitetu Historycznego Badania Zbrodni Katyńskiej', in *W Przeddzień Zbrodni Katyńskiej*, Warsaw: NKHBZK, 1999, pp. 98–114.

133 See Bożena Łojek, 'Polska Fundacja Katyńska', in *Zbrodnia Katyńska próba bilansu*, Warsaw: NKHBZK, 2001, pp. 161–78.

134 See Bożena Łojek, Stanisław Mikke, Zdzisław Sawicki and Jacek Trznadel, *Muzeum Katyńskie w Warszawie*, Warsaw: MON, 2000.

135 Sławomir Błażewicz, 'Muzeum Katyński, 1993–2000: Próba bilansu i dalsze perspektywy', in *Zbrodnia Katyńska próba bilansu*, pp. 179–92.

136 Bożena Łojek, 'Muzeum Katyńskie walka o miejsce pamięci', in *Zbrodnia Katyńska po 60 latach*, Warsaw: NKHBZK, 2000, pp. 139–61.

137 Cf. Stanisław Broniewski-Orsza, 'Upamiętnienie ofiar zbrodni katyńskiej w programie działanie ROPWiM', in *Zbrodnia nie ukarana: Katyń – Twer – Charków*, Warsaw: NKHBZK, 1996.

138 See the interview with Antoni Majorowicz, the chairman of the Konin branch, the first of these to be legally registered, on their organisational and membership difficulties and lack of agreement as to their role, *Polityka*, 10 June 1989, p. 14.

139 Włodzimierz Dusiewicz, 'Rodziny Katyńskie w Polsce', in *Zbrodnia Katyńska po 60 latach*, pp. 162–84.

140 Second Sejm PR, II Kadencja, *Informacja o działalności Semu*, Warsaw: Kancelaria Sejmu, 1995, p. 142. Reproduced in *Zbrodnia nie Ukarana: Katyń – Twer – Charków*, p. 468.

141 Full texts of Sejm resolution of 13 April 2000 and Senate resolution of 12 April 2000 in *Zbrodnia Katyńska po 60 latach*, pp. 205–8.

142 Speech at the Tomb of the Unknown Soldier, 13 April 2000, *Zbrodnia Katyńska po 60 latach*, pp. 209–11.

143 For his account and justification of the episode, see Jan Piątkowski, *Dotyk zbrodni – Katyń*, Warsaw: PRO ARTE, 2002.

144 See George Sanford, *Democratic Government in Poland: Constitutional Politics Since 1989*, Basingstoke: Palgrave, 2002, pp. 219–25.

145 Łojek letter of 26 March 2001 to Kieres and Kieres reply of 6 April 2001 in *Zbrodnia Katyńska: Pytania pozostałe bez odpowiedzi*, pp. 41–5.

146 http://dziennik.pap.com.pl/index.html?dzial=POS&poddzial=SPN&id_depeszy=14777330. The Government of the Ukraine responded positively to the Russian request that they make their material available to them. What this involved was unclear at the time that this book went to press although it was reported as involving the bodies of 270 Polish officers discovered at Bykovna near Kiev.

Conclusion
Closure of the 1940 Soviet Massacre Issue

Truth – what still remains to be revealed?

The long drawn out search for the truth about Katyn and the 1940 massacre resembles a detective story in many respects. The issue was further complicated because, as Congressman Ray Madden said when chairing the 1952 committee, 'the Katyn massacre is the only international crime in world history where two nations disputed the guilt'.[1] The general outline of the Kozelsk-Katyn, Starobelsk-Kharkov and Ostashkov-Mednoe aspects of the 1940 massacre has been revealed in the extensive detail covered in this book by the political admissions, archival revelations, judicial investigations and exhumations of the early 1990s. The exhumations, however, were only able to resolve the commemoration issue on a largely group not individual basis. Although much progress was made it did not prove possible to identify all the Polish bodies individually in the three burial sites nor to establish fully comprehensive lists of all the Poles buried there. Beyond that, as we saw in Chapter Five, the burial sites of the victims associated with the 1940 massacre in the Ukraine and Belarus still have not been established while the names of those killed in Belarus remain even hazier. Although probably hardly anyone who had participated in carrying out the 1940 massacre was still alive by 2004 only the names of the top planners and middle-level organisers as well as the main executioners had been established while most of the lower-level incidental assistants and escort guards had vanished into oblivion. Finally, one doubts if any new documentation will emerge about the motivation behind the top leadership decision. At most some scraps of hearsay or diary evidence concerning some NKVD functionary involved or a forgotten copy of a list or order may emerge in due course. One doubts if anything new still remains to be discovered about Stalin himself. It is also unlikely if anything major concerning the Western cover-up and its convoluted consequences, despite the Hess speculation and the question marks over Allied wartime intelligence material, still remains to be exposed. The fundamental general issues, however, still remain for further discussion so the interpretation of the material will continue to be fought over.

One can also ask, but not necessarily provide satisfactory answers to, the following questions: Why was the massacre not extended or completed to include all Polish officer PoWs in the USSR? What lessons, if any, did the Stalinist leadership draw from the massacre? Why, apart from the German invasion, was it not repeated in the Baltic States? Relatives and Polish specialists are also unhappy that it has proved impossible to establish the names of all the Poles buried in the three main burial sites or to establish beyond doubt that all, as opposed to the overwhelming bulk, of those named on the camp transportation lists are actually buried in their respective burial sites. In addition it is unclear whether some individuals withdrawn from the camps in the period immediately preceding the main massacre were actually returned to be disposed of within them or whether they were killed, or even buried, elsewhere. This type of problem looms even larger in the case of those shot in the Belarusan and Ukrainian prisons.

Memory – commemoration and closure

The issue of memory has two quite separate aspects. The first, the conflict between Polish society's search for the truth about the 1940 massacre and the PZPR which was forced to support the Soviet Burdenko version, has been discussed in Chapter Eight. The evidence is that the 1940 massacre was a malignant cancer poisoning the Polish–Soviet relationship. It reinforced other factors which rendered the stabilisation of the PRL problematic. Another aspect is whether the revelation of historical truth provides sufficient satisfaction for such an atrocity or whether it has to be accompanied by judicial acts. As we have seen, the Russian Procuracy investigations of the early 1990s contributed a little towards rounding off the historical truth. They did nothing in terms of satisfying any possible desire for vengeance in the form of the trial, condemnation and punishment of surviving perpetrators.

The other main aspect of memory is commemoration, aptly defined as 'a way of marking out a space in the public sphere'.[2] This took the form in the 1990s of political declarations, media publicity and academic studies and debate asserting the truth about the 1940 massacre in Poland and the West and to a lesser degree in Russia. With the passing of communism and the emergence of the truth, however, a lively debate occurred within the Katyn community in Poland as to how memory should be commemorated in the form of graves, cemeteries, chapels and other physical memorials. From the time of Roman Catholic Primate Józef Glemp's visit to Katyn in December 1988 onwards a large number of crosses and other temporary memorials were set up in all three burial sites. A variety of religious memorial services and other forms of consecration were held at various times over the years during the visits of relatives and varied delegations.

Polish–Russian negotiations began in 1992. Their joint agreement of 22

February 1994 on Cemeteries and War Memorials, however, proved difficult to implement. The soundings and drillings taken during the
1994–1996 exhumations allowed the Polish side to identify the location of
individual burial pits and to suggest territorial limits for the proposed
cemeteries within which all the Poles were buried. Preliminary agreement
was reached on their construction by March 1995. Their foundation
stones, consecrated by Pope John Paul II, were laid at Katyn and Mednoe
in June 1995. ROPWiM then organised an architects' competition which
produced various plans. Prime Minister Chernomyrdin's Russian Government passed resolution number 1247 on the subject in October 1996 but
definite planning decisions and actual construction were delayed until
1998–1999.

The above activity finally culminated in 2000 with the ceremonial
opening and consecration of military cemeteries in Katyn and Mednoe in
Russia and Kharkov in the Ukraine under the patronage of Prime Minister
Jerzy Buzek.[3] As a result of the efforts of the Katyn pressure groups,
notably ROPWiM, the cemeteries were given federal status. This, in
theory, meant that their upkeep and preservation became a responsibility
of the Russian and Ukrainian central Governments. The Poles had,
however, resisted Russian and Ukrainian suggestions that joint memorials
should be erected to all the NKVD victims buried there, irrespective of
nationality.[4]

Justice – forgiveness and reconciliation

Individuals affected by a crime can have their feelings of grievance
assuaged by the trial and punishment of the perpetrators. The rancour of
whole societies has also been dealt with in the same way with the implementation of ideas of international justice in the 20th century. The concepts of War Crimes and of Crimes against Humanity were applied against
the Nazi and Japanese leaderships at the end of the Second World War.
An uneven beginning was also made in the same direction in handling the
Yugoslav conflicts of the 1990s. Whether practice will be improved by the
establishment of the International Criminal Court with a general remit
wider than the specific courts established for post-Yugoslavia and Rwanda
remains to be seen. Another subject in its own right is whether individuals
or nations forgive and ask for forgiveness as the basis for reconciliation.
How nations forgive past grievances and reconcile with historical opponents is an issue which has been boosted by the post-Second World War
movement towards European Union. At present, however, one can only
pose the question whether examples of reconciliation such as the Franco-
German in the 1960s or the Polish–German in the 1990s can be emulated
by the future Polish–Russian relationship.

Such developments have come too late for the judicial punishment of
the perpetrators of the 1940 massacre to be dealt with in this way, particu-

larly as the Russian republic did not move quickly enough to use its national courts for this purpose. How then can closure be brought about for the issue? In theory, either an international or an *ad hoc* tribunal could hear and weigh up the evidence and conclude with an authoritative declaration. This study has shown how such proposals were resisted by Western, as well as communist, Governments during 1943–1990. This road is now even less likely. There is considerable dispute over the choice of relevant tribunal or the judicial, political and academic character of any alternative or *ad hoc* substitute. Bodies such as the United Nations also have more pressing business than to issue declarations on historical, as against current, atrocities. Given this situation, the only alternative, in the first instance, is for the matter to be examined and revealed in full by the academic community and to be publicised thoroughly by the mass media. Joint historical conferences, publications and archive exchanges played an important role after the fall of communism.

Ultimately, the Russian Republic, as the direct successor to the USSR, will need to build on the consequences of accepting responsibility for this particular crime. This was done, to an extent, by the political and judicial elites in the early 1990s although not sufficiently wholeheartedly to convince all of Russian society and public opinion. President Boris Yeltsin and his adviser Sergei Stankevich apologised for Katyn in 1992–1993 but such declarations were little publicised in Russia. In addition, all the relevant documentation will have to be made available to scholars and through them to public opinion. A new Russian generation will also need to come to terms with the Stalinist past in order to overcome its inheritance in the same way that the Germans had their similar debate over Nazism after 1950. Only when this is done will Polish public opinion accept the same level of national reconciliation which has been achieved with Germany since 1990.

The issue of political forgiveness has been much discussed by the academic community in recent years.[5] The Katyn *milieu* got onto this question once other issues had been exhausted but found it philosophically difficult to relate it to the wider debate and to get beyond a constraining framework of Polish Christianity.[6] Questionnaires distributed within Katyn Family circles in 2003 revealed an overwhelming majority (190 out of 200 respondents) against unconditional forgiveness although 5 per cent were willing to do so. About a third were willing to forgive if suitable contrition or compensation were offered while another third would do so if, additionally, forgiveness was requested directly. A sixth considered that the following conditions needed to be fulfilled. These were the completion of judicial investigations, that all documentation be made available, the ending of secrecy so that Russian public opinion would become conscious of the crime, and the moral condemnation of the atrocity and its perpetrators by an international judicial tribunal. Only a tenth considered that the massacre could not be forgiven under any circumstances.[7] Other questionnaires revealed significant divisions about whether the act of forgiveness should be carried out solely by the Federation of Katyn Families or whether it should take the form of a declaration worked out jointly with the President of the Republic and the Sejm and Senate.[8] Numerous responses indicated dissatisfaction with the absence of a full and unreserved apology by the President and Duma of the Russian Republic and with the level of financial commitments accepted.

The long drawn out and painful crusade for the truth about the whole of the 1940 massacre from 1943 to 1990 challenges a whole raft of Western democratic shibboleths. Realists still argue that the compromises or necessities of foreign-policy-making statecraft relativise the purely objective historical truth. What was held to be the truth about Katyn, for example, varied for the Americans in 1943, 1945, 1952 or 1992. Historically, political elites camouflaged or distorted inconvenient truths in the light of the overriding priority of *raison d'état*. But modern democratic and mass media frameworks have eroded the conditions which allowed secrecy and Machiavellianism to dominate foreign policy making. The question, therefore, arises – do or should noble lies and secrecy be resorted to, in extreme cases, in order to manoeuvre democratic electorates into accepting unethical measures dictated by the statecraft of protecting the national interest? Could Roosevelt and Churchill have openly told their publics that Stalin was a tyrant who had murdered and imprisoned millions of his own citizens in addition to shooting 22 000 Polish PoWs in 1940 without foreclosing their longer-term aims? Would democratic opinion have accepted the necessity of making a deal with him in order to win the war against Nazi Germany and in the hope of establishing a new post-war order?

If cynical realism undermines the moral bases of a democratic polity then, as we have seen from our case study of how the British Foreign Office handled the Katyn issue, it also led to self-delusion by the policy makers themselves. If the truth of an issue such as the 1940 Soviet massacre or the threat posed by an Iraqi dictator and his alleged weapons of mass destruction in 2003 proves inconvenient then it becomes both a psychological and practical necessity to reshape it into a more acceptable form. In retrospect, the diplomatic and military reports supported by the 1943 exhumations at Katyn provided what would normally have been accepted as a more than sufficient amount of evidence to prove Soviet guilt. As the conclusion ran counter to longer-term Western political priorities the various levels and types of evidence were challenged and undermined by the British Foreign Office in order to produce an open verdict suspending judgement. This allowed both foreign policy makers and administrators to maintain their self-respect as honourable and moral individuals and to pursue their favoured course while fending off external and public opinion challenges. The self-delusion that this was both a moral and correct approach meant that successive generations of Foreign

Office officials repeated the same arguments and confirmed the same line right up until 1990. Unlike the more flexible Americans, British decision makers really found difficulty in accepting the relativity of the Katyn truth. After all, according to their own lights they were moral and honourable individuals, maintaining the highest standards of public service. Such trite phrases as were trotted out again by the Hutton and Butler Inquiries in 2003–2004 reinforced elite self-delusions and confused public opinion just sufficiently to ensure the survival of the Blair Government.

This study has demonstrated the dual character of the 1940 massacre *aka* Katyn issue. Apart from the Ukrainian and Belarusan dimensions of the massacre, a plateau seems to have been reached by 1993 in revealing and documenting the truth about the central Kozelsk-Katyn, Starobelsk-Kharkov and Ostashkov-Mednoe aspects of the massacre. This has been presented to the reader, in the first half of the book, in strictly academic terms as an illustrative case study of the processes and mechanisms involved in carrying out a Stalinist crime and situated in its historical and explanatory context. The second half of the study has, however, explained why what would otherwise be a long-forgotten massacre remained a sensitive and controversial issue after 1943 which still has not been satisfactorily resolved in Polish–Russian relations and which, incidently, reveals much about British policy making. How the truth about often politically embarrassing atrocities should be handled by democratic governments in relation to modern mass-media-driven public opinion is a burning issue of the age. The same question mark also applies to the balance to be struck between pragmatic realism and idealist morality and between national interests and wider principles of international law. How nations can reconcile in terms of European, if not global, community by admitting the truth of past atrocities and offering apologies to each other and, where appropriate restitution and compensation is a key issue on the political agenda of the early 21st century.

Notes

1 *Hearings*, Part 7, p. 1943.
2 George Schopflin, *Nations, Identity, Power*, London: Hurst, 2000, p. 74.
3 For descriptions of the statuary, inscriptions, area and territorial limits of the Katyn and Mednoe cemeteries see Jolanta Adamska, 'Katyń, Miednoje 1940–2000', in *Zbrodnia Katyńska: Próba bilansu*, Warsaw: 2001, pp. 62–5.
4 There is an interesting echo and inversion of the Auschwitz controversy here. Some Jews argued that the extermination camp represented a peculiarly and specifically Jewish tragedy while the Poles in this instance argued that Nazi victims had been drawn from all humanity although Jews suffered most.
5 See Peter Digesser, *Political Forgiveness*, Ithaca, NY: Cornell UP, 2001. Cf. Martha Minow (ed.), *Breaking the Cycles of Hatred: Memory, Law and Repair*, Princeton, NJ: Princeton UP, 2002.
6 See the contributions by various Polish clerics in *Zbrodnia Katyńska: Problem przebaczenia*, Warsaw: NKHBZK, 2003. The Oxford-based philosopher Leszek

Kołakowski distinguishes between bureaucratic forgiveness by state or public bodies and forgiveness by individuals according to the Christian spiritual canon, ibid., pp. 22–7.

7   Bożena Łojek, 'Czy zbrodnię Katyńską można przebaczyć? Wyniki ankiety son-dażowej', ibid., pp. 70–4.

8   Ibid., pp. 76–9.

Select bibliography

Archival

Archiwum Akt Nowych (Warsaw)

Hoover Institution's Eastern Archive
Akta Janusza Zawodnego (Zawodny Papers)

Centralne Archiwum Wojskowe (Warsaw)

Kolekcja Akt z Archiwów Rosyjskich (Documentary Collections from the Russian Archives)
CAW. VIII. 800. 20. Zarząd Główny ds Jeńców Wojennych Internowanych 1939–1945 i Podległych Jednostek (Main Department for Prisoners of War Interned 1939–1945 and Subordinate Organisations)
CAW. VIII. 800.21. Komisja Burdenki (Burdenko Commission)

Muzeum Katyńskie, oddział Muzeum Wojska Polskiego (Warsaw)

Public Record Office (London)

CAB 66 War Cabinet memoranda
CAB 92 Polish Forces (Official) Committee
FCO 28 Foreign and Commonwealth Office
FO 181 Embassy and Consular Archives, Russia
FO 371 Foreign Office General Correspondence
GFM 33 Captured Records
HS 4 Special Operations Executive
HW 1, 12, 19 General Communications Head Quarters (GCHQ intercepts)
LCO 2 Lord Chancellor's Office
PREM 3 Prime Minister's Office
WO 106 War Office. Directorate of Military Operations and Intelligence
WO 208 Military Intelligence Directorate

Instytut Polski i Muzeum Sikorskiego (London)

Protocols and Testimonies before the Special Military Court of Polish PoWs held in the USSR during the Second World War

Published primary sources

Agresja sowiecka na Polskę w świetle dokumentów: 17 września 1939r, Warsaw: Centralne Archiwum Wojskowe/Bellona, vols 1–3, 1994–1996. Vol. 1. Eugeniusz Kozłowski (ed.), *Geneza i skutki agresji*, 1994. Vol. 2. Stanisław Jaczyński (ed.), *Działania wojsk Frontu Ukraińskiego*, 1996. Vol. 3. Czesław Grelak (ed.), *Działania wojsk Frontu Białoruskiego*, 1995.

Amtliches Material zum Massenmord von Katyn, Berlin: F. Eher Nachf., 1943.

Armia Krajowa w dokumentach, 1939–1945, London: Gryf, vols 1–4, 1970–1976.

Centre for Information and Documentation of the Polish Government, *The German Invasion of Poland: Polish Black Book*, London-Melbourne, 1941.

Cyprian, Tadeusz, and Jerzy Sawicki (eds), *Sprawy Polskie w Procesie Norymberskim*, Poznań: Instytut Zachodni, 1956.

Czarna Księga Cenzury PRL, London: ANEKS, 1977.

Degras, Jane (ed.), *Soviet Documents on Foreign Policy*, London: RIIA, 3 vols, 1951–1953.

Documents on German Foreign Policy, Series D, 1937–1945, vols 8, 9, 10, 11, 12, London: HMSO, 1954–1964.

Dokumenty i materiały do historii stosunków polsko-radzieckich, vol. 7, *styczeń 1939–grudzień 1943*, Warsaw: KiW, 1973.

'Dokumenty Katyńskie', *Wojskowy Przegląd Historyczny*, vol. 35, nos 3–4 (1990).

Foreign Office, Historical Notes and Occasional Papers, *British Reactions to the Katyn Massacre, 1943–2003* (Butler Memorandum), London, 2003. www.fco.gov.uk/servlet/Front?pagename=OpenMarket/Xcelerate/ShowPage&c=Page&cid=1049114089000.

Foreign Relations of the United States: Diplomatic Papers, Washington, DC: Government Printing Office. Volumes for: 1939, 1, 2 (1956), 1940, II (1957), 1941, 1 (1958), 1942, III (1961), 1943, III (1963), 1944, III (1963).

General Sikorski Historical Institute (London), *Documents on Polish–Soviet Relations, 1939–45*, London: Heinemann, 1961 and 1967. Vol. 1, *1939–1943*, vol. 2, *1943–1945*.

Gieysztor, Aleksander and Rudolf Pichoja, (chief eds), *Katyń: Dokumenty Zbrodni*, Warsaw: Naczelna Dyrekcja Archiwów Państwowych/Wydawnictwo Trio. Vol. 1. *Jeńcy nie wypowiedzianej wojny, sierpień 1939–marzec 1940* (1995). Vol. 2. *Zagłada, marzec–czerwiec 1940* (1998). Vol. 3. *Losy Ocalałych, lipiec 1940–marzec 1943* (2001).

Jędrzejewicz, Wacław (ed.), *Poland in the British Parliament, 1939–1945: Documentary Material Relating to the Cause of Poland in World War Two*, New York: Józef Piłsudski Institute, 3 vols, 1946–1959.

Jegliński, Piotr (ed.), *Pamiętniki znalezione w Katyniu*, introduction by Janusz K. Zawodny, Paris: Spotkania, 1989.

KARTA, *Rosja a Katyń: Biuletyn HAI*, Warsaw: KARTA, 1994.

Katyń, Starobielsk, Ostaszków, Kozielsk: Najnowsze Dokumenty NKWD, Paris: Editions Dembinski, 1990.

Katyń: Wybór publicystyki 1943–1988 i lista Katyńska, introduction by Alexandra Kwiatkowska-Viatteau, London: Polonia, 1988.

The Katyn Forest Massacre: Hearings before the Select Committee to Conduct an Investigation of the Facts, Evidence and Circumstances of the Katyn Forest Massacre, 82nd Congress, Washington, DC: US Government Printing Office, 7 vols, 1952.

The Katyn Forest Massacre: Interim Report of the Select Committee to Conduct an Investigation of the Facts, Evidence and Circumstances of the Katyn Forest Massacre, 82nd Congress, Washington, DC: US Government Printing Office, 1952.

The Katyn Forest Massacre: Final Report of the Select Committee to Conduct an Investigation of the Facts, Evidence and Circumstances of the Katyn Forest Massacre, House Report 2505, 82nd Congress, 2nd session, Washington, DC: US Government Printing Office, 1952.

Komisja Historyczna Polskiego Sztabu Głównego Polskich Sił Zbrojnych, *Polskie Siły Zbrojne w drugiej wojnie światowej,* Vol. 1, *Kampania Wrześniowa 1939,* Vol. 3, *Armia Krajowa,* London: Sikorski Institute, 1950–1951.

Lutoborski, Anna and Tadeusz (eds), *Pamiętniki znalezione w Katyniu,* Paris-Warsaw: n.p., 2nd edn with foreword by Janusz Zawodny, 1990.

Materski, Wojciech (ed.), *Katyń: Dokumenty ludobójstwa: Dokumenty i materiały archiwalne przekazane Polsce 14 października 1992 r.,* Warsaw: ISP PAN, 1992.

—— (ed.), *Documents of Genocide: Documents and Materials from the Soviet Archives Turned Over to Poland on October 14, 1992,* Warsaw: ISP PAN, 1993.

—— (ed.), *Kremlin versus Poland, 1939–1945: Documents from the Soviet Archives,* Warsaw: ISP PAN, 1996.

Ministère des Affaires Etrangères, *Documents Diplomatiques Français 1939 (2 Séptembre–31 Décembre),* Brussels: Peter Lang, 2002.

Ministerstwo Spraw Wewnętrznych, *Polskie podziemie 1939–1941: Lwów, Kołomyja, Stryj, Złoczów,* Warsaw: MSW, 1998.

——, *Śladem zbrodni katyńskiej,* Warsaw: MSW, 1998.

——, *Zachodnia Białoruś 17 ix 1939–22 vi 1941,* Warsaw: MSW, 1998.

——, *Naznaczeni piętnem Ostaszkowa,* Warsaw: MSW, 2000.

Moszyński, Adam (ed.), *Lista Katyńska: Jeńcy obozów Kozielsk, Ostaszków, Starobielsk zaginieni w Rosji Sowieckiej,* Warsaw: OmnipressPolskie Towarzystwo Historyczne, 1989.

Nazi Conspiracy and Aggression, 8 vols and 2 supplements. Washington, DC: Government Printing Office, 1946–1948.

O'Malley, Owen, 'Disappearance of Polish Officers in the Union of Soviet Socialist Republics', Memoranda from Sir Owen O'Malley to Sir Anthony Eden, London: Polish Cultural Foundation, 1972; Paris: Editions Spotkania, 1980.

Polish White Book: Official Documents Concerning Polish–German and Polish–Soviet Relations, 1933–1939, London: Hutchinson, 1940.

Polish–Soviet Relations, 1939–1943, New York: Polish Information Centre, 1943.

Słowa tęsknoty: Zachowane listy jeńców Kozielska, Ostaszkowa i Starobielska, Szczecin: Stowarzyszenie Katyńskie w Szczecine, 1996.

Snopkiewicz, Jacek, and Andrzej Zakrzewski, *Decyzja: Dokumenty Katynia,* Warsaw: PAI Interpress, 1992.

Sontag, James and James Beddie (eds), *Nazi–Soviet Relations, 1939–1941: Documents from the Archives of the German Foreign Office,* Westport, CT: Greenwood Press, 1976.

Sprawa polska w czasie drugiej wojny światowej na arenie międzynarodowej: Zbiór dokumentów, Warsaw: PWN, 1965.

Strzembosz, Tomasz (ed.), *Okupacja sowiecka (1939–1941) w świetle tajnych dokumen-*

tów: obywatele polscy na kresach północno-wschodnich II Rzeczypospolitej pod okupacją sowiecką w latach 1939–1941, Warsaw: ISP PAN, 1996.

Szcześniak, Andrzej Leszek (ed.), *Katyń: Tło historyczne, fakty, dokumenty*, Warsaw: ALFA, 1989.

——. *Zmowa: IV rozbiór Polski*, Warsaw: ALFA, 1990.

Trial of the Major War Criminals before the International Military Tribunal, Nuremberg, Nuremberg International Tribunal, 42 vols, 1948.

Z archiwów sowieckich series, Warsaw: ISP PAN, vols 1–5, 1992–1995. Vol. 1, Wojciech Materski (ed.), *Polscy jeńcy wojenni w ZSSR, 1939–1941*, 1992. Vol. 2, Wojciech Materski (ed.), *Armia Polska w ZSSR, 1941–1942*, 1992. Vol. 3, Wojciech Roszkowski (ed.), *Konflikty polsko-sowieckie, 1942–1944*, 1993. Vol. 4, Tomasz Strzembosz (ed.), *Stalin a Powstanie Warszawskie, 1944*. Vol. 5, Andrzej Paczkowski (ed.), *Powrót z sowieckich lagrów*, 1995.

Zbrodnia Katyńska w świetle dokumentów, foreword by Władysław Anders, London: Gryf, 12 editions, 1948–1989. English language version, *The Crime of Katyn*, London: Polish Cultural Foundation, 1965.

Memoirs

Anders, Władysław, *An Army in Exile: The Story of the Second Polish Corps*, London: Macmillan, 1949.

——, *Bez ostatniego rozdziału: wspomniena z lat 1939–1946*, London: Gryf, 10th edn, 1989.

Bohusz-Szyszko, Zygmunt, *Czerwony Sfinks*, Rome: Polski Dom Wydawniczy, 1946.

Bór-Komorowski, Tadeusz, *The Secret Army*, Nashville, TENN: Battery Press, 1984.

Churchill, Winston, *The Second World War*, Vol. IV, *The Hinge of Fate*, London: Cassel, 1951.

Ciechanowski, Jan, *Defeat in Victory*, Garden City, NY: Doubleday & Co., 1947.

Czapski, Józef, *Wspomnienia Starobielskie*, Rome: White Eagle, 1944.

——, *The Inhuman Land*, London: Chatto & Windus, 1951.

Goetel, Ferdynand, *Czasy Wojny*, London: Veritas, 1955.

Klimkowski, J[erzy], *Byłem adiutantem gen.Andersa*, Warsaw: MON, 1959.

Korbonski, Stefan, *The Polish Underground State: A Guide to the Underground, 1939–1945*, New York: Columbia UP, 1978.

Kot, Stanisław, *Conversations with the Kremlin and Dispatches from Russia*, London: Oxford UP, 1963.

Lane, Arthur Bliss, *I Saw Poland Betrayed*, Indianapolis, IN: Bobbs-Merrill, 1948.

Lochner, Louis (ed.), *The Goebbels Diaries*, New York: Doubleday, 1948.

Łopianowski, Narcyz, *Rozmowy z NKWD, 1940–1941*, Warsaw: PAX, 1990.

Maisky, Ivan, *Memoirs of a Soviet Ambassador*, New York: Charles Scribner, 1968.

Mikołajczyk, Stanisław, *The Rape of Poland: Pattern of Soviet Aggression*, New York: McGraw-Hill, 1948.

Młynarski, Bronisław, *W niewoli sowieckiej*, London: Gryf, 1974. English language edition, Casimir, Zdziechowski *The 79th Survivor: Bronisław Młynarski*, London: Bachman & Turner, 1976.

Peszkowski, Zdzisław, *Memoirs of a Prisoner of War in Kozielsk*, Wrocław: Polish Katyń Foundation, 2nd edn, 1994.

——, *Droga Krzyżowa: polska Golgota Wschodu*, Warsaw: 'Soli Deo', 1994.

Raczyński, Edward, *In Allied London*, London: Weidenfeld & Nicolson, 1962.

Slowes, Salomon, *The Road to Katyn: A Soldier's Story*, Oxford: Blackwell, 1992.

Sudoplatov, Pavel, *Special Tasks: The Memoirs of an Unwanted Witness: A Soviet Spymaster*, London: Warner Books, 1995.

Świaniewicz, Stanisław, *W cieniu Katynia*, Paris: Instytut Literacki, 1976; Warsaw: Officyna Literatów, 1991. English Language edition, *In the Shadow of Katyn*, Calgary, Alberta: Bunker & Bunker, 2002.

Zabiełło, Stanisław (ed.), *Sprawa Polska podczas II Wojny Światowej w świetle pamiętników*, Warsaw: PISM, 1958.

Bibliographies

Harz, Maria, 'Bibliografia zawartości *Zeszytów Katyńskich* za lata 1990–1996', in *Ku cmentarzom Polskim w Katyniu, Miednoje i Charkowie*, Warsaw: NKHBZK, 1997, pp. 142–52.

——, 'Bibliografia zbrodni Katyńskiej: Materiały z lat 1993–1997', in *Zbrodnia Katyńska: Upamiętnienie ofiar i zadośćuczynienie*, Warsaw, 1998.

——, 'Bibliografie i Przeglądy Publikacji', in *Zbrodnia Katyńska po 60 latach: Polityka, Nauka, Moralność*, Warsaw: NKHBZK, 2000.

Jagodziński, Zdzisław, *Bibliografia Katyńska (książki i broszury)*, London: The Polish Library, 1st edn, 1976; rev. 2nd edn, 1982.

Olech, Urszula, and Elżbieta, Pawińska *Bibliografia zbrodni Katyńskiej: Materiały z lat 1993–2000*, Warsaw: Centralna Biblioteka Wojskowa, 2000.

Secondary sources

Abarinov, Vladimir, *The Murderers of Katyn: A Russian Journalist Investigates the 1940 Massacre of 15,000 Polish Officers in Soviet Captivity*, New York: Hippocrene, 1993.

Adler, Nancy, *Victims of Soviet Terror: The Story of the Memorial Movement*, Westport, CT: Greenwood, 1993.

Applebaum, Anne, *GULAG: A History of the Soviet Camps*, London: Allen Lane, 2003.

Azborovskaa, Inessa, Anatolii Ablokov and Valentina Parsadanova, *Katinskij sindrom v sovetsko-pol'skih i rossijsko-pol'skih otnoseniah*, Moscow: ROSSPEN, 2001.

Basak, Adam, *Historia pewnej mistyfikacji: Zbrodnia Katyńska przed Trybunałem Norymberskim*, Wrocław: Wydawnictwo Uniwersytetu Wrocławskiego, 1993.

Bass, Gary, *Stay the Hand of Vengeance: The Politics of War Crimes Tribunals*, Princeton, NJ: Princeton, 2000.

Bell, Philip, *John Bull and the Bear: British Public Opinion, Foreign Policy and the Soviet Union, 1941–1945*, London: Arnold, 1990.

Bernas, Franciszek and Jacek Wilczur, *Piekielny krąg: Z dziejów Czeka, GPU, NKWD*, Warsaw: Zespół Badawczo-Naukowy do Spraw Zagłady Kresów Wschodnich, 1996.

Blum, Ignacy, *Żołnierze Armii Polskiej w ZSRR*, Warsaw: Wojskowy Instytut Historyczny, 1967.

Borak, Mečislav, *Vraždy v Katynskem lese*, Ostrava: Petit, 1993.

Bratko, Józef, *Dlaczego zginąłeś, prokuratorze?*, Kraków: Stowarzyszenie Twórcze. Krakowski Klub Artystyczno-Literacki, 1998.

Bregman, Aleksander, *Najlepszy sojusznik Hitlera: Studium o współpracy niemiecko-sowieckiej, 1939–1941*, London: Orbis, 1958.

Brickhill, Paul, *The Great Escape*, New York: Norton, 1950.

Budurowycz, Bohdan, *Polish–Soviet Relations, 1932–1939*, New York: Columbia UP, 1963.

Carrier, Capucine, *Filling in the Blank Spots*, Brussels: University Libre de Bruxelles CERI/CSIR. Topical Papers No. 1, June 1989.

Ciesielski, Stanisław, Wojciech Materski and Andrzej Paczkowski, *Represje Sowieckie wobec Polaków i Obywateli Polskich*, Warsaw: Ministerstwo Sprawiedliwości RP/KARTA, 2000.

Conquest, Robert (ed.), *Justice and the Legal System in the USSR*, London: Bodley Head, 1968.

——, (ed.), *The Soviet Police System*, London: Bodley Head, 1968.

——, *The Nation-Killers: The Soviet Deportation of Nationalities*, London: Macmillan, 1970.

——, *The Great Terror: Stalin's Purge in the 1930s*, London: Macmillan, rev. edn, 1973.

——, *Kolyma: The Arctic Death Camps*, London: Macmillan, 1978.

——, *Inside Stalin's Secret Police: NKVD politics, 1936–1939*, Basingstoke: Macmillan, 1985.

——, *The Great Terror: A Reassessment*, London: Hutchinson, 1990.

Coutividis, John and Jaime Reynolds, *Poland, 1939–1947*, Leicester, UK: Leicester UP, 1986.

Cygan, Wiktor, *Kresy w ogniu: Wojna polsko-sowiecka, 1939*, Warsaw: Gryf, 1990.

Czapska, Maria (ed.), *Polacy w ZSSR, 1939–1942: Antologia*, Paris: Instytut Literacki, 1963.

Digesser, Peter, *Political Forgiveness*, Ithaca, NY: Cornell UP, 2001.

Dziewanowski, Marian K., *The Communist Party of Poland*, Cambridge, MA: Harvard UP, 1976.

Epstein, Julius, *The Mysteries of the Van Vliet Report*, Chicago: Polish American Congress, 1951.

Fainsod, Merle, *Smolensk under Soviet Rule*, New York: Random House, 1963.

——, *How Russia is Ruled*, Cambridge, MA: Harvard UP, 1964.

FitzGibbon, Louis, *Katyn – A Crime Without Parallel*, London: Tom Stacey, 1971. Also Torrance, CA: Noontide Press, 1979.

——, *The Katyn Cover-Up*, London: Tom Stacey, 1972.

——, *Unpitied and Unknown: Katyn – Bologoye – Dergachi*, London: Bachman & Turner, 1975.

——, *Katyn Memorial*, London: SPK/Gryf, 1977. Polish language edition, *O Prawdę i Sprawiedliwość: Pomnik Katyński w Londynie*, London: SPK-Gryf, 1977.

Foreign Office, Library and Records Department, *The Katyn Massacre: An SOE Perspective*, London: LRD, 1996.

Frącki, Edward, 'Dokumenty polskie i Polski dotyczące w archiwach rosyjskich', *Dzieje Najnowsze*, vol. 25, no. 1 (1993), pp. 93–104.

Gajowniczek, Zuzanna (ed.), *Śladem zbrodni Katyńskiej*, Warsaw: Centralne Archiwum MSW i Administracji RP, 1998.

——, *Ukraiński ślad Katynia*, Warsaw: Ministerstwo Spraw Wewnętrznych, 1995.

Garliński, Józef, *Poland in the Second World War*, Basingstoke: Macmillan, 1985.

Garrett, C. and S., 'Death and Politics: The Katyn Forest Massacre and American Foreign Policy', *East European Quarterly*, 20, 4 (January 1987), pp. 429–46.

Godziemba-Maliszewski, Wacław, *Katyń: An Interpretation of Aerial Photographs Considered with Facts and Documents*, Warsaw: Polskie Towarzystwo Geograficzne/Klub Teledetekcji Środowiska, 1995.

Gross, Jan, *Revolution from Abroad: The Soviet Conquest of Poland's Western Ukraine and Western Belorussia*, Princeton, NJ: Princeton UP, 1988.

—— and Irena Grudzińska-Gross (eds), *W czterdziestym nas matko na Sybir zesłali...*, London: Aneks, 1983.

Gruner-Zarnoch, Ewa, *Starobielsk w oczach ocalałych jeńców*, Szczecin: ROPWiM, 2001.

—— and Ryszard Wołągiewicz (eds), *Słowa tęsknoty: Zachowane listy jeńców Kozielska, Ostaszkowa i Starobielska*, Szczecin: Stowarzyszenie Katynskie w Szczecinie, 1996.

Hudson, G., 'A Polish Challenge: A Review Article', *International Affairs*, 36, 2 (April 1950), pp. 214–21.

Jaczyński, Stanisław, *Zygmunt Berling: Między Sławą a Potępieniem*, Warsaw: KiW, 1993.

——, *Obozy Jenieckie NKWD, ix 1939–viii 1941*, Warsaw: Bellona, 1995.

——, *Zagłada oficerów Wojska Polskiego na Wschodzie, Wrzesień 1939–Maj 1940*, Warsaw: Bellona, 2000.

Jakubowski, Anthony (pseud. Anthony Alexander James), *Katyn: A Whisper in the Trees*, Santa Maria, CA: Kuma Publishing, 1991.

Jakubowski, Grzegorz, *et al.*, *Naznaczeni piętnem Ostaszkowa: Wykazy jeńców obozu Ostaszkowa i ich rodzin*, Warsaw: RYTM, 2000.

Jankowski, Stanisław, and Edward Miszczak, *Powrót do Katynia*, Rzeszów: KAW, 1990.

Jasiewicz, Krzysztof, *Zagłada polskich kresów: Ziemiaństwo polskie na Kresach Północno-Wschodnich Rzeczypospolitej pod okupacją sowiecką 1939–1941*, Warsaw: Volumen/ISP PAN, 1998.

Jażborowska, Inessa, Anatolij Jabłokow and Jurij Zoria, *Katyń: Zbrodnia chroniona tajemnicą państwową*, Warsaw: KiW, 1998.

Kacewicz, George, *Great Britain, the Soviet Union and the Polish Government-in-Exile (1939–1945)*, The Hague: Martinus Nijhof, 1979.

Kadell, Franz, *Die Katyn Luge: Geschichte einer Manipulation: Fakten, Dokumenten und Zeugen*, Munich: F.A. Herbig, 1991.

Kaiser, Gerd, and Andrzej Leszek Szcześniak, *Katyn: Der Masemmord an polnischen offizieren*, Berlin: Links Verlag, 1991.

——, *Katyn: Das staatsverbrechen – das staatsgeheimnis*, Berlin: Afbau Taschenbuch Verlag, 2002.

Kalbarczyk, Sławomir, *Polscy pracownicy nauki: ofiary zbrodni sowieckich w latach II wojny światowej: zamordowani – więzieni – deportowani*, Warsaw: Neriton, 2001.

Karpus, Zbigniew, *Jeńcy i internowanych rosyjscy i ukraińcy na terenie Polski w latach 1918–1924*, Toruń: Adam Marszałek, 1997.

Kola, Andrzej, and Andrzej Przewoźnik (eds), *Katyń, Miednoje, Charków: ziemia oskarża: z prac badawczych i ekshumacyjnych prowadzonych w 1994 roku na oficerach polskich zamordowanych na wschodzie*, Warsaw: Rada Ochrony Pamięci Walk i Męczeństwa, 1996.

Krzyżanowski, Jerzy, *Katyń w literaturze: międzynarodowa antologia poezji, dramatu i prozy*, Lublin: Norbertinum, 1995.

Kwiatkowska-Viatteau, Alexandra, *1940–1943, Katyn: L'Armée Polonaise Assassinée*, Brussels: Editions Complexes, 1982.

Lauck, John, *Katyn Killings in the Record*, Clifton, NJ: Kingston Press, 1999.

Lebediewa (Lebedeva), Natalia, *Katyń: Zbrodnia przeciwko ludzkości*, Warsaw: Bellona, 1997. The original Russian version is *Katyn: prestuplenie protiv chelovechestva*, Moscow: Progress/Kultura, 1994.

Łojek, Bożena, Stanisław, Mikke, Zdzisław Sawicki, and Jacek Trznadel, *Muzeum Katyńskie w Warszawie*, Warsaw: MON, 2000.

Łojek, Jerzy (pseud. Leopold Jerzewski), *Dzieje sprawy Katynia*, Białystok: Versus, 1989.

Łossowski, Piotr, *Litwa a sprawy Polskie, 1939–1940*, Warsaw: PWN, 2nd edn, 1985.

Lukas, Richard, *The Strange Allies: The United States and Poland, 1941–1945*, Knoxville, TENN: University of Tennessee Press, 1978.

——, *The Forgotten Holocaust: The Poles under German Occupation, 1939–1944*, Lexington, KY: UP of Kentucky, 1986.

Maciszewski, Jarema, *Wydrzeć prawdę*, Warsaw: BGW, 1993.

Mackiewicz, Józef, *The Katyn Wood Murders*, London: Hollis & Carter, 1951.

——, *Katyń: Zbrodnia bez Sądu i Kary*, Warsaw: PFK–Antyk, 1997.

Madajczyk, Czesław, *Dramat Katyński*, Warsaw: KiW, 1989.

McLoughlin, Barry, and McDermott, Kevin (eds), *Stalin's Terror: High Politics and Mass Repression in the Soviet Union*, Basingstoke: Palgrave Macmillan, 2003.

Merridale, Catherine, *Night of Stone: Death and Memory in Russia*, London: Granta, 2000.

Mikke, Stanisław, *Spij mężny w Katyniu, Charkowie i Miednoj*, Warsaw: Rada Ochrony Pamięci Walk i Męczeństwa, 1998.

Mikulski, Teofil, *Biogramy jeńców: Kozielsk, Starobielsk, Ostaszków, Ukraina, Zaginieni*, Wrocław: Wydawnictwo UWr, 1999.

Ministerstwo Spraw Wewnętrznych, *Ukraiński ślad Katynia*, Warsaw: MSW, 1995.

Minow, Martha, *Between Vengeance and Forgiveness: Facing History after Genocide and Mass Violence*, Boston: Beacon Press, 1999.

Misiuk, Andrzej (ed.), *Lista Ostaszkowska*, Szczytno: Wydawnictwo Wyższej Szkoły Policji, 1993.

Montfort, Henri de, *Le Massacre de Katyn: Crime Russe ou Crime Allemand?*, Paris: Editions de la Table Ronde, 1966.

Mora, S. (pseud. Kazimierz Zamorski), and Piotr Zwierniak (pseud. Stanisław Starzewski), *Sprawiedliwość sowiecka*, Rome: n.p., 1945.

Moszyński, Adam (ed.), *Lista Katyńska*, Warsaw: CDN, 1988.

Mukhin, Jurij, *Katynskij detektiv*, Moscow: Struve, 1995.

National Committee of Americans of Polish Descent, *Death at Katyn*, NCAPD, 5th edn. 1945.

Nowak, Edmund (ed.), *Jeńcy wojenni II wojny światowej: Stan archiwów i najnowszych badań*, Opole: Centralne Muzeum Jeńców Wojennych w Łambinowicach-Opole, 1996.

Ochotin, Nikita, and Arsenii Roginsky (eds), *Łagry: przewodnik encyklopedyczny*, Warsaw: KARTA/Memorial, 1998.

Paczkowski, Andrzej, *Pół wieku dziejów Polski, 1939–1989*, Warsaw: PWN, 1995.

Parrish, Michael, *The Lesser Terror: Soviet State Security, 1939–1953*, Westport, CT: Praeger, 1996.

Paul, Allen, *Katyn: Stalin's Massacre and the Seeds of Polish Resurrection*, Annapolis MD: Naval Institute Press, 1996.

Pobóg-Malinowski, Władysław, *Najnowsza historia polityczna Polski, 1864–1945*, London: n.p., vol. 2, 1981.

Podoski, Bogdan (P.B.), *Polska Wschodnia, 1939–1941*, Rome: Odział Kultury i Prasy 2 Korpusu, 1945.

Popiński, Krzysztof, Aleksander Kokurin and Aleksander Gurjanow, *Drogi Smierca: Ewakuacja więzień sowieckich z kresów Wschodnich II RP w czerwcu i lipcu 1941*, Warsaw: KARTA, 1995.

Prazmowska, Anita, *Britain and Poland, 1939–1943: The Betrayed Ally*, Cambridge: Cambridge UP, 1995.

——, *Civil War in Poland, 1942–1948*, Basingstoke: Palgrave, 2004.

Rekulski, Antoni, *Czy drugi Katyń?*, Paris: Instytut Literacki, 1980.

Roszkowski, Wojciech, *Historia Polski, 1918–1980*, Warsaw: PWN, 1992.

Rozek, Edward, *Allied Wartime Diplomacy*, London: John Wiley, 1958.

Siedlecki, Julian, *Losy Polaków w ZSSR w latach 1939–1986*, London: Gryf, 1987.

Siemaszko, Władysław and Ewa (eds), *Ludobójstwo dokonane przez nacjonalistów ukraińskich na ludności polskiej Wołynia, 1939–1945*, Warsaw: Von Borowiecky, 3 vols, 2000.

Siemaszko, Zbigniew, 'Jeńcy Wojenni (ZSRR 1939–1941)', *Zeszyty Historyczne*, Paris, no. 82, 1987, pp. 86–105.

——, *W sowieckim osaczeniu, 1939–1943*, London: Polska Fundacja Kulturalna, 1991.

Sword, Keith (ed.), *The Soviet Takeover of the Polish Eastern Provinces, 1939–1941*, Basingstoke: Macmillan, 1991.

——, *Deportation and Exile: Poles in the Soviet Union, 1939–48*, Cambridge: Cambridge UP, 2nd edn, 1996.

Szawłowski, Ryszard (Karol Liszewski), *Wojna polsko-sowiecka, 1939*, London: Polish Cultural Foundation, 1986; Warsaw: Antyk, 1997.

Szcześniak, Andrzej, *Katyń. Tło historyczne, fakty, dokumenty*, Warsaw: ALFA, 1989.

Szczygielski, Andrzej (ed.), *Pomnik Katyński w Adelajdzie*, Happy Valley, South Australia: Stowarszyszenie Polskich Kombatantów w Australia, 1981.

Szymczak, Robert, *The Unquiet Dead: The Katyn Forest Massacre as an Issue in American Diplomacy and Politics*, Doctor of Arts Dissertation, Carnegie-Mellon University, 1980, Ann Arbor, MI: University Microfilms International no. 4012, 1985.

Tarczyński, Marek (ed. unless otherwise stated), *Zeszyty Katyńskie* Warsaw: Niezależny Komitet Historyczny Badania Zbrodni Katyńskiej/Polska Fundacja Katyńska.

1. *Katyń: problemy i zagadki*, 1990, ed. Jerzy Jackl.
2. *Zbrodnia Katyńska: droga do prawdy: historia – archeologia – kryminalistyka – polityka – prawo*, 1992.
3. *Zeznanie Tokariewa*, 1994.
4. *Listy Katyńskiej ciąg dalszy: Straceni na Ukrainie*, 1994.
5. *II Półwiecze zbrodni: Katyń – Twer – Charków*, 1995.
6. *Zbrodnia nie ukarana: Katyń – Twer – Charków*, 1996.
7. Mackiewicz, Józef (ed. Jacek Trznadel), *Zbrodnia bez sądu i kary*, 1997.
8. *Ku cmentarzom Polskim w Katyniu, Miednoje, Charkowie*, 1997.
9. *Zbrodnia Katyńska: Upamiętnienie ofiar i zadośćuczynienie*, 1998.
10. *W Przeddzień Zbrodni Katyńskiej: Agresja Sowiecka 17 września 1939 roku*, 1999.
11. Montfort, Henri de, *Masakra w Katyniu*, 1999.
12. *Zbrodnia Katyńska po 60 latach: Polityka, Nauka, Moralność*, 2000.
13. *Zbrodnia Katyńska: proba bilansu*, 2001.
14. Jankowski, Stanisław M. (ed. Marek Tarczyński), *Czterdziestu co godzinę*, 2002.
15. *Zbrodnia Katyńska: pytania pozostają bez odpowiedzi*, 2002.

16. *Kaplica Katyńska w katedrze polowej Wojska Polskiego*, 2002.

17. *Zbrodnia Katyńska: Problem przebaczenia*, 2003.

18. Jankowski, Stanisław M., *Dzień rozpoczął się szczególnie. . .*, 2003.

Terry, Sarah M., *Poland's Place in Europe: General Sikorski and the Origin of the Oder–Neisse Line, 1939–1943*, Princeton, NJ: Princeton UP, 1983.

Toynbee, Arnold and Veronica Toynbee (eds), *Survey of International Affairs, 1939–1946: Hitler's Europe*, London: RIIA/OUP, 1954.

Trznadel, Jacek, *Powrót rozstrzelanej Armii (Katyń – fakty – rewizje poglądy)*, Warsaw: Antyk, 1994.

——, *The Crime of Katyn*, Warsaw: Central Club of the Polish Army, 2000.

Umiastowski, Roman, *Poland, Russia and Great Britain, 1941–1945*, London: Hollis & Carter, 1946

Tucholski, Jędrzej, *Mord w Katyniu: Kozielsk, Ostaszków, Starobielsk: lista ofiar*, Warsaw: PAX, 1991.

Walichnowski, Tadeusz (ed.), *Deportacje i przemieszczenia lucdności polskiej w głąb ZSRR, 1939–1945*, Warsaw: PWN, 1989.

Weydenthal, Jan B. de, *The Communists of Poland: An Historical Outline*, Stanford, CA: Hoover Institution Press, 1978.

Wielhorski, W., *Los Polaków w niewoli sowieckiej*, London: Rada Ziem Wschodnich RP, 1956.

Wilamowski, Jacek, *Kłamstwo Stulecia: W Cieniu Katynia*, Warsaw: Agencja Wydawnicza CB, 2003.

Wittlin, Tadeusz, *Time Stopped at 6.30: The Untold Story of the Katyn Massacre*, Indianapolis, IN: Bobbs-Merrill, 1965.

Wołągiewicz, Ryszard, *Katyń w albumach rodzinnych*, Szczecin: Stowarzyszenie 'Katyń' w Szczecinie, 1991.

Zajdlerowa, Zoe, *The Dark Side of the Moon*, eds John Coutouvidis and Thomas Lane, London: HarvesterWheatsheaf, 1989.

Żaroń, Piotr, *Obozy jeńców polskich w ZSRR w latach, 1939–1941*, London: Unicorn, 1994.

——, *Agresja Związku Radzieckiego na Polskę, 17 września 1939r. Los Jeńców Polskich*, Toruń: Adam Marszałek, 1998.

Zaslavsky, Victor, 'The Katyn Massacre: "Class Cleansing" as Totalitarian Praxis', *Telos*, no. 114 (Winter 1999), pp. 67–107.

——, *Le Massacre de Katyn: Crime et Mensonge*, Paris: Editions Rocher, 2003.

Zawodny, J.K., *Death in the Forest: The Story of the Katyn Forest Massacre*, Notre Dame, IN: University of Notre Dame Press, 1962; London: Macmillan, 1971.

——, *Katyń*, foreword by Zbigniew Brzezinski. Paris: Spotkania, rev. edn, 1989.

——, 'Sprawa Katyńska w polityce Amerykańskiej', *Wojskowy Przegląd Historyczny*, 36, 1 (1991), pp. 279–83.

Index

Lightning Source UK Ltd.
Milton Keynes UK
UKOW031319171111

182222UK00003B/56/P